Mint Chocolate

4

MAMI ORIKASA

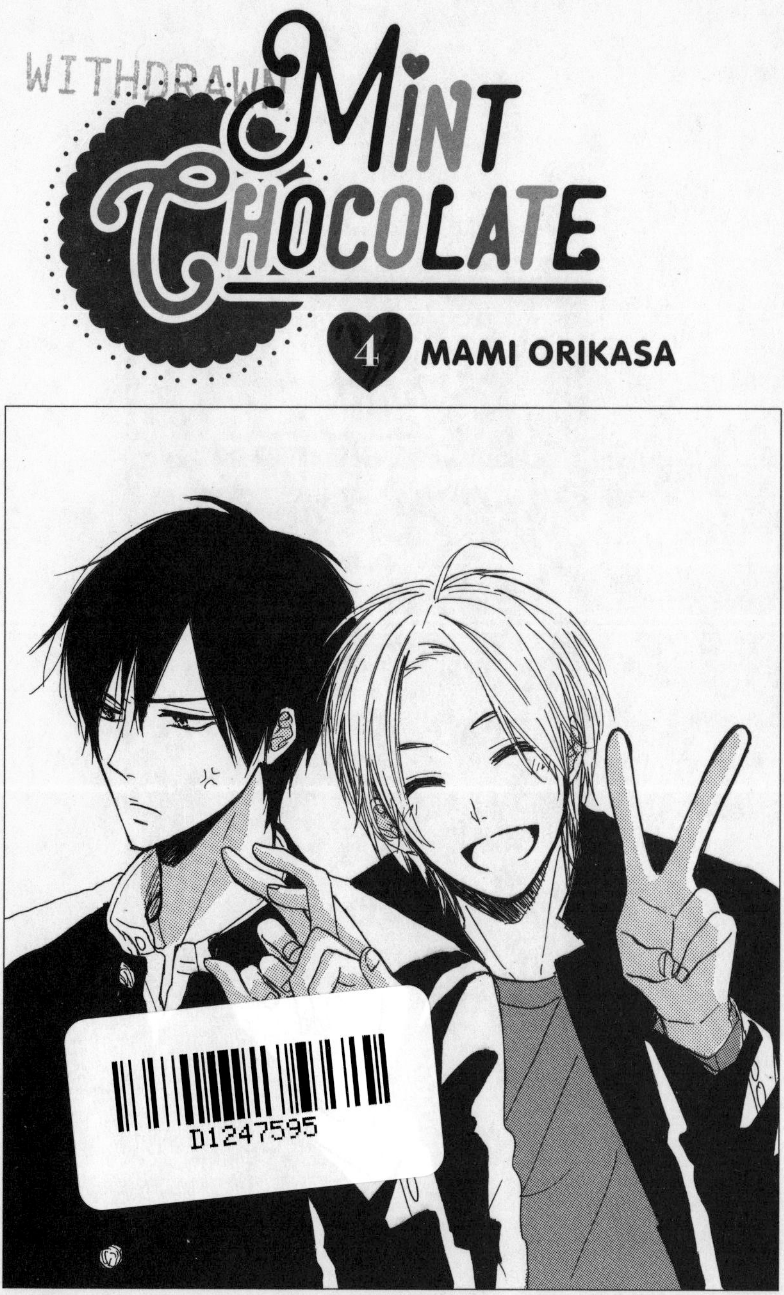

Mint Chocolate

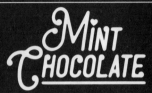

CONTENTS

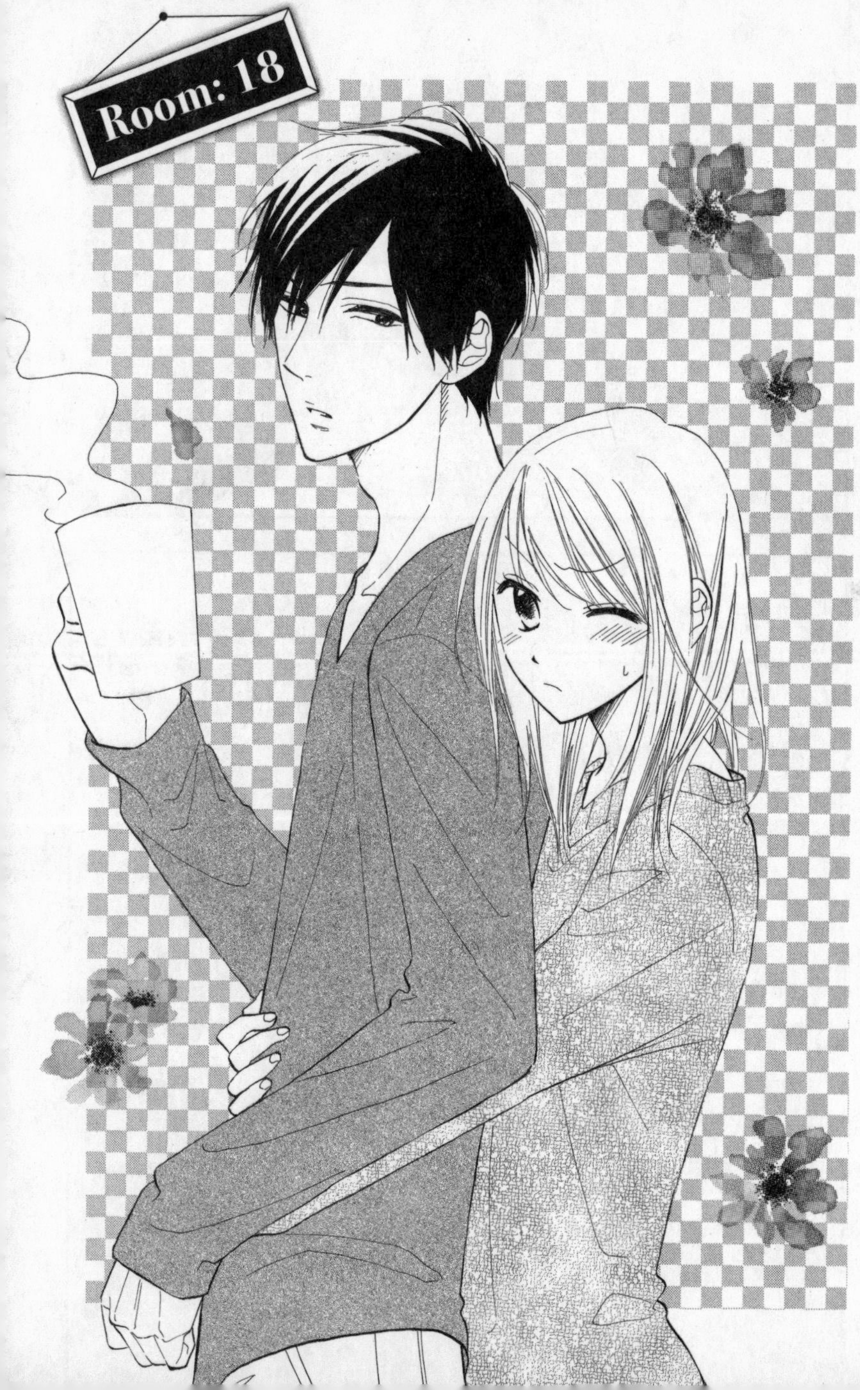
Room: 18

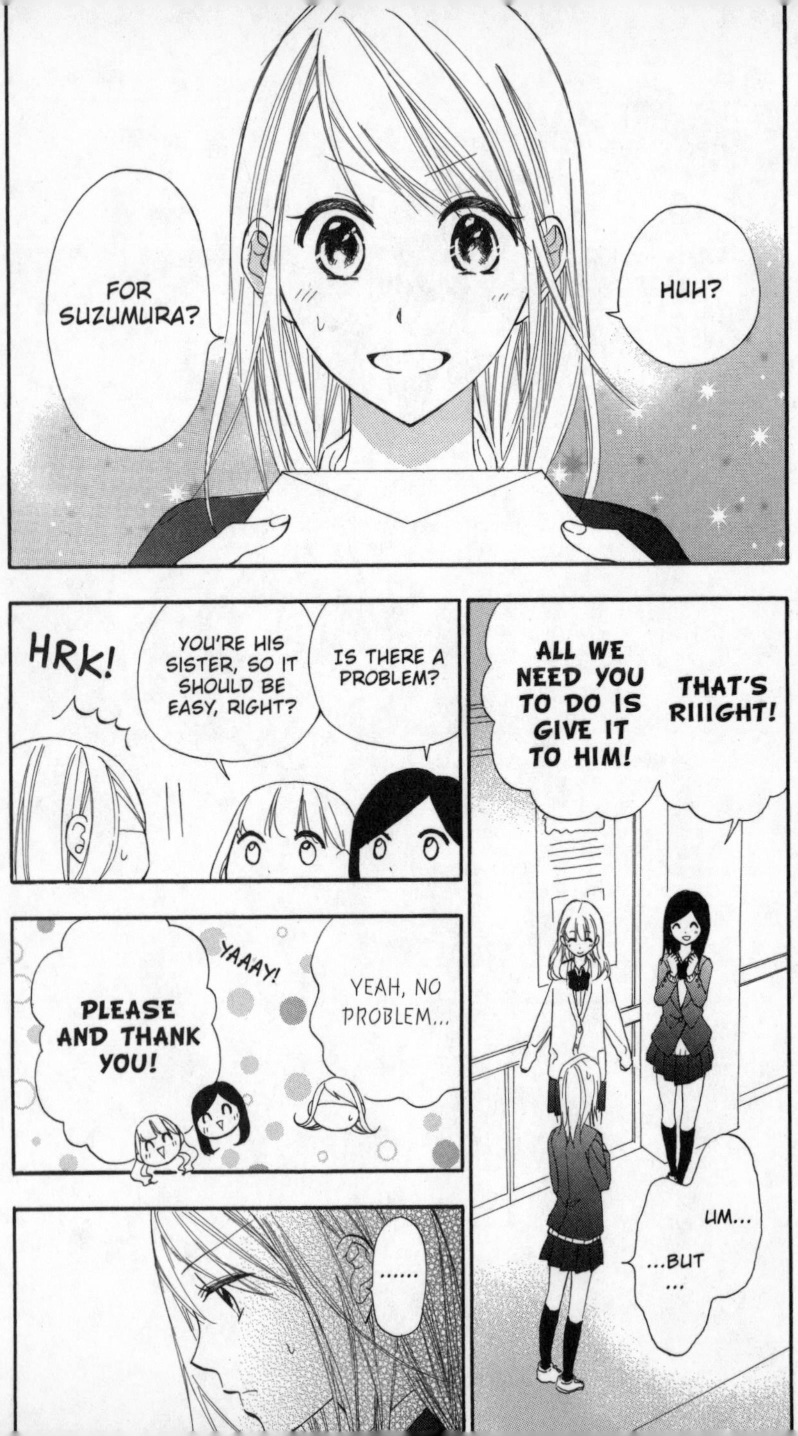
HUH?
FOR SUZUMURA?
THAT'S RIIIGHT!
ALL WE NEED YOU TO DO IS GIVE IT TO HIM!
UM...
...BUT ...
IS THERE A PROBLEM?
YOU'RE HIS SISTER, SO IT SHOULD BE EASY, RIGHT?
HRK!
YEAH, NO PROBLEM...
YAAAY!
PLEASE AND THANK YOU!
......

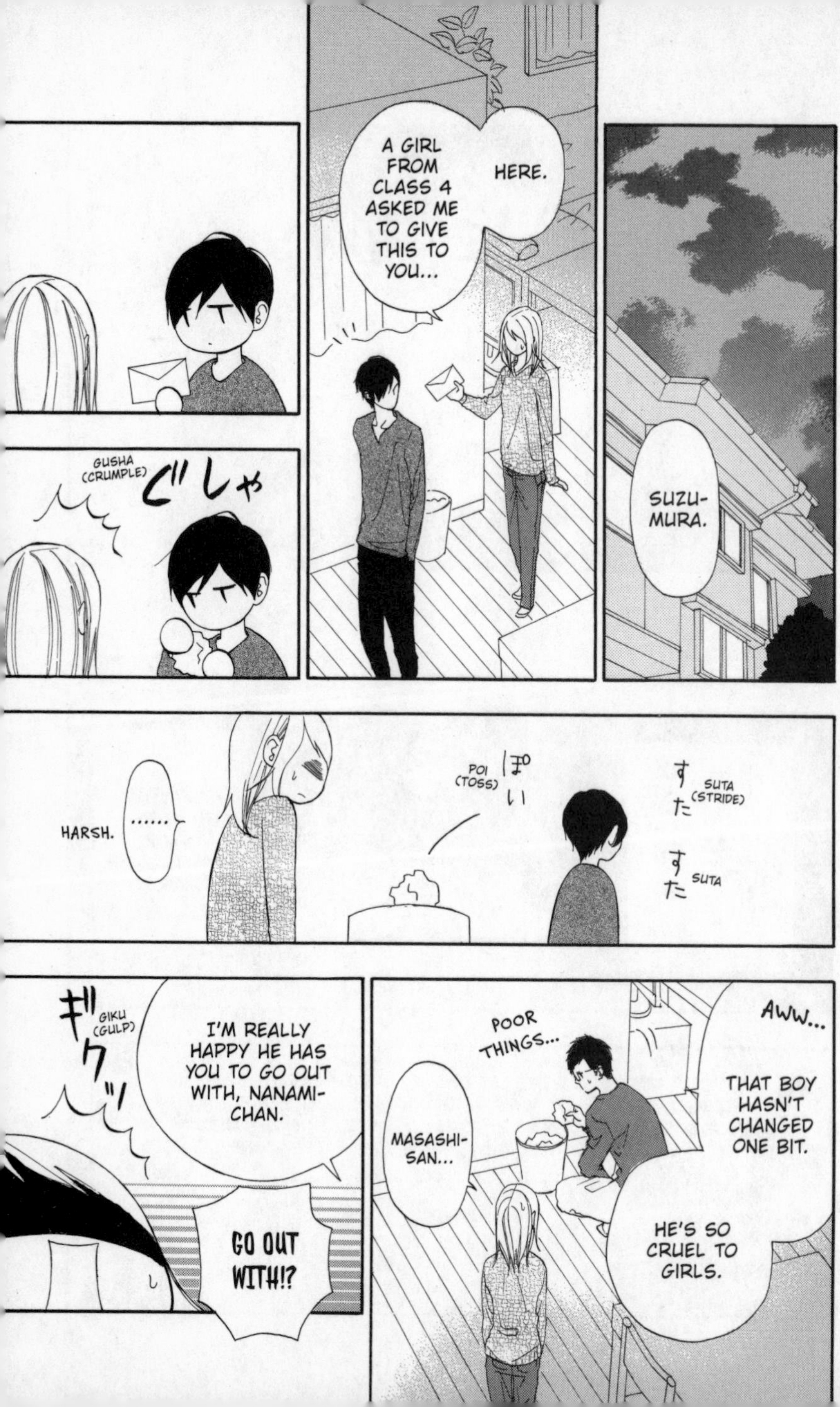
SUZU-MURA.
HERE.
A GIRL FROM CLASS 4 ASKED ME TO GIVE THIS TO YOU...
ぐしゃ
GUSHA (CRUMPLE)
すた
SUTA (STRIDE)
すた
SUTA
ぽい
POI (TOSS)
......
HARSH.
AWW...
THAT BOY HASN'T CHANGED ONE BIT.
HE'S SO CRUEL TO GIRLS.
POOR THINGS...
MASASHI-SAN...
I'M REALLY HAPPY HE HAS YOU TO GO OUT WITH, NANAMI-CHAN.
ギクッ
GIKU (GULP)
GO OUT WITH!?

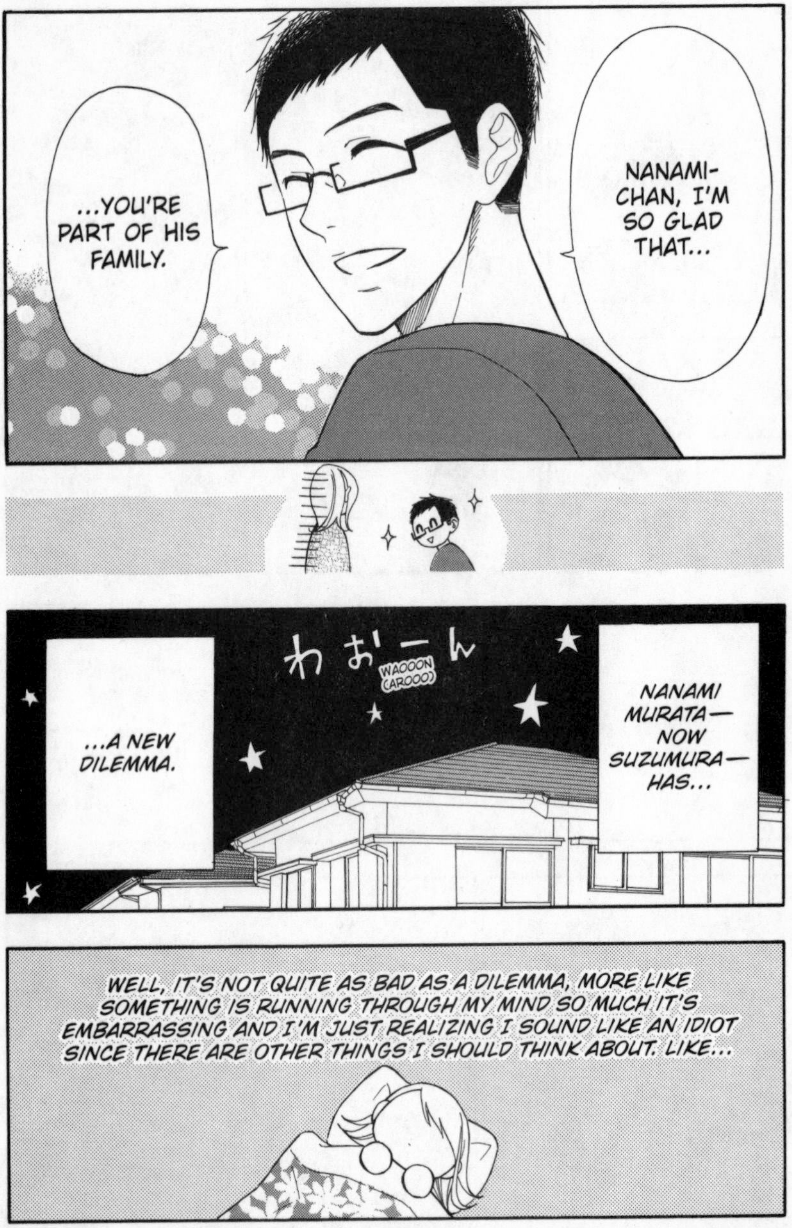
NANAMI-CHAN, I'M SO GLAD THAT...
...YOU'RE PART OF HIS FAMILY.
NANAMI MURATA—NOW SUZUMURA—HAS...
わおーん
WAOOON (AROOO)
...A NEW DILEMMA.
WELL, IT'S NOT QUITE AS BAD AS A DILEMMA, MORE LIKE SOMETHING IS RUNNING THROUGH MY MIND SO MUCH IT'S EMBARRASSING AND I'M JUST REALIZING I SOUND LIKE AN IDIOT SINCE THERE ARE OTHER THINGS I SHOULD THINK ABOUT. LIKE...

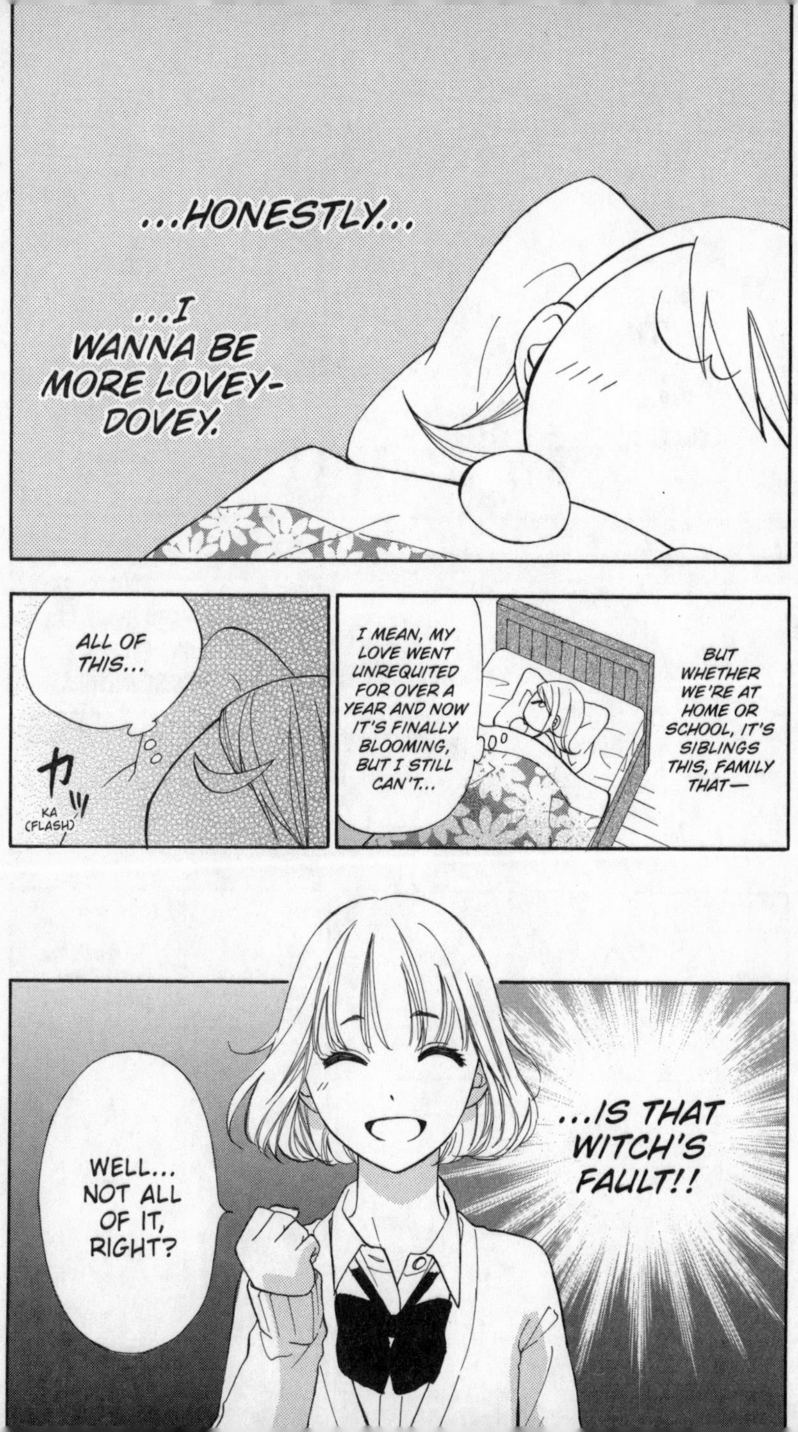
...HONESTLY...
...I WANNA BE MORE LOVEY-DOVEY.
I MEAN, MY LOVE WENT UNREQUITED FOR OVER A YEAR AND NOW IT'S FINALLY BLOOMING, BUT I STILL CAN'T...
BUT WHETHER WE'RE AT HOME OR SCHOOL, IT'S SIBLINGS THIS, FAMILY THAT—
ALL OF THIS...
カッ
KA (FLASH)
...IS THAT WITCH'S FAULT!!
WELL... NOT ALL OF IT, RIGHT?

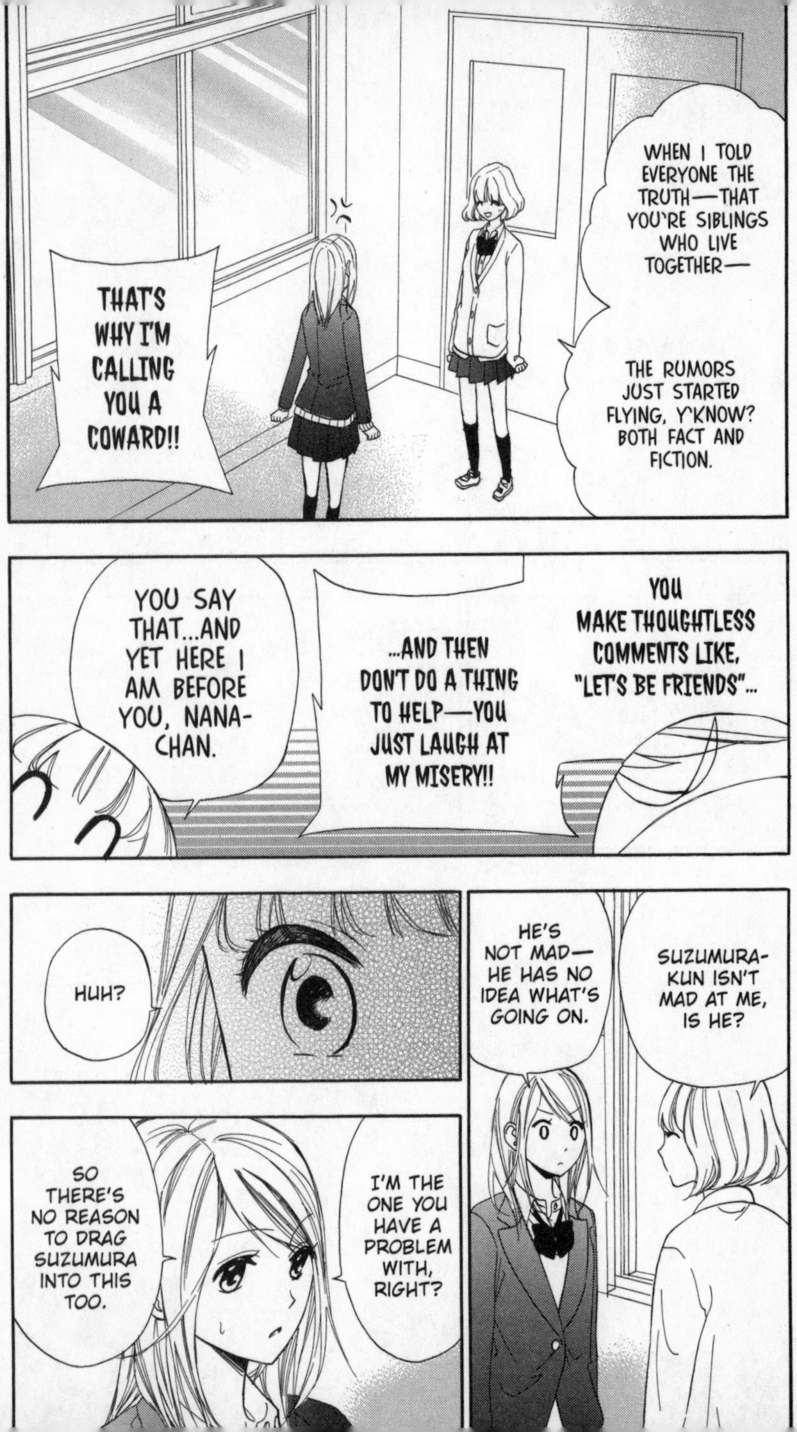
WHEN I TOLD EVERYONE THE TRUTH—THAT YOU'RE SIBLINGS WHO LIVE TOGETHER—
THE RUMORS JUST STARTED FLYING, Y'KNOW? BOTH FACT AND FICTION.
THAT'S WHY I'M CALLING YOU A COWARD!!
YOU MAKE THOUGHTLESS COMMENTS LIKE, "LET'S BE FRIENDS"...
...AND THEN DON'T DO A THING TO HELP—YOU JUST LAUGH AT MY MISERY!!
YOU SAY THAT...AND YET HERE I AM BEFORE YOU, NANA-CHAN.
SUZUMURA-KUN ISN'T MAD AT ME, IS HE?
HE'S NOT MAD—HE HAS NO IDEA WHAT'S GOING ON.
HUH?
I'M THE ONE YOU HAVE A PROBLEM WITH, RIGHT?
SO THERE'S NO REASON TO DRAG SUZUMURA INTO THIS TOO.

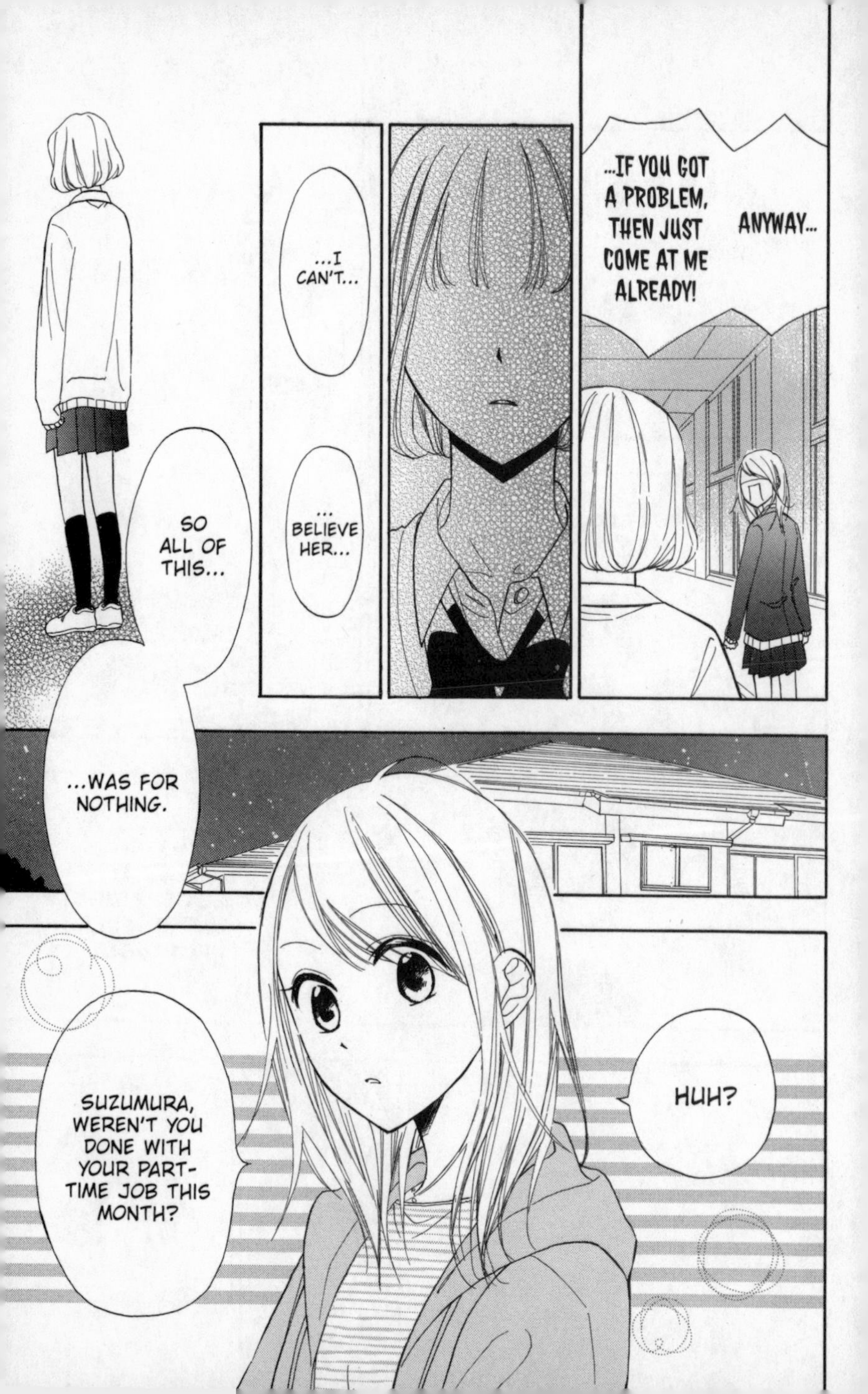
ANYWAY...
...IF YOU GOT A PROBLEM, THEN JUST COME AT ME ALREADY!
...I CAN'T...
...BELIEVE HER...
SO ALL OF THIS...
...WAS FOR NOTHING.
HUH?
SUZUMURA, WEREN'T YOU DONE WITH YOUR PART-TIME JOB THIS MONTH?

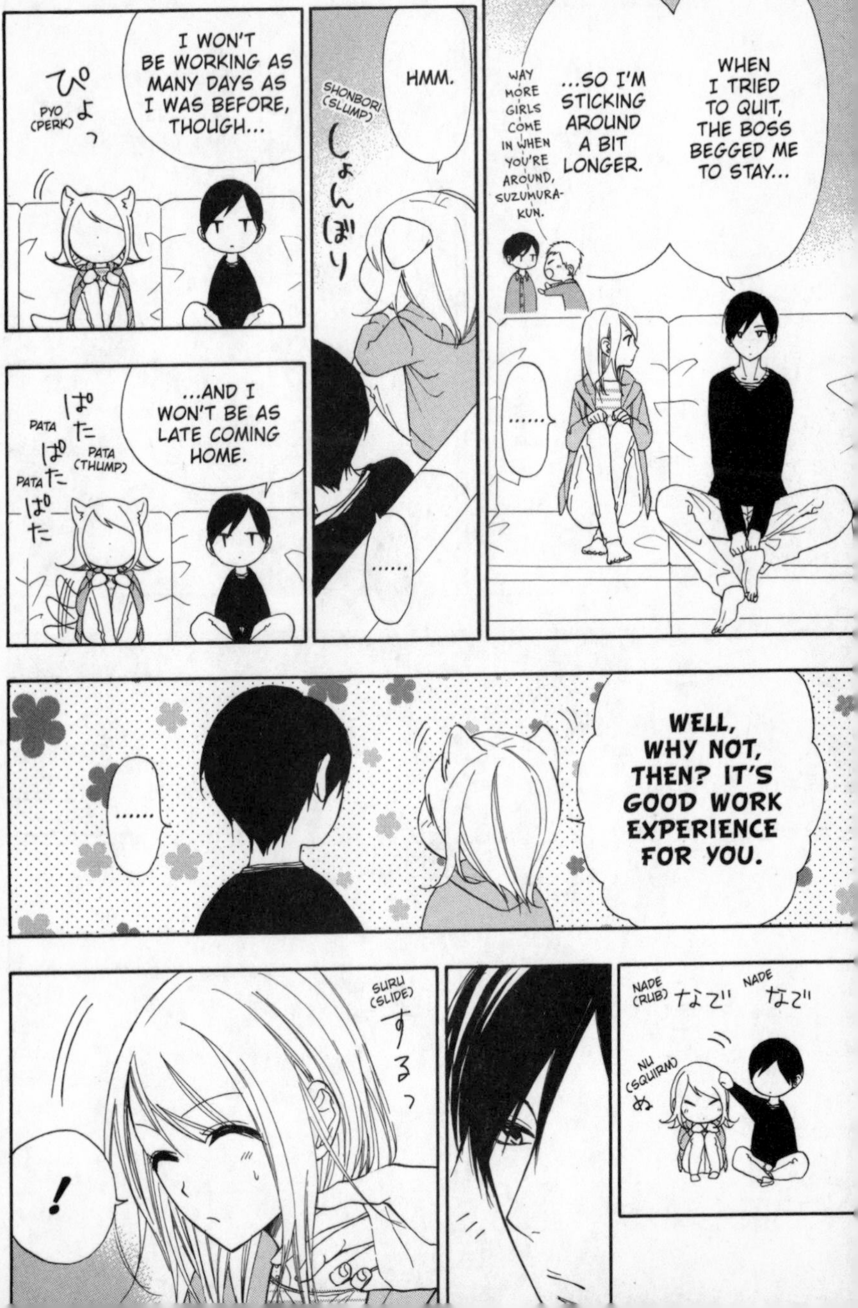
WHEN I TRIED TO QUIT, THE BOSS BEGGED ME TO STAY...
...SO I'M STICKING AROUND A BIT LONGER.
WAY MORE GIRLS COME IN WHEN YOU'RE AROUND, SUZUMURA-KUN.
......
HMM.
SHONBORI (SLUMP) しょんぼり
......
I WON'T BE WORKING AS MANY DAYS AS I WAS BEFORE, THOUGH...
PYO (PERK) ぴよっ
...AND I WON'T BE AS LATE COMING HOME.
PATA PATA PATA (THUMP) ぱたぱたぱた
WELL, WHY NOT, THEN? IT'S GOOD WORK EXPERIENCE FOR YOU.
......
NADE (RUB) なで NADE なで
NU (SQUIRM) ぬ
SURU (SLIDE) するっ
!

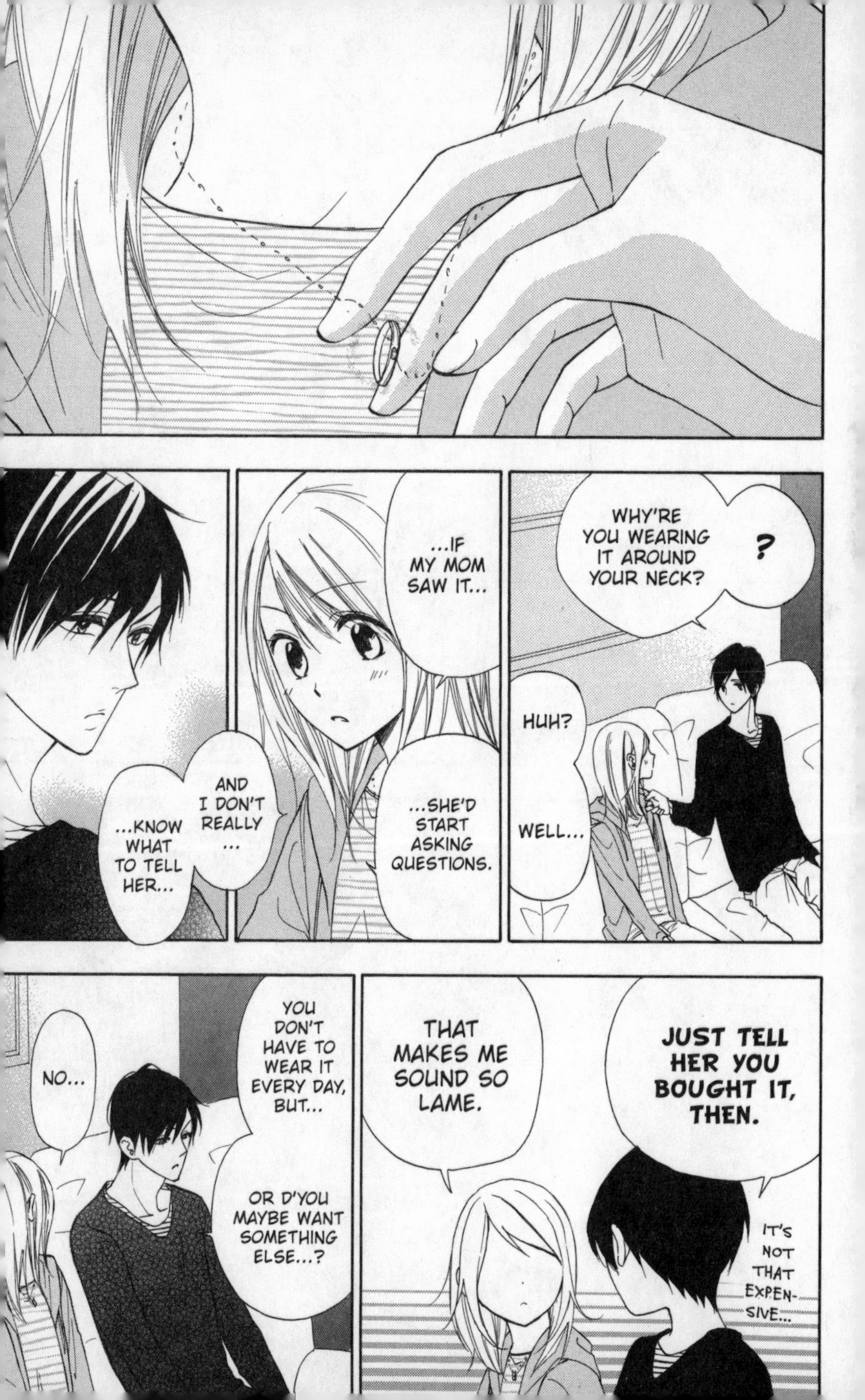
WHY'RE YOU WEARING IT AROUND YOUR NECK?
?
HUH?
WELL...
...IF MY MOM SAW IT...
...SHE'D START ASKING QUESTIONS.
AND I DON'T REALLY ...
...KNOW WHAT TO TELL HER...
JUST TELL HER YOU BOUGHT IT, THEN.
THAT MAKES ME SOUND SO LAME.
IT'S NOT THAT EXPENSIVE...
YOU DON'T HAVE TO WEAR IT EVERY DAY, BUT...
NO...
OR D'YOU MAYBE WANT SOMETHING ELSE...?

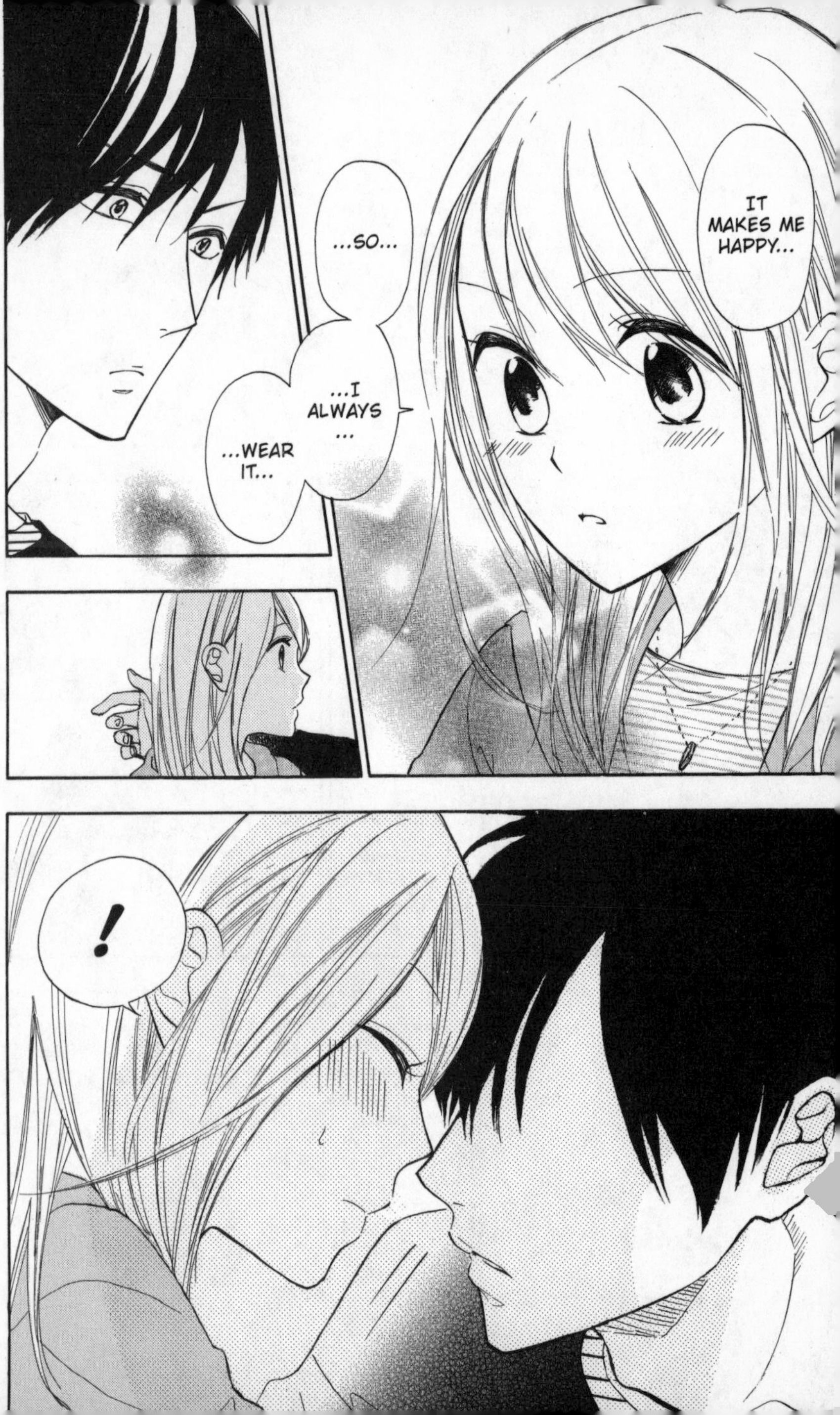
IT MAKES ME HAPPY...
...SO...
...I ALWAYS ...
...WEAR IT...
!

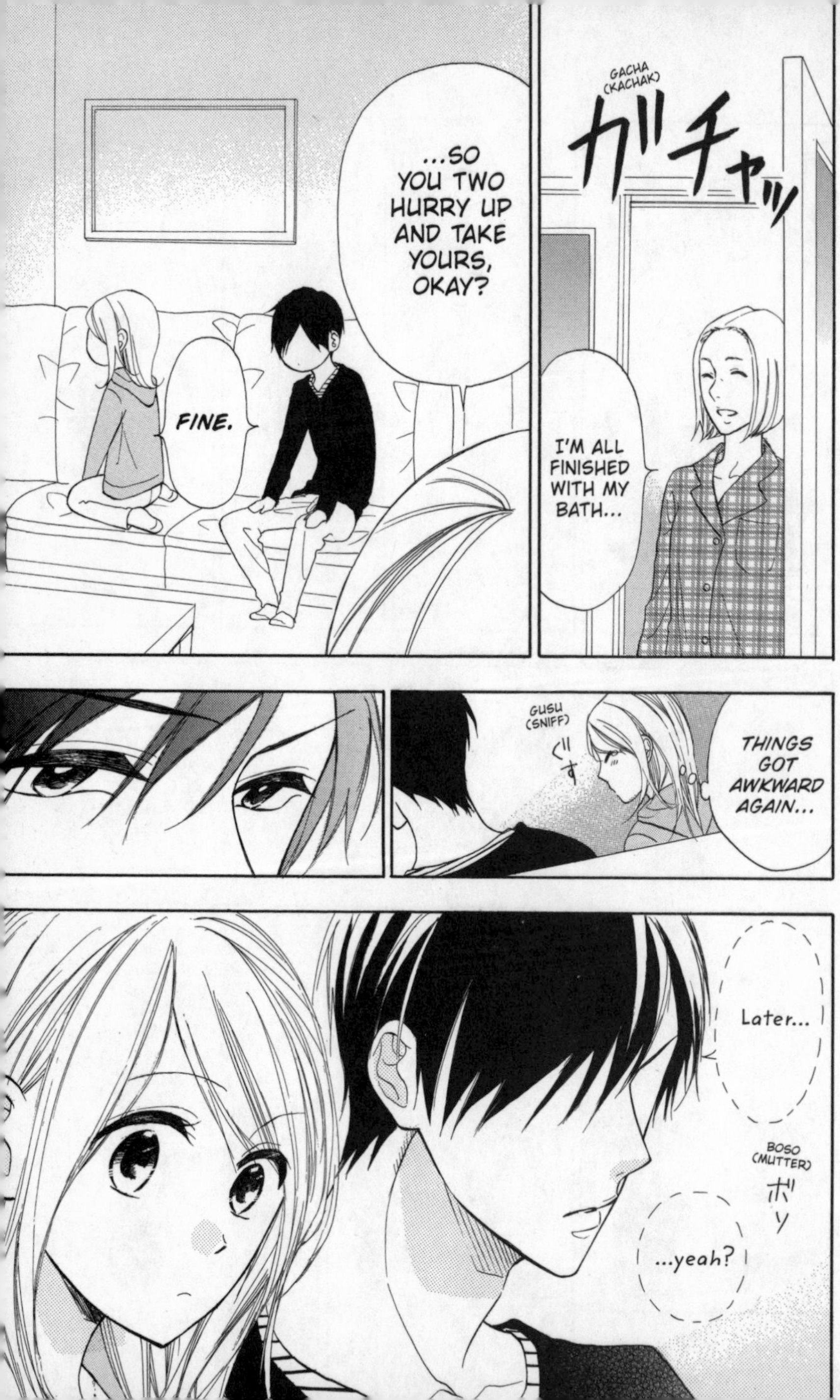
GACHA (KACHAK)
ガチャッ
I'M ALL FINISHED WITH MY BATH...
...SO YOU TWO HURRY UP AND TAKE YOURS, OKAY?
FINE.
GUSU (SNIFF)
ぐす
THINGS GOT AWKWARD AGAIN...
Later...
BOSO (MUTTER)
ボソ
...yeah?

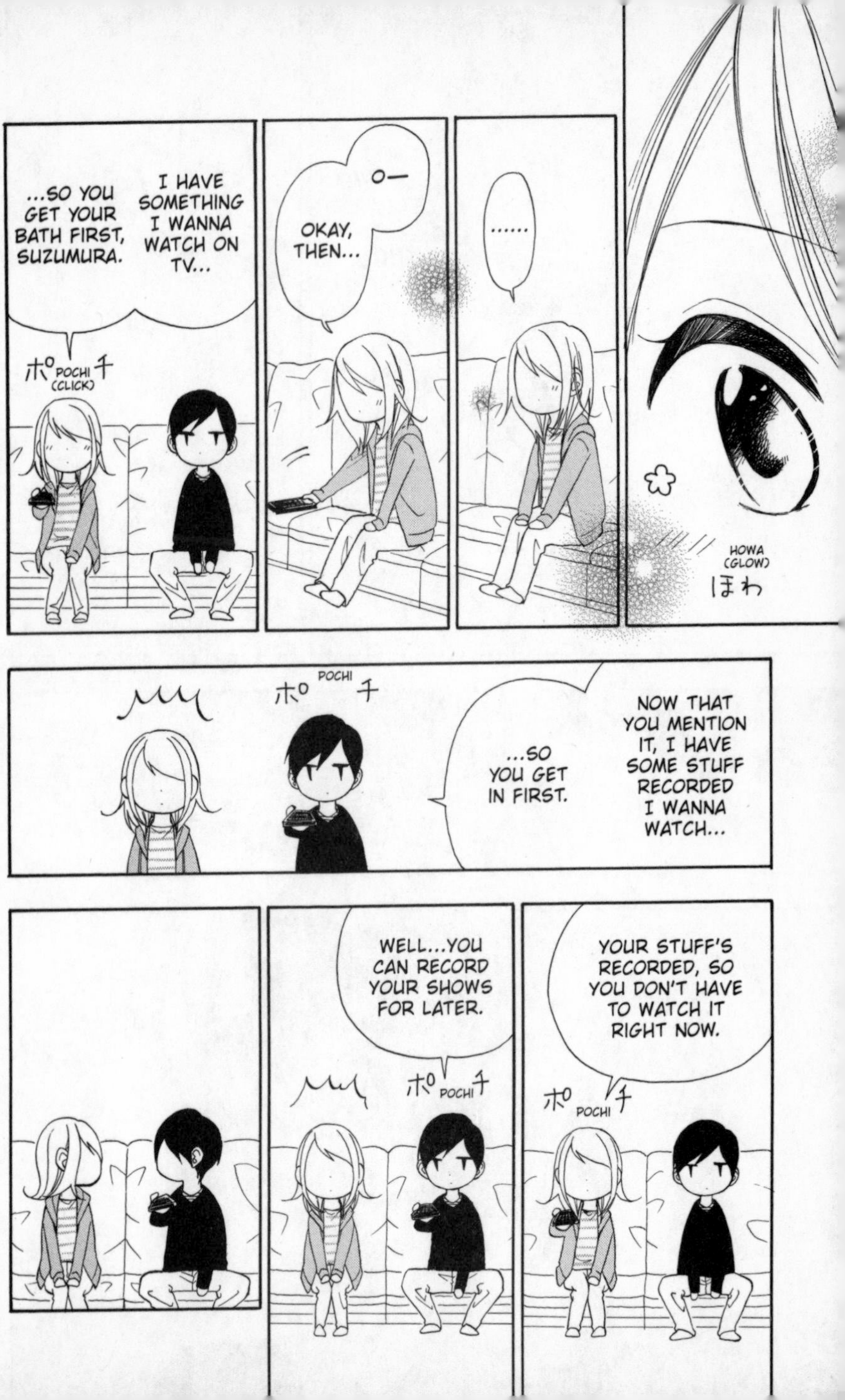
HOWA (GLOW)
ほわ
......
O—
OKAY, THEN...
I HAVE SOMETHING I WANNA WATCH ON TV...
...SO YOU GET YOUR BATH FIRST, SUZUMURA.
ポ POCHI チ (CLICK)
NOW THAT YOU MENTION IT, I HAVE SOME STUFF RECORDED I WANNA WATCH...
...SO YOU GET IN FIRST.
ポ POCHI チ
YOUR STUFF'S RECORDED, SO YOU DON'T HAVE TO WATCH IT RIGHT NOW.
ポ POCHI チ
WELL...YOU CAN RECORD YOUR SHOWS FOR LATER.
ポ POCHI チ

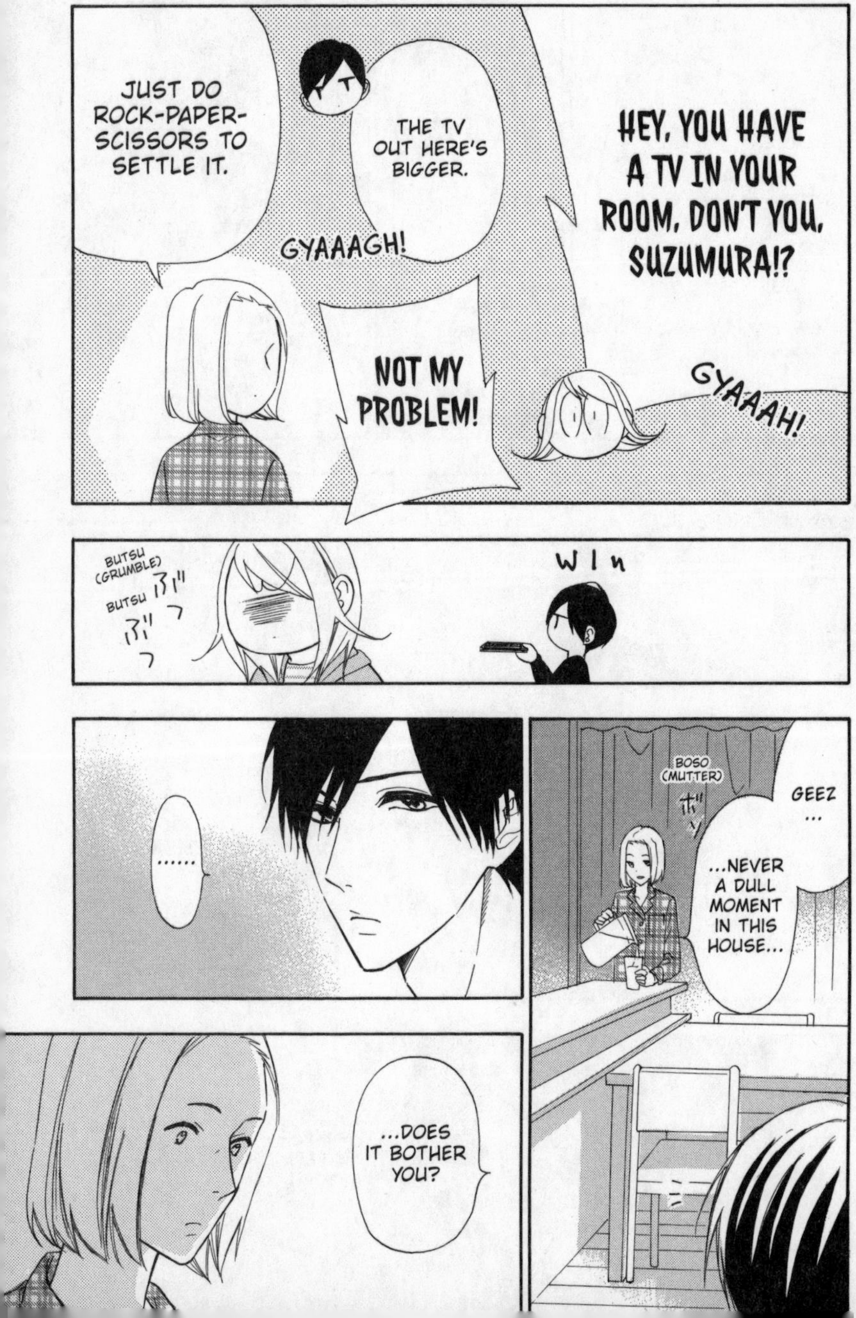
HEY, YOU HAVE A TV IN YOUR ROOM, DON'T YOU, SUZUMURA!?
GYAAAH!
NOT MY PROBLEM!
THE TV OUT HERE'S BIGGER.
GYAAAGH!
JUST DO ROCK-PAPER-SCISSORS TO SETTLE IT.
WIn
BUTSU (GRUMBLE)
BUTSU ぶつぶつ
BOSO (MUTTER)
ボソ
GEEZ...
...NEVER A DULL MOMENT IN THIS HOUSE...
......
...DOES IT BOTHER YOU?

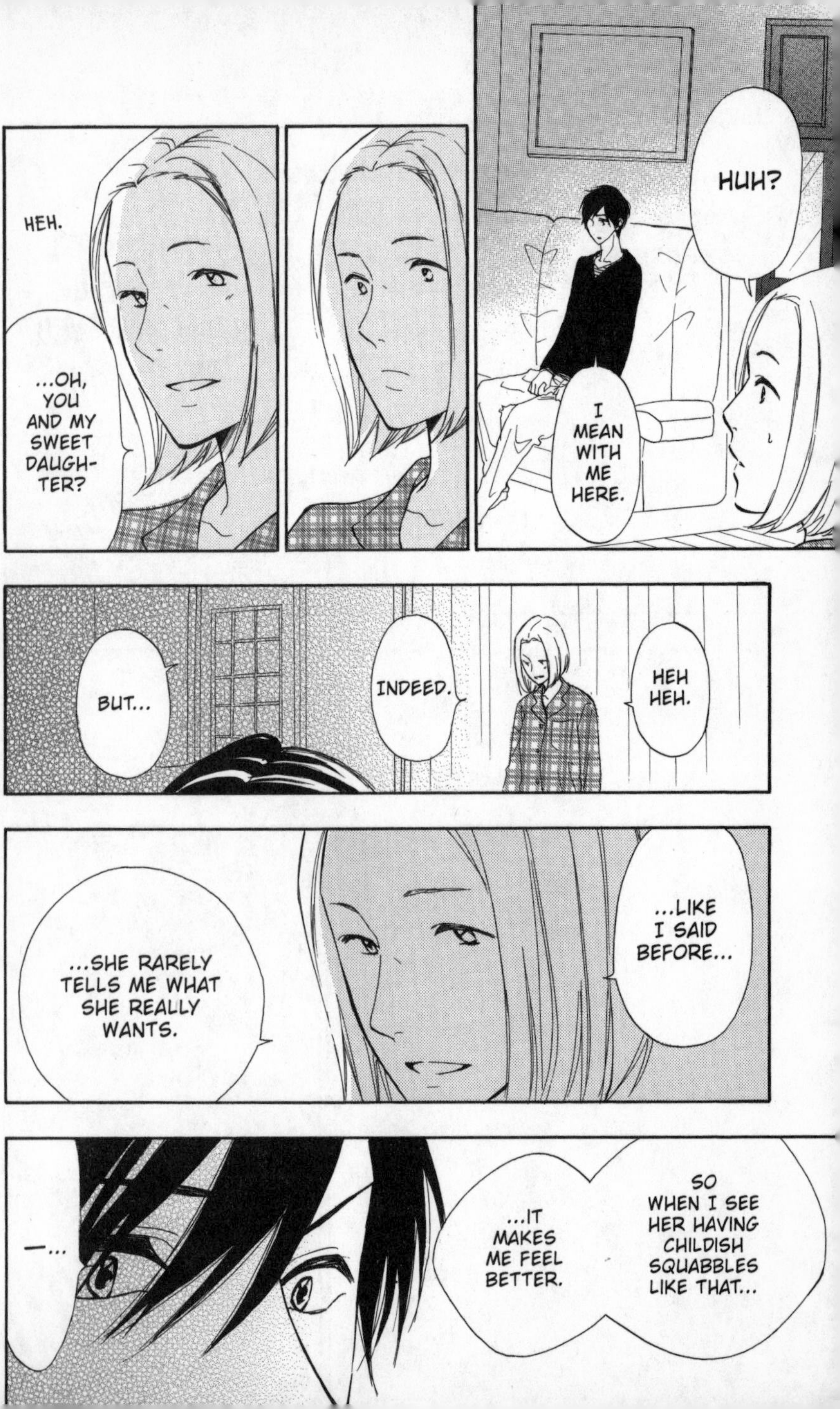
HUH?
I MEAN WITH ME HERE.
HEH.
...OH, YOU AND MY SWEET DAUGHTER?
HEH HEH.
INDEED.
BUT...
...LIKE I SAID BEFORE...
...SHE RARELY TELLS ME WHAT SHE REALLY WANTS.
SO WHEN I SEE HER HAVING CHILDISH SQUABBLES LIKE THAT...
...IT MAKES ME FEEL BETTER.
—...

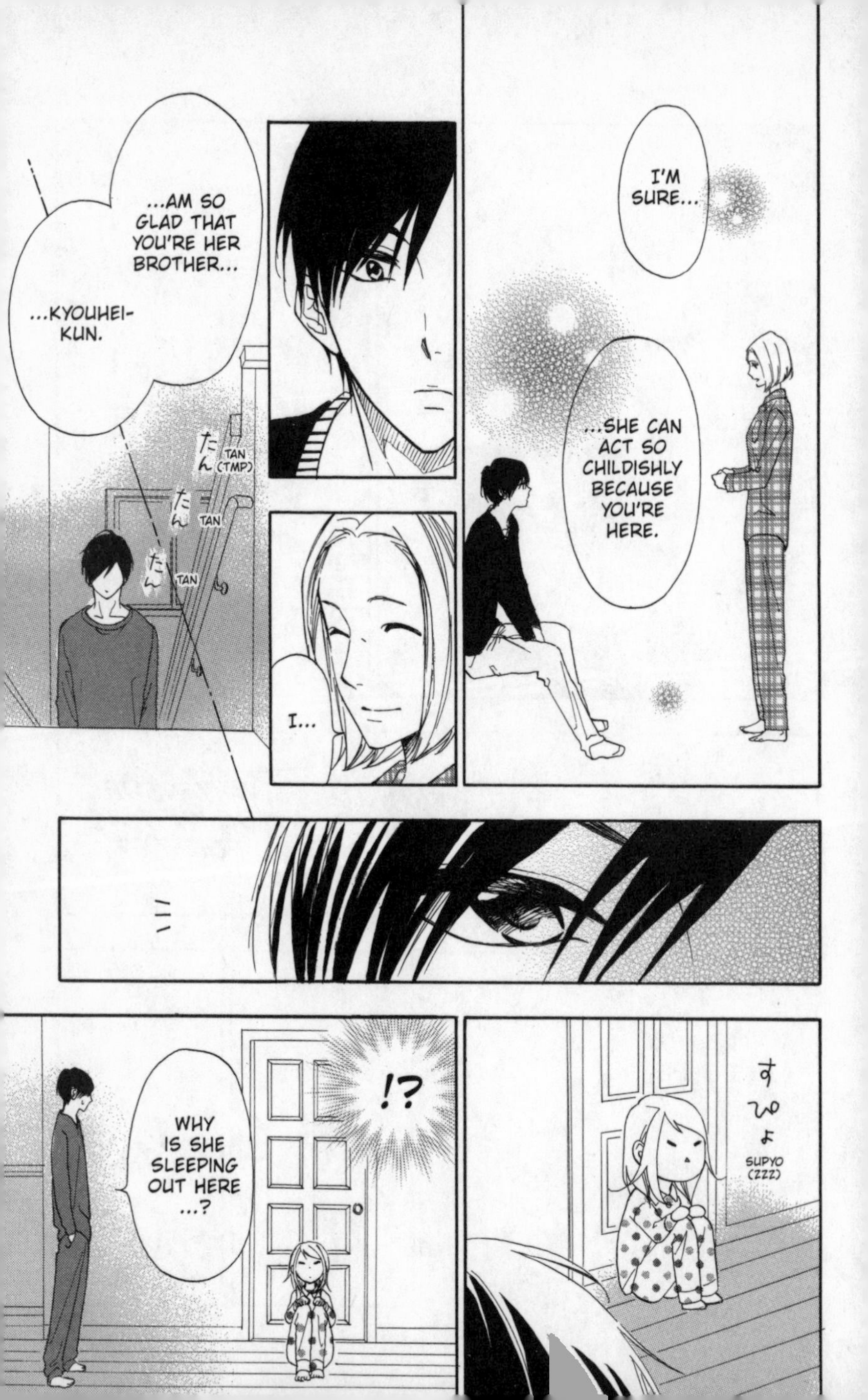

I'M SURE...
...SHE CAN ACT SO CHILDISHLY BECAUSE YOU'RE HERE.
I...
...AM SO GLAD THAT YOU'RE HER BROTHER...
...KYOUHEI-KUN.
たん TAN (TMP)
たん TAN
たん TAN
すぴょ
SUPYO (ZZZ)
!?
WHY IS SHE SLEEPING OUT HERE ...?

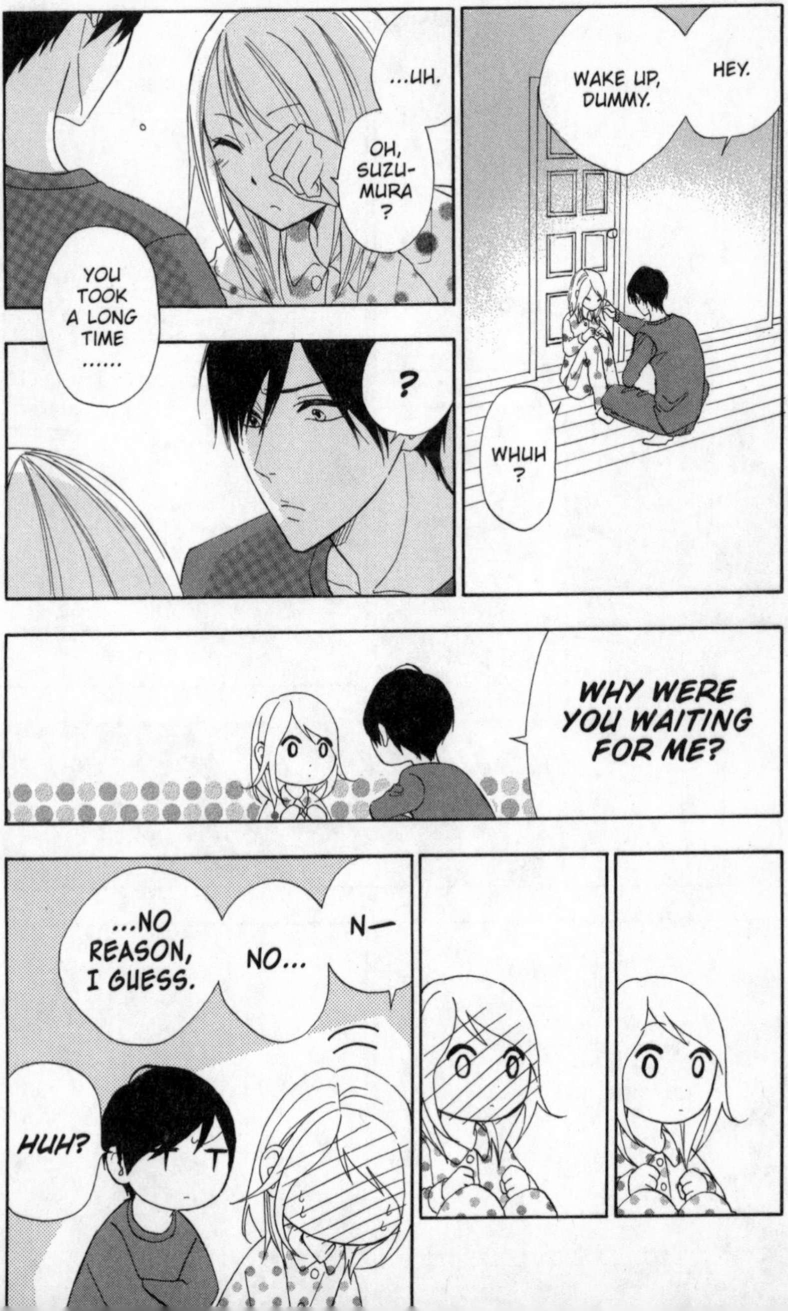
HEY.
WAKE UP, DUMMY.
WHUH?
...UH.
OH, SUZUMURA?
YOU TOOK A LONG TIME ......
?
WHY WERE YOU WAITING FOR ME?
N—
NO...
...NO REASON, I GUESS.
HUH?

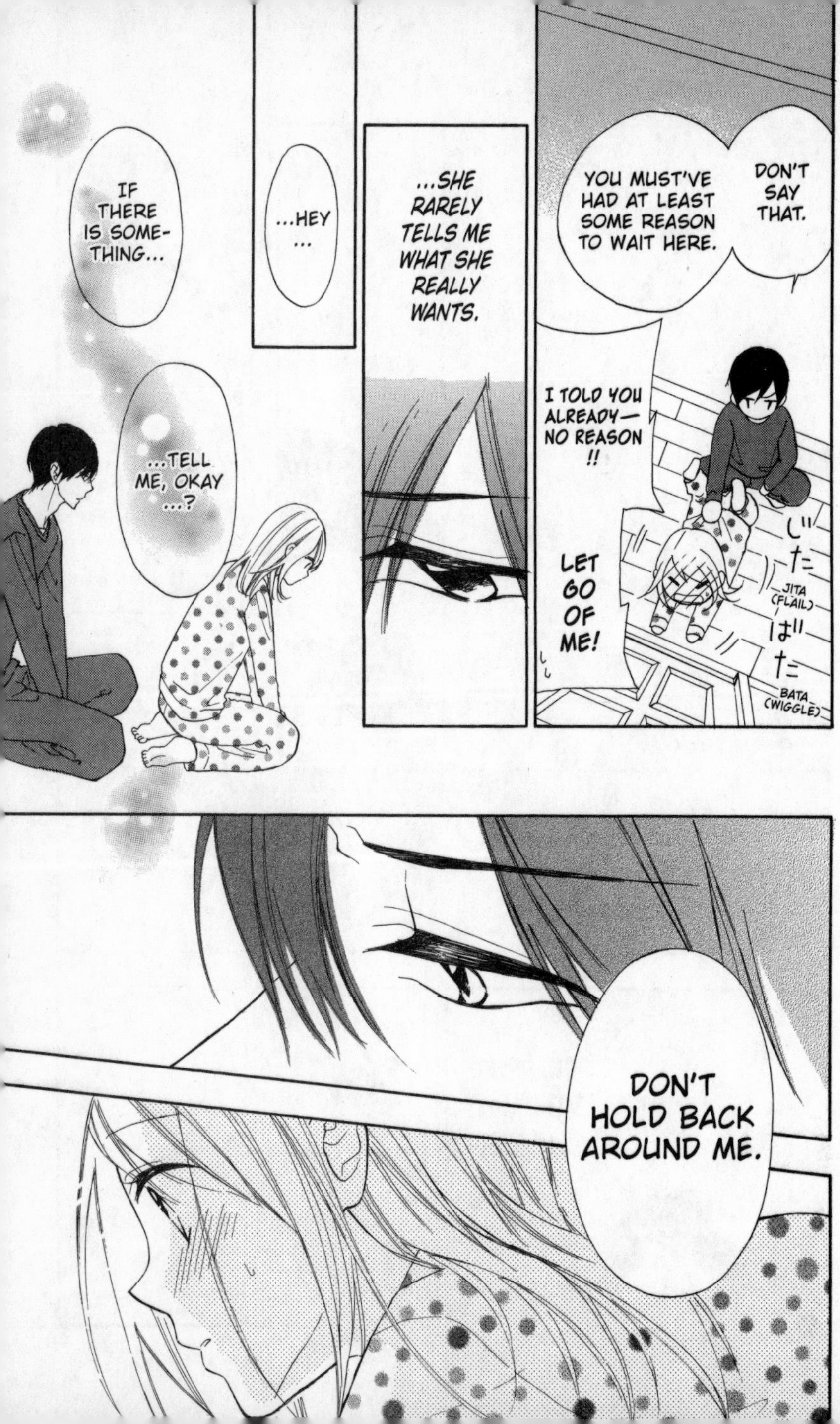
DON'T SAY THAT.
YOU MUST'VE HAD AT LEAST SOME REASON TO WAIT HERE.
I TOLD YOU ALREADY—NO REASON!!
LET GO OF ME!
じた
JITA (FLAIL)
ばた
BATA (WIGGLE)
...SHE RARELY TELLS ME WHAT SHE REALLY WANTS.
...HEY...
IF THERE IS SOMETHING...
...TELL ME, OKAY...?
DON'T HOLD BACK AROUND ME.

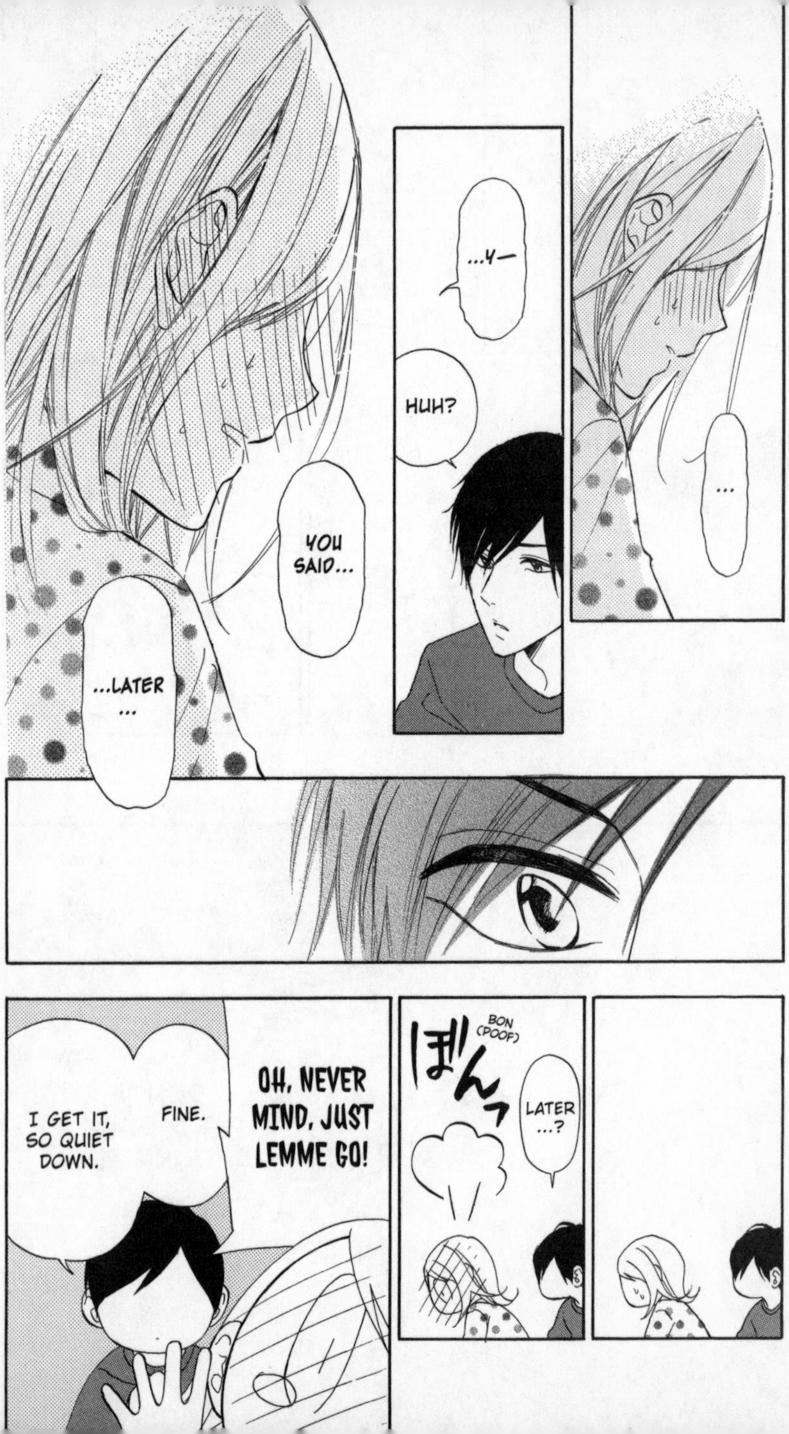
...
...Y—
HUH?
YOU SAID...
...LATER ...
ぼんっ
BON (POOF)
LATER ...?
OH, NEVER MIND, JUST LEMME GO!
FINE.
I GET IT, SO QUIET DOWN.

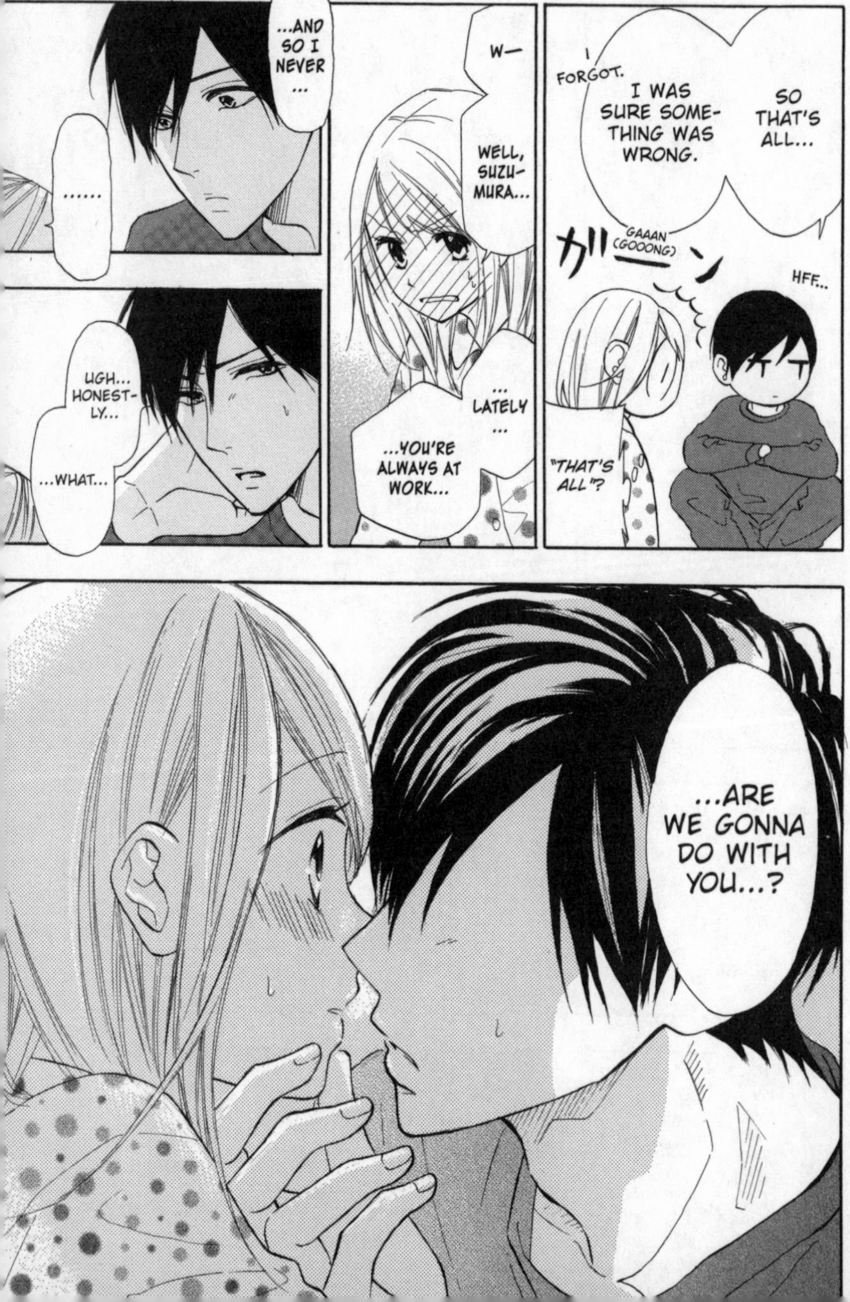
SO THAT'S ALL...
I FORGOT. I WAS SURE SOME-THING WAS WRONG.
GAAAN (GOOONG)
HFF...
"THAT'S ALL"?
W—
WELL, SUZU-MURA...
... LATELY ...
...YOU'RE ALWAYS AT WORK...
...AND SO I NEVER ...
......
UGH... HONEST-LY...
...WHAT...
...ARE WE GONNA DO WITH YOU...?

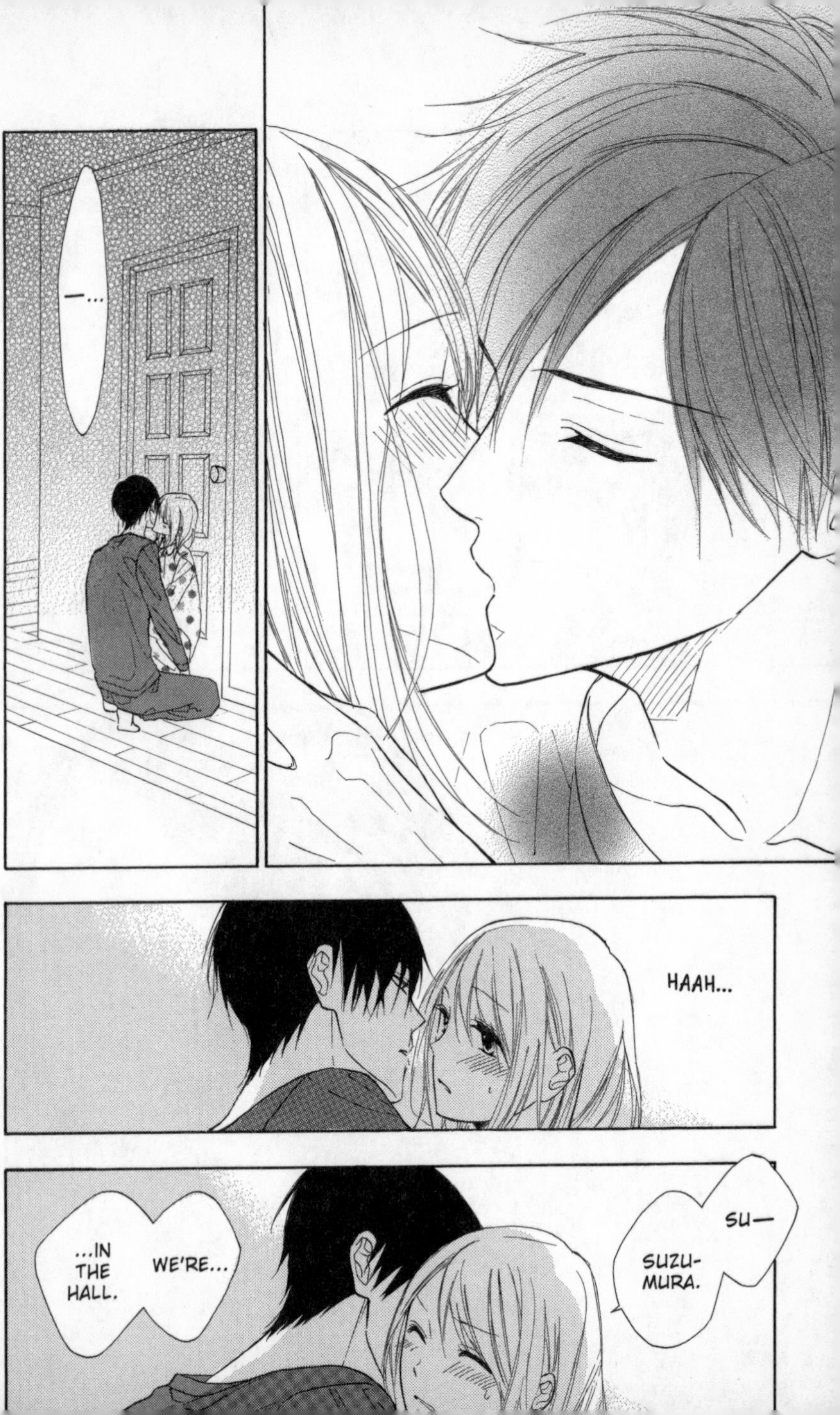
—...
HAAH...
SU—
SUZU-MURA.
WE'RE...
...IN THE HALL.

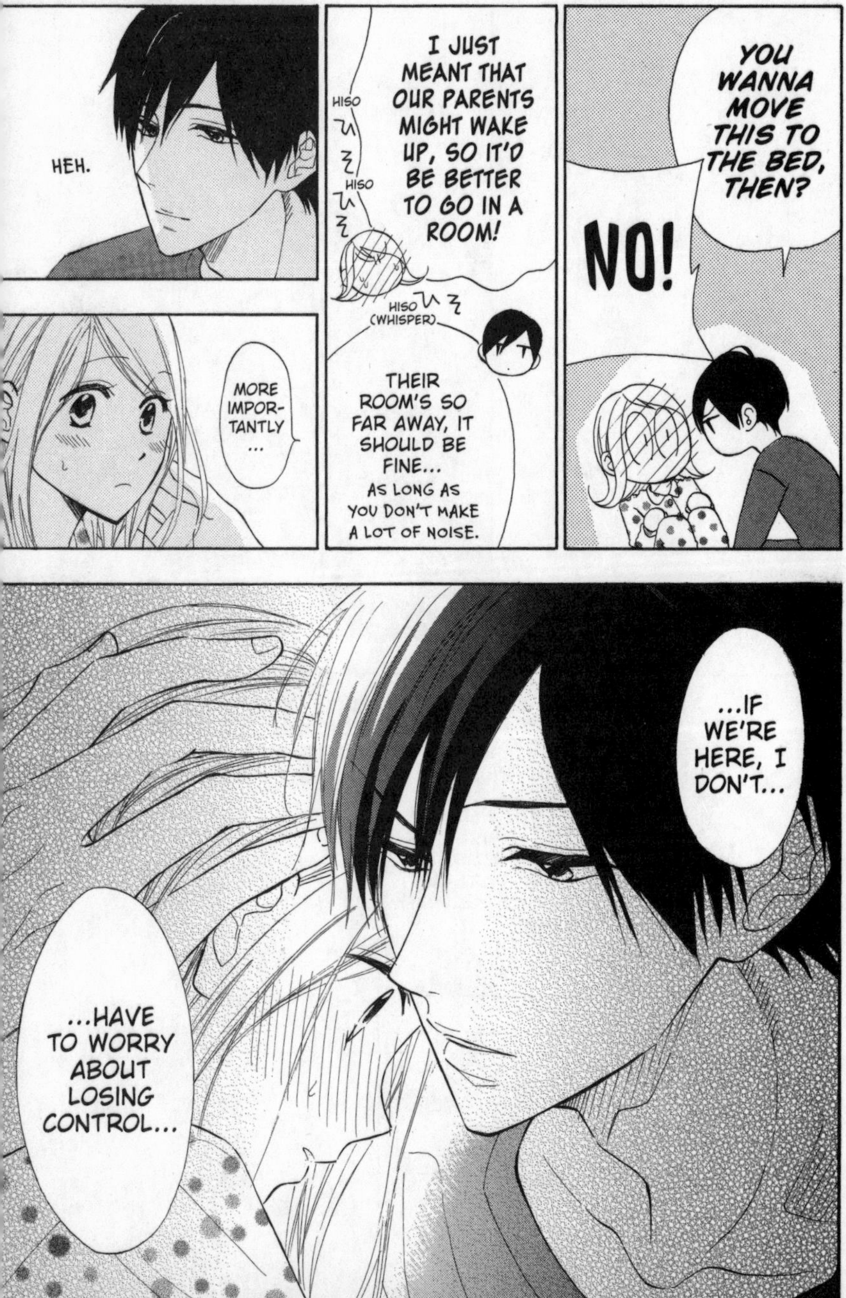
YOU WANNA MOVE THIS TO THE BED, THEN?
NO!
I JUST MEANT THAT OUR PARENTS MIGHT WAKE UP, SO IT'D BE BETTER TO GO IN A ROOM!
HISO HISO
HISO (WHISPER)
THEIR ROOM'S SO FAR AWAY, IT SHOULD BE FINE... AS LONG AS YOU DON'T MAKE A LOT OF NOISE.
HEH.
MORE IMPOR-TANTLY ...
...IF WE'RE HERE, I DON'T...
...HAVE TO WORRY ABOUT LOSING CONTROL...

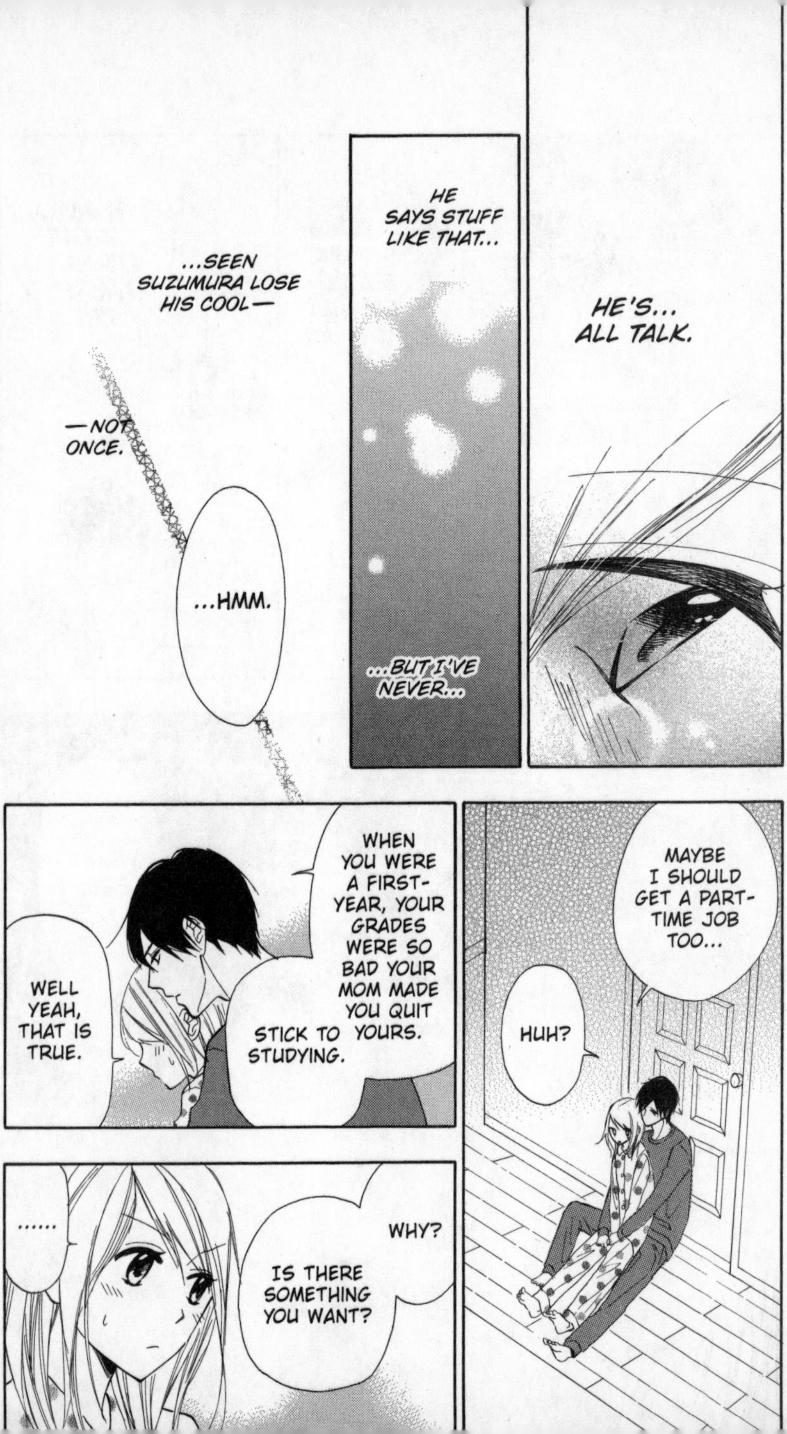
HE'S... ALL TALK.
HE SAYS STUFF LIKE THAT...
...BUT I'VE NEVER...
...SEEN SUZUMURA LOSE HIS COOL—
—NOT ONCE.
...HMM.
MAYBE I SHOULD GET A PART-TIME JOB TOO...
HUH?
WHEN YOU WERE A FIRST-YEAR, YOUR GRADES WERE SO BAD YOUR MOM MADE YOU QUIT YOURS.
STICK TO STUDYING.
WELL YEAH, THAT IS TRUE.
WHY?
IS THERE SOMETHING YOU WANT?
......

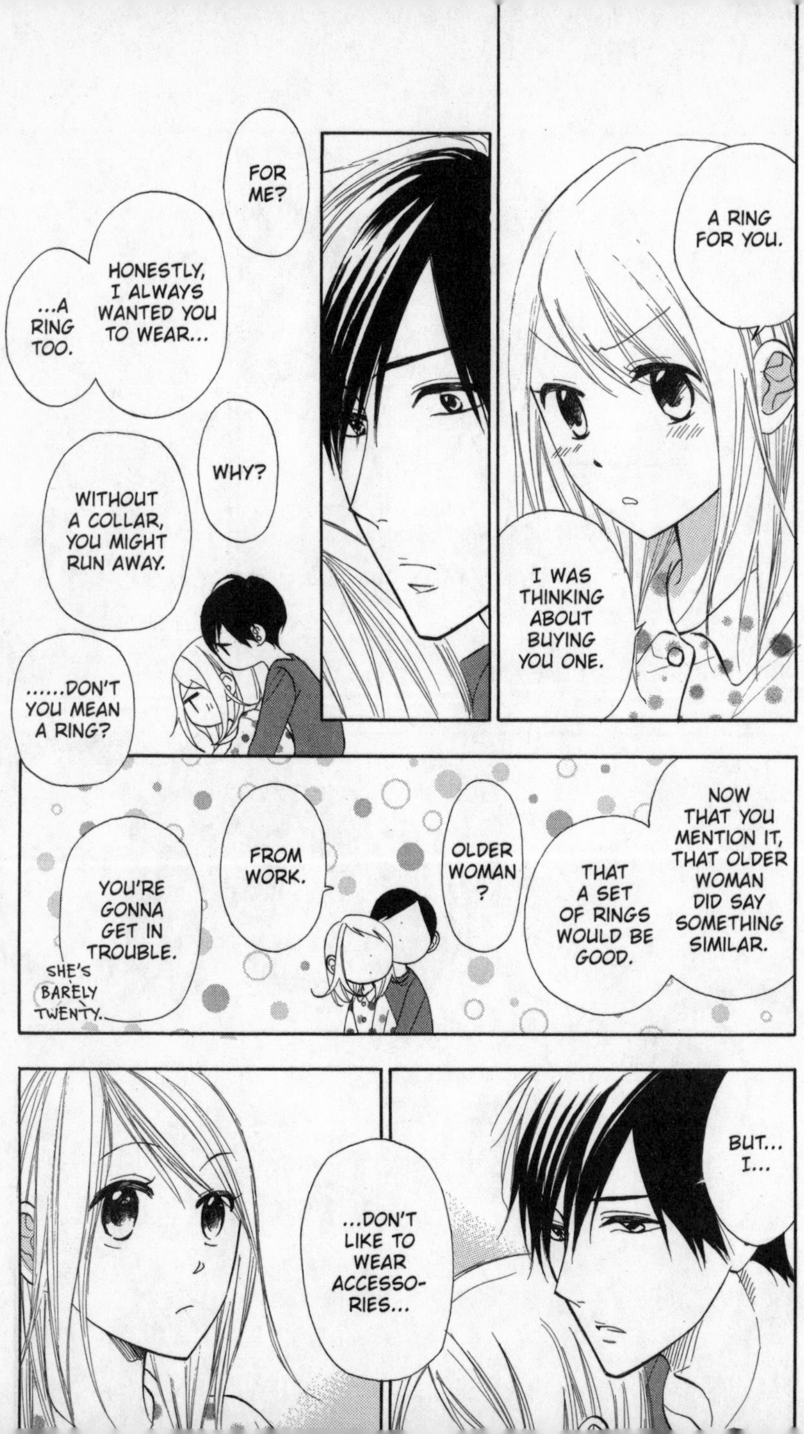
A RING FOR YOU.
I WAS THINKING ABOUT BUYING YOU ONE.
FOR ME?
HONESTLY, I ALWAYS WANTED YOU TO WEAR...
...A RING TOO.
WHY?
WITHOUT A COLLAR, YOU MIGHT RUN AWAY.
......DON'T YOU MEAN A RING?
NOW THAT YOU MENTION IT, THAT OLDER WOMAN DID SAY SOMETHING SIMILAR.
THAT A SET OF RINGS WOULD BE GOOD.
OLDER WOMAN?
FROM WORK.
YOU'RE GONNA GET IN TROUBLE.
SHE'S BARELY TWENTY.
BUT... I...
...DON'T LIKE TO WEAR ACCESSORIES...

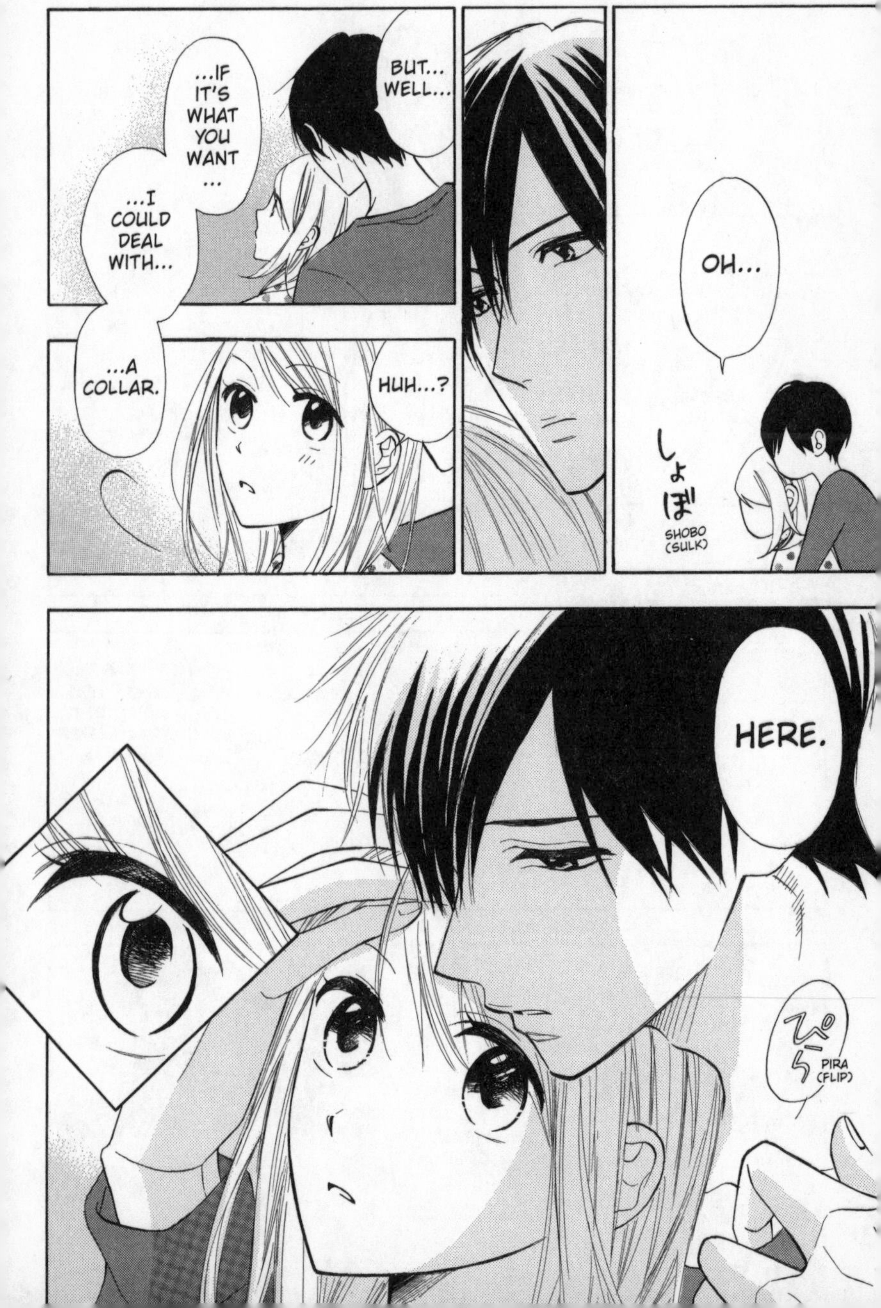
OH...
しょぼ
SHOBO (SULK)
BUT... WELL...
...IF IT'S WHAT YOU WANT...
...I COULD DEAL WITH...
...A COLLAR.
HUH...?
HERE.
ぴら
PIRA (FLIP)

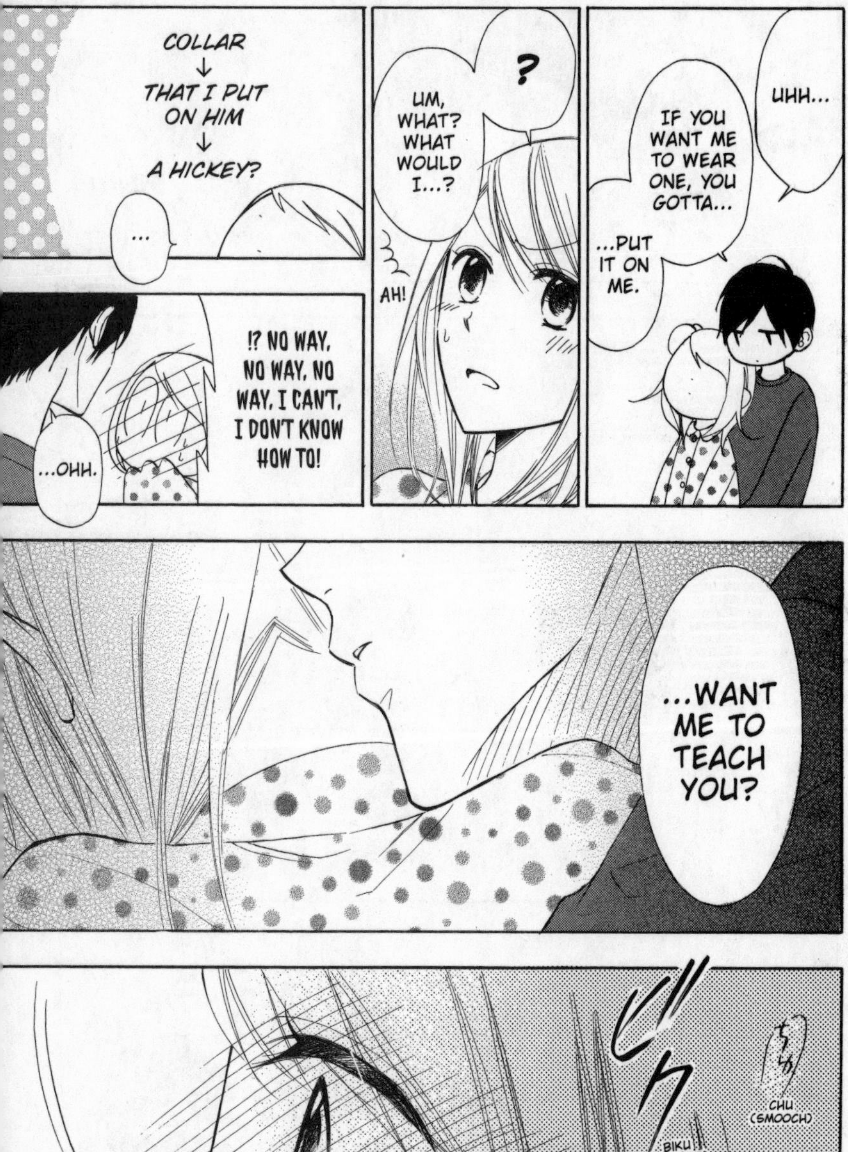
UHH...
IF YOU WANT ME TO WEAR ONE, YOU GOTTA...
...PUT IT ON ME.
?
UM, WHAT? WHAT WOULD I...?
AH!
COLLAR ↓ THAT I PUT ON HIM ↓ A HICKEY?
...
!? NO WAY, NO WAY, NO WAY, I CAN'T, I DON'T KNOW HOW TO!
...OHH.
...WANT ME TO TEACH YOU?
CHU (SMOOCH)
BIKU (QUIVER)

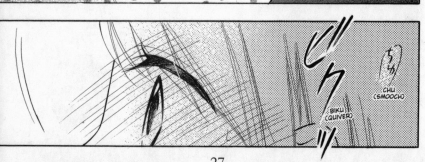

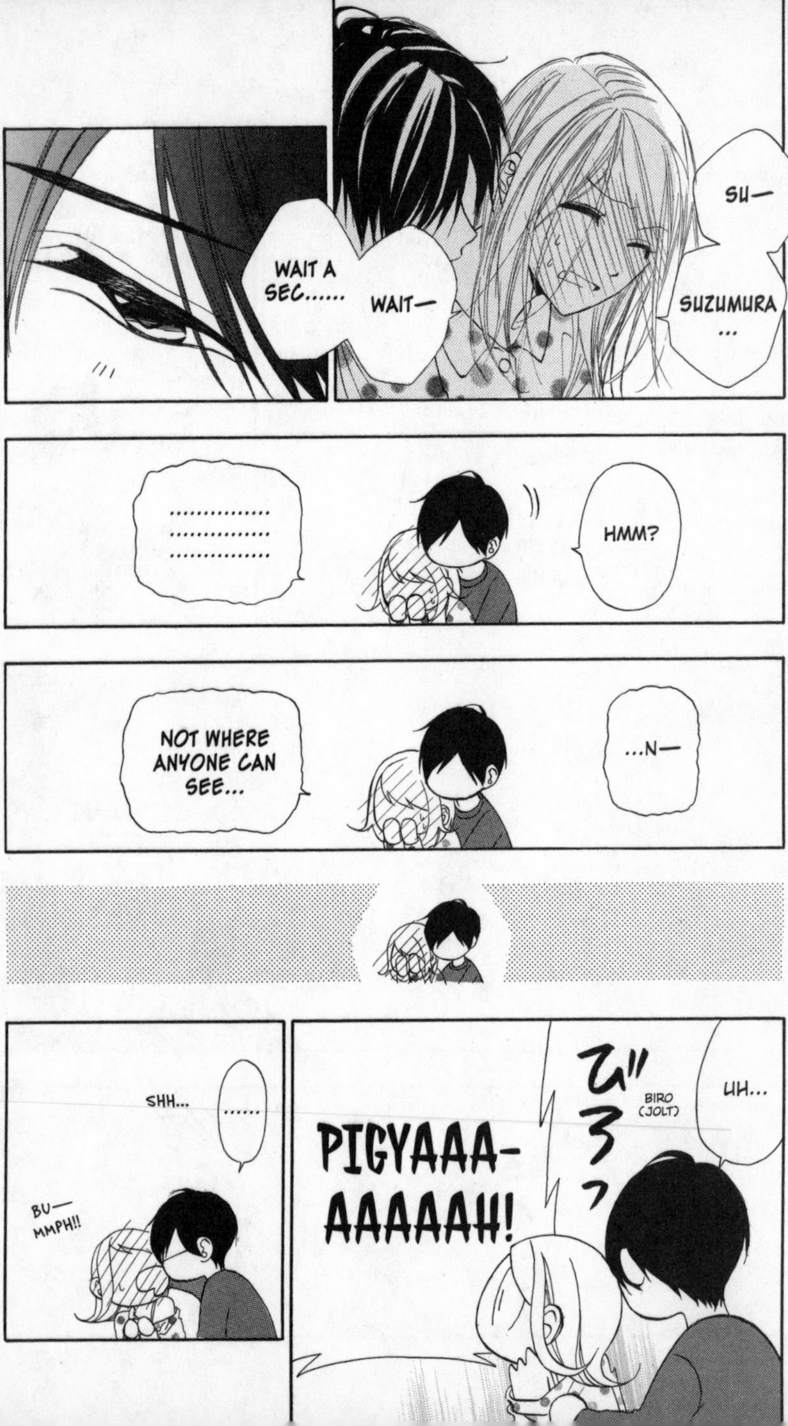
SU—
SUZUMURA...
WAIT—
WAIT A SEC......
HMM?
....
....
....
...N—
NOT WHERE ANYONE CAN SEE...
UH...
BIRO (JOLT)
PIGYAAA-AAAAAH!
......
SHH...
BU—MMPH!!

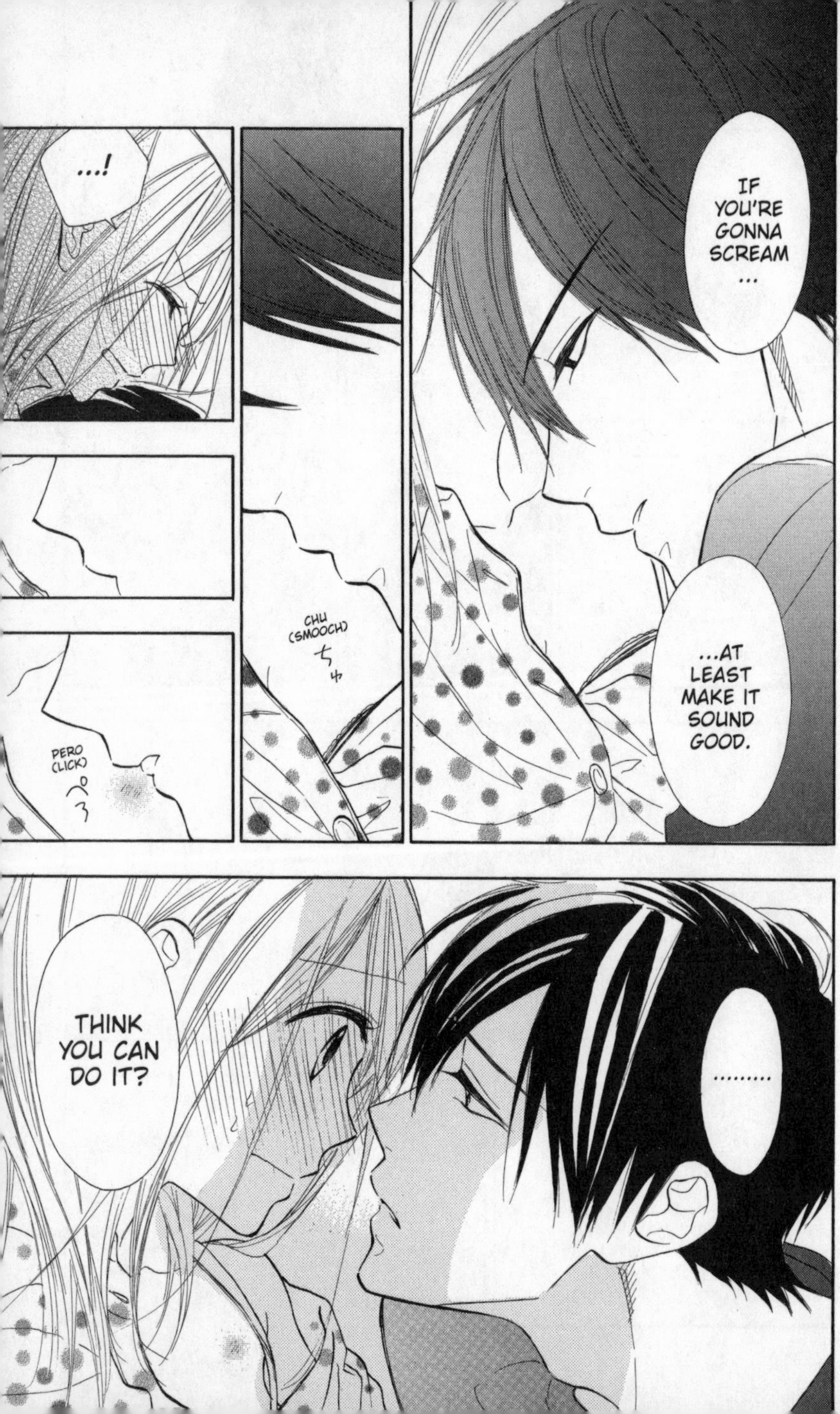
IF YOU'RE GONNA SCREAM ...
...AT LEAST MAKE IT SOUND GOOD.
CHU (SMOOCH)
ちゅ
...!
PERO (LICK)
ぺろ
....
THINK YOU CAN DO IT?

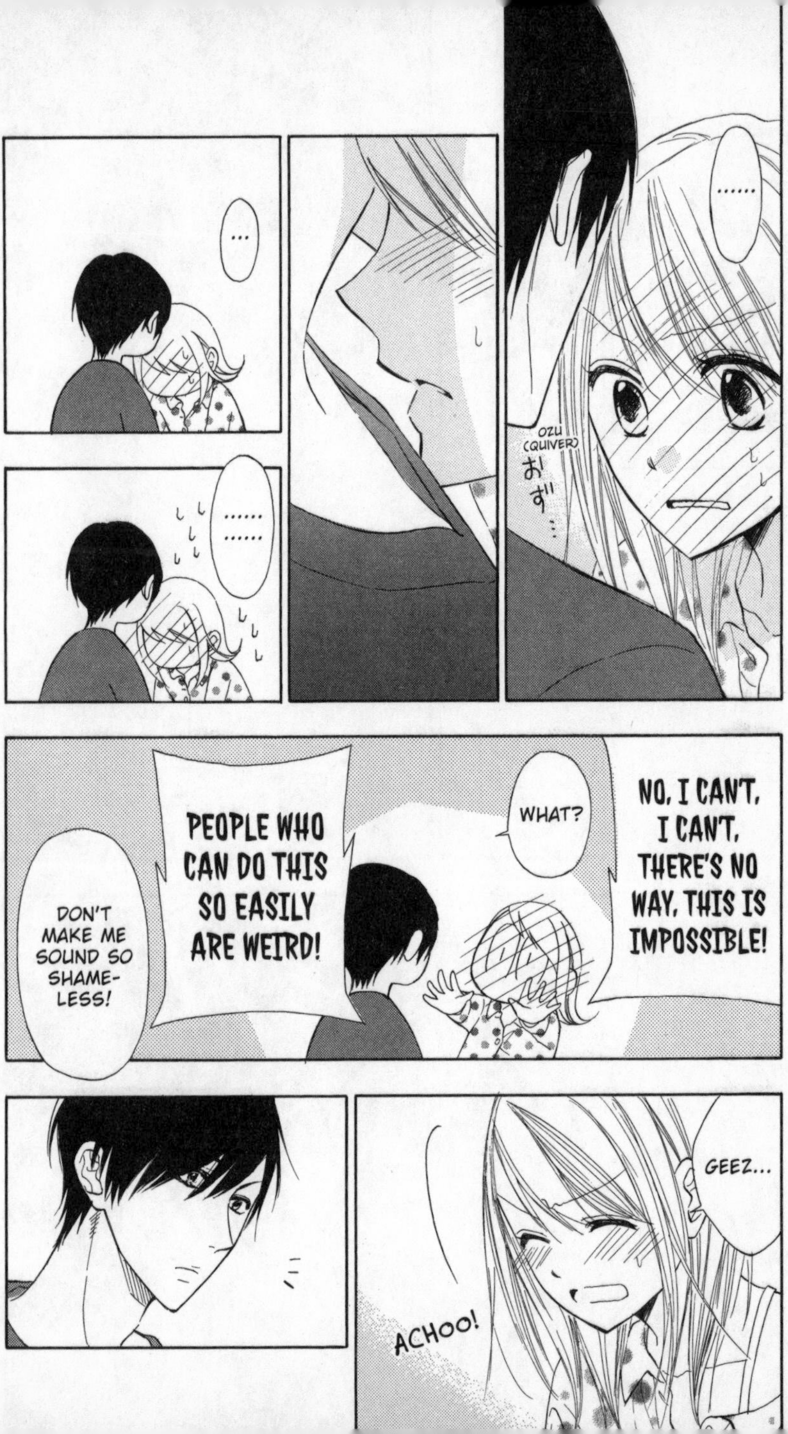
......
OZU (QUIVER)
おず…
...
......
......
NO, I CAN'T, I CAN'T, THERE'S NO WAY, THIS IS IMPOSSIBLE!
WHAT?
PEOPLE WHO CAN DO THIS SO EASILY ARE WEIRD!
DON'T MAKE ME SOUND SO SHAME-LESS!
GEEZ...
ACHOO!

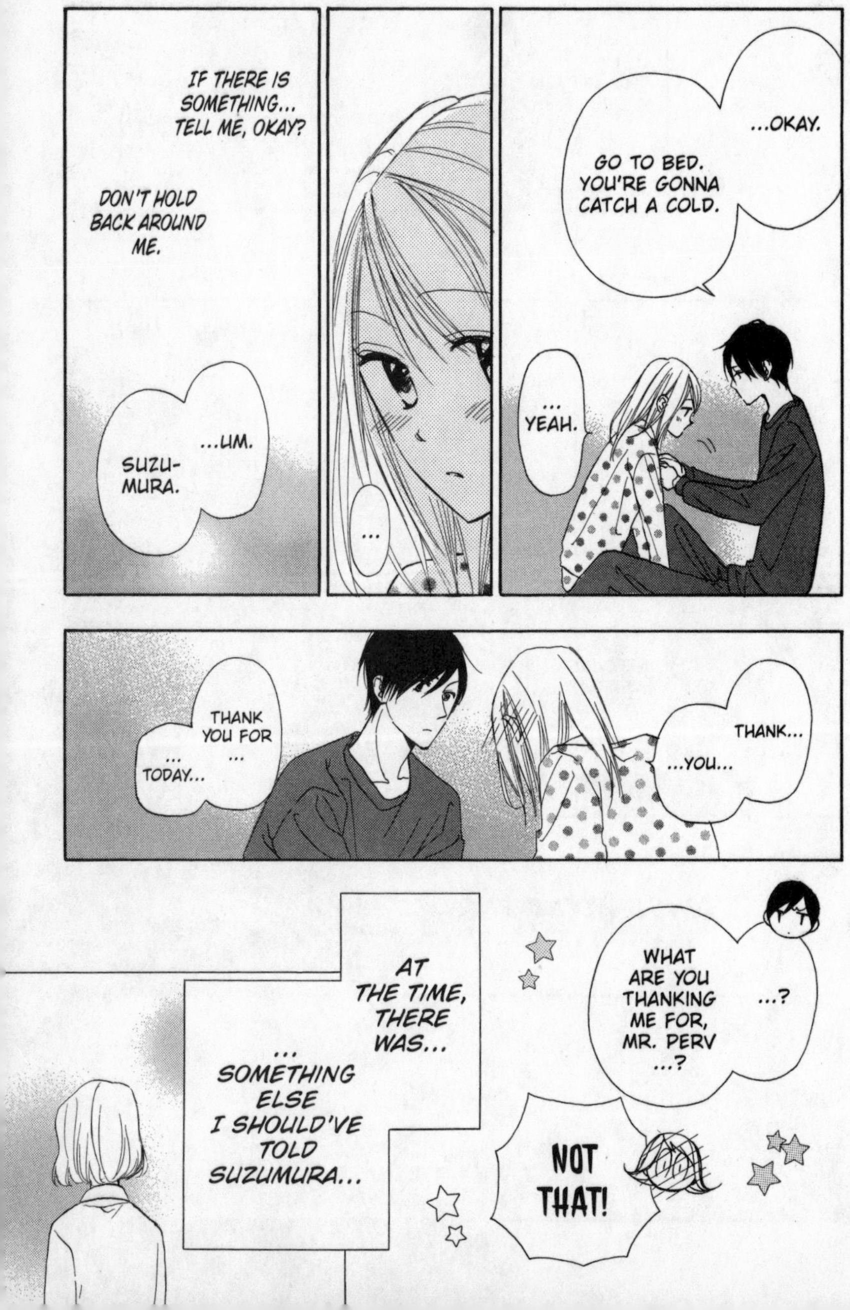
...OKAY.
GO TO BED. YOU'RE GONNA CATCH A COLD.
... YEAH.
...
IF THERE IS SOMETHING... TELL ME, OKAY?
DON'T HOLD BACK AROUND ME.
...UM.
SUZUMURA.
THANK...
...YOU...
THANK YOU FOR ... ... TODAY...
WHAT ARE YOU THANKING ME FOR, MR. PERV ...?
...?
NOT THAT!
AT THE TIME, THERE WAS...
... SOMETHING ELSE I SHOULD'VE TOLD SUZUMURA...

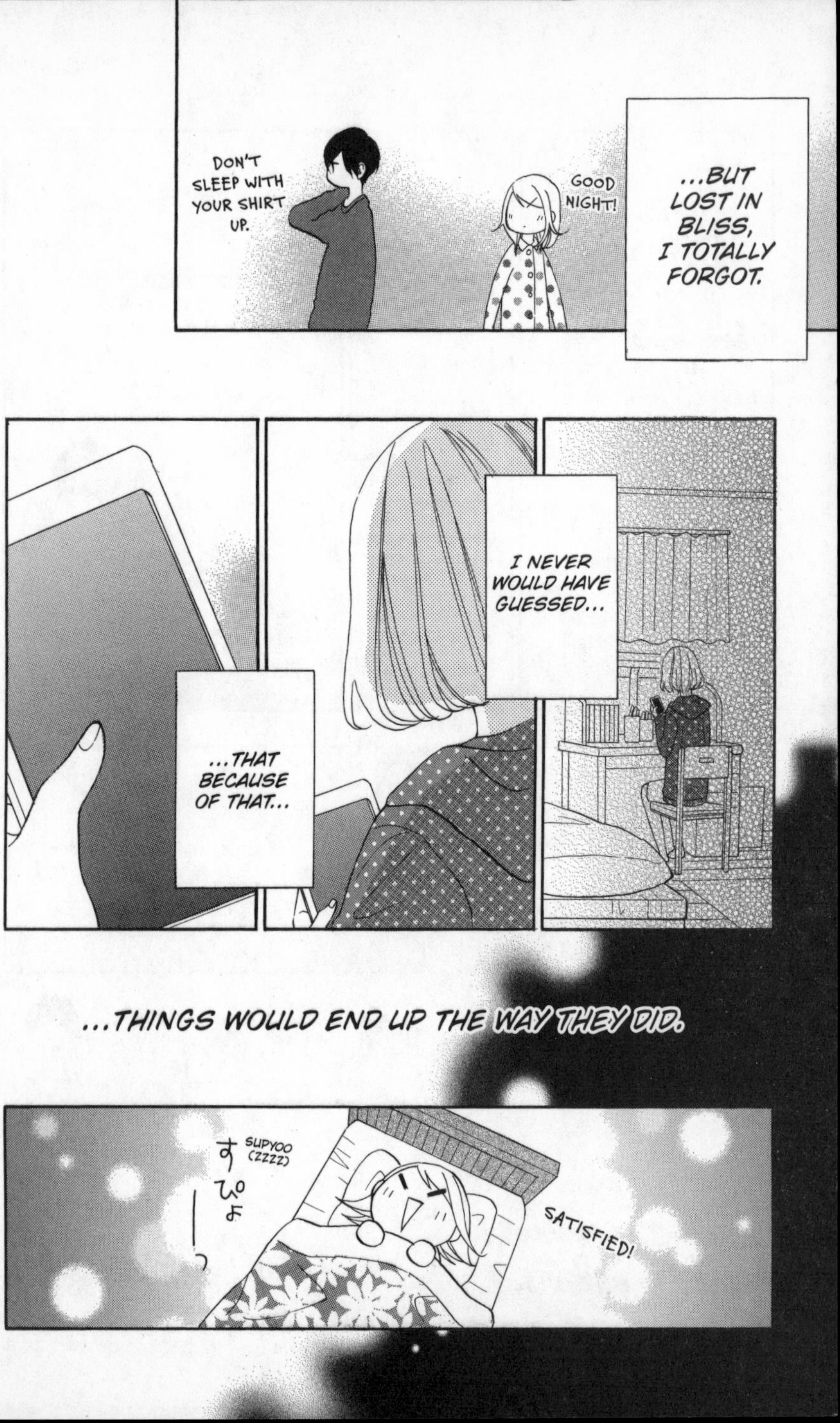
...BUT LOST IN BLISS, I TOTALLY FORGOT.
GOOD NIGHT!
DON'T SLEEP WITH YOUR SHIRT UP.
I NEVER WOULD HAVE GUESSED...
...THAT BECAUSE OF THAT...
...THINGS WOULD END UP THE WAY THEY DID.
SATISFIED!
すぴょーっ
SUPYOO (ZZZZ)

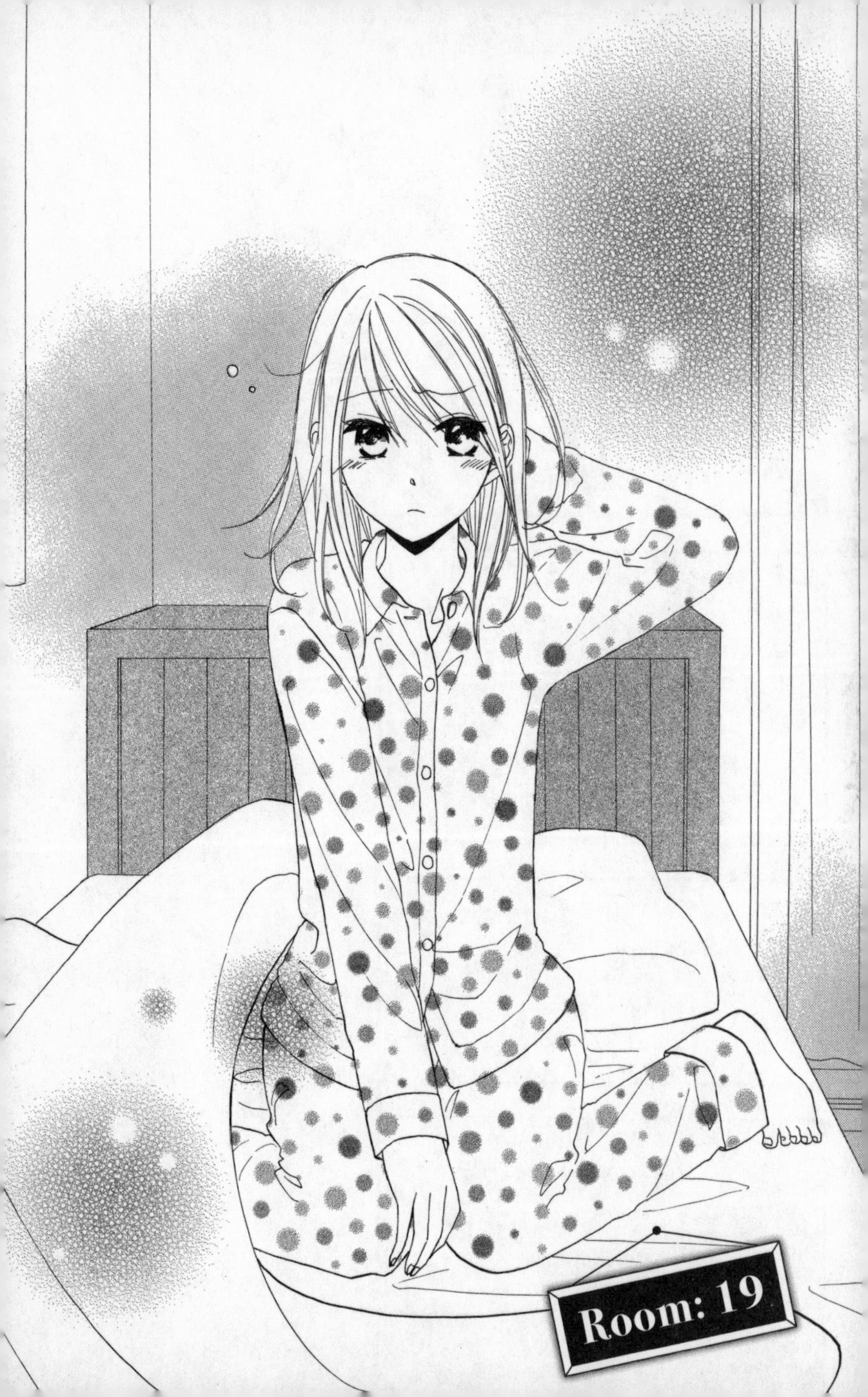
Room: 19

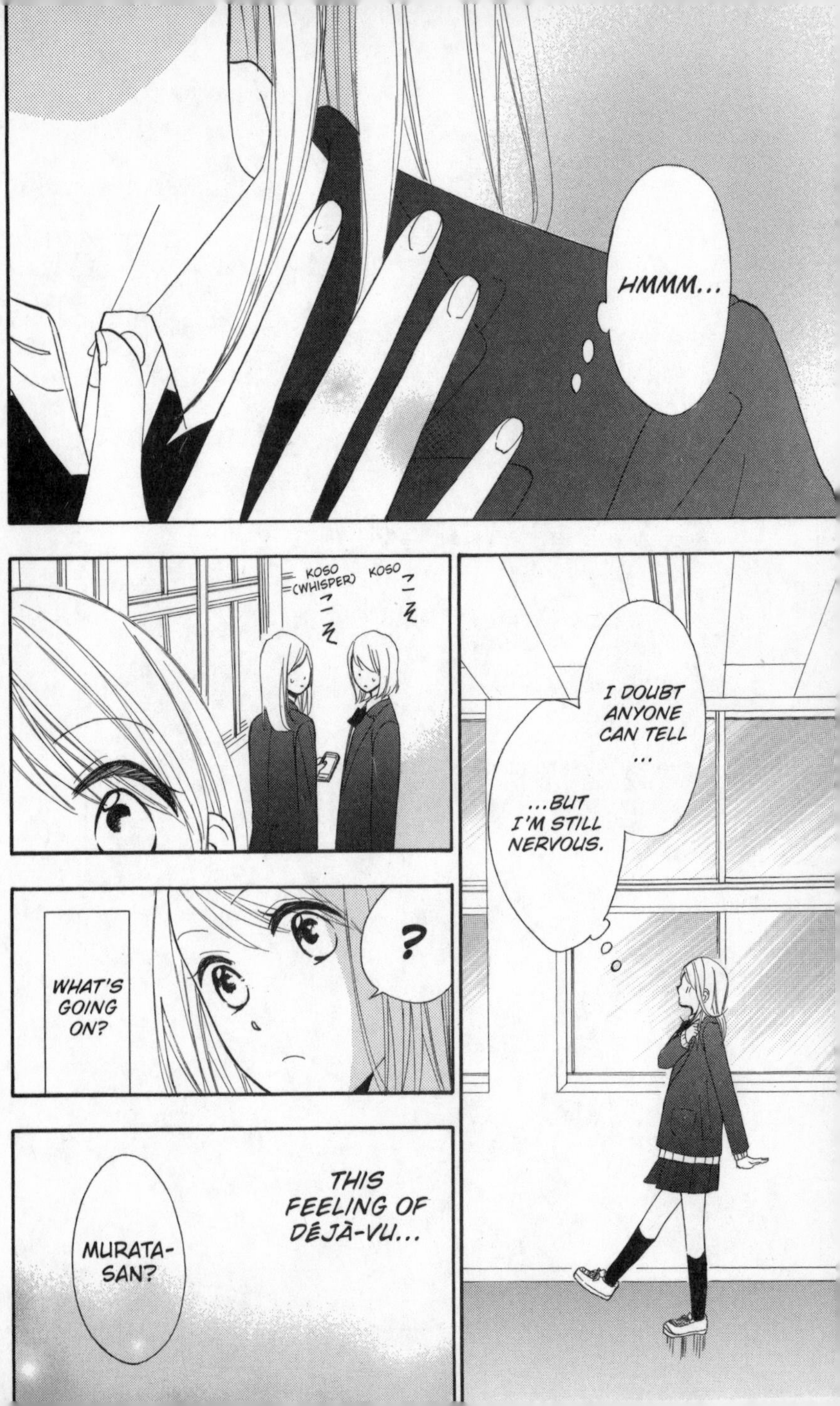
HMMM...
I DOUBT ANYONE CAN TELL...
...BUT I'M STILL NERVOUS.
KOSO (WHISPER) KOSO
こそ こそ
?
WHAT'S GOING ON?
THIS FEELING OF DÉJÀ-VU...
MURATA-SAN?

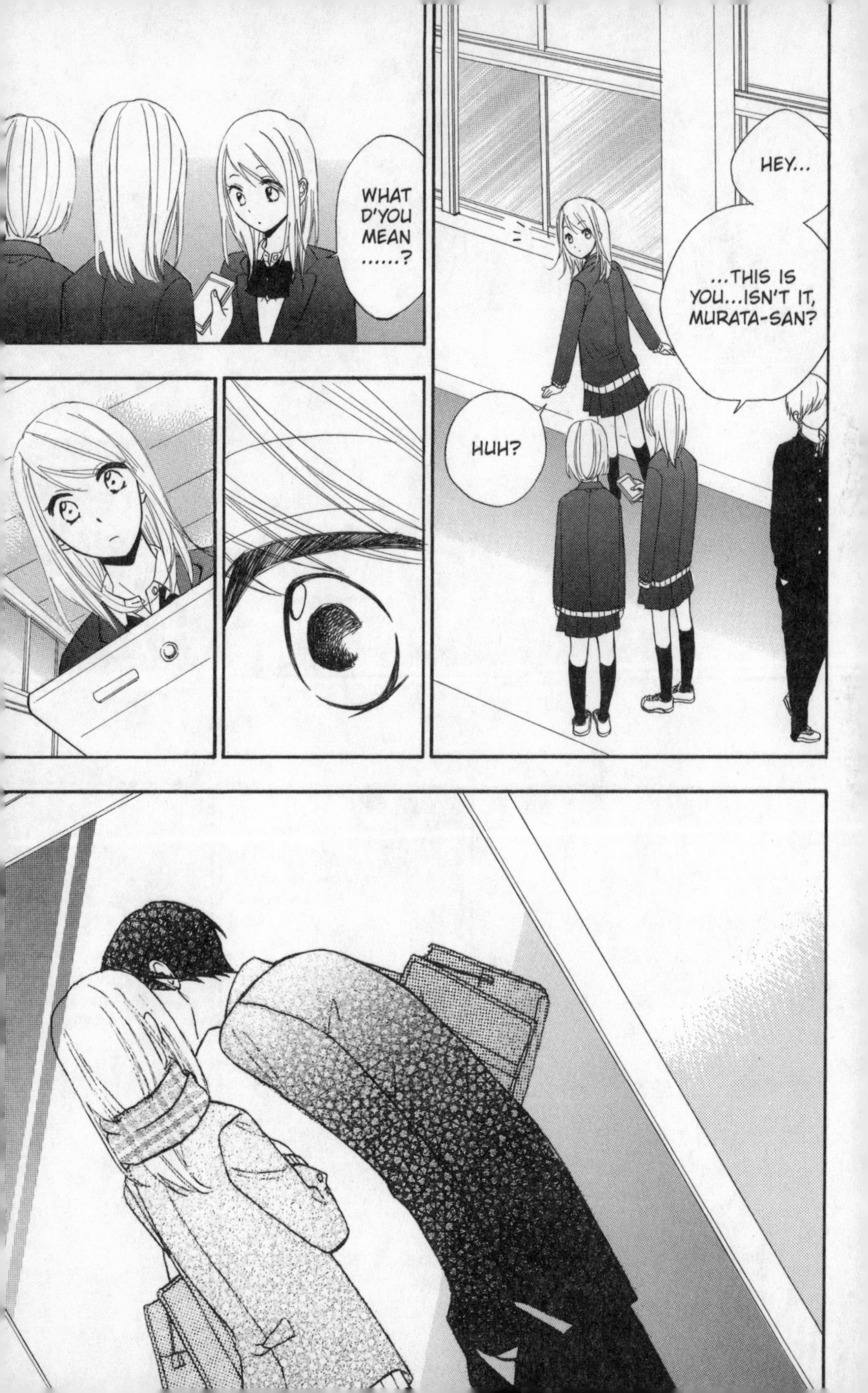
HEY...
...THIS IS YOU...ISN'T IT, MURATA-SAN?
HUH?
WHAT D'YOU MEAN ......?

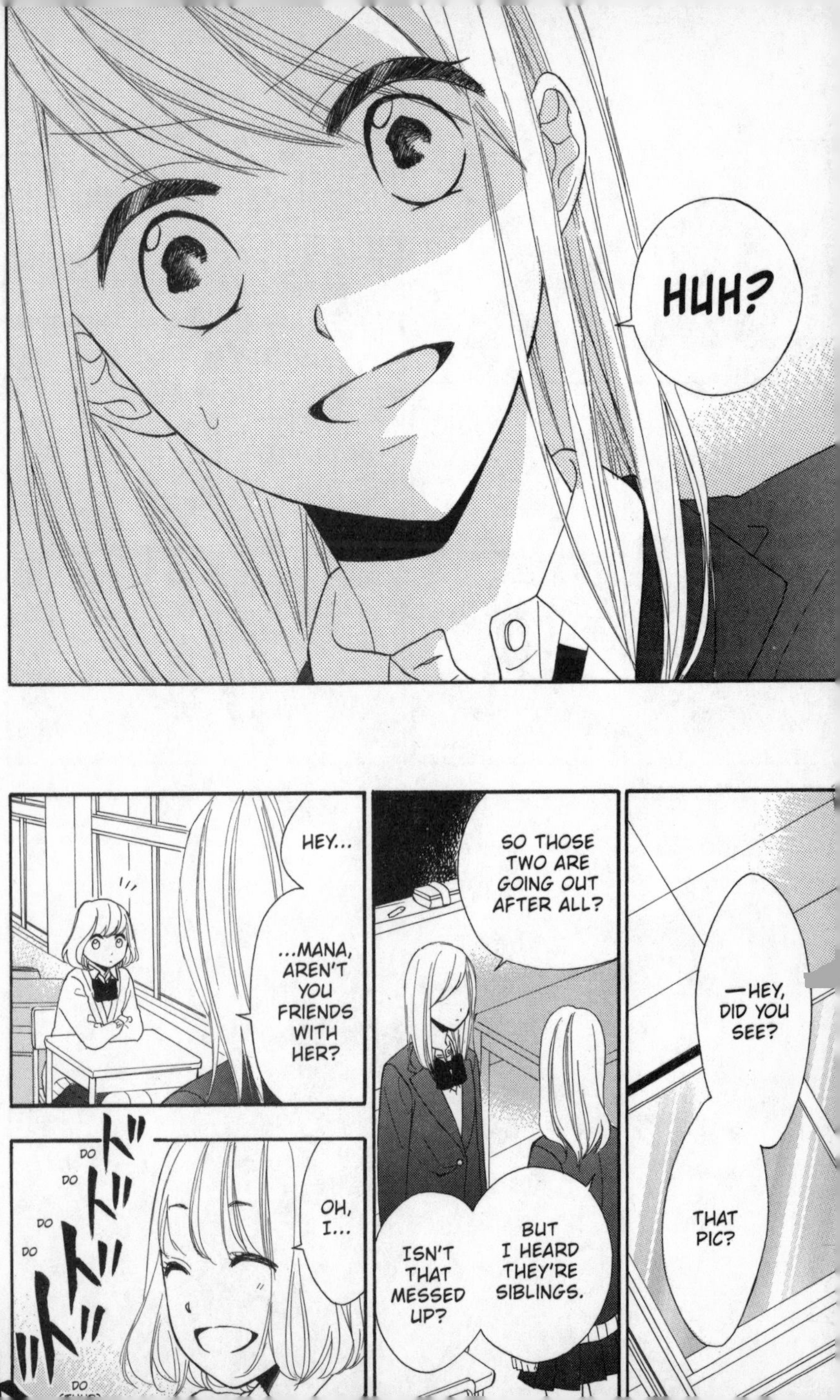
HUH?
—HEY, DID YOU SEE?
THAT PIC?
SO THOSE TWO ARE GOING OUT AFTER ALL?
BUT I HEARD THEY'RE SIBLINGS.
ISN'T THAT MESSED UP?
HEY...
...MANA, AREN'T YOU FRIENDS WITH HER?
OH, I...
DO
DO
DO
DO
DO

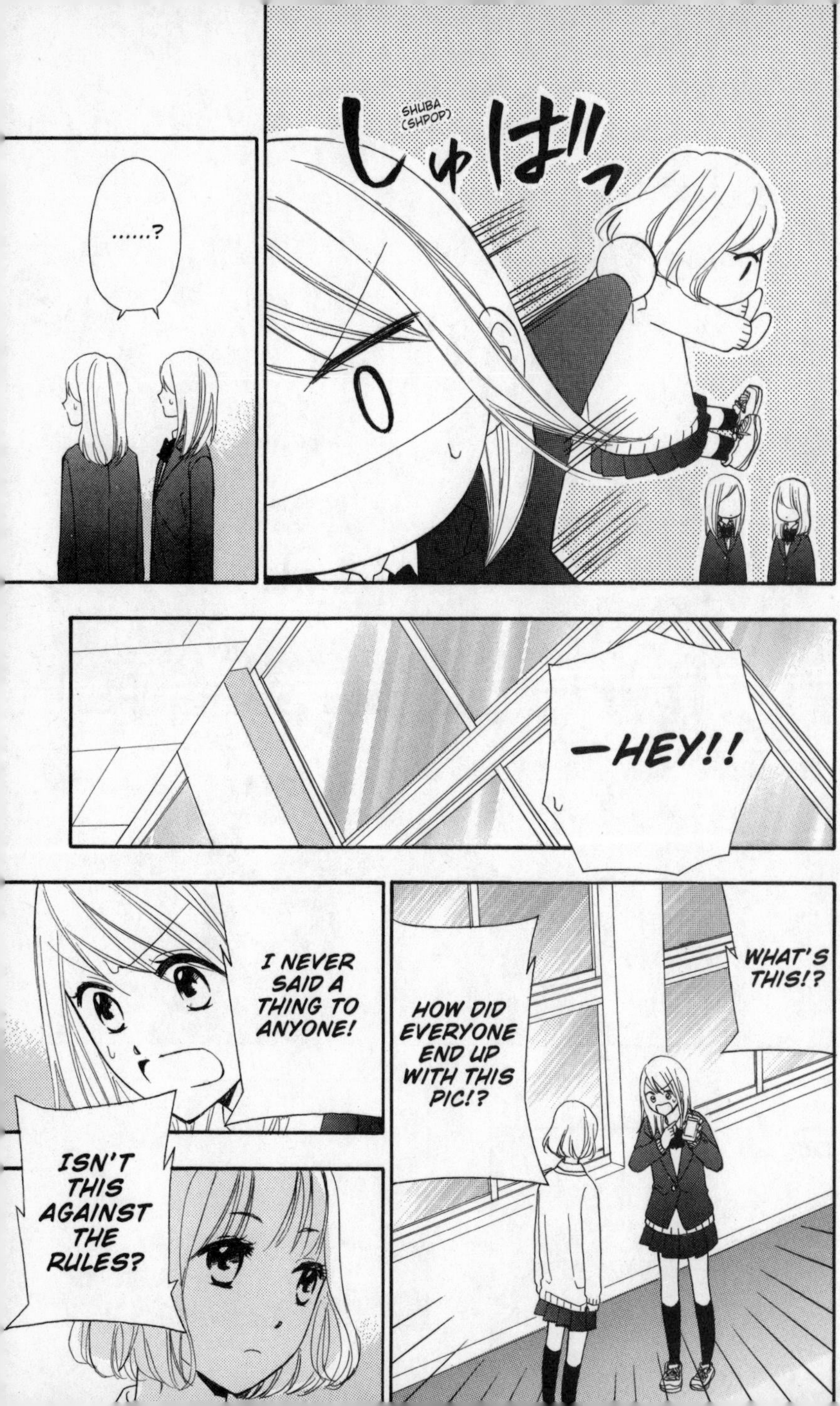
しゅばっ
SHUBA (SHPOP)
......?
—HEY!!
WHAT'S THIS!?
HOW DID EVERYONE END UP WITH THIS PIC!?
I NEVER SAID A THING TO ANYONE!
ISN'T THIS AGAINST THE RULES?

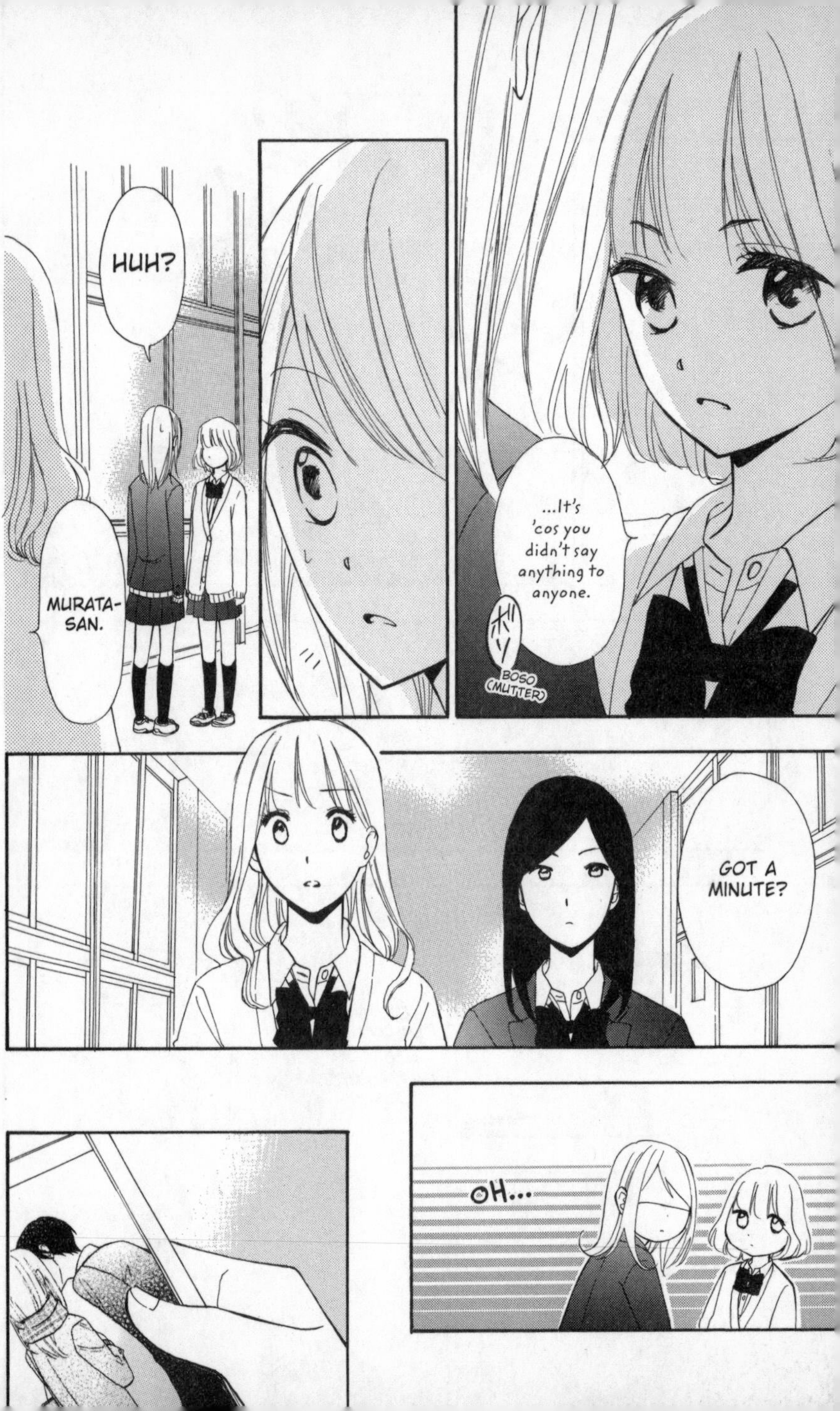
...It's 'cos you didn't say anything to anyone.
ボソ
BOSO (MUTTER)
HUH?
MURATA-SAN.
GOT A MINUTE?
OH...

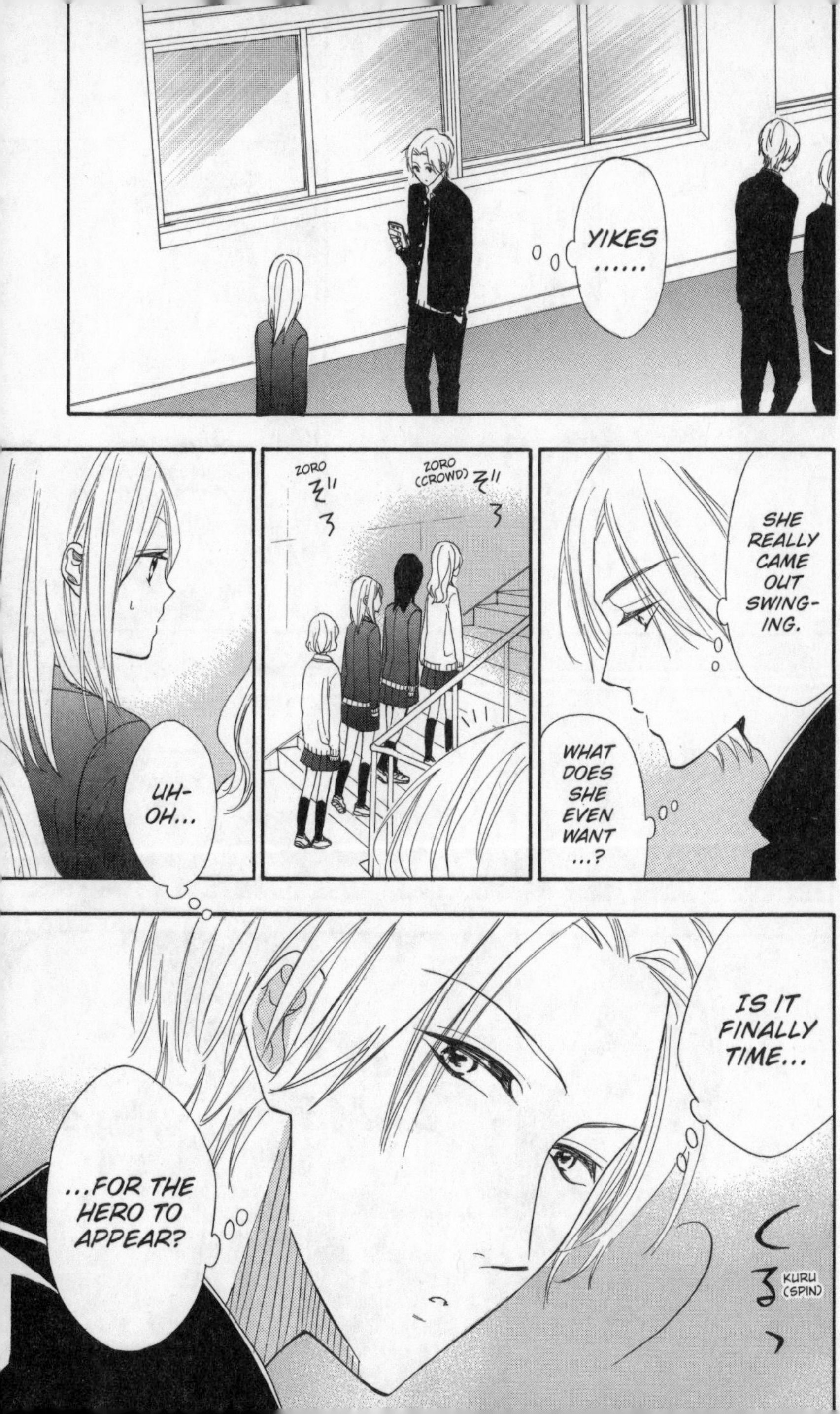
YIKES ......
SHE REALLY CAME OUT SWING-ING.
WHAT DOES SHE EVEN WANT ...?
ZORO (CROWD)
ZORO
UH-OH...
IS IT FINALLY TIME...
...FOR THE HERO TO APPEAR?
KURU (SPIN)

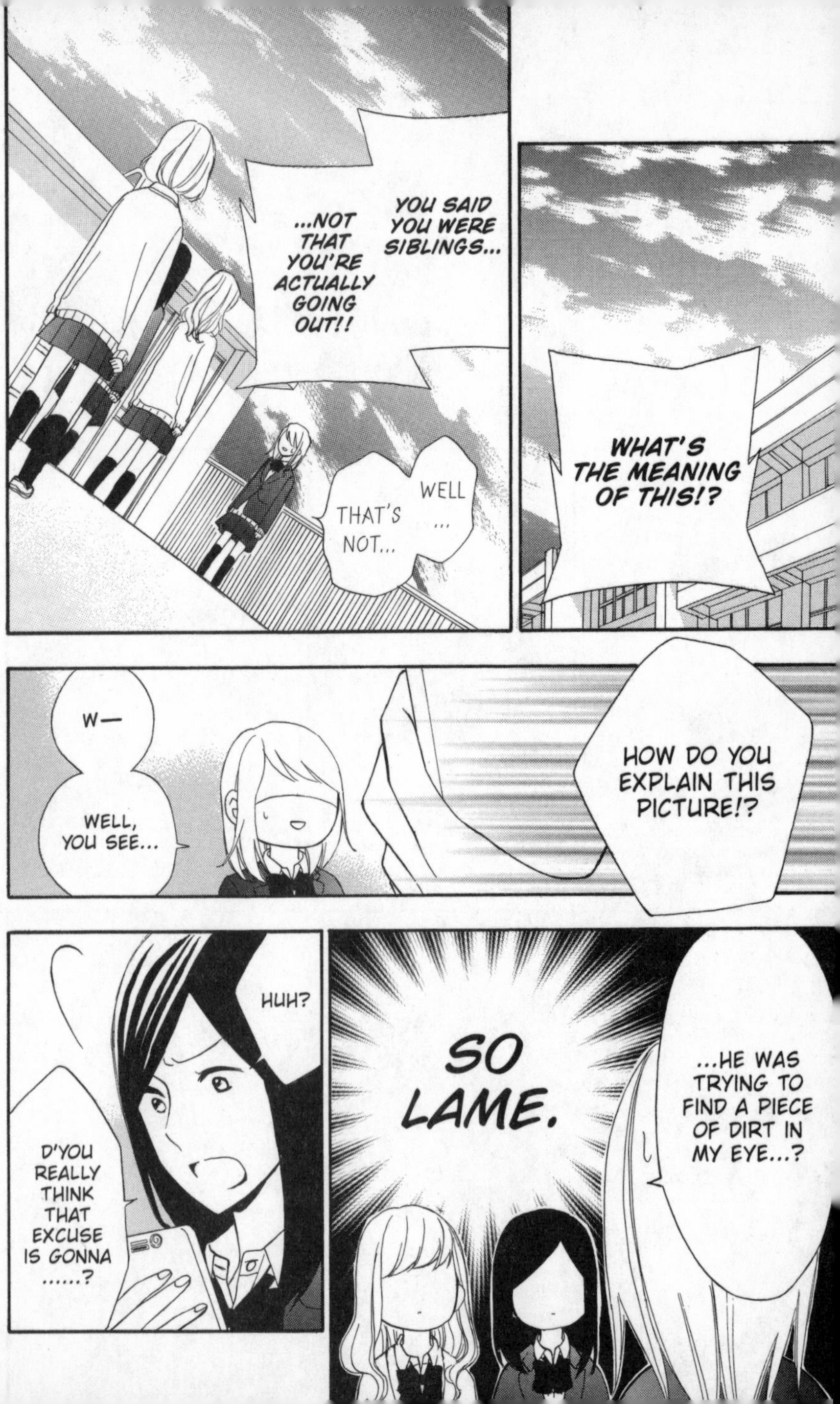
WHAT'S THE MEANING OF THIS!?
YOU SAID YOU WERE SIBLINGS...
...NOT THAT YOU'RE ACTUALLY GOING OUT!!
WELL...
THAT'S NOT...
HOW DO YOU EXPLAIN THIS PICTURE!?
W—
WELL, YOU SEE...
...HE WAS TRYING TO FIND A PIECE OF DIRT IN MY EYE...?
SO LAME.
HUH?
D'YOU REALLY THINK THAT EXCUSE IS GONNA ......?

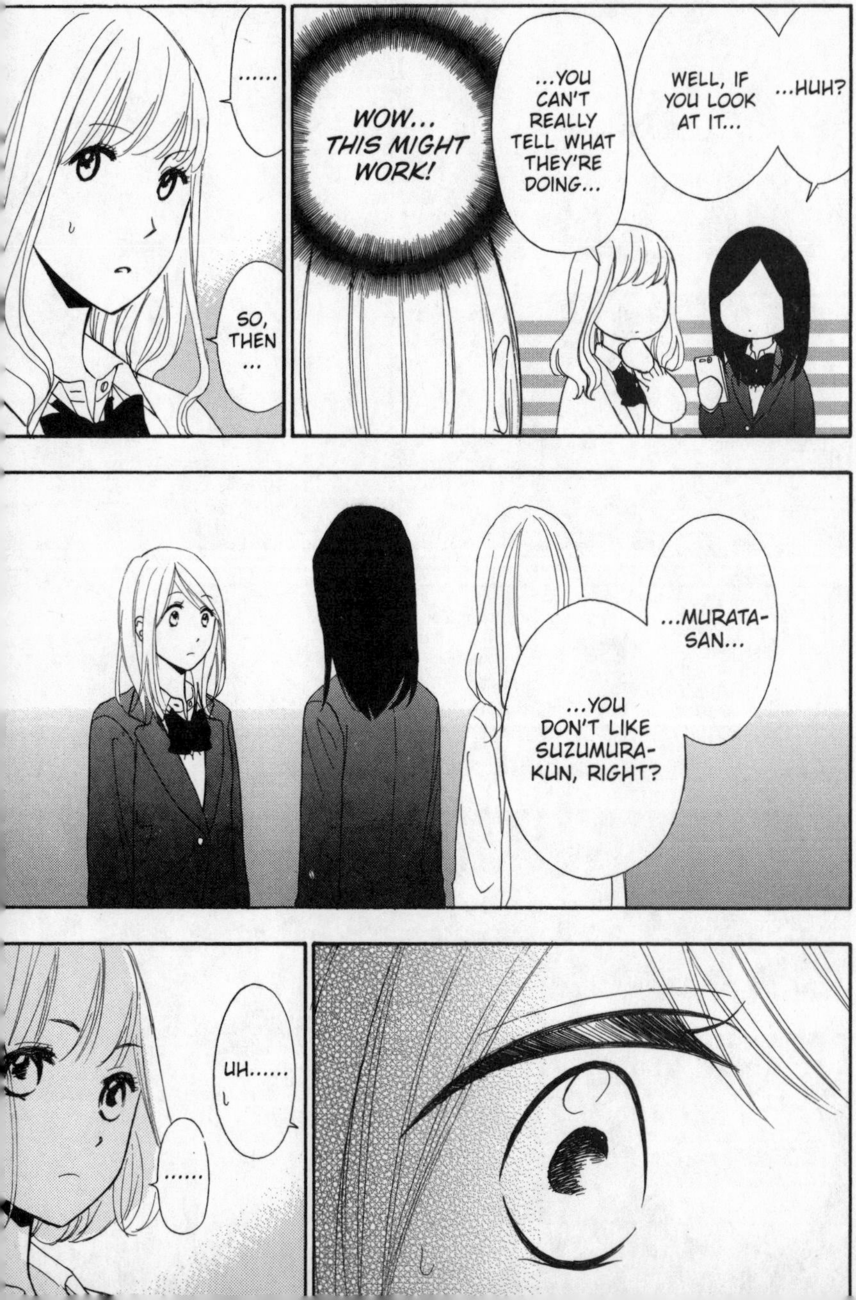
...HUH?
WELL, IF YOU LOOK AT IT...
...YOU CAN'T REALLY TELL WHAT THEY'RE DOING...
WOW... THIS MIGHT WORK!
......
SO, THEN ...
...MURATA-SAN...
...YOU DON'T LIKE SUZUMURA-KUN, RIGHT?
UH......
......

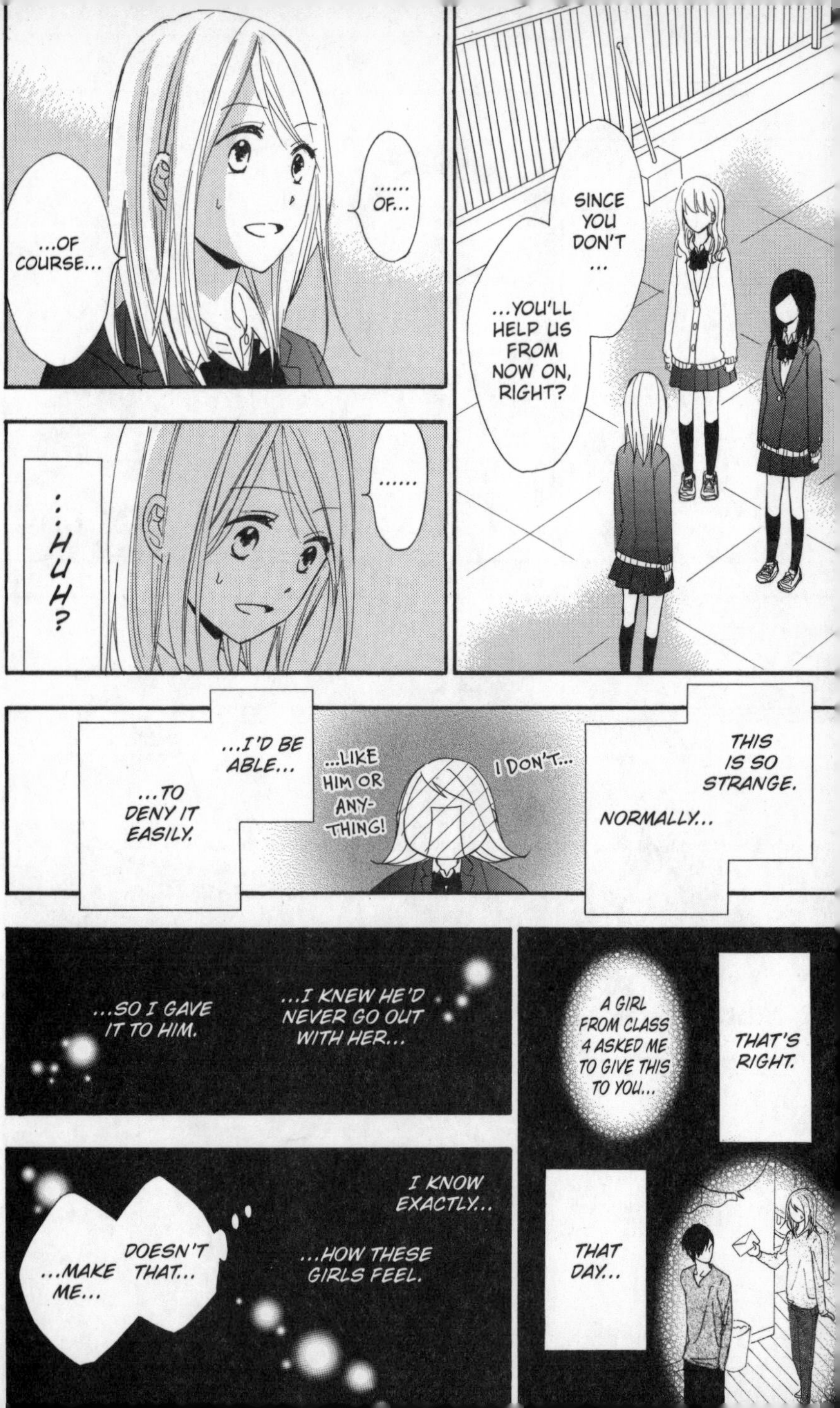
SINCE YOU DON'T ...
...YOU'LL HELP US FROM NOW ON, RIGHT?
...... OF...
...OF COURSE...
......
...HUH?
THIS IS SO STRANGE.
NORMALLY...
I DON'T...
...LIKE HIM OR ANY-THING!
...I'D BE ABLE...
...TO DENY IT EASILY.
THAT'S RIGHT.
A GIRL FROM CLASS 4 ASKED ME TO GIVE THIS TO YOU...
THAT DAY...
...I KNEW HE'D NEVER GO OUT WITH HER...
...SO I GAVE IT TO HIM.
I KNOW EXACTLY...
...HOW THESE GIRLS FEEL.
DOESN'T THAT...
...MAKE ME...

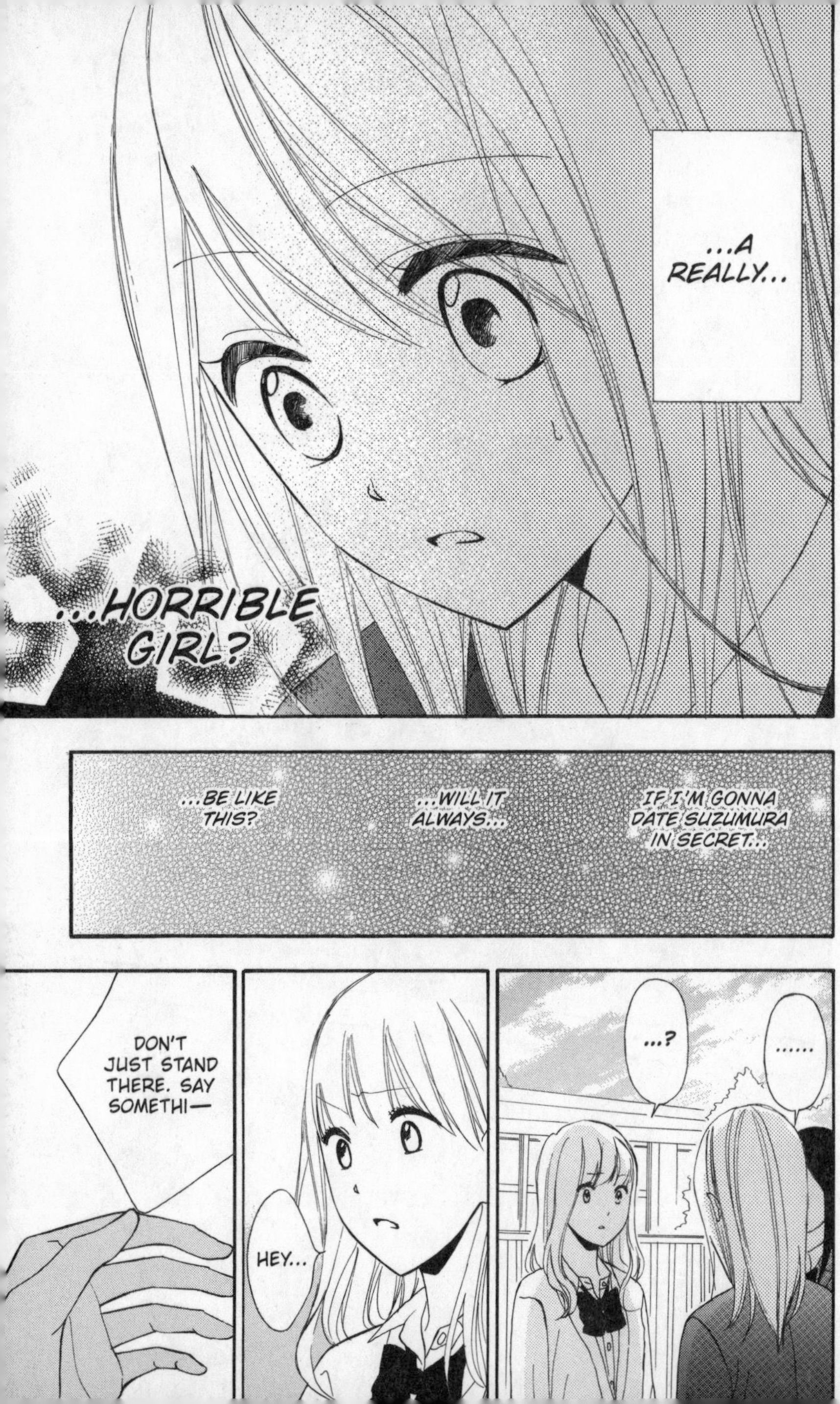
...A REALLY...
...HORRIBLE GIRL?
IF I'M GONNA DATE SUZUMURA IN SECRET...
...WILL IT ALWAYS...
...BE LIKE THIS?
......
...?
HEY...
DON'T JUST STAND THERE. SAY SOMETHI—

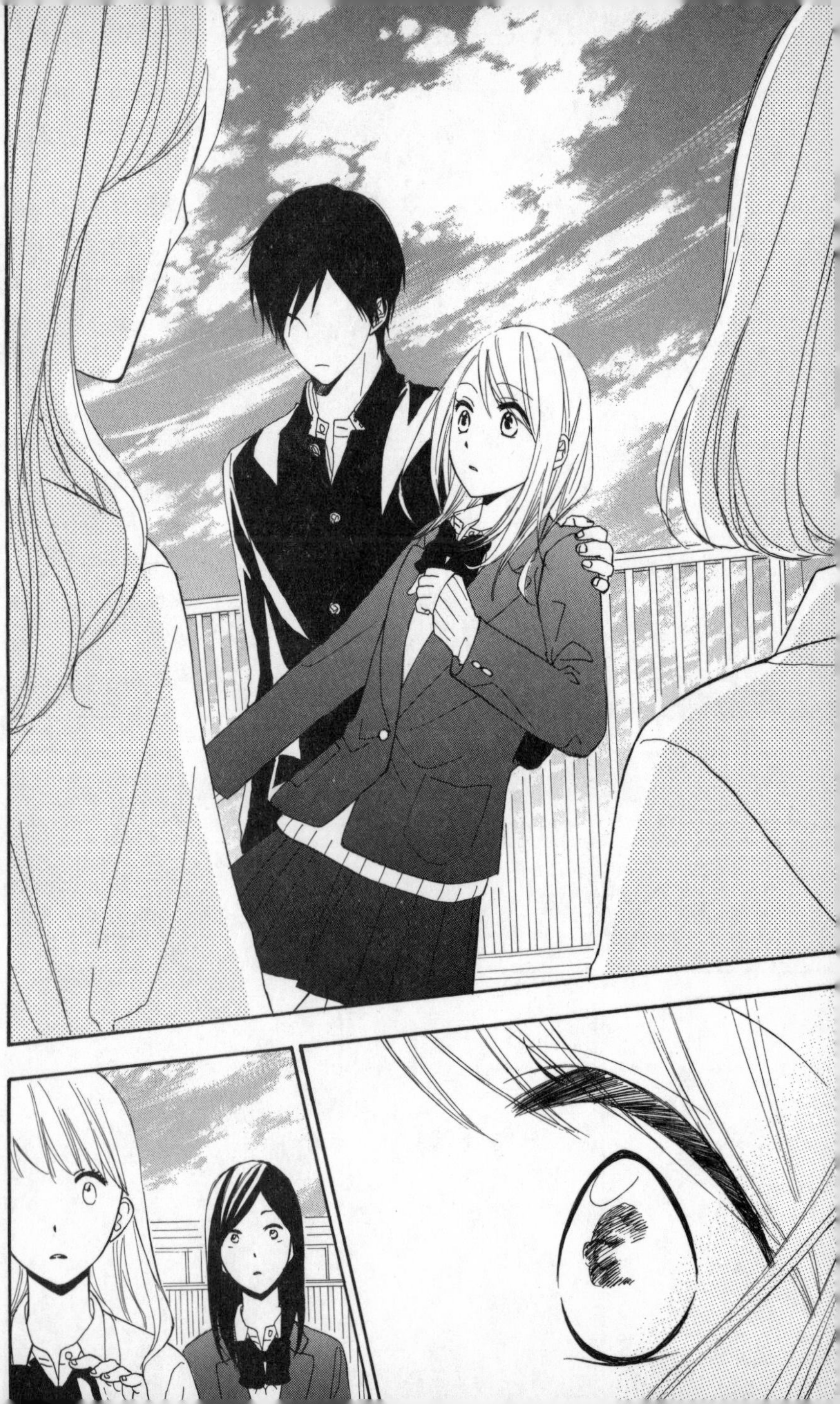

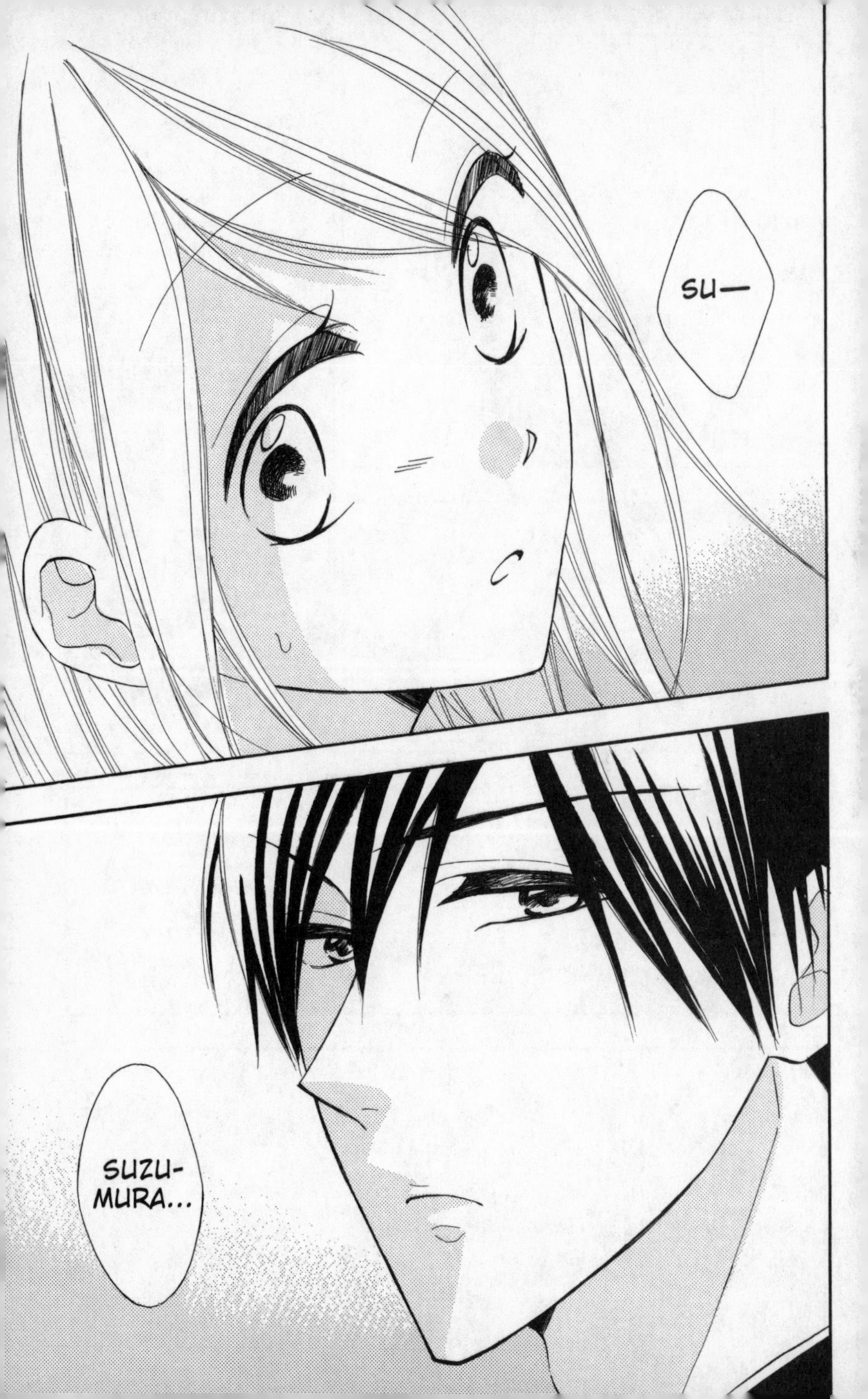
SU—
SUZU-
MURA...

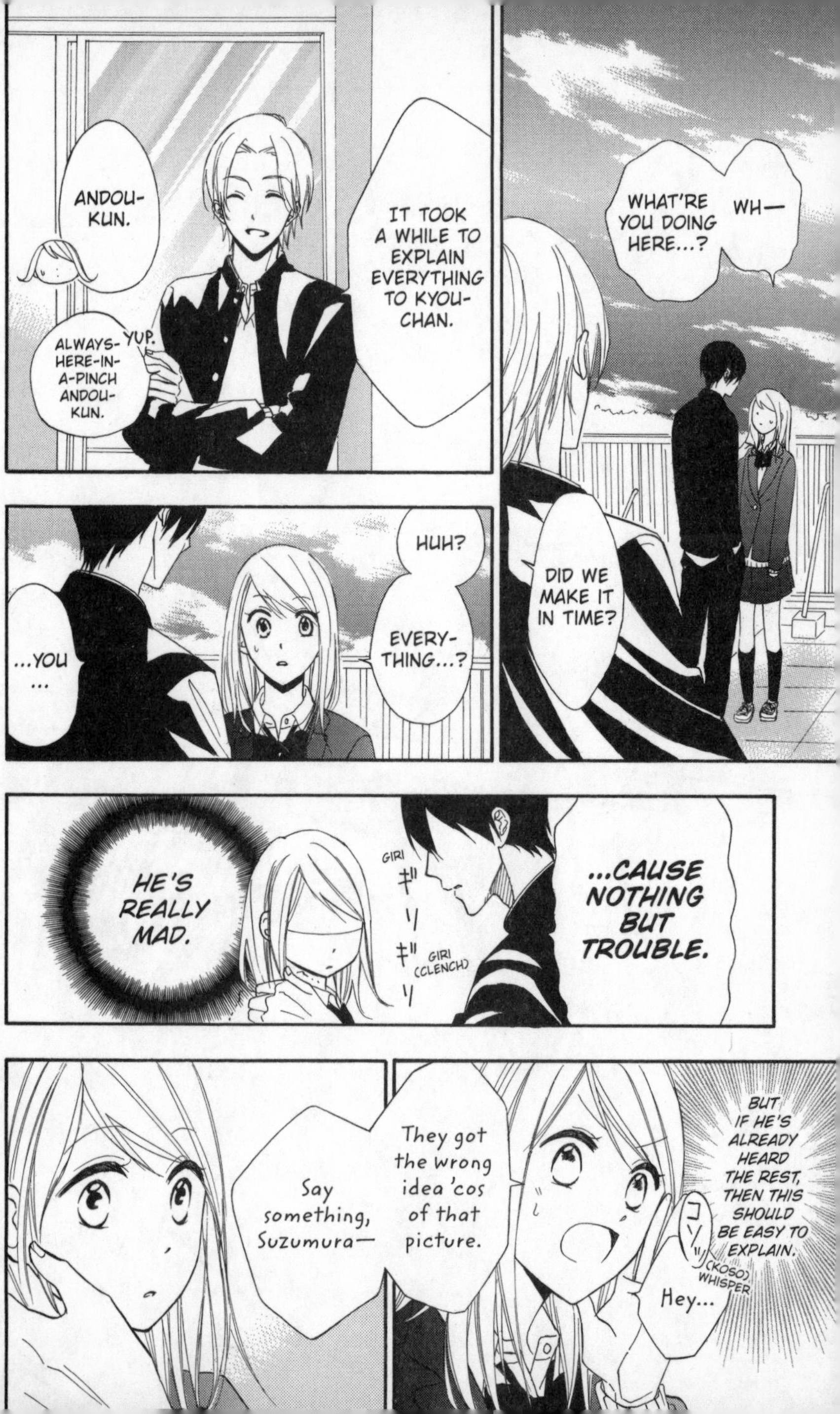
WH—
WHAT'RE YOU DOING HERE...?
DID WE MAKE IT IN TIME?
IT TOOK A WHILE TO EXPLAIN EVERYTHING TO KYOU-CHAN.
ANDOU-KUN.
YUP.
ALWAYS-HERE-IN-A-PINCH ANDOU-KUN.
HUH?
EVERY-THING...?
...YOU ...
...CAUSE NOTHING BUT TROUBLE.
GIRI GIRI (CLENCH)
HE'S REALLY MAD.
BUT IF HE'S ALREADY HEARD THE REST, THEN THIS SHOULD BE EASY TO EXPLAIN.
(KOSO) WHISPER
Hey...
They got the wrong idea 'cos of that picture.
Say something, Suzumura—

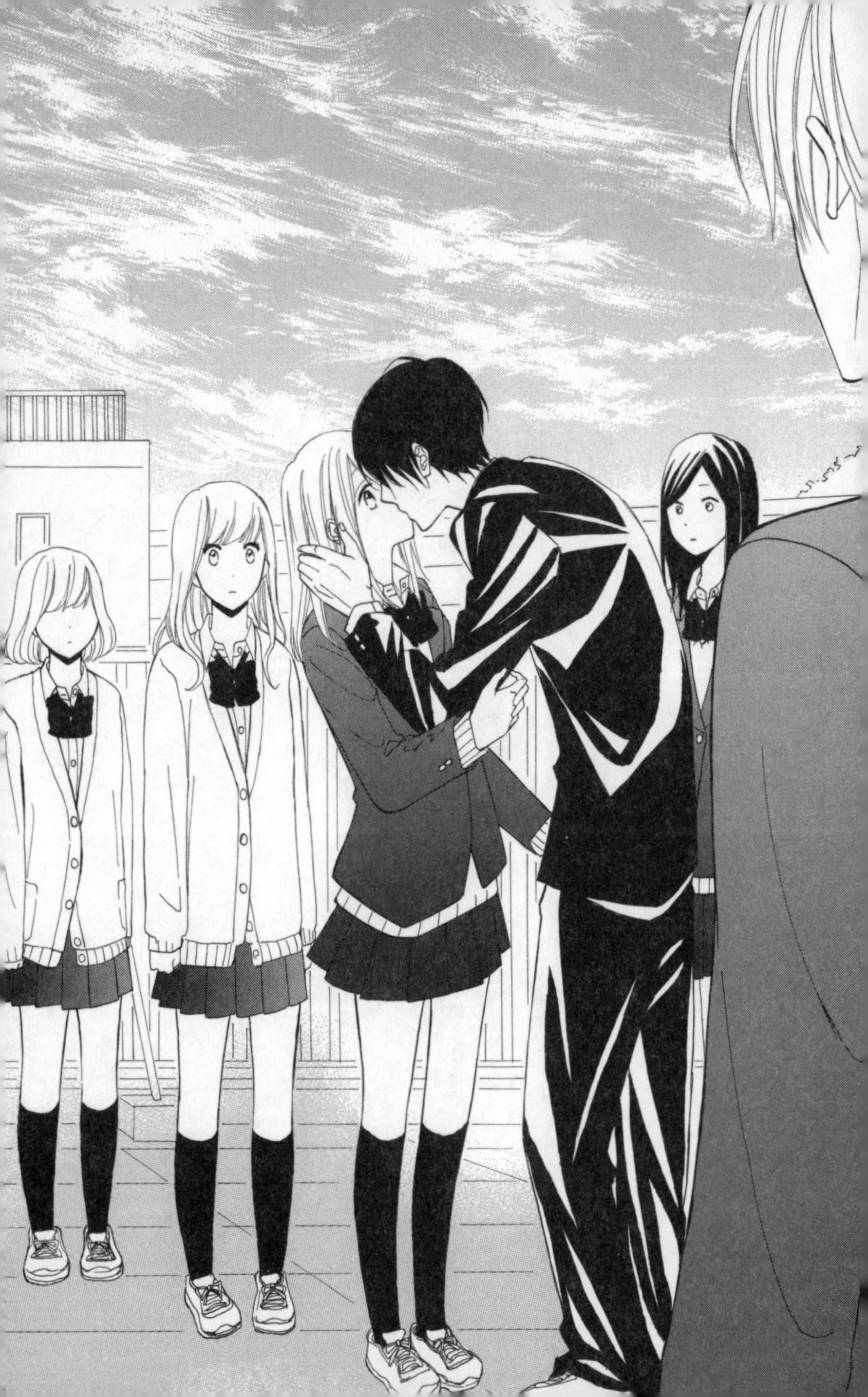

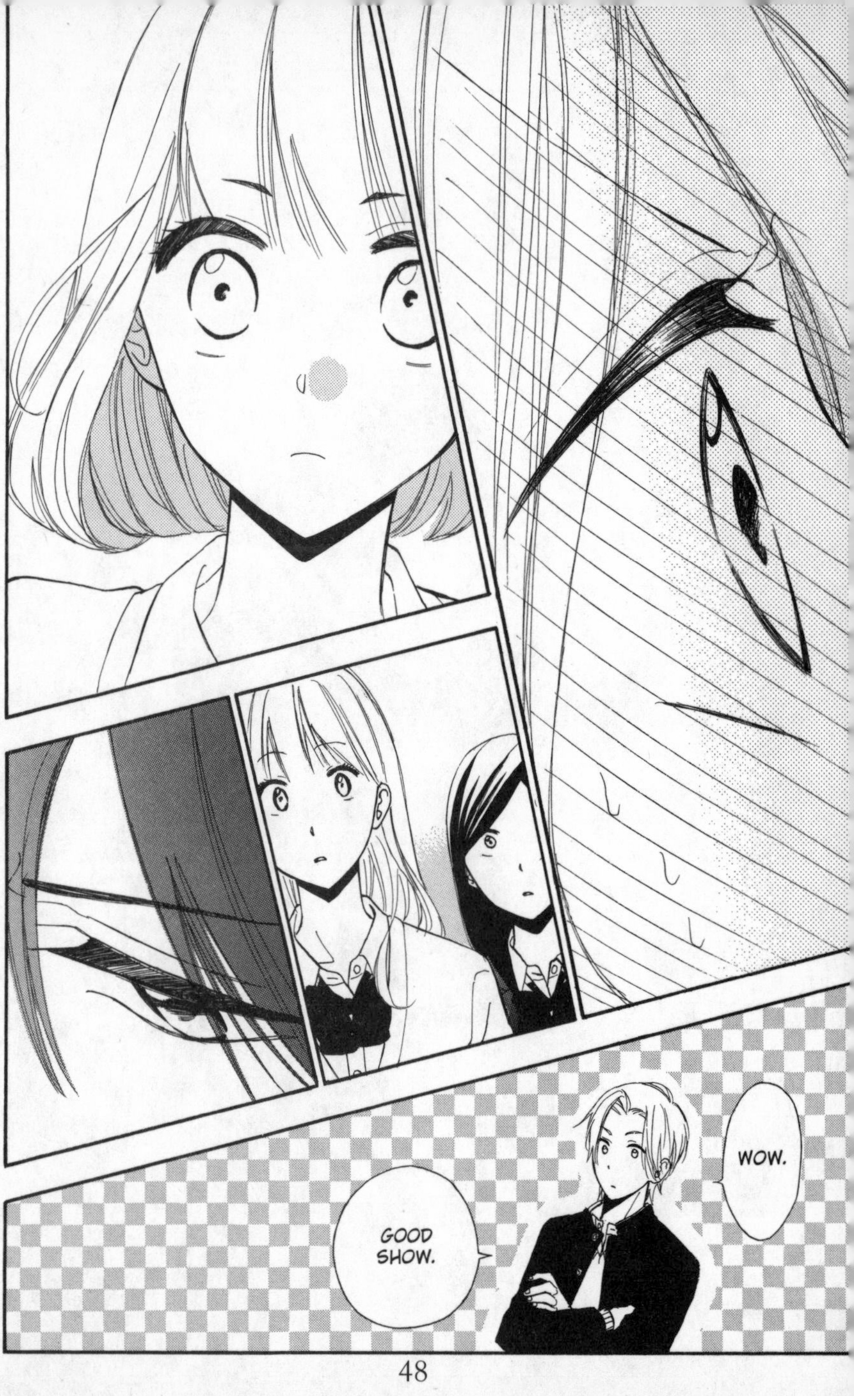
WOW.
GOOD SHOW.

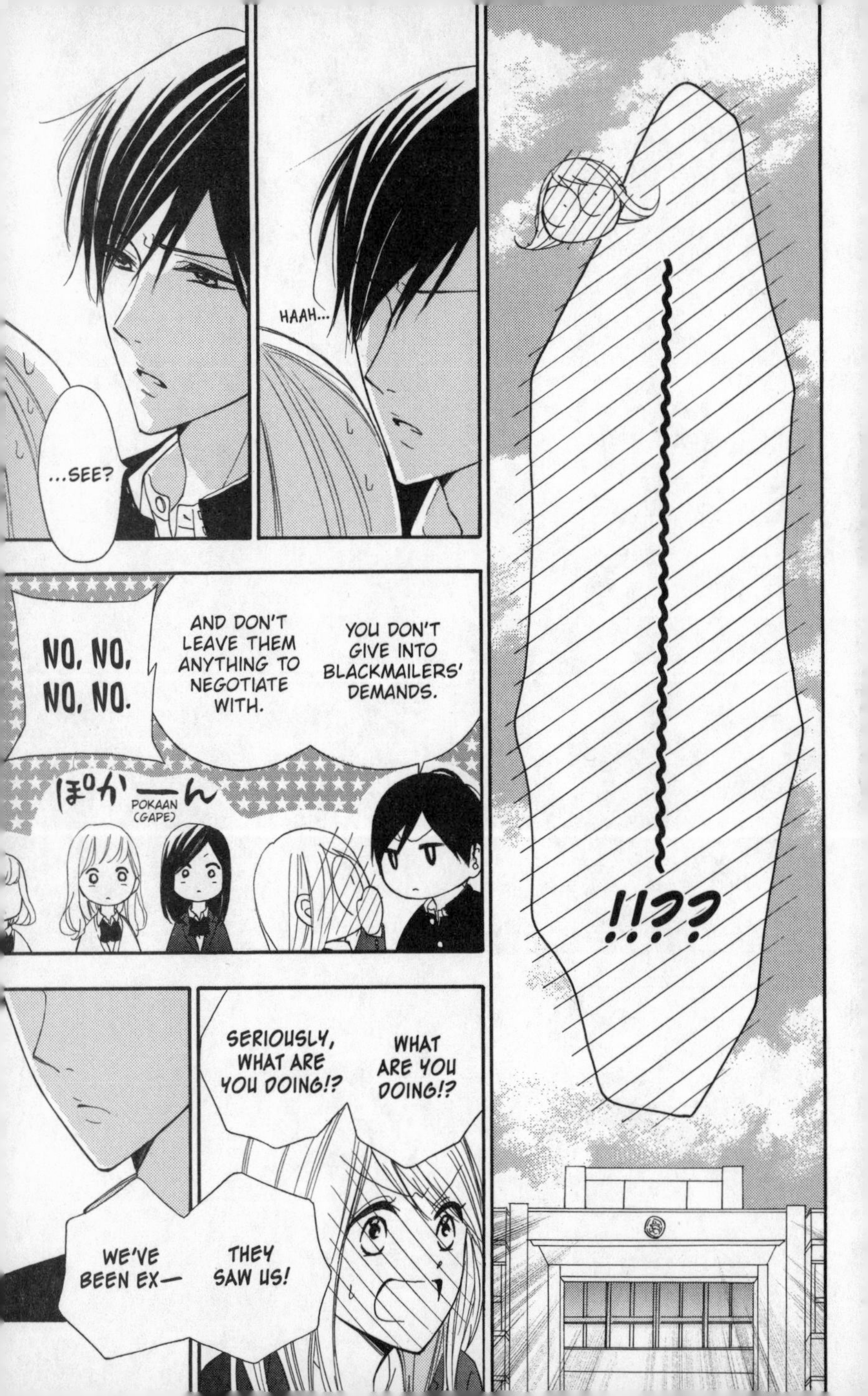
!!??
HAAH...
...SEE?
YOU DON'T GIVE INTO BLACKMAILERS' DEMANDS.
AND DON'T LEAVE THEM ANYTHING TO NEGOTIATE WITH.
NO, NO, NO, NO.
ぽかーん
POKAAN (GAPE)
WHAT ARE YOU DOING!?
SERIOUSLY, WHAT ARE YOU DOING!?
THEY SAW US!
WE'VE BEEN EX—

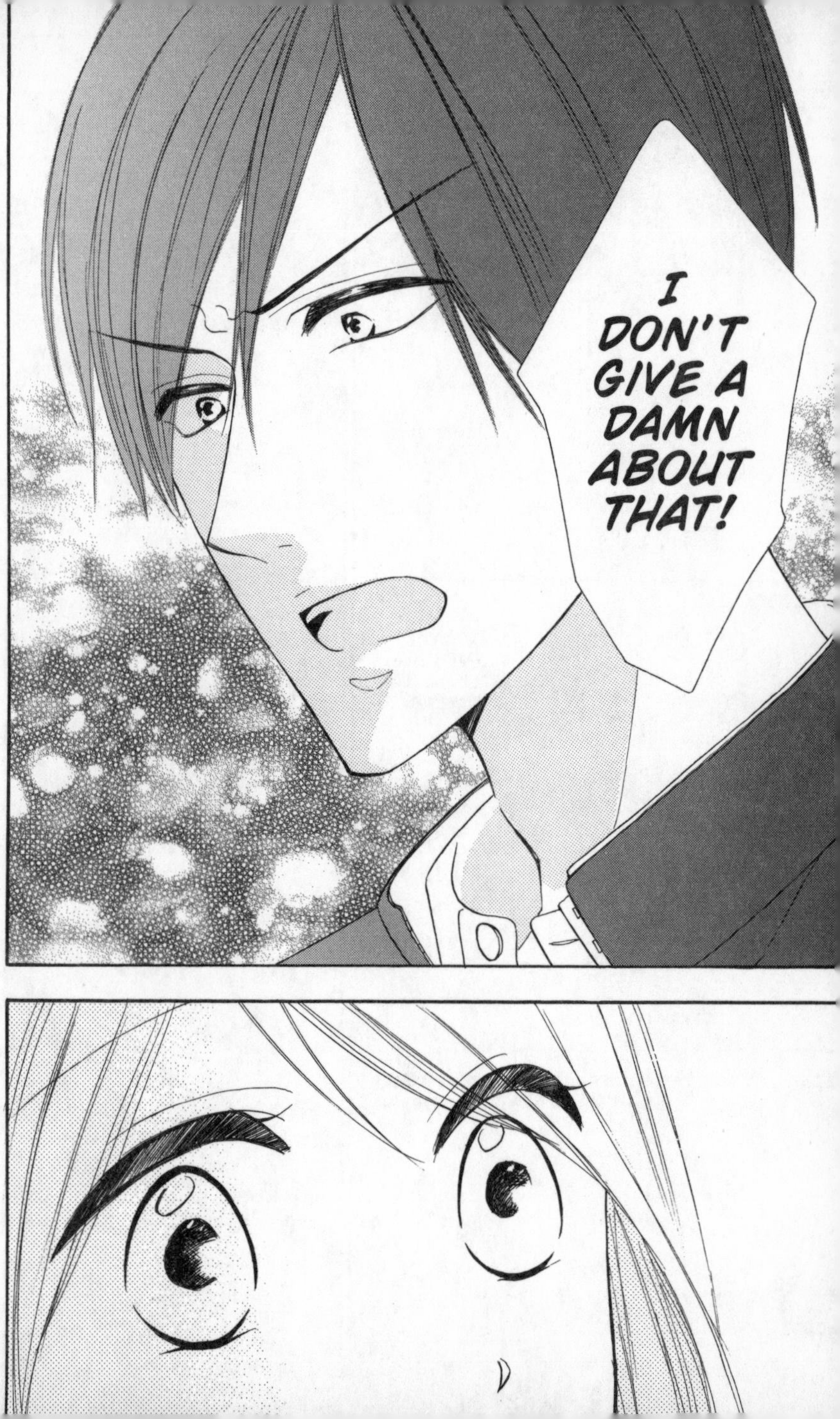
I DON'T GIVE A DAMN ABOUT THAT!

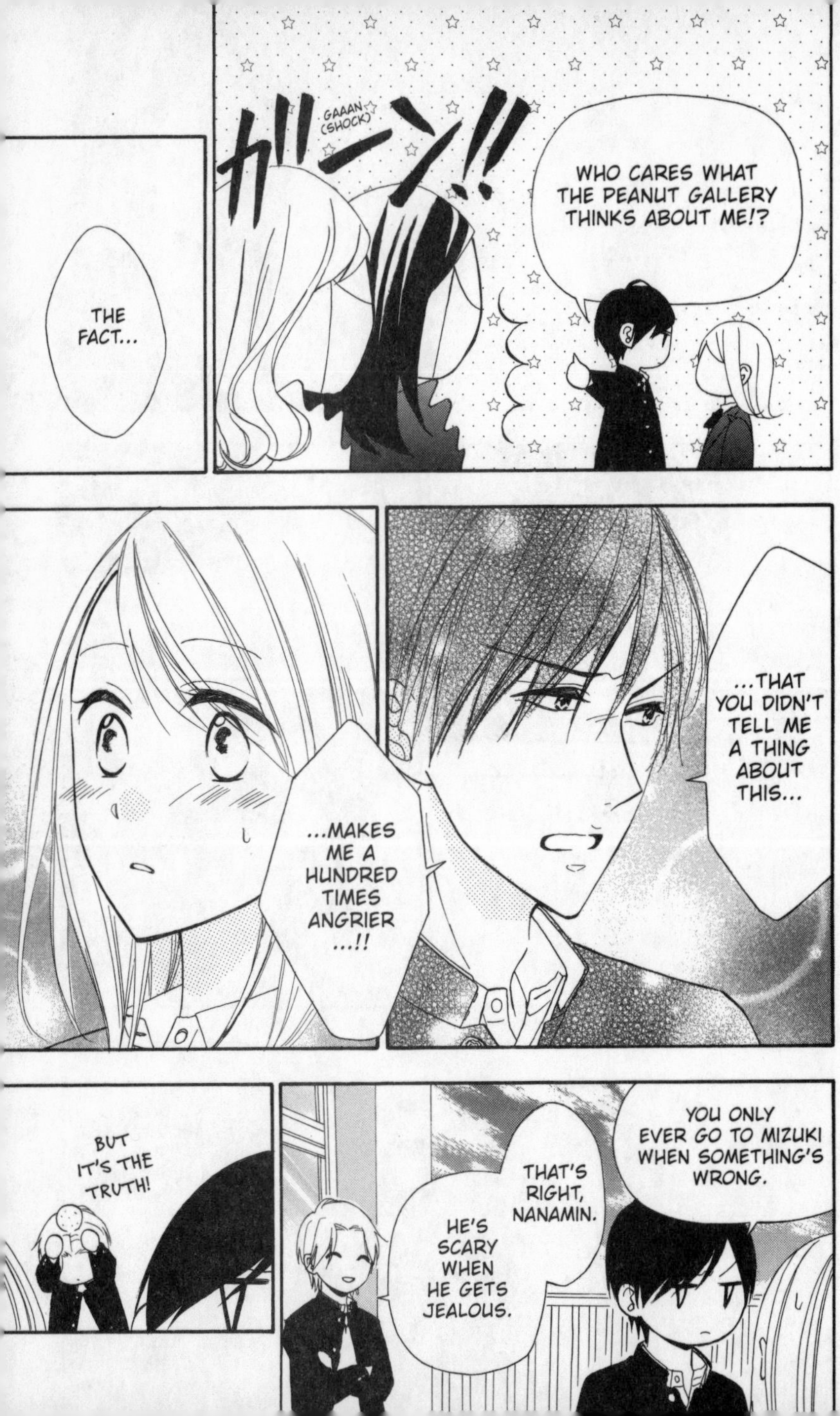
WHO CARES WHAT THE PEANUT GALLERY THINKS ABOUT ME!?
GAAAN (SHOCK)
THE FACT...
...THAT YOU DIDN'T TELL ME A THING ABOUT THIS...
...MAKES ME A HUNDRED TIMES ANGRIER ...!!
YOU ONLY EVER GO TO MIZUKI WHEN SOMETHING'S WRONG.
THAT'S RIGHT, NANAMIN.
HE'S SCARY WHEN HE GETS JEALOUS.
BUT IT'S THE TRUTH!

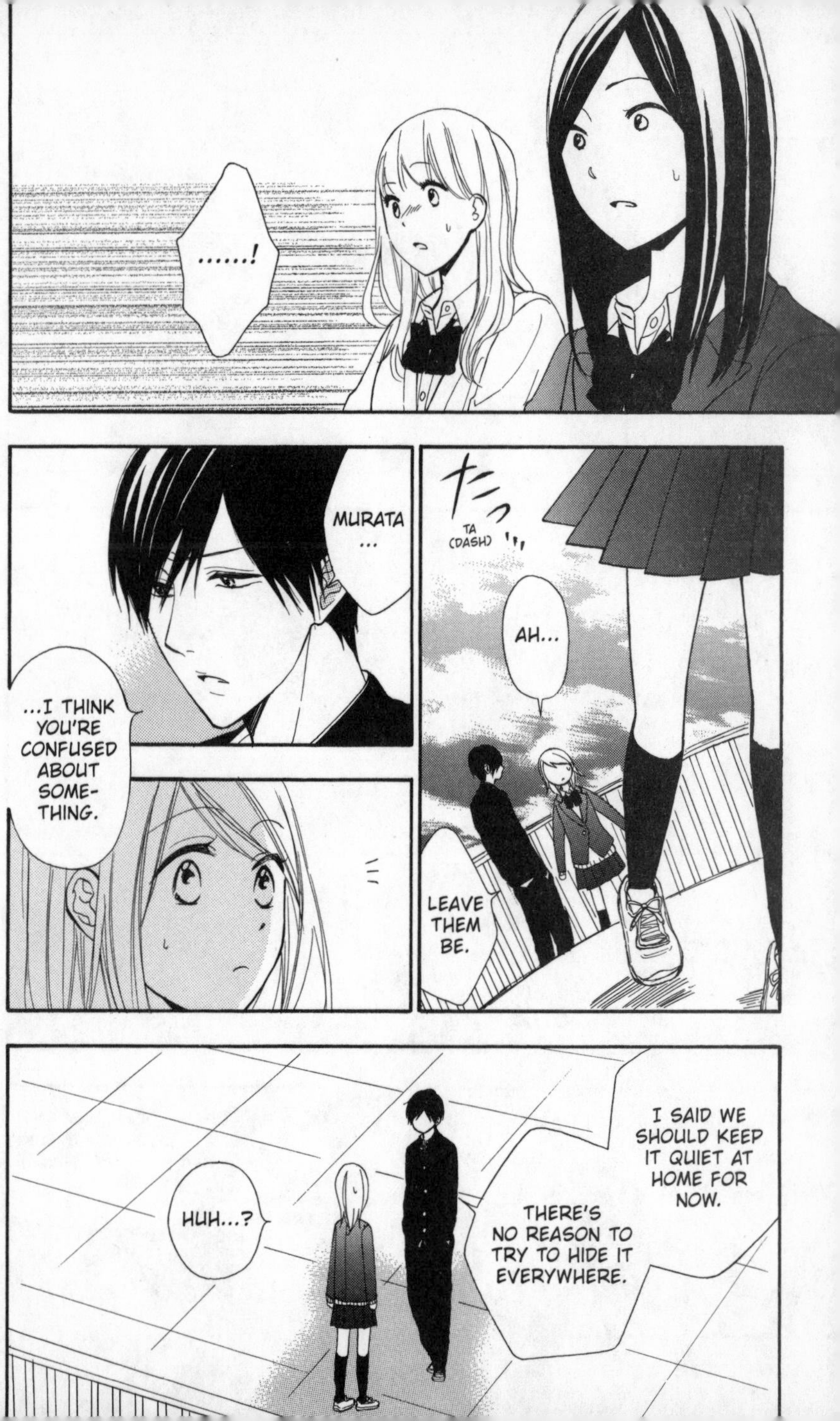
......!
TA (DASH)
AH...
LEAVE THEM BE.
MURATA ...
...I THINK YOU'RE CONFUSED ABOUT SOMETHING.
I SAID WE SHOULD KEEP IT QUIET AT HOME FOR NOW.
THERE'S NO REASON TO TRY TO HIDE IT EVERYWHERE.
HUH...?

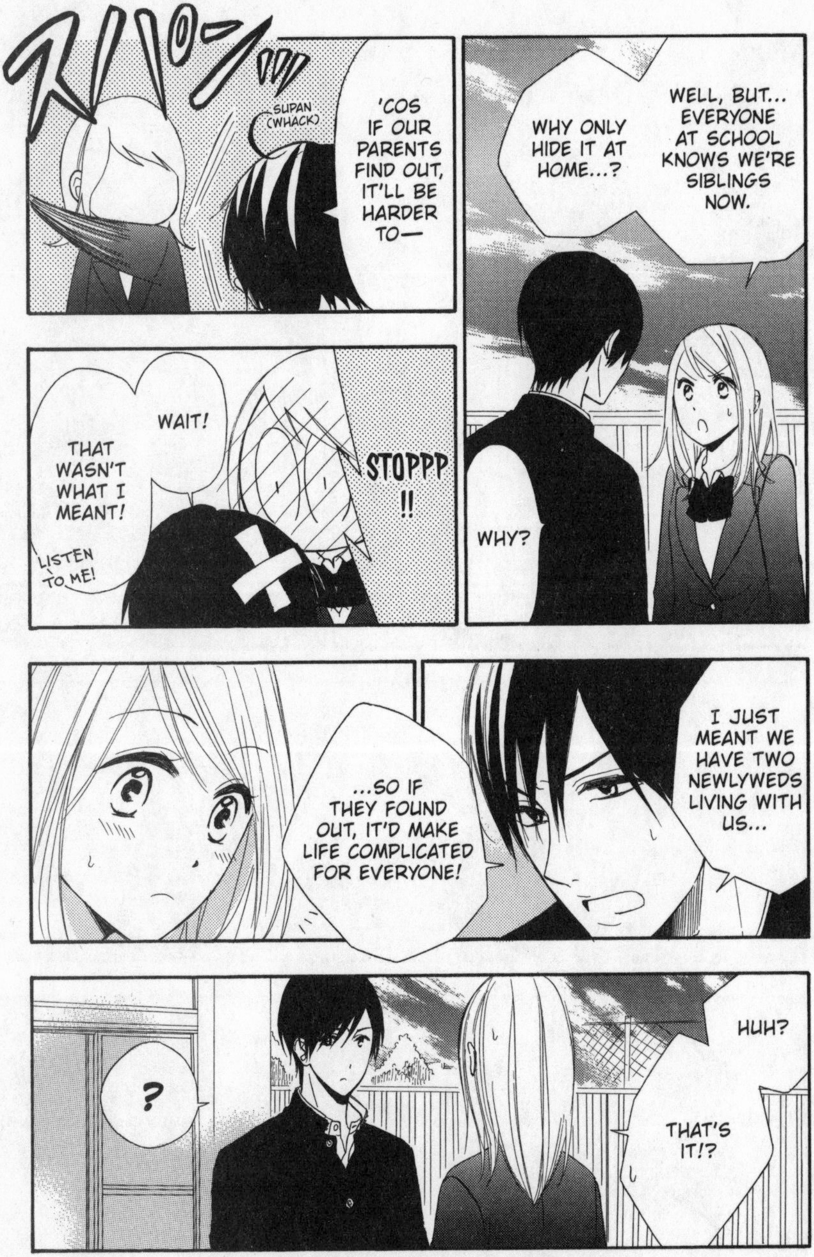
WELL, BUT... EVERYONE AT SCHOOL KNOWS WE'RE SIBLINGS NOW.
WHY ONLY HIDE IT AT HOME...?
WHY?
'COS IF OUR PARENTS FIND OUT, IT'LL BE HARDER TO—
スパーン
SUPAN (WHACK)
STOPPP!!
WAIT!
THAT WASN'T WHAT I MEANT!
LISTEN TO ME!
I JUST MEANT WE HAVE TWO NEWLYWEDS LIVING WITH US...
...SO IF THEY FOUND OUT, IT'D MAKE LIFE COMPLICATED FOR EVERYONE!
HUH?
THAT'S IT!?
?

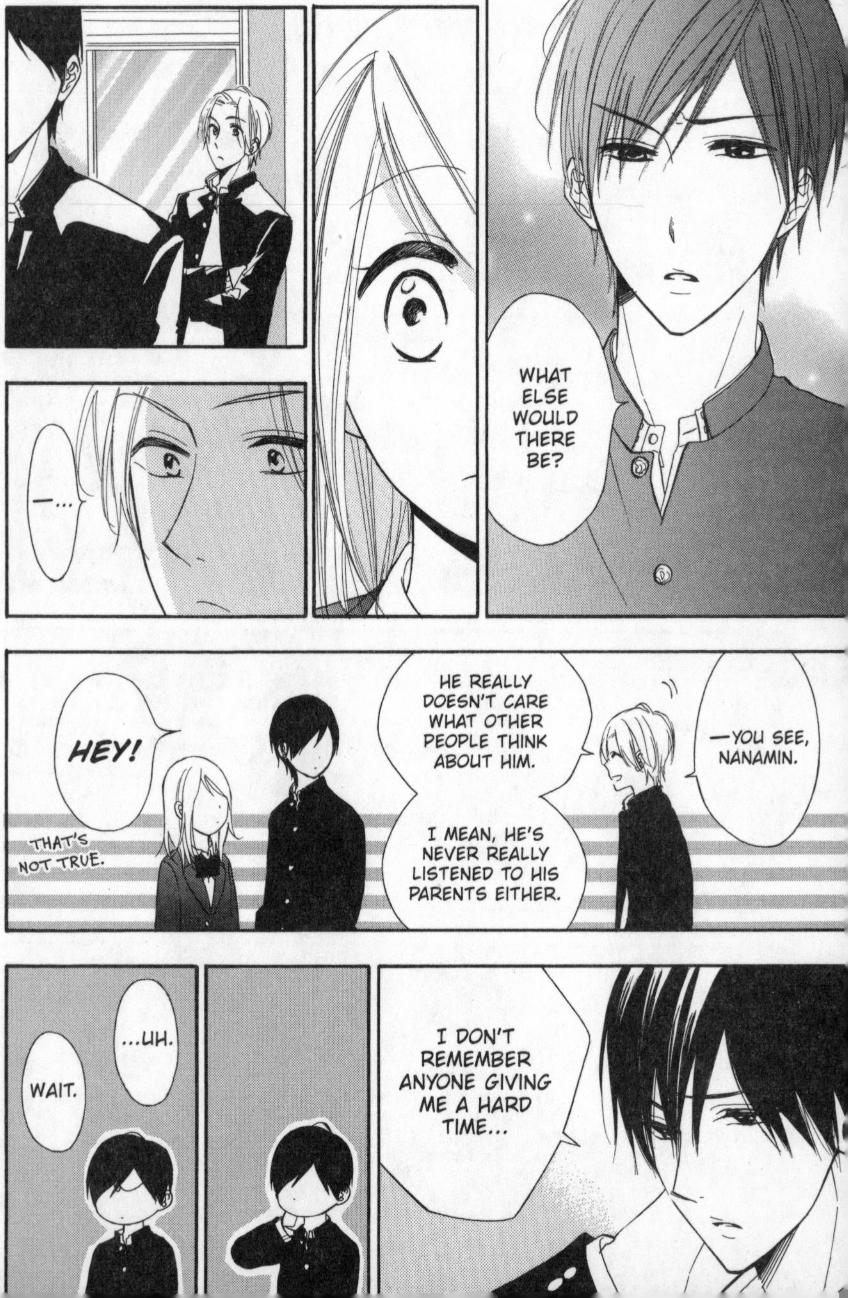
WHAT ELSE WOULD THERE BE?
—...
—YOU SEE, NANAMIN.
HE REALLY DOESN'T CARE WHAT OTHER PEOPLE THINK ABOUT HIM.
I MEAN, HE'S NEVER REALLY LISTENED TO HIS PARENTS EITHER.
HEY!
THAT'S NOT TRUE.
I DON'T REMEMBER ANYONE GIVING ME A HARD TIME...
...UH.
WAIT.

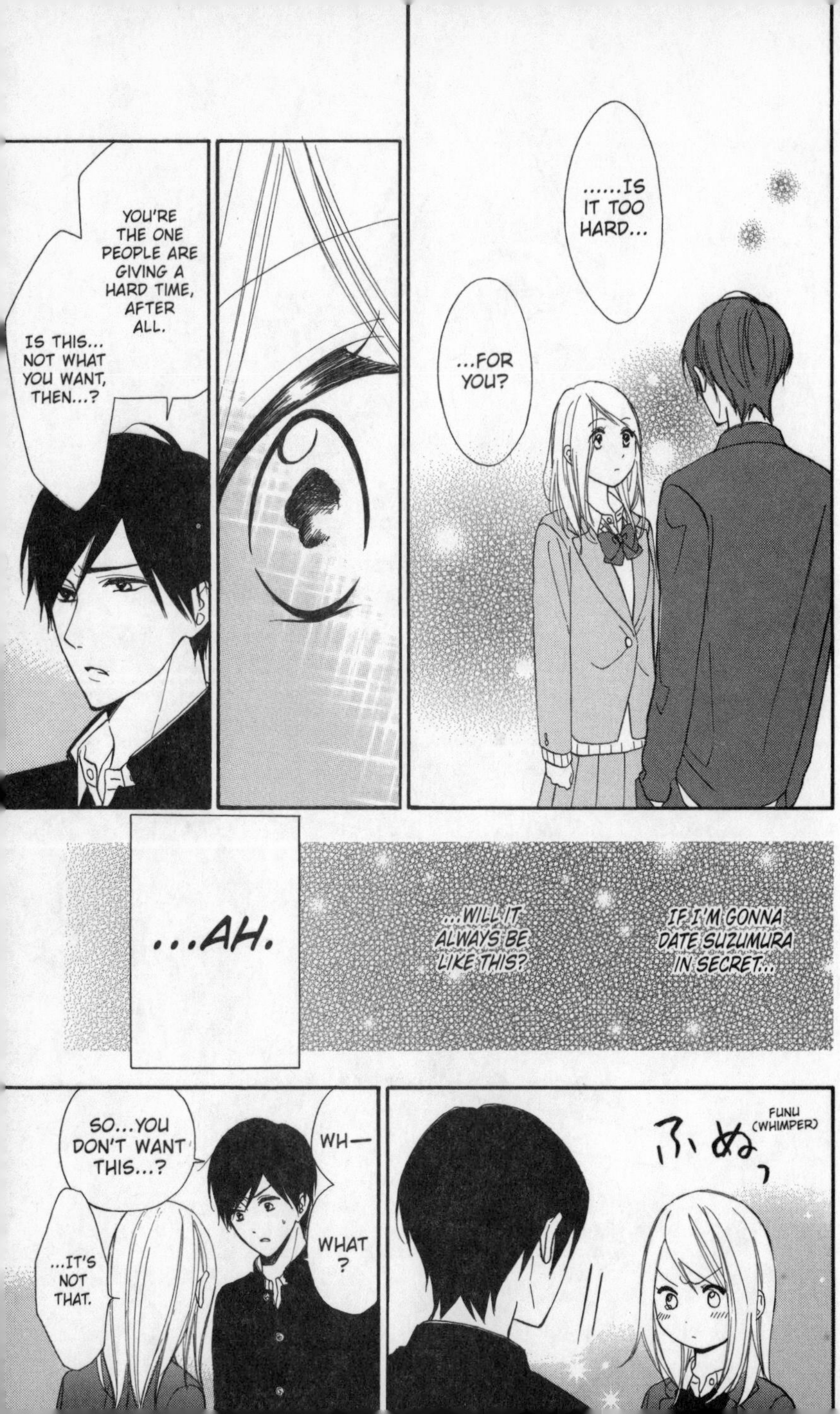
......IS IT TOO HARD...
...FOR YOU?
YOU'RE THE ONE PEOPLE ARE GIVING A HARD TIME, AFTER ALL.
IS THIS... NOT WHAT YOU WANT, THEN...?
IF I'M GONNA DATE SUZUMURA IN SECRET...
...WILL IT ALWAYS BE LIKE THIS?
...AH.
ふぬ
FUNU (WHIMPER)
WH—
WHAT?
SO...YOU DON'T WANT THIS...?
...IT'S NOT THAT.

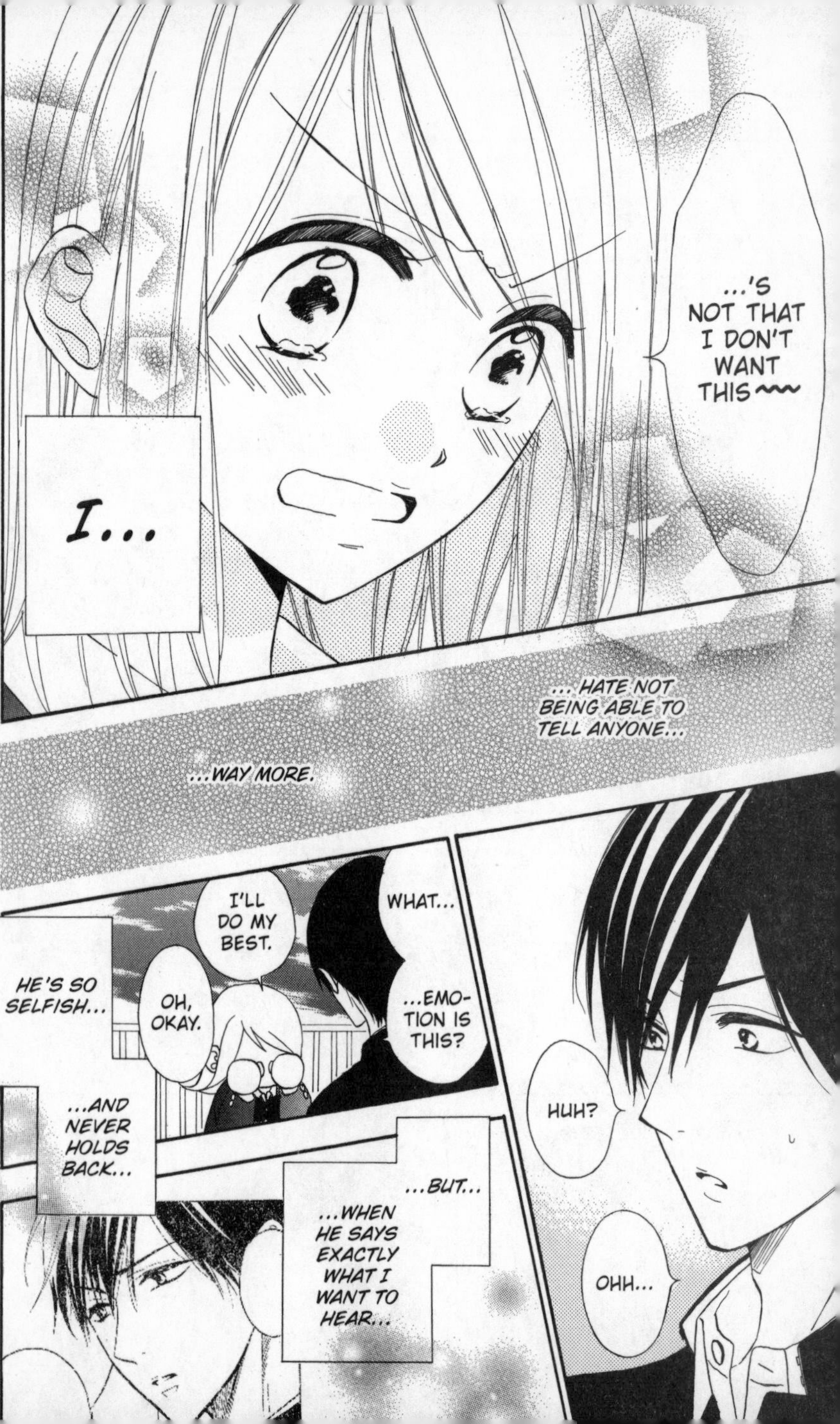

...'S NOT THAT I DON'T WANT THIS~
I...
... HATE NOT BEING ABLE TO TELL ANYONE...
...WAY MORE.
HUH?
OHH...
WHAT...
...EMO-TION IS THIS?
I'LL DO MY BEST.
OH, OKAY.
HE'S SO SELFISH...
...AND NEVER HOLDS BACK...
...BUT...
...WHEN HE SAYS EXACTLY WHAT I WANT TO HEAR...

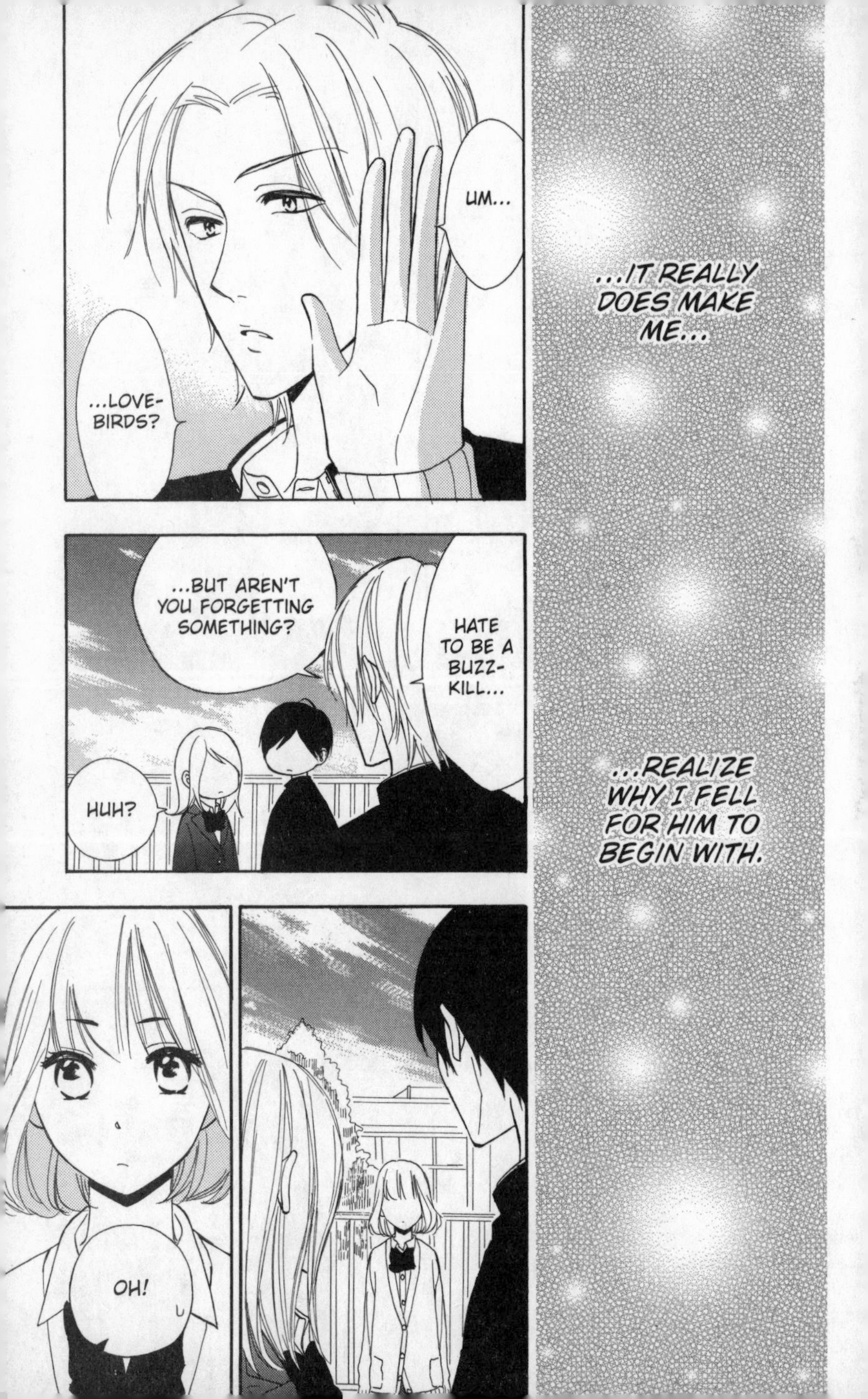
...IT REALLY DOES MAKE ME...
...REALIZE WHY I FELL FOR HIM TO BEGIN WITH.
UM...
...LOVE-BIRDS?
HATE TO BE A BUZZ-KILL...
...BUT AREN'T YOU FORGETTING SOMETHING?
HUH?
OH!

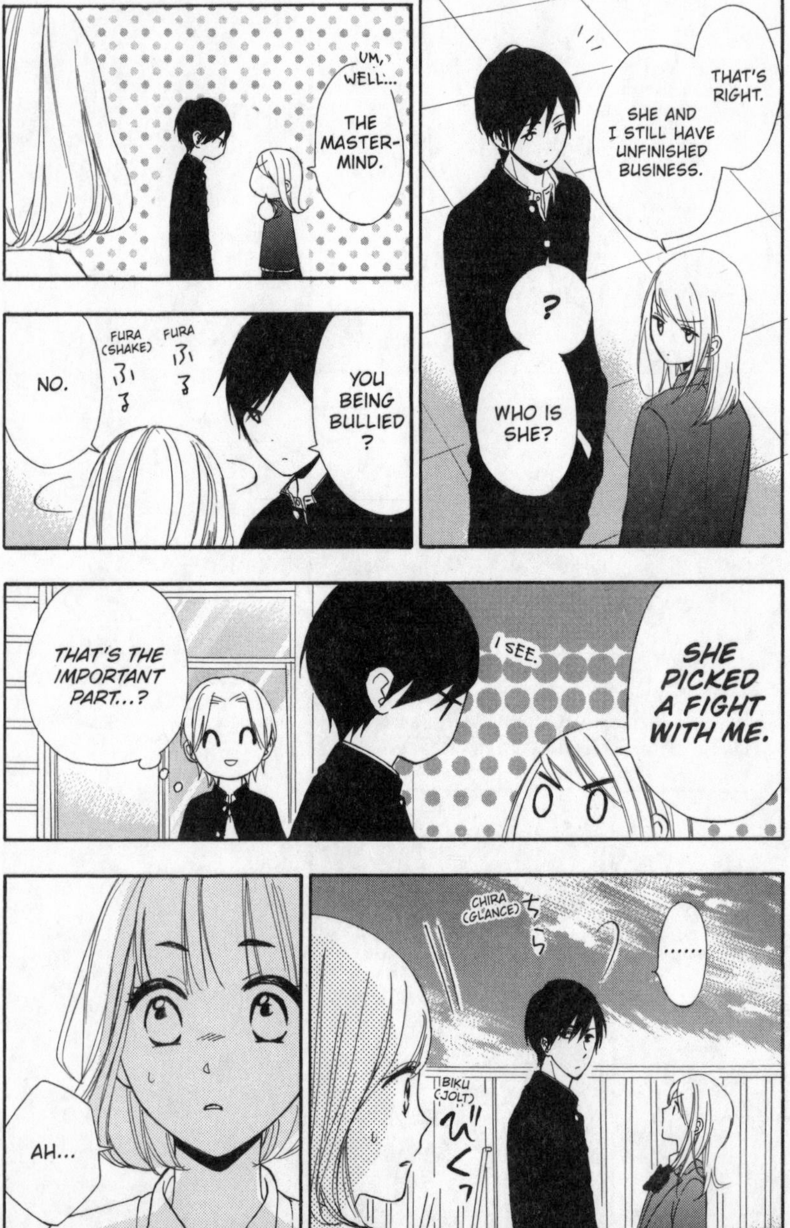
THAT'S RIGHT.
SHE AND I STILL HAVE UNFINISHED BUSINESS.
?
WHO IS SHE?
UM, WELL...
THE MASTER-MIND.
YOU BEING BULLIED?
FURA ふる
FURA (SHAKE) ふる
NO.
SHE PICKED A FIGHT WITH ME.
I SEE.
THAT'S THE IMPORTANT PART...?
......
CHIRA (GLANCE) ちら
BIKU (JOLT) びくっ
AH...

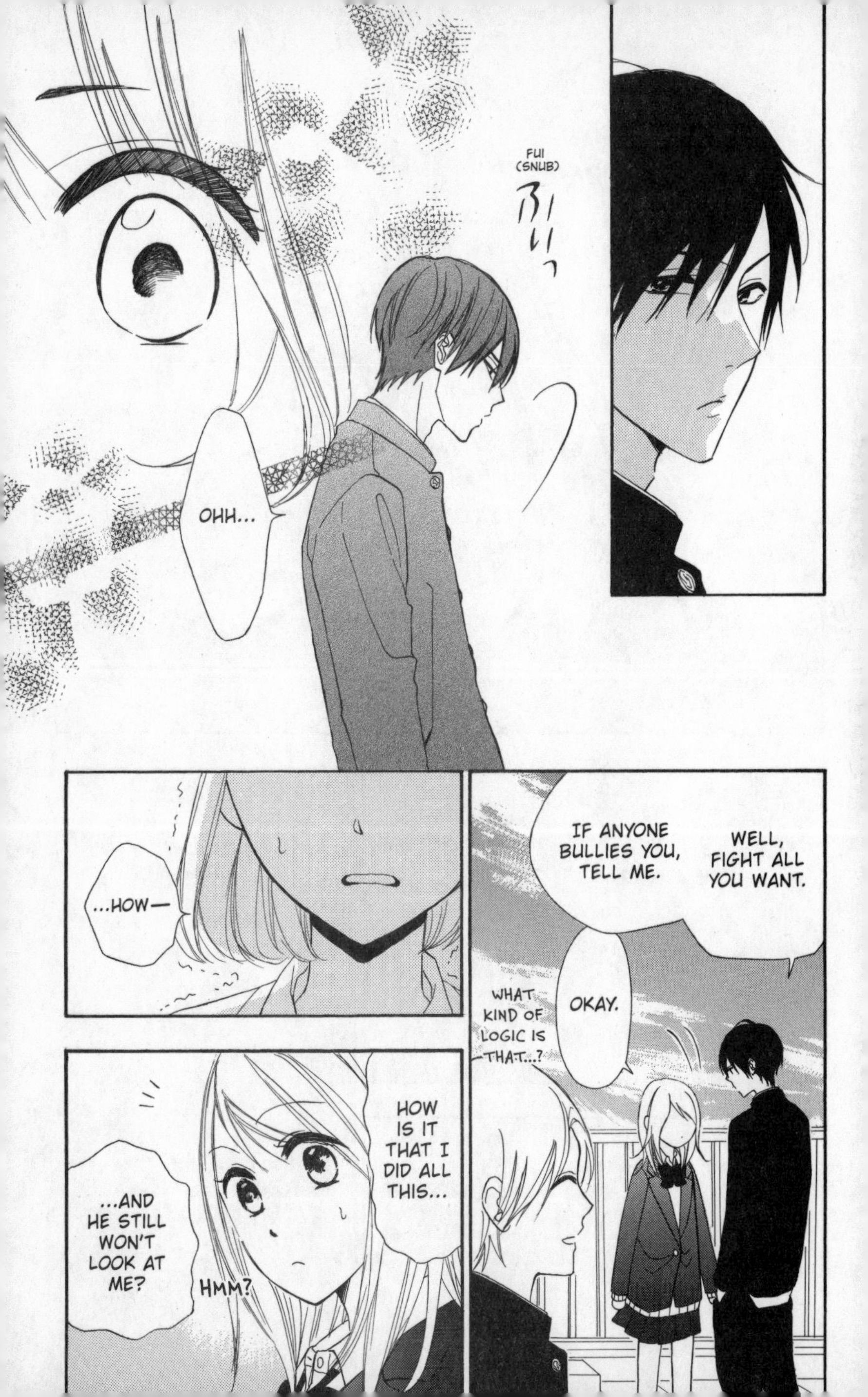
FUI (SNUB)
ふいっ
OHH...
WELL, FIGHT ALL YOU WANT.
IF ANYONE BULLIES YOU, TELL ME.
OKAY.
WHAT KIND OF LOGIC IS THAT...?
...HOW—
HOW IS IT THAT I DID ALL THIS...
...AND HE STILL WON'T LOOK AT ME?
HMM?

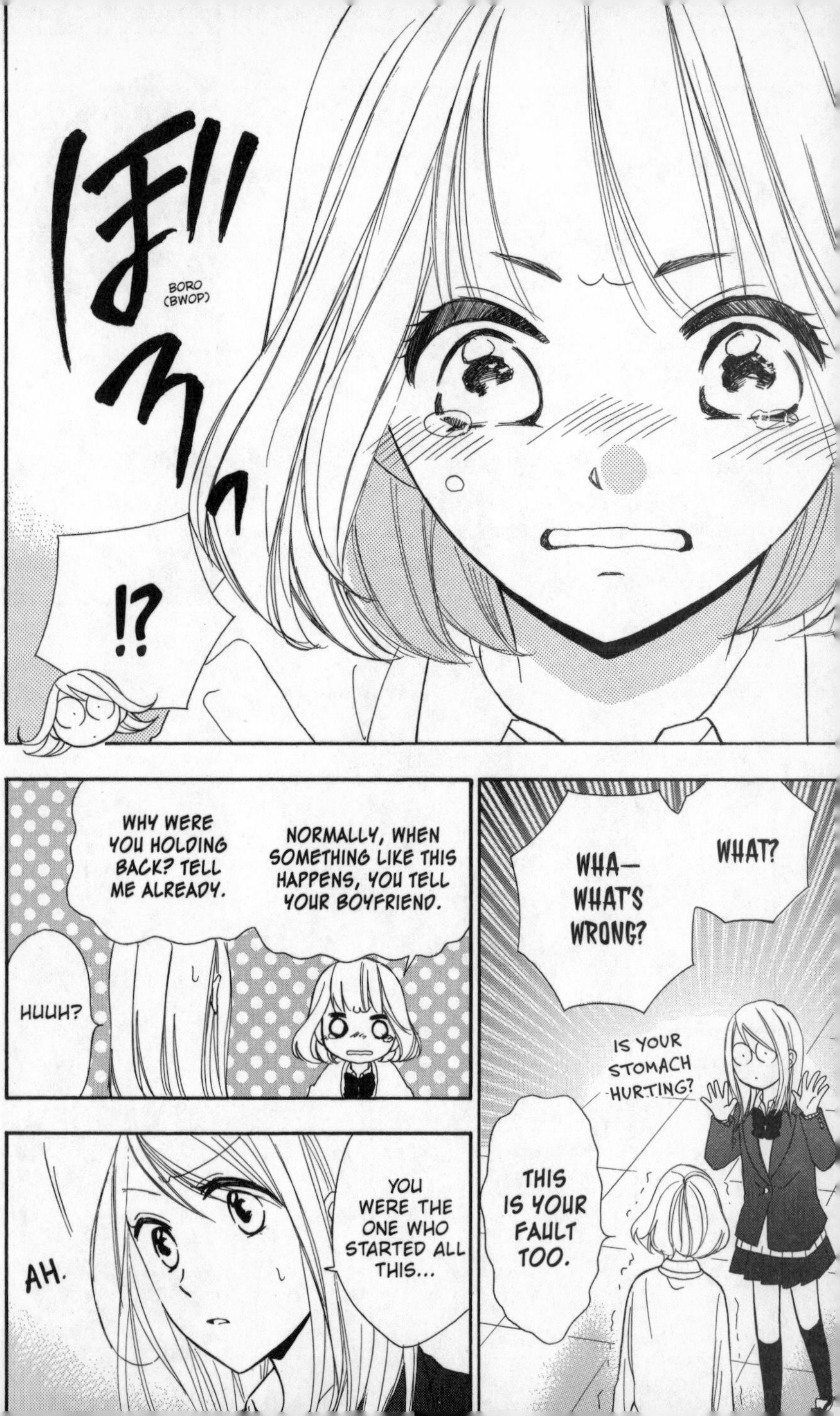
ぼろっ
BORO (BWOP)
!?
WHAT?
WHA— WHAT'S WRONG?
IS YOUR STOMACH HURTING?
THIS IS YOUR FAULT TOO.
NORMALLY, WHEN SOMETHING LIKE THIS HAPPENS, YOU TELL YOUR BOYFRIEND.
WHY WERE YOU HOLDING BACK? TELL ME ALREADY.
HUUH?
YOU WERE THE ONE WHO STARTED ALL THIS...
AH.

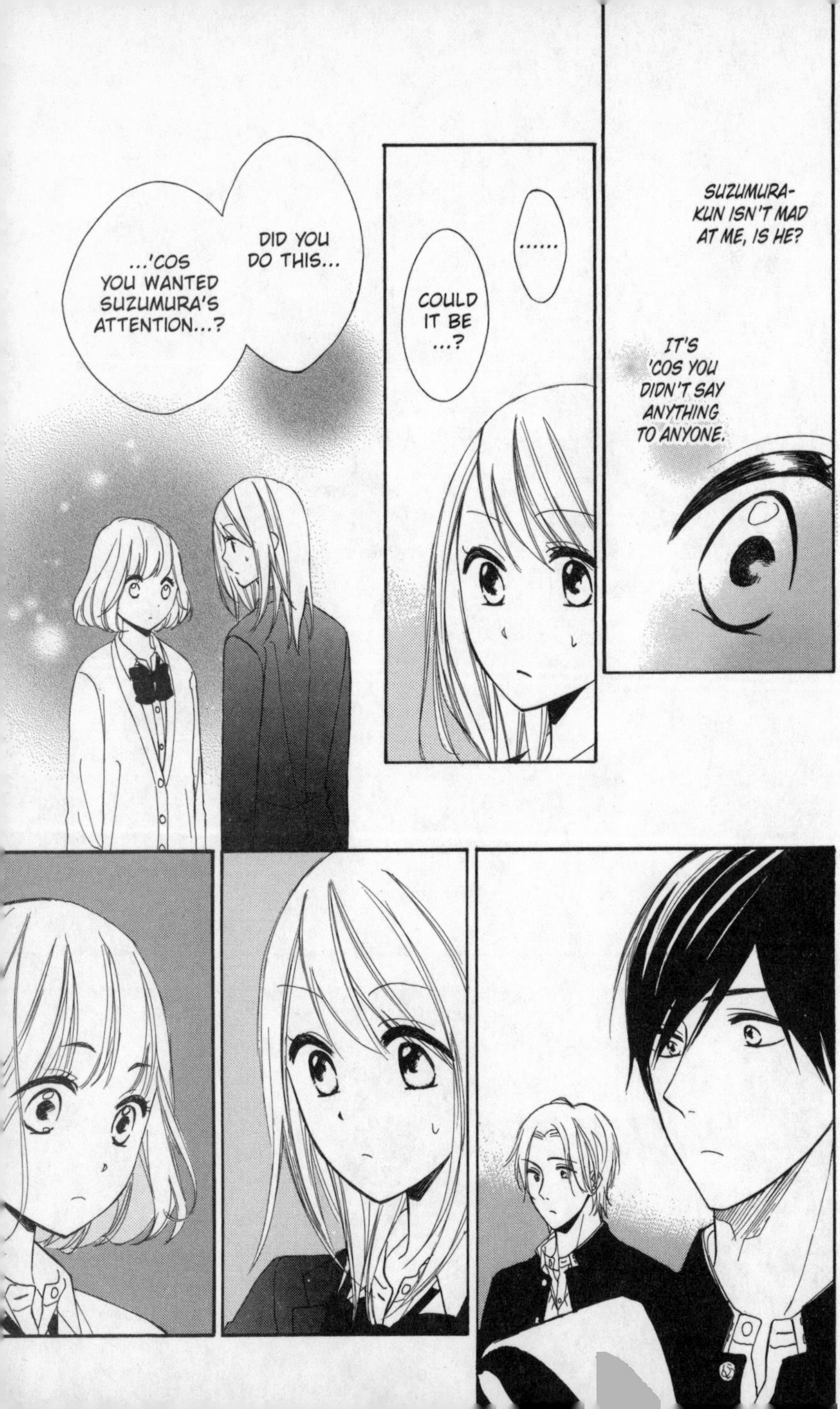
SUZUMURA-KUN ISN'T MAD AT ME, IS HE?
IT'S 'COS YOU DIDN'T SAY ANYTHING TO ANYONE.
......
COULD IT BE ...?
DID YOU DO THIS...
...'COS YOU WANTED SUZUMURA'S ATTENTION...?

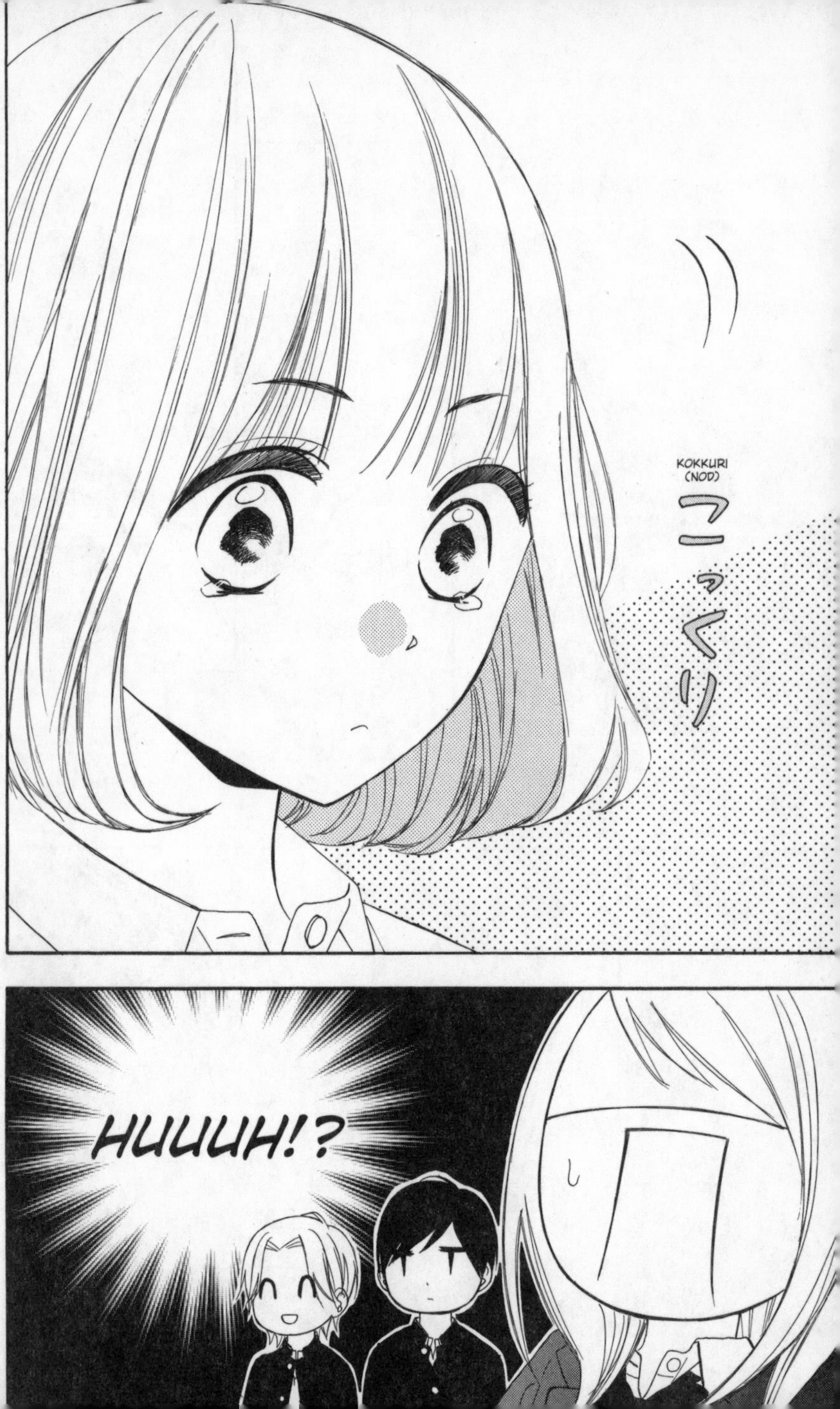
KOKKURI (NOD)
こっくり
HUUUH!?

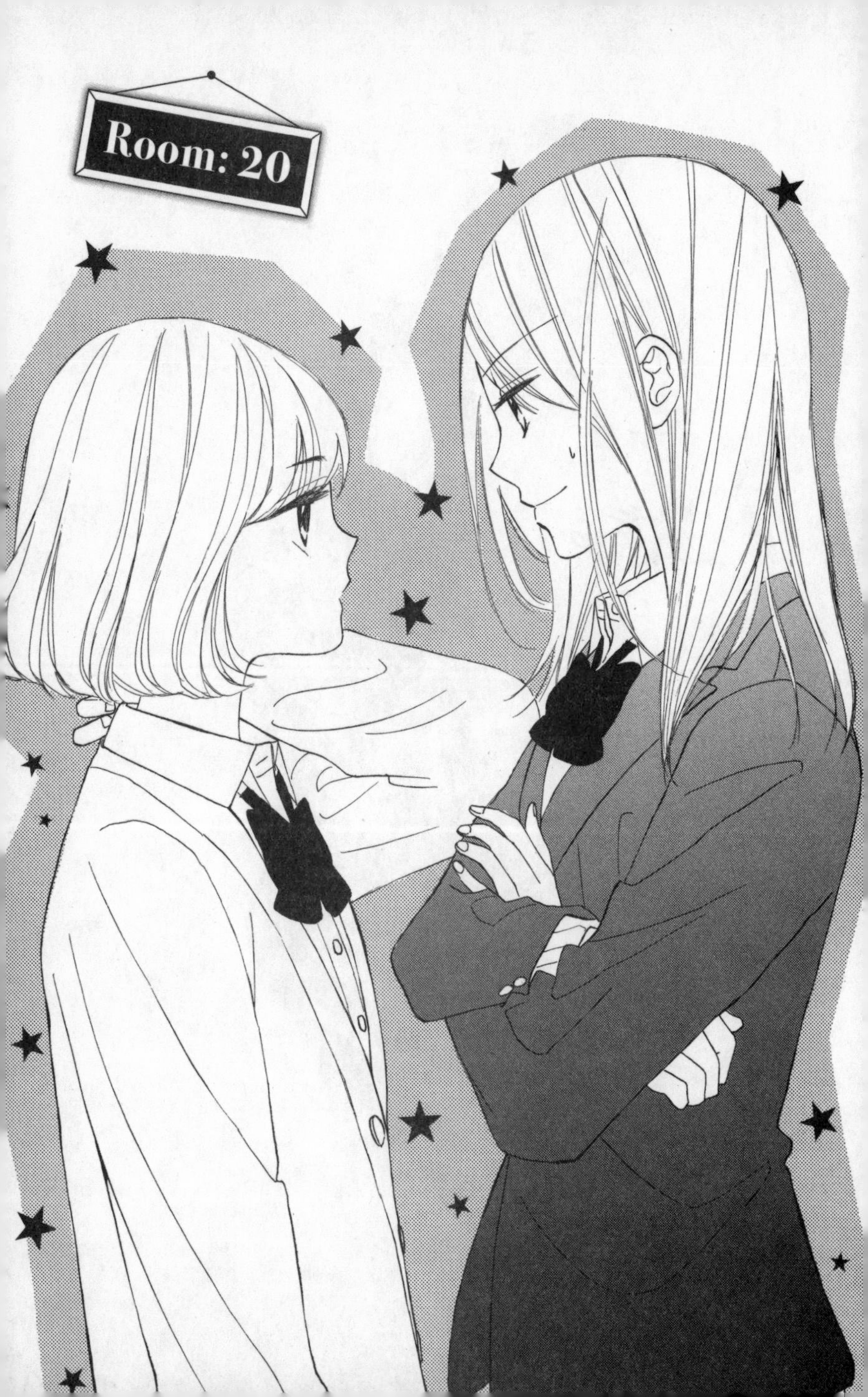
Room: 20

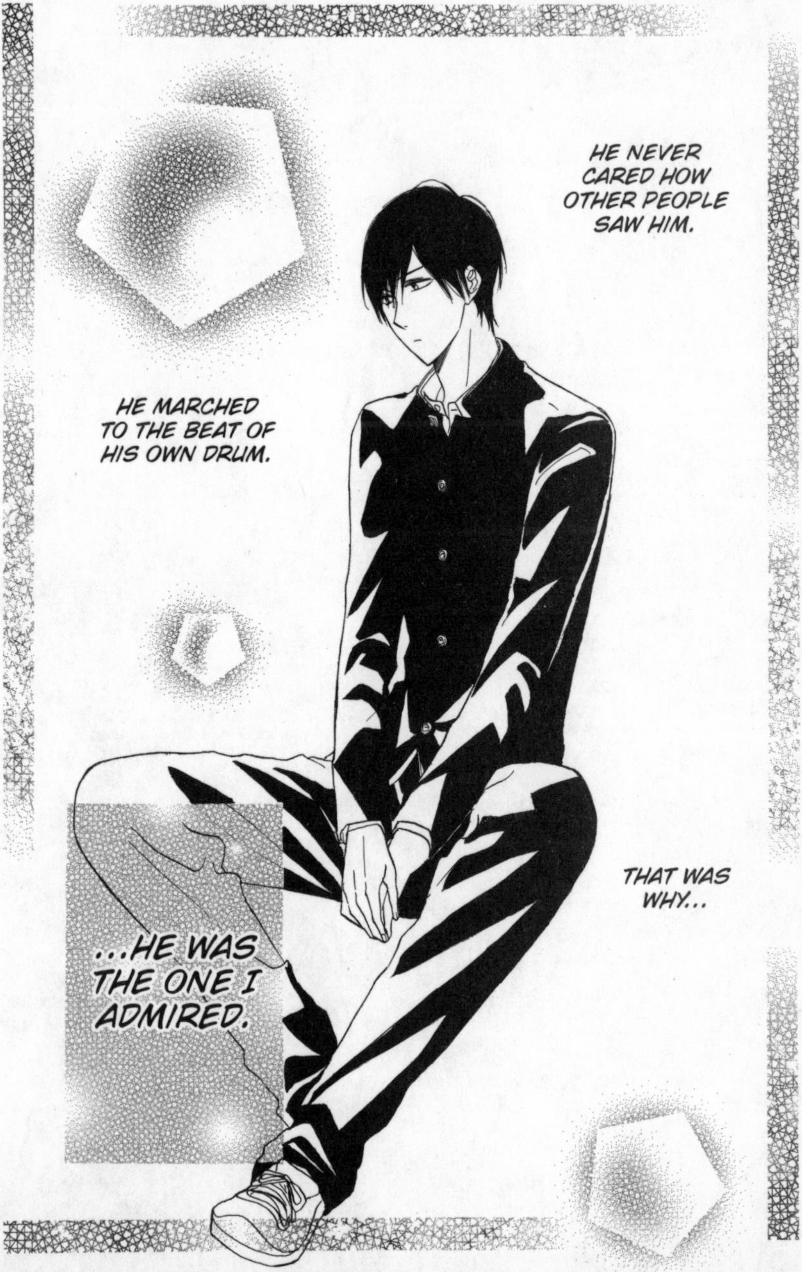
HE NEVER CARED HOW OTHER PEOPLE SAW HIM.
HE MARCHED TO THE BEAT OF HIS OWN DRUM.
THAT WAS WHY...
...HE WAS THE ONE I ADMIRED.

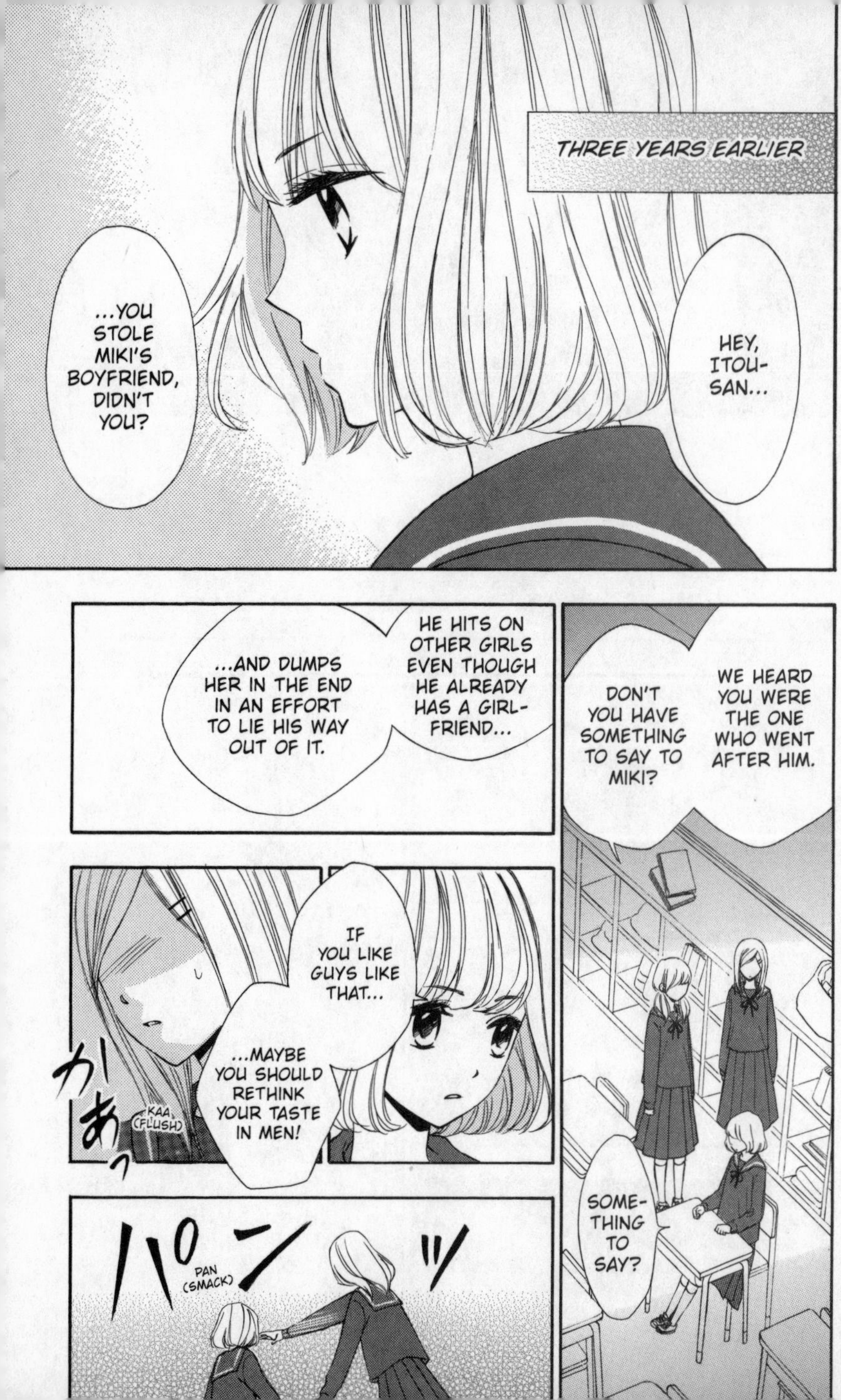
THREE YEARS EARLIER
HEY, ITOU-SAN...
...YOU STOLE MIKI'S BOYFRIEND, DIDN'T YOU?
WE HEARD YOU WERE THE ONE WHO WENT AFTER HIM.
DON'T YOU HAVE SOMETHING TO SAY TO MIKI?
SOME-THING TO SAY?
HE HITS ON OTHER GIRLS EVEN THOUGH HE ALREADY HAS A GIRL-FRIEND...
...AND DUMPS HER IN THE END IN AN EFFORT TO LIE HIS WAY OUT OF IT.
IF YOU LIKE GUYS LIKE THAT...
...MAYBE YOU SHOULD RETHINK YOUR TASTE IN MEN!
かぁっ
KAA (FLUSH)
パーンッ
PAN (SMACK)

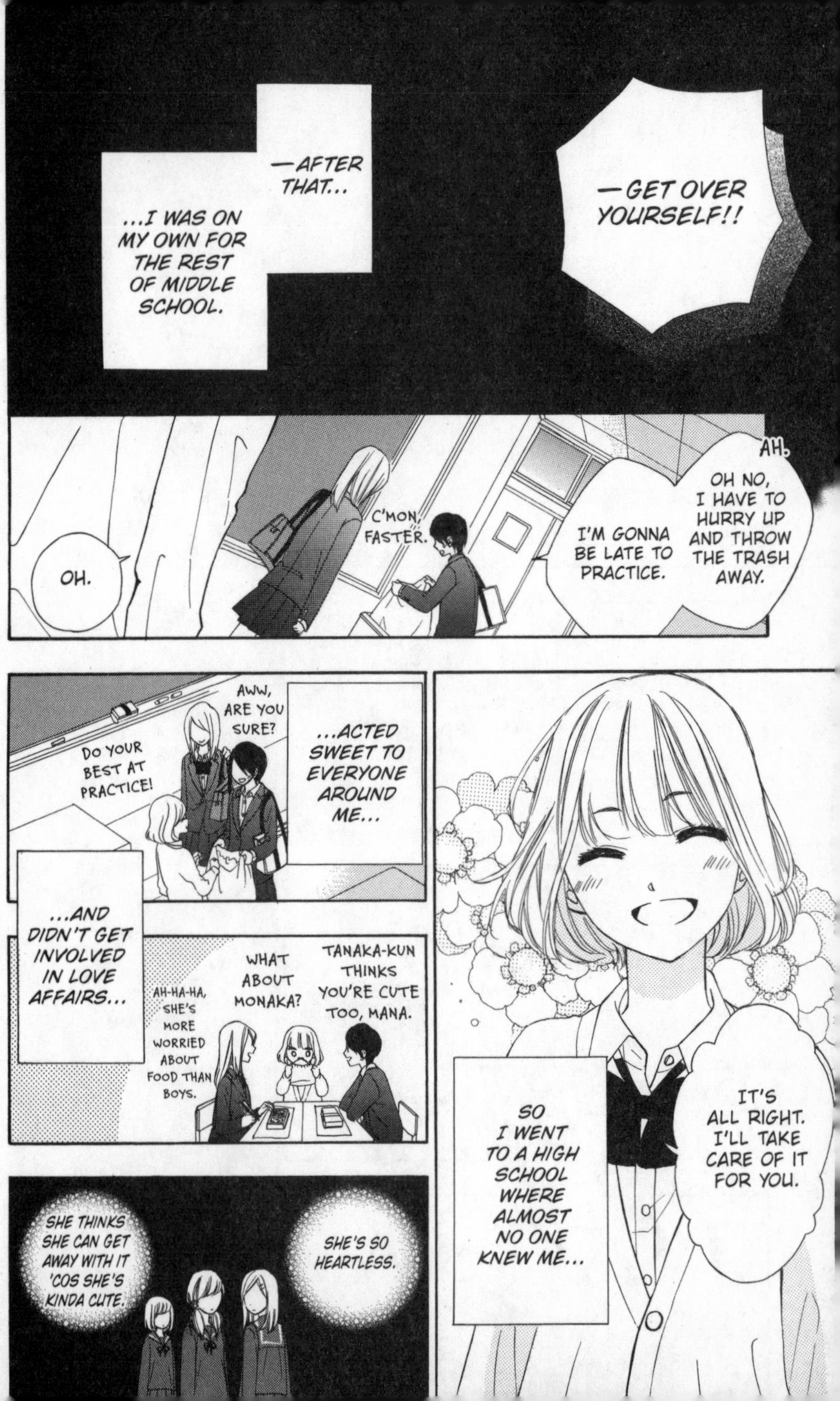
—GET OVER YOURSELF!!
—AFTER THAT...
...I WAS ON MY OWN FOR THE REST OF MIDDLE SCHOOL.
AH.
OH NO, I HAVE TO HURRY UP AND THROW THE TRASH AWAY.
I'M GONNA BE LATE TO PRACTICE.
C'MON, FASTER.
OH.
IT'S ALL RIGHT. I'LL TAKE CARE OF IT FOR YOU.
AWW, ARE YOU SURE?
...ACTED SWEET TO EVERYONE AROUND ME...
DO YOUR BEST AT PRACTICE!
...AND DIDN'T GET INVOLVED IN LOVE AFFAIRS...
TANAKA-KUN THINKS YOU'RE CUTE TOO, MANA.
WHAT ABOUT MONAKA?
AH-HA-HA, SHE'S MORE WORRIED ABOUT FOOD THAN BOYS.
SHE'S SO HEARTLESS.
SHE THINKS SHE CAN GET AWAY WITH IT 'COS SHE'S KINDA CUTE.
SO I WENT TO A HIGH SCHOOL WHERE ALMOST NO ONE KNEW ME...

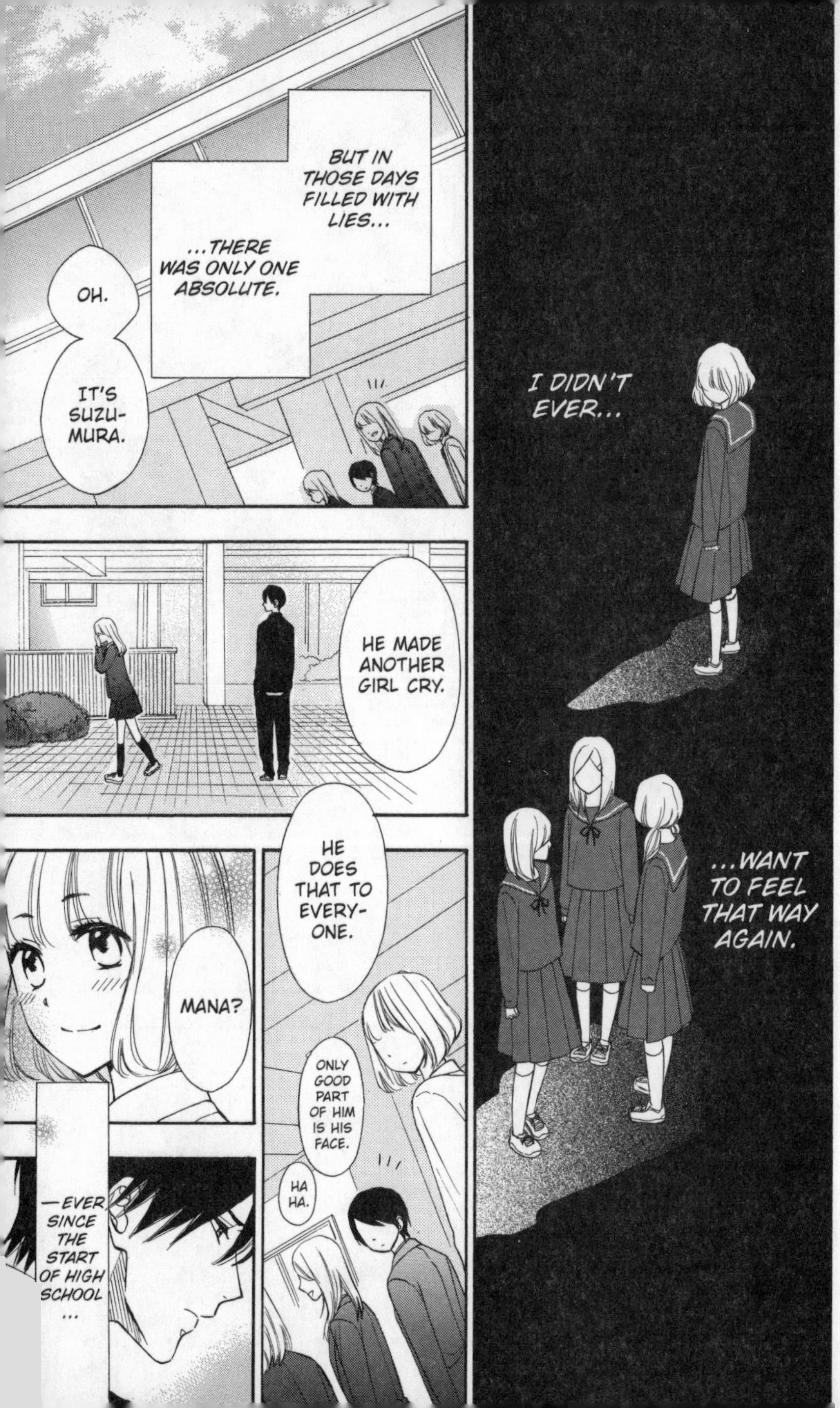
I DIDN'T EVER...
...WANT TO FEEL THAT WAY AGAIN.
BUT IN THOSE DAYS FILLED WITH LIES...
...THERE WAS ONLY ONE ABSOLUTE.
OH.
IT'S SUZU-MURA.
HE MADE ANOTHER GIRL CRY.
HE DOES THAT TO EVERY-ONE.
ONLY GOOD PART OF HIM IS HIS FACE.
HA HA.
MANA?
—EVER SINCE THE START OF HIGH SCHOOL...

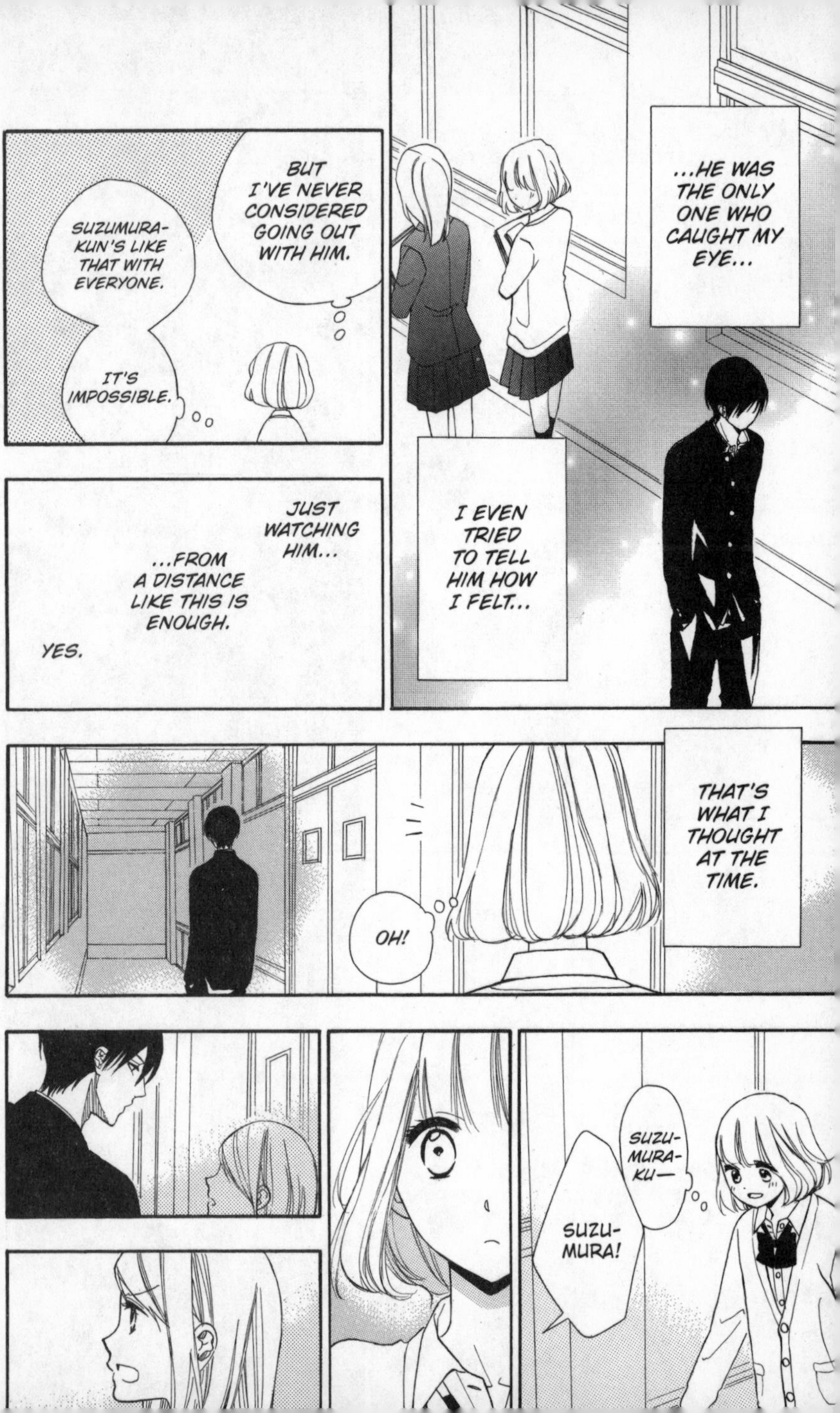
...HE WAS THE ONLY ONE WHO CAUGHT MY EYE...
I EVEN TRIED TO TELL HIM HOW I FELT...
BUT I'VE NEVER CONSIDERED GOING OUT WITH HIM.
SUZUMURA-KUN'S LIKE THAT WITH EVERYONE.
IT'S IMPOSSIBLE.
JUST WATCHING HIM...
...FROM A DISTANCE LIKE THIS IS ENOUGH.
YES.
THAT'S WHAT I THOUGHT AT THE TIME.
OH!
SUZU-MURA-KU—
SUZU-MURA!

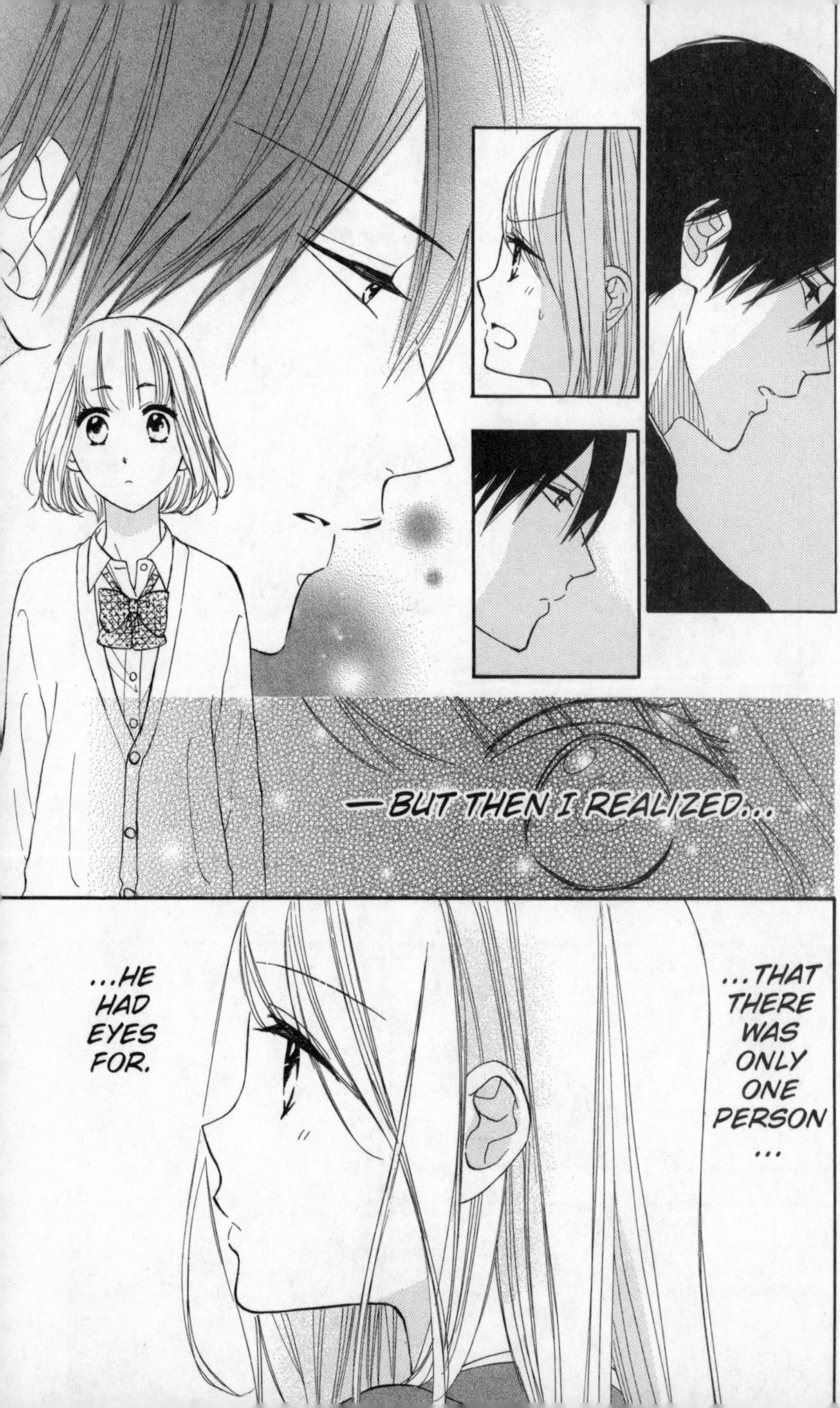
—BUT THEN I REALIZED...
...THAT THERE WAS ONLY ONE PERSON...
...HE HAD EYES FOR.

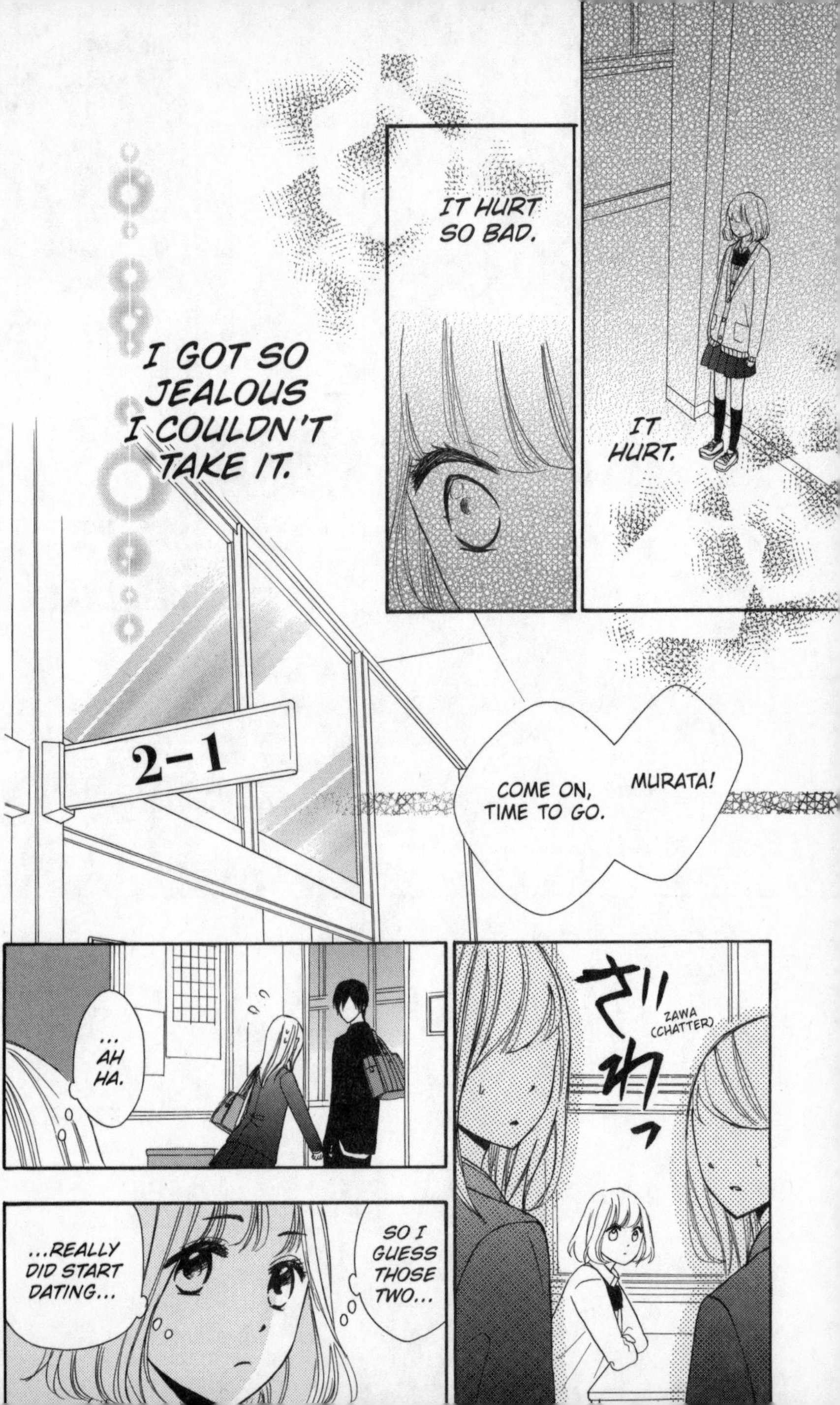
IT HURT.
IT HURT SO BAD.
I GOT SO JEALOUS I COULDN'T TAKE IT.
2-1
MURATA!
COME ON, TIME TO GO.
ざわっ
ZAWA (CHATTER)
...AH HA.
SO I GUESS THOSE TWO...
...REALLY DID START DATING...

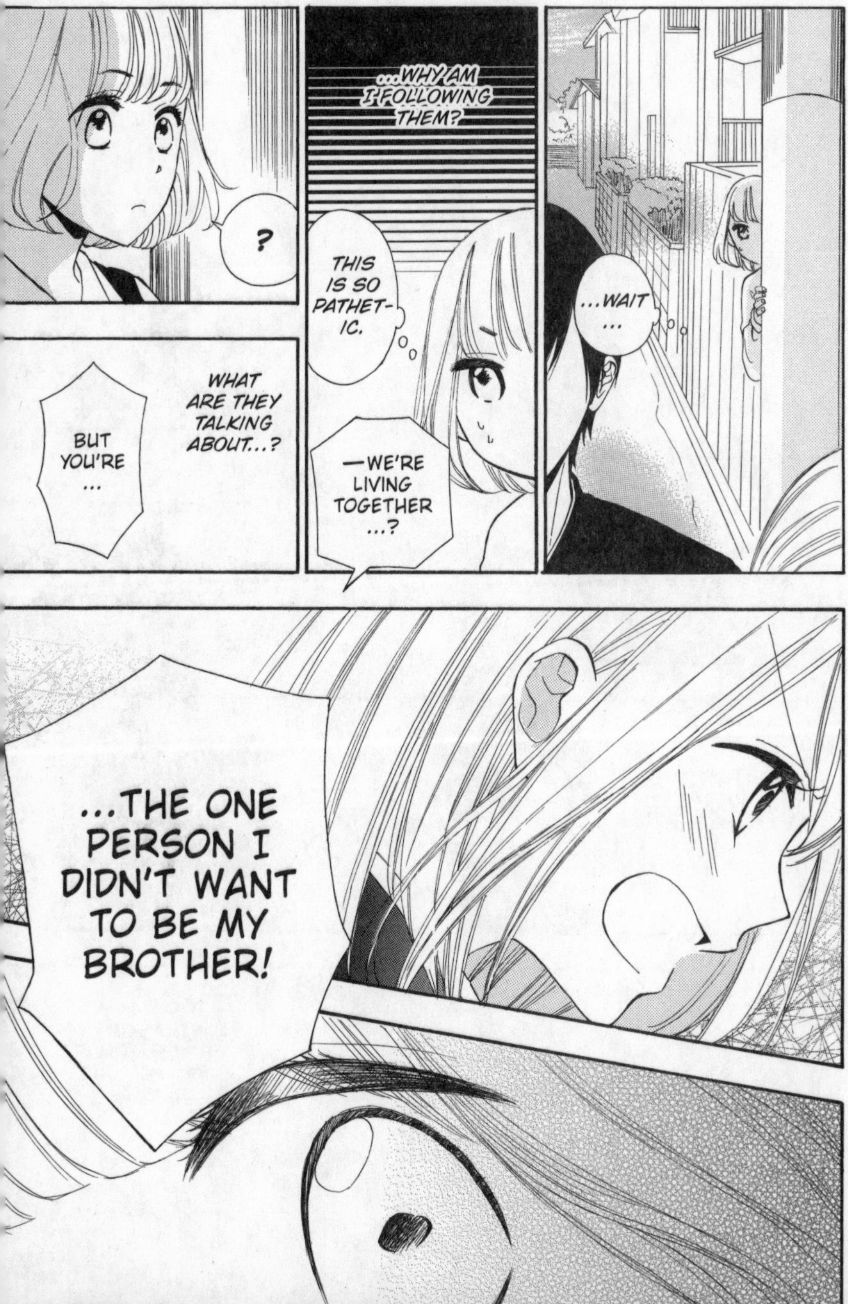
...WAIT ...
...WHY AM I FOLLOWING THEM?
THIS IS SO PATHETIC.
—WE'RE LIVING TOGETHER ...?
?
WHAT ARE THEY TALKING ABOUT...?
BUT YOU'RE ...
...THE ONE PERSON I DIDN'T WANT TO BE MY BROTHER!

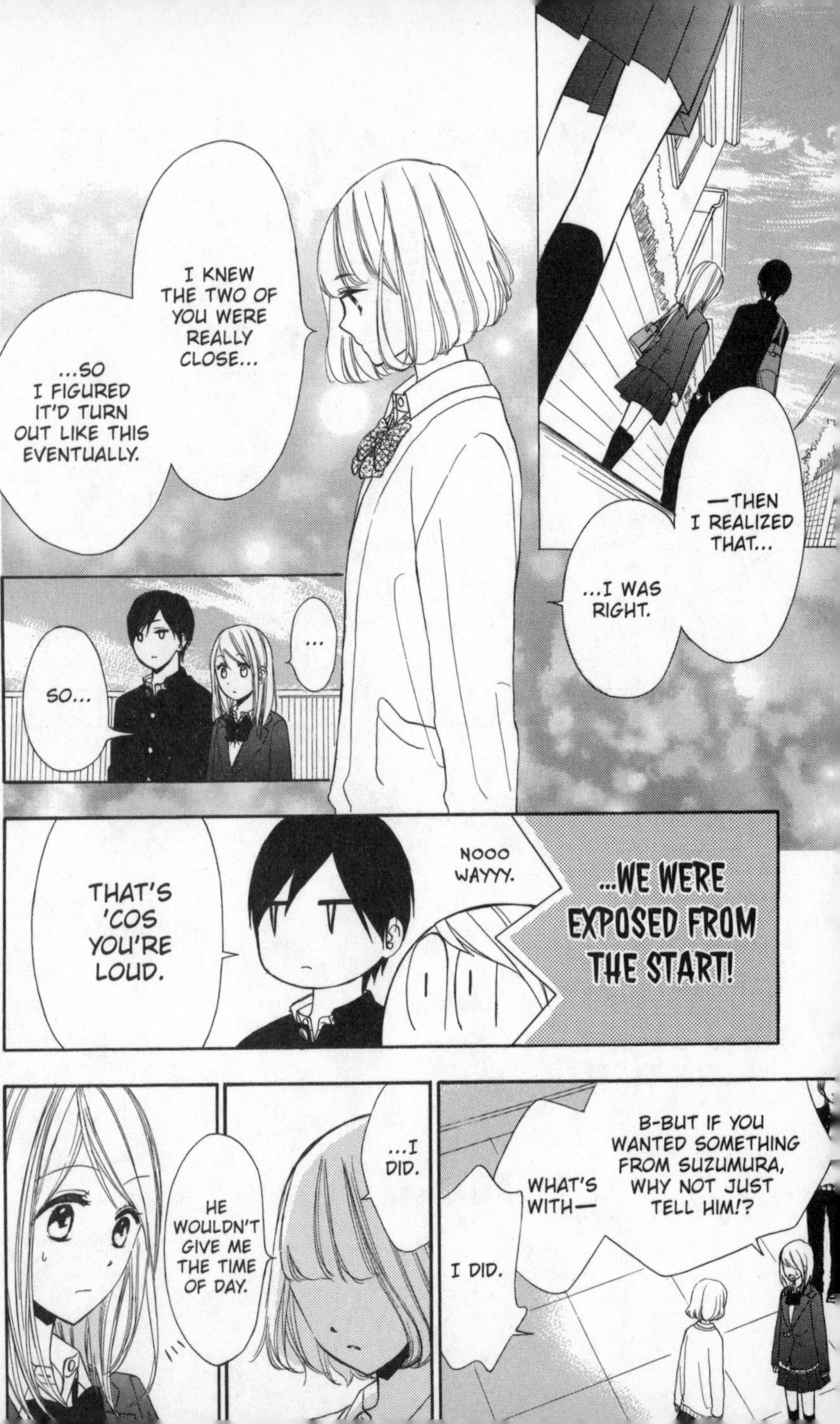
—THEN I REALIZED THAT...
...I WAS RIGHT.
I KNEW THE TWO OF YOU WERE REALLY CLOSE...
...SO I FIGURED IT'D TURN OUT LIKE THIS EVENTUALLY.
...
SO...
...WE WERE EXPOSED FROM THE START!
NOOO WAYYY.
THAT'S 'COS YOU'RE LOUD.
B-BUT IF YOU WANTED SOMETHING FROM SUZUMURA, WHY NOT JUST TELL HIM!?
WHAT'S WITH—
I DID.
...I DID.
HE WOULDN'T GIVE ME THE TIME OF DAY.

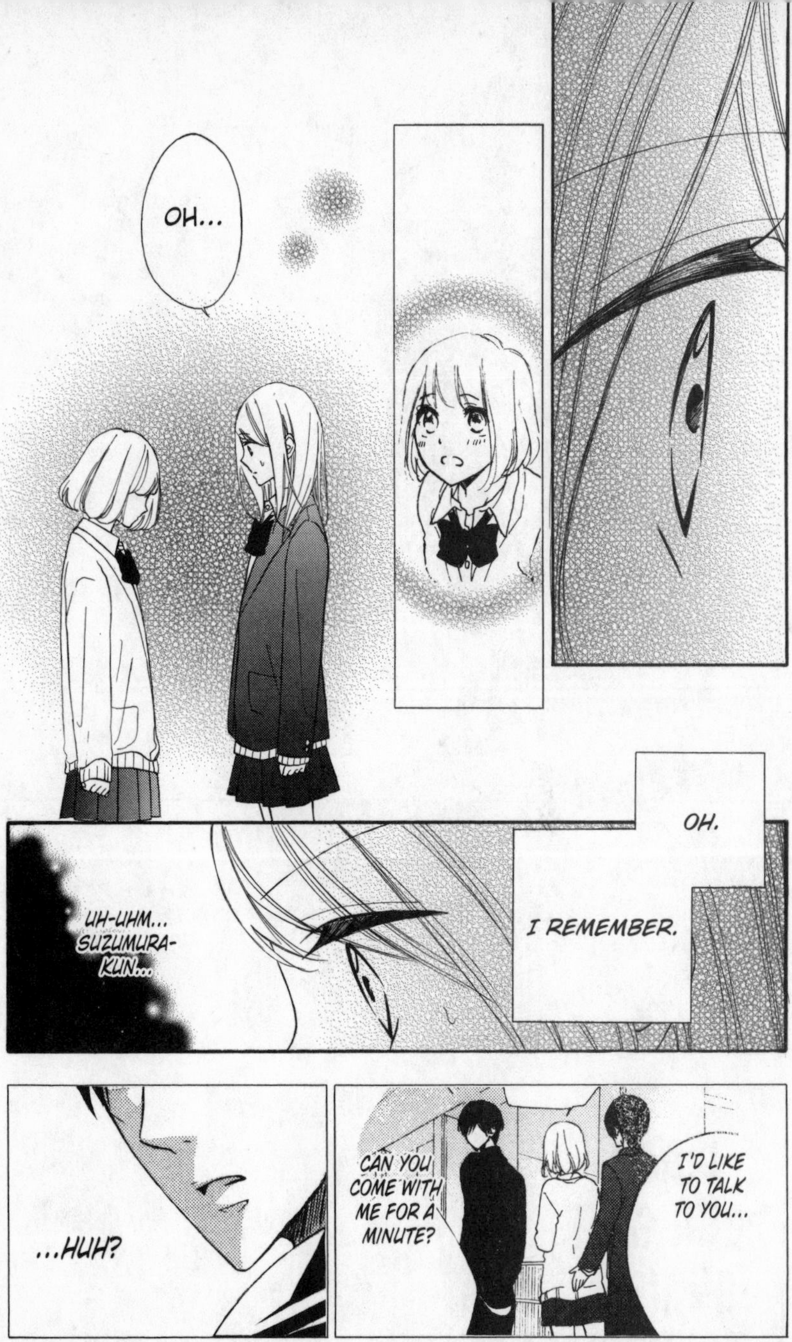
OH...
OH.
I REMEMBER.
UH-UHM... SUZUMURA-KUN...
I'D LIKE TO TALK TO YOU...
CAN YOU COME WITH ME FOR A MINUTE?
...HUH?

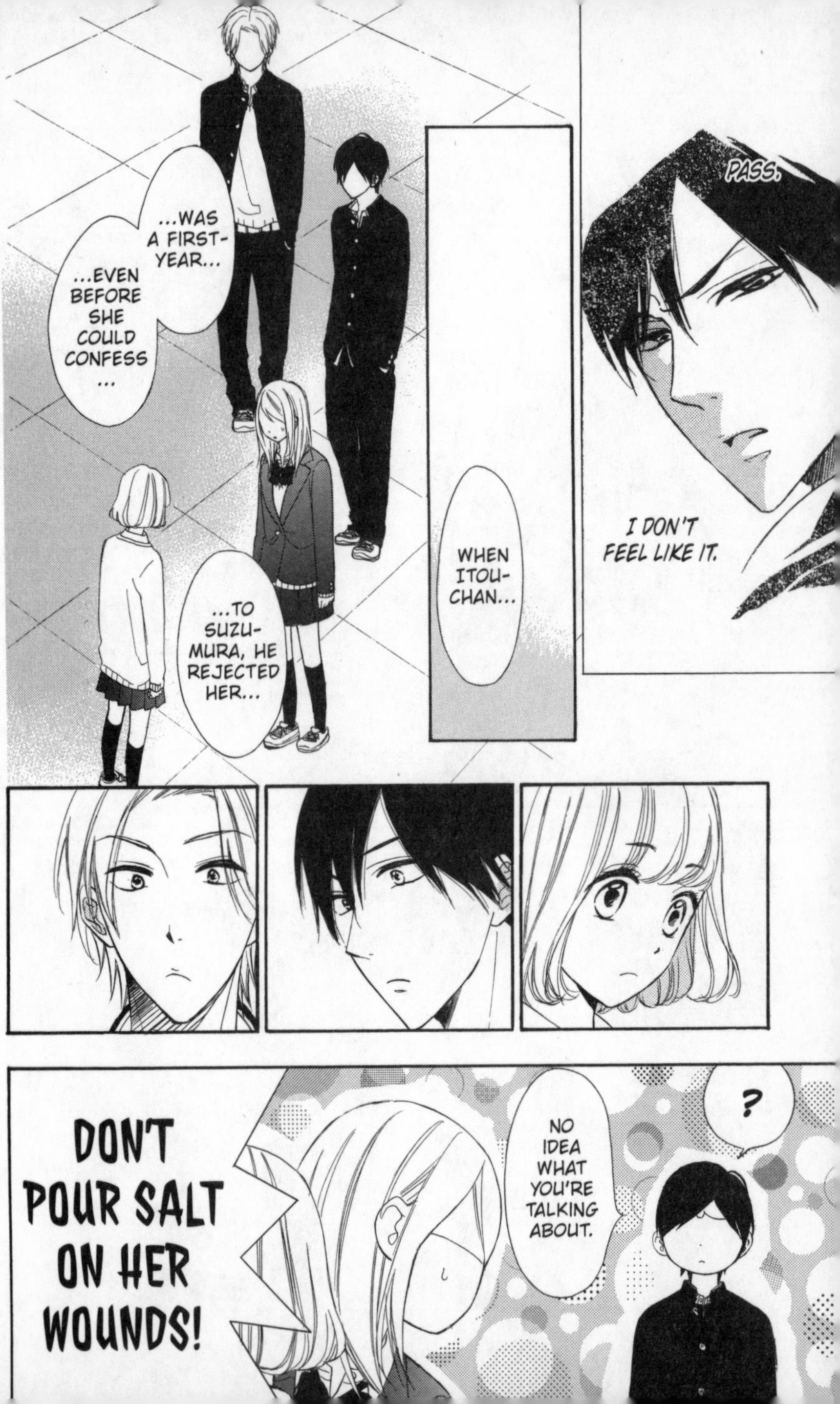
PASS.
I DON'T FEEL LIKE IT.
WHEN ITOU-CHAN...
...WAS A FIRST-YEAR...
...EVEN BEFORE SHE COULD CONFESS...
...TO SUZUMURA, HE REJECTED HER...
?
NO IDEA WHAT YOU'RE TALKING ABOUT.
DON'T POUR SALT ON HER WOUNDS!

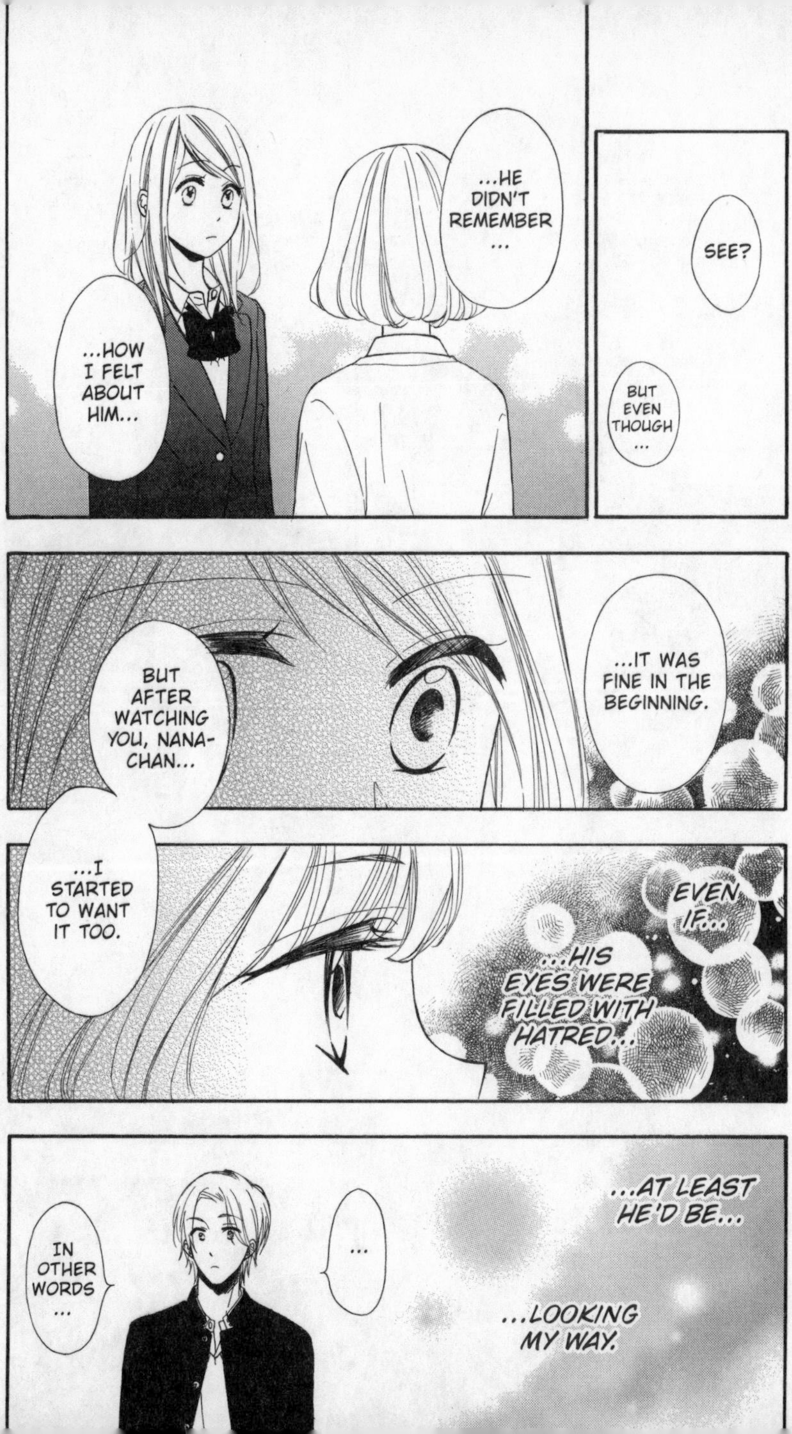
SEE?
BUT EVEN THOUGH...
...HE DIDN'T REMEMBER...
...HOW I FELT ABOUT HIM...
...IT WAS FINE IN THE BEGINNING.
BUT AFTER WATCHING YOU, NANA-CHAN...
...I STARTED TO WANT IT TOO.
EVEN IF...
...HIS EYES WERE FILLED WITH HATRED...
...AT LEAST HE'D BE...
...LOOKING MY WAY.
...
IN OTHER WORDS...

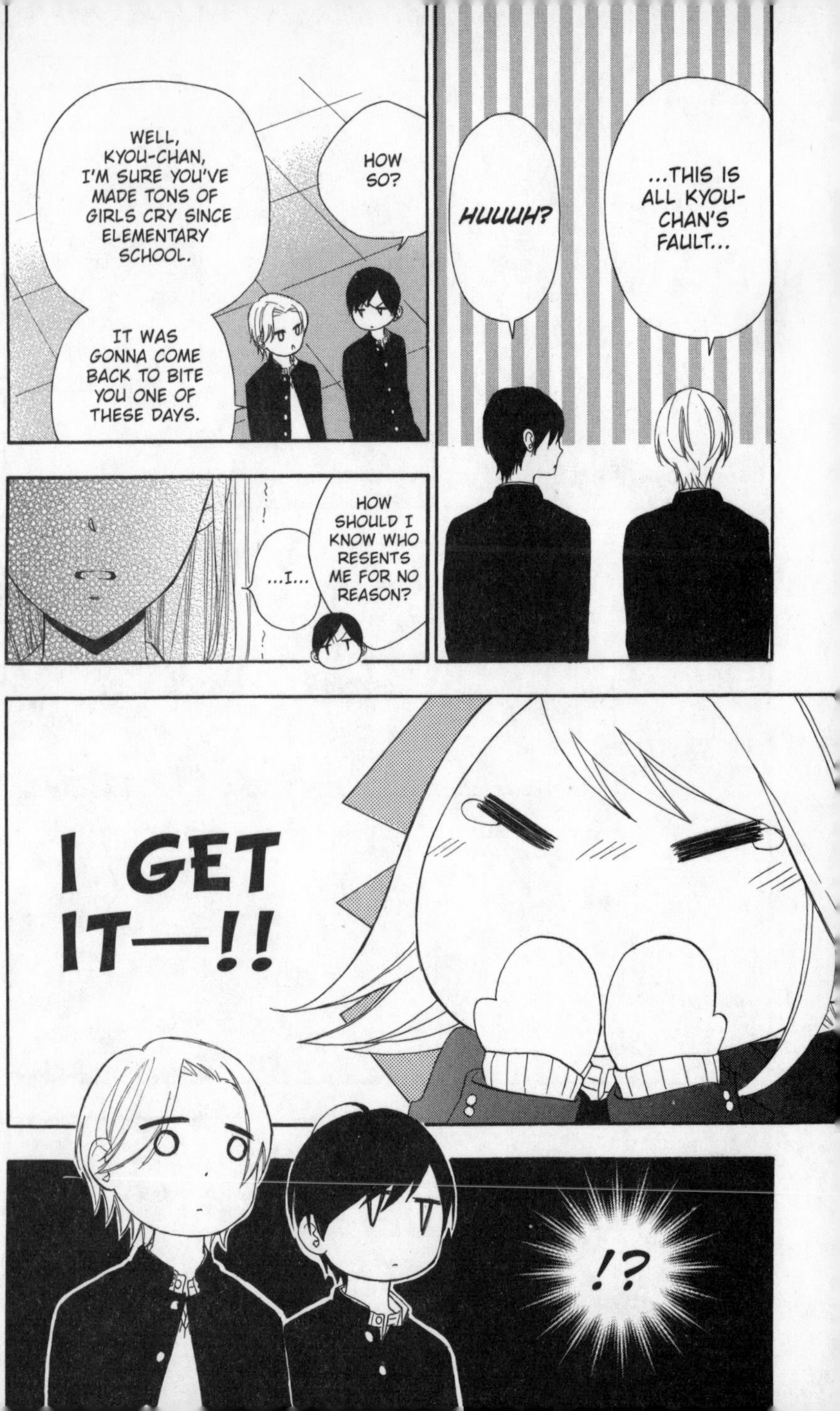
...THIS IS ALL KYOU-CHAN'S FAULT...
HUUUH?
HOW SO?
WELL, KYOU-CHAN, I'M SURE YOU'VE MADE TONS OF GIRLS CRY SINCE ELEMENTARY SCHOOL.
IT WAS GONNA COME BACK TO BITE YOU ONE OF THESE DAYS.
HOW SHOULD I KNOW WHO RESENTS ME FOR NO REASON?
...I...
I GET IT—!!
!?

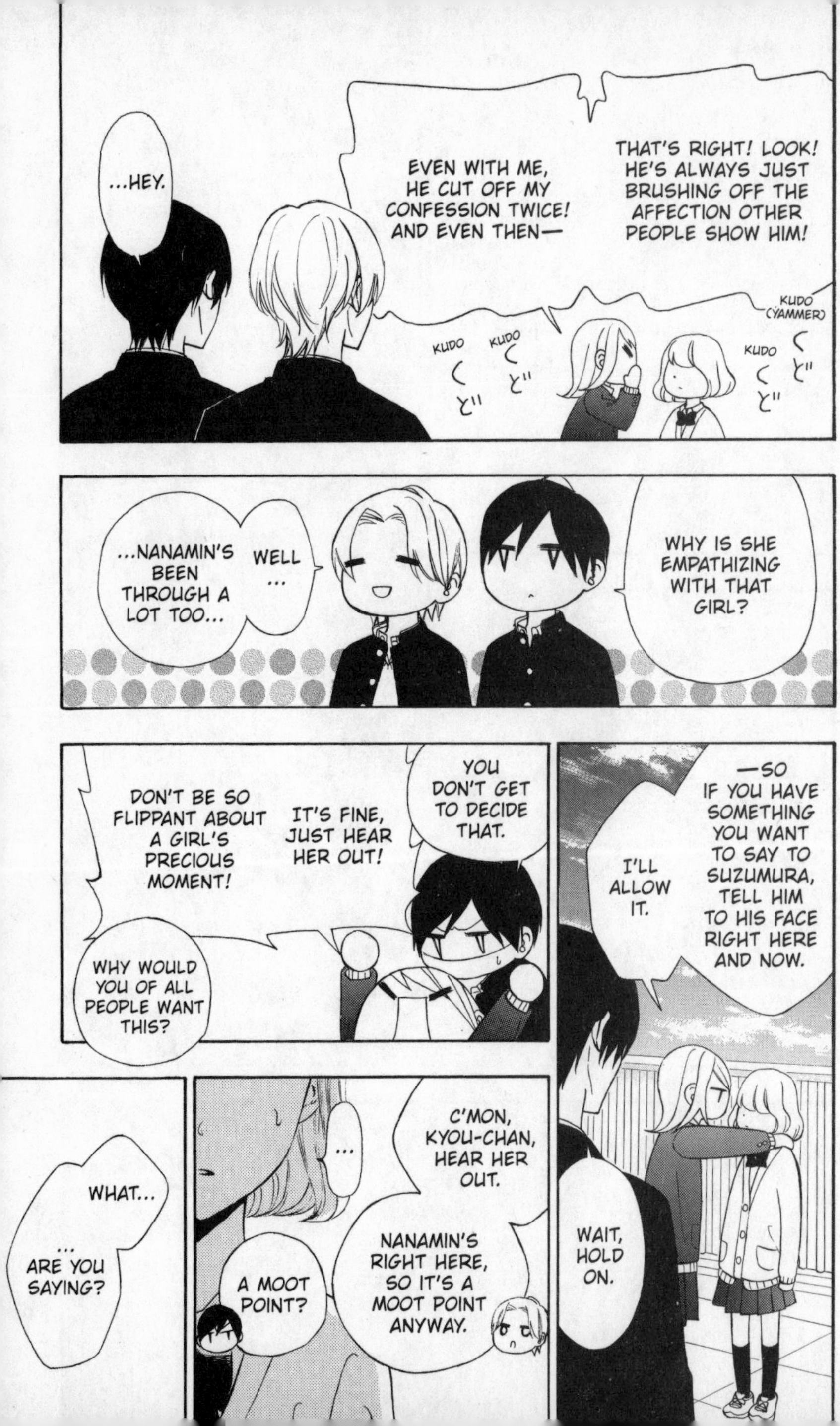
THAT'S RIGHT! LOOK! HE'S ALWAYS JUST BRUSHING OFF THE AFFECTION OTHER PEOPLE SHOW HIM!
EVEN WITH ME, HE CUT OFF MY CONFESSION TWICE! AND EVEN THEN—
KUDO (YAMMER)
KUDO
KUDO
KUDO
...HEY.
WHY IS SHE EMPATHIZING WITH THAT GIRL?
WELL ...
...NANAMIN'S BEEN THROUGH A LOT TOO...
—SO IF YOU HAVE SOMETHING YOU WANT TO SAY TO SUZUMURA, TELL HIM TO HIS FACE RIGHT HERE AND NOW.
I'LL ALLOW IT.
WAIT, HOLD ON.
YOU DON'T GET TO DECIDE THAT.
IT'S FINE, JUST HEAR HER OUT!
DON'T BE SO FLIPPANT ABOUT A GIRL'S PRECIOUS MOMENT!
WHY WOULD YOU OF ALL PEOPLE WANT THIS?
C'MON, KYOU-CHAN, HEAR HER OUT.
...
NANAMIN'S RIGHT HERE, SO IT'S A MOOT POINT ANYWAY.
A MOOT POINT?
WHAT...
... ARE YOU SAYING?

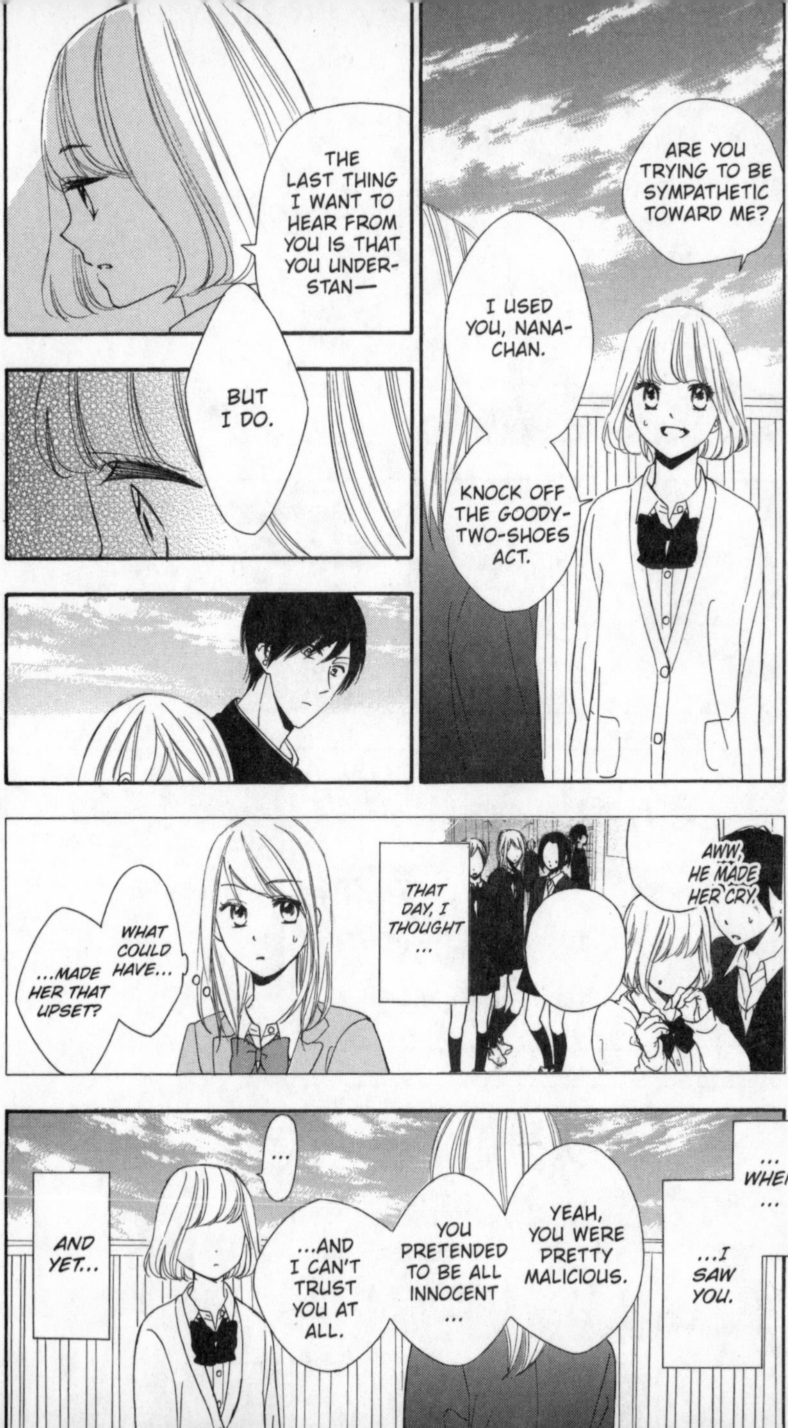
ARE YOU TRYING TO BE SYMPATHETIC TOWARD ME?
I USED YOU, NANA-CHAN.
KNOCK OFF THE GOODY-TWO-SHOES ACT.
THE LAST THING I WANT TO HEAR FROM YOU IS THAT YOU UNDERSTAN—
BUT I DO.
AWW, HE MADE HER CRY.
THAT DAY, I THOUGHT ...
WHAT COULD HAVE...
...MADE HER THAT UPSET?
... WHEN ...
...I SAW YOU.
YEAH, YOU WERE PRETTY MALICIOUS.
YOU PRETENDED TO BE ALL INNOCENT ...
...AND I CAN'T TRUST YOU AT ALL.
...
AND YET...

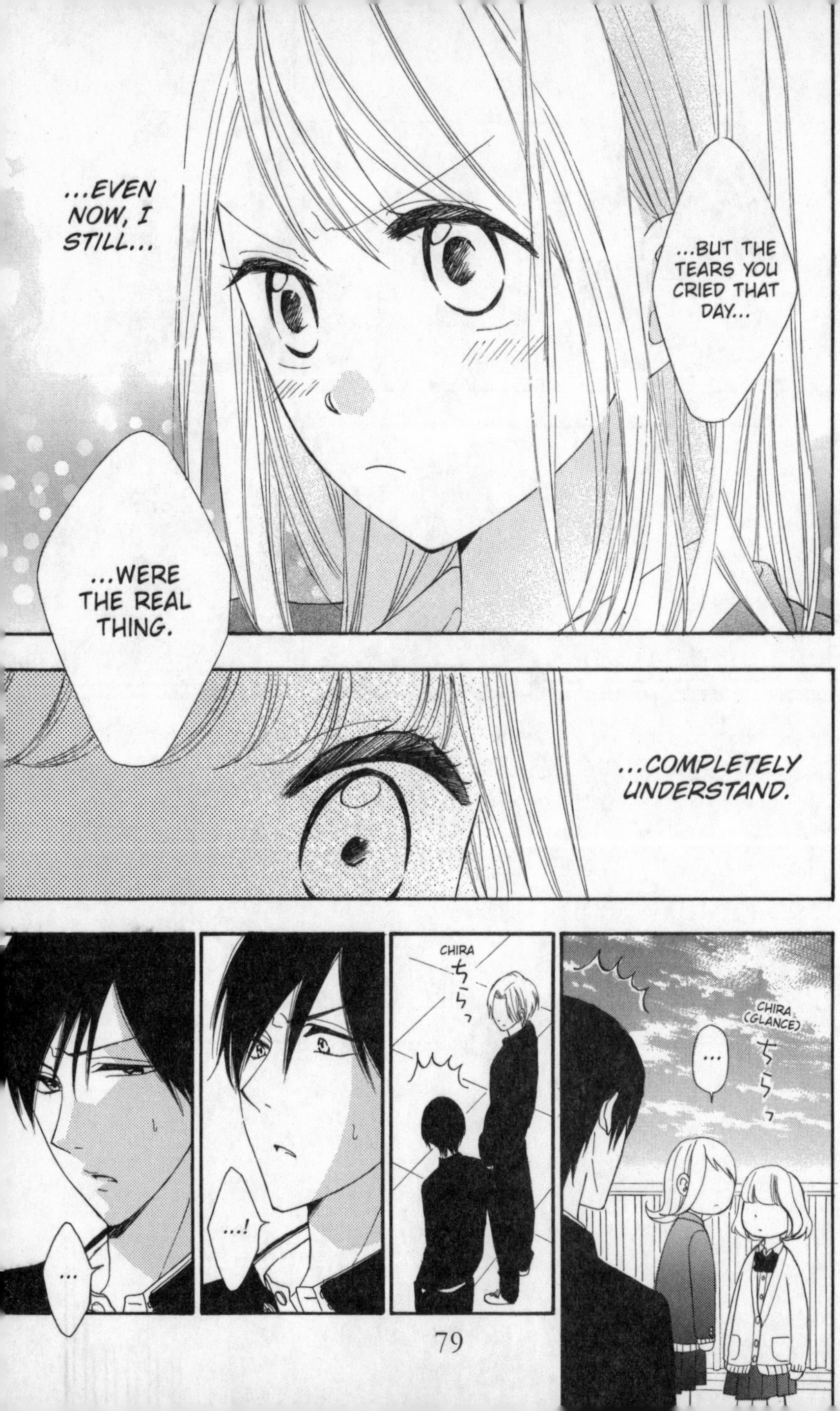
...BUT THE TEARS YOU CRIED THAT DAY...
...EVEN NOW, I STILL...
...WERE THE REAL THING.
...COMPLETELY UNDERSTAND.
CHIRA (GLANCE)
ちらっ
...
CHIRA
ちらっ
...!
...

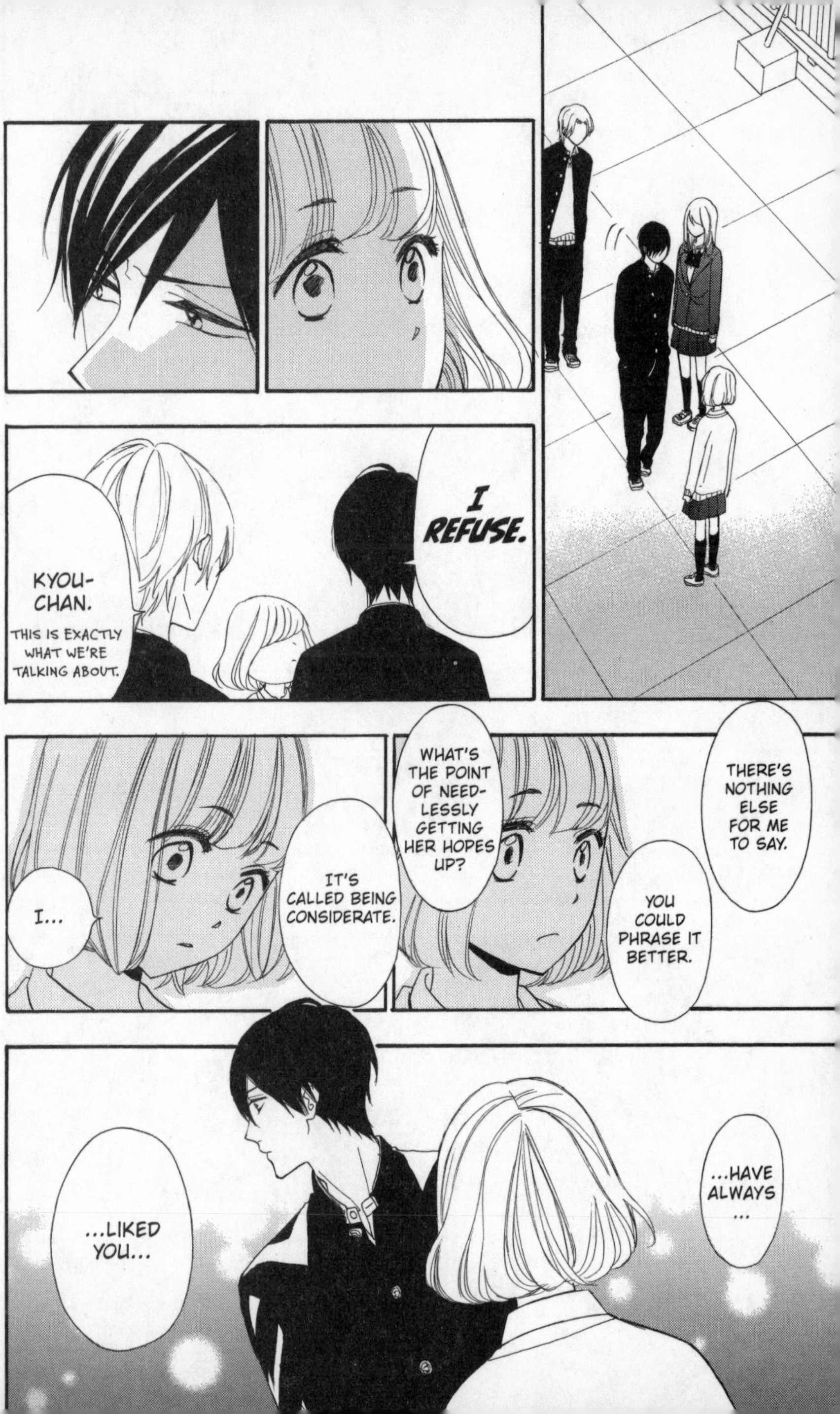
I REFUSE.
KYOU-CHAN.
THIS IS EXACTLY WHAT WE'RE TALKING ABOUT.
THERE'S NOTHING ELSE FOR ME TO SAY.
WHAT'S THE POINT OF NEED-LESSLY GETTING HER HOPES UP?
YOU COULD PHRASE IT BETTER.
IT'S CALLED BEING CONSIDERATE.
I...
...HAVE ALWAYS...
...LIKED YOU...

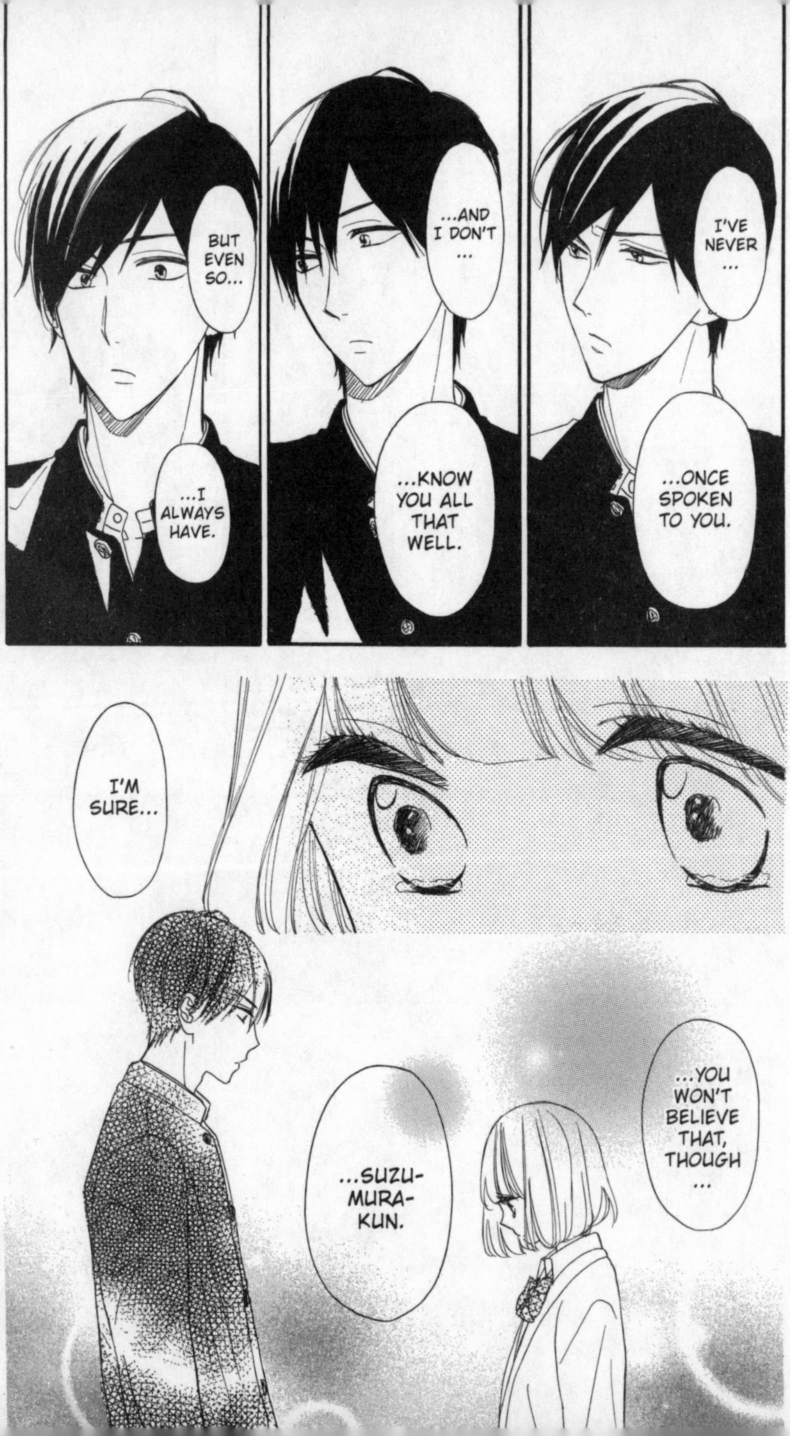
I'VE NEVER...
...ONCE SPOKEN TO YOU.
...AND I DON'T...
...KNOW YOU ALL THAT WELL.
BUT EVEN SO...
...I ALWAYS HAVE.
I'M SURE...
...YOU WON'T BELIEVE THAT, THOUGH...
...SUZUMURA-KUN.

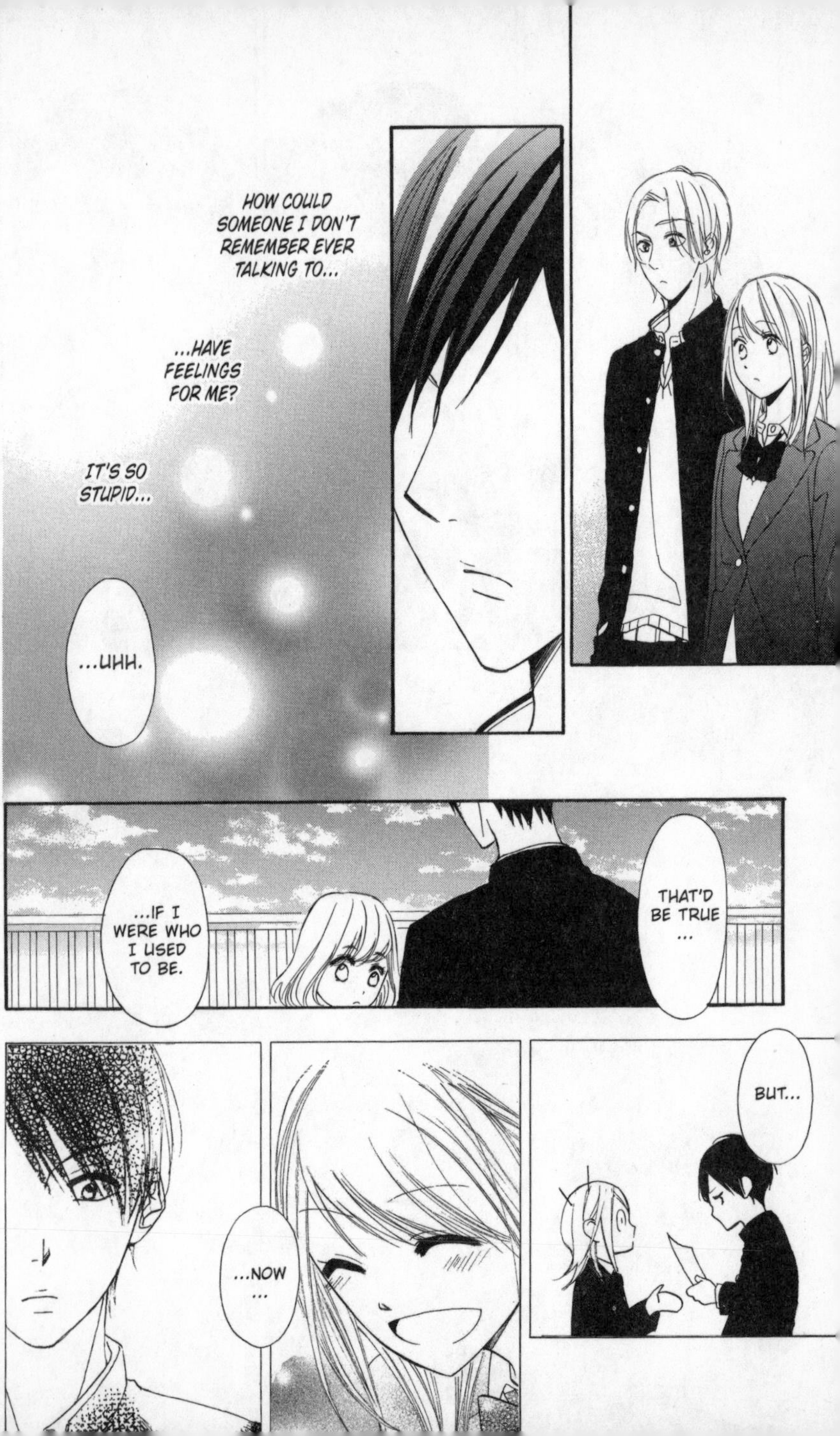
HOW COULD SOMEONE I DON'T REMEMBER EVER TALKING TO...
...HAVE FEELINGS FOR ME?
IT'S SO STUPID...
...UHH.
THAT'D BE TRUE...
...IF I WERE WHO I USED TO BE.
BUT...
...NOW...

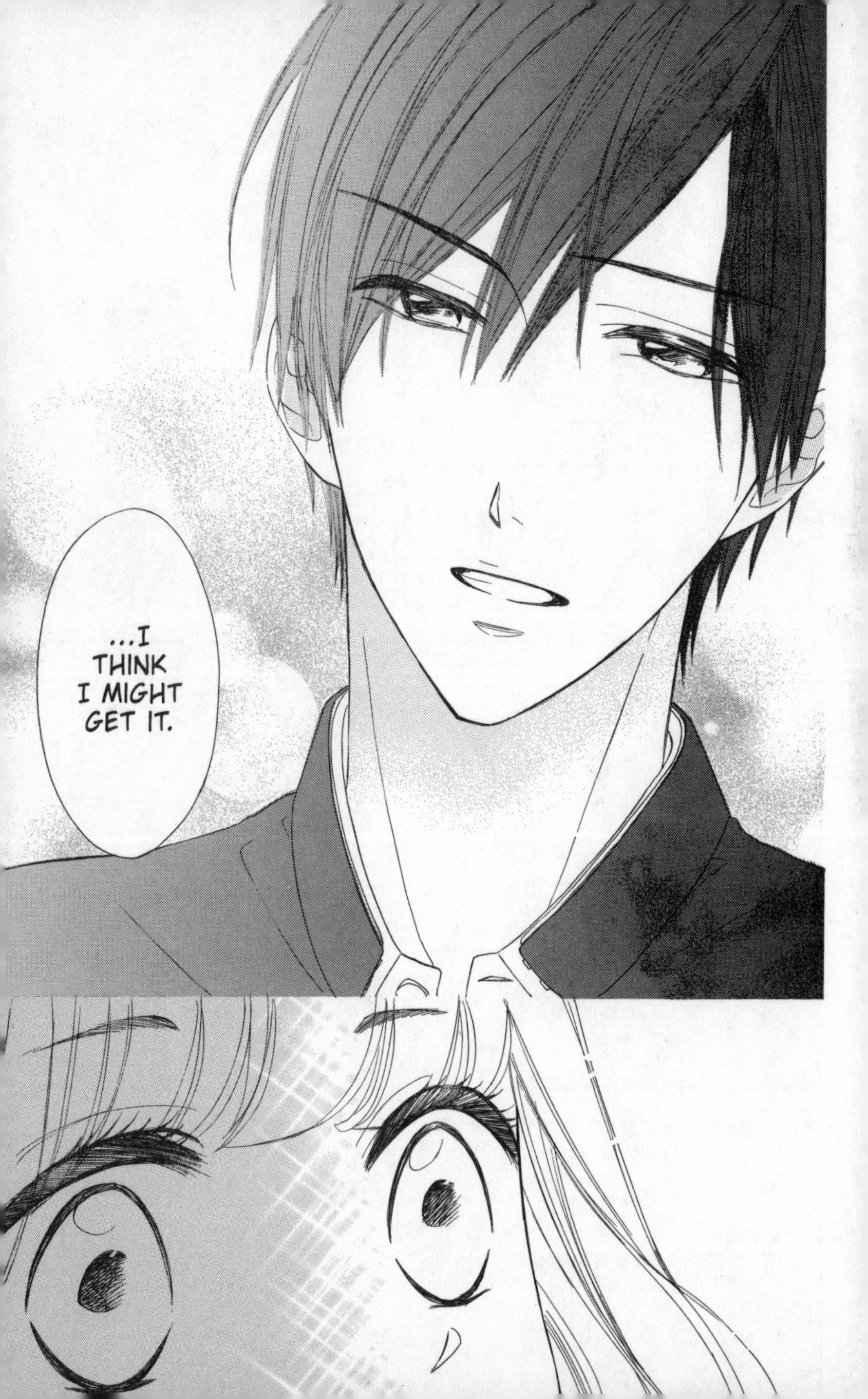
...I THINK I MIGHT GET IT.

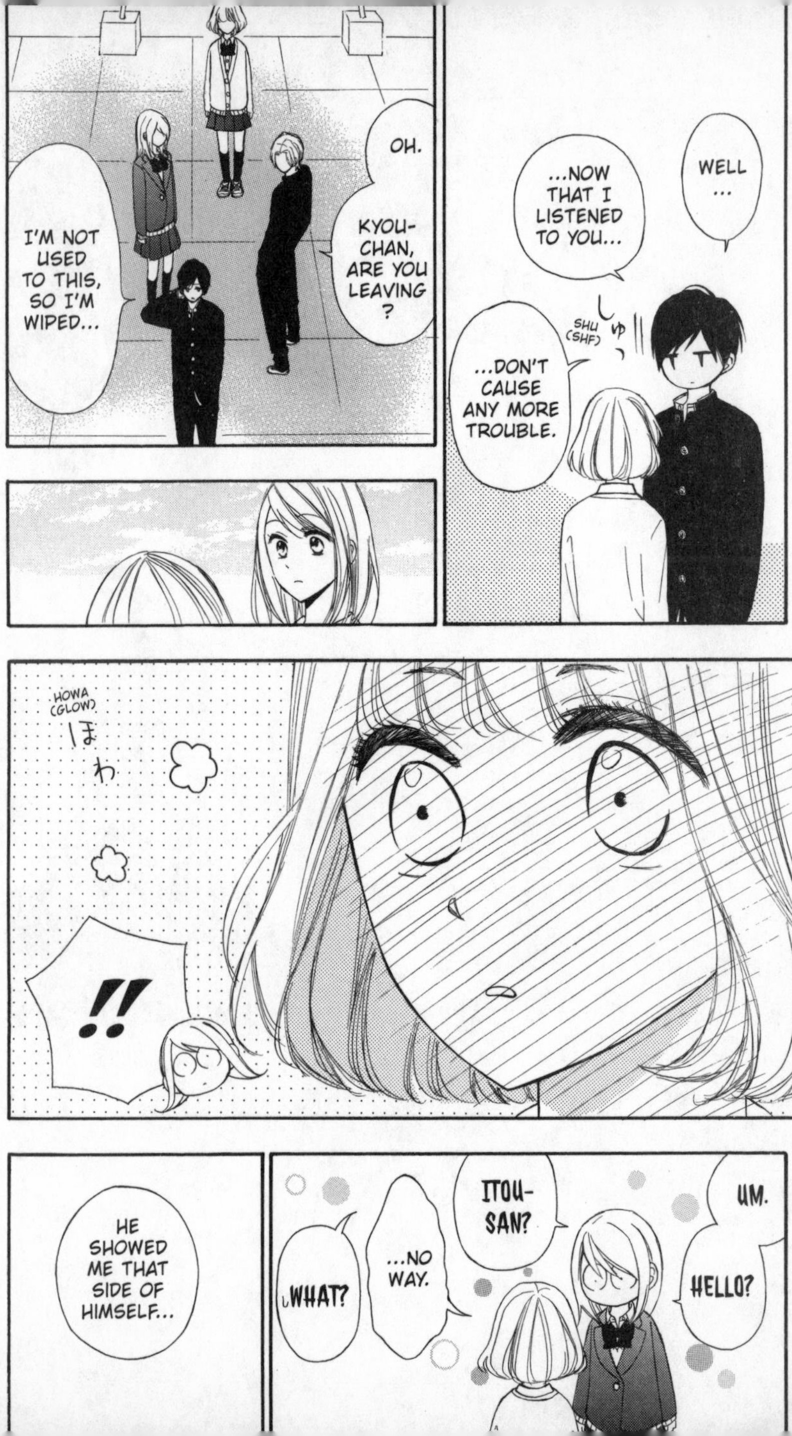
WELL ...
...NOW THAT I LISTENED TO YOU...
SHU (SHF)
しゅっ
...DON'T CAUSE ANY MORE TROUBLE.
OH.
KYOU-CHAN, ARE YOU LEAVING?
I'M NOT USED TO THIS, SO I'M WIPED...
HOWA (GLOW)
ほわ
!!
UM.
HELLO?
ITOU-SAN?
...NO WAY.
WHAT?
HE SHOWED ME THAT SIDE OF HIMSELF...

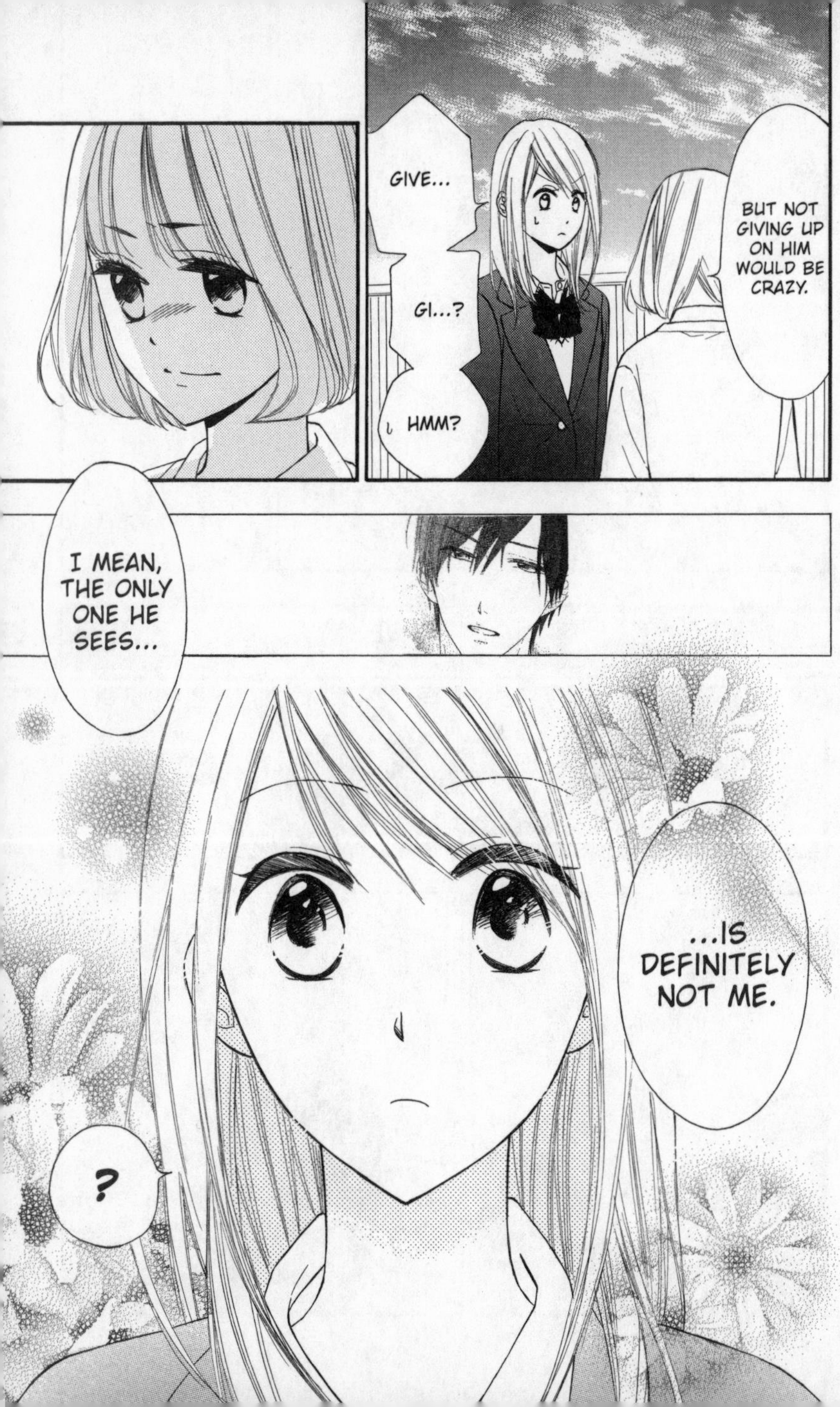
BUT NOT GIVING UP ON HIM WOULD BE CRAZY.
GIVE...
GI...?
HMM?
I MEAN, THE ONLY ONE HE SEES...
...IS DEFINITELY NOT ME.
?

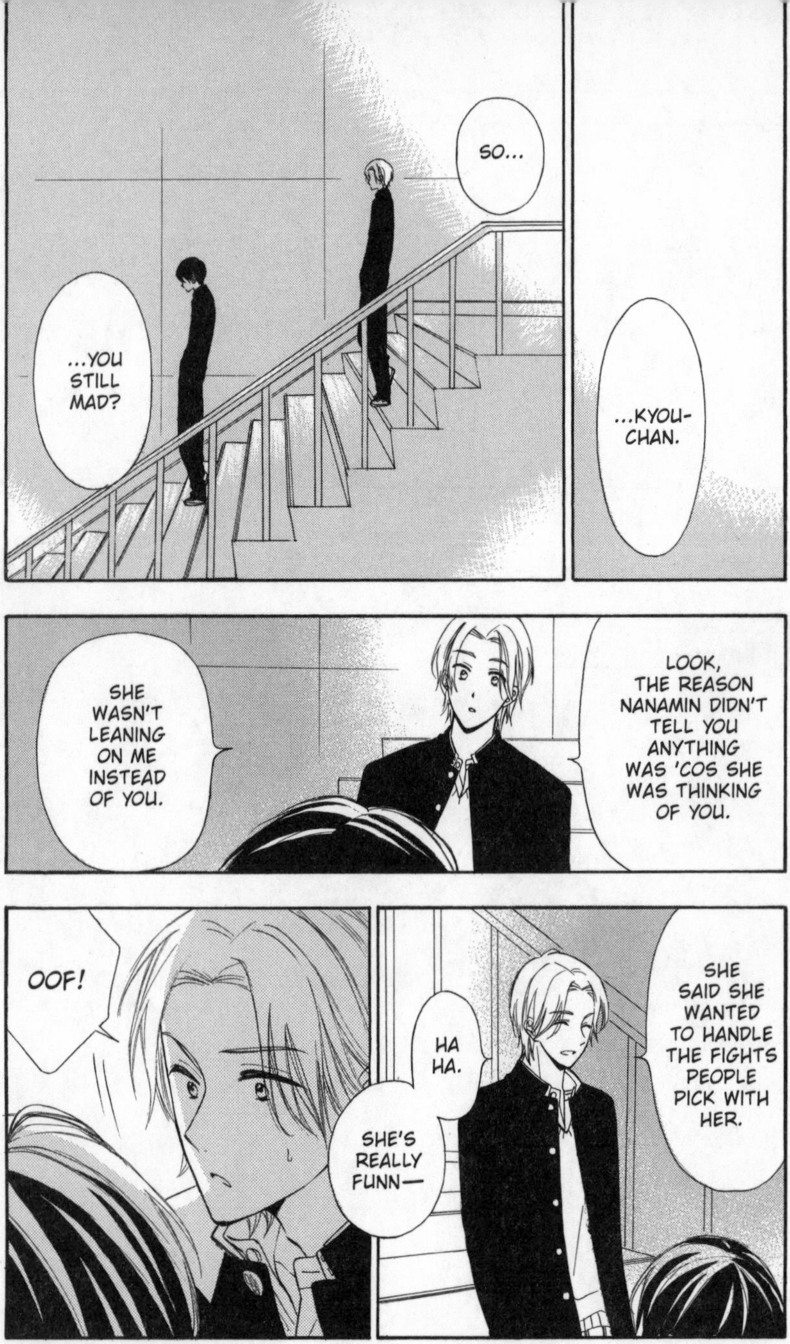
...KYOU-CHAN.
SO...
...YOU STILL MAD?
LOOK, THE REASON NANAMIN DIDN'T TELL YOU ANYTHING WAS 'COS SHE WAS THINKING OF YOU.
SHE WASN'T LEANING ON ME INSTEAD OF YOU.
SHE SAID SHE WANTED TO HANDLE THE FIGHTS PEOPLE PICK WITH HER.
HA HA.
SHE'S REALLY FUNN—
OOF!

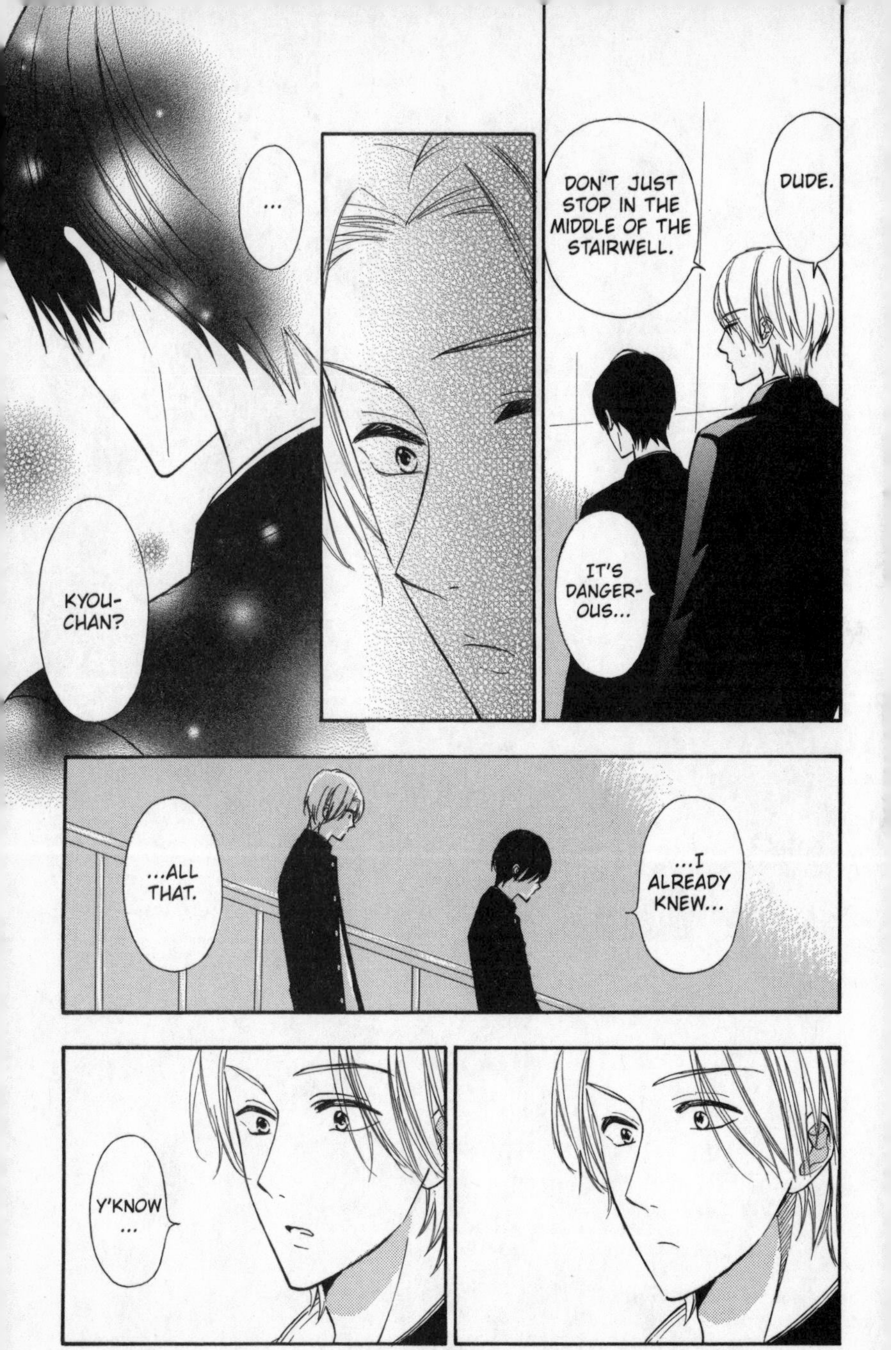
DUDE.
DON'T JUST STOP IN THE MIDDLE OF THE STAIRWELL.
IT'S DANGER-OUS...
...
KYOU-CHAN?
...I ALREADY KNEW...
...ALL THAT.
Y'KNOW ...

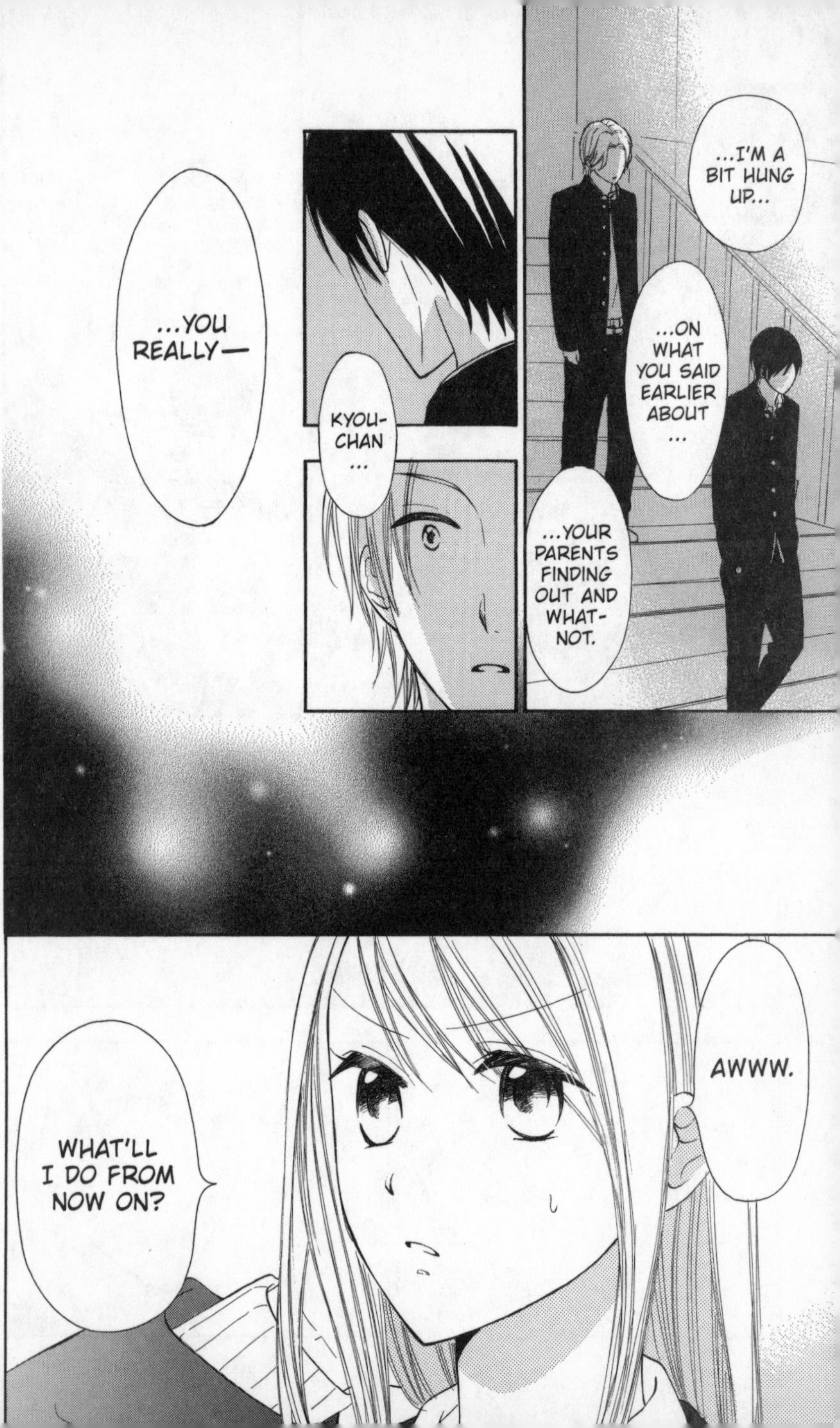
...I'M A BIT HUNG UP...
...ON WHAT YOU SAID EARLIER ABOUT...
...YOUR PARENTS FINDING OUT AND WHAT-NOT.
KYOU-CHAN...
...YOU REALLY—
AWWW.
WHAT'LL I DO FROM NOW ON?

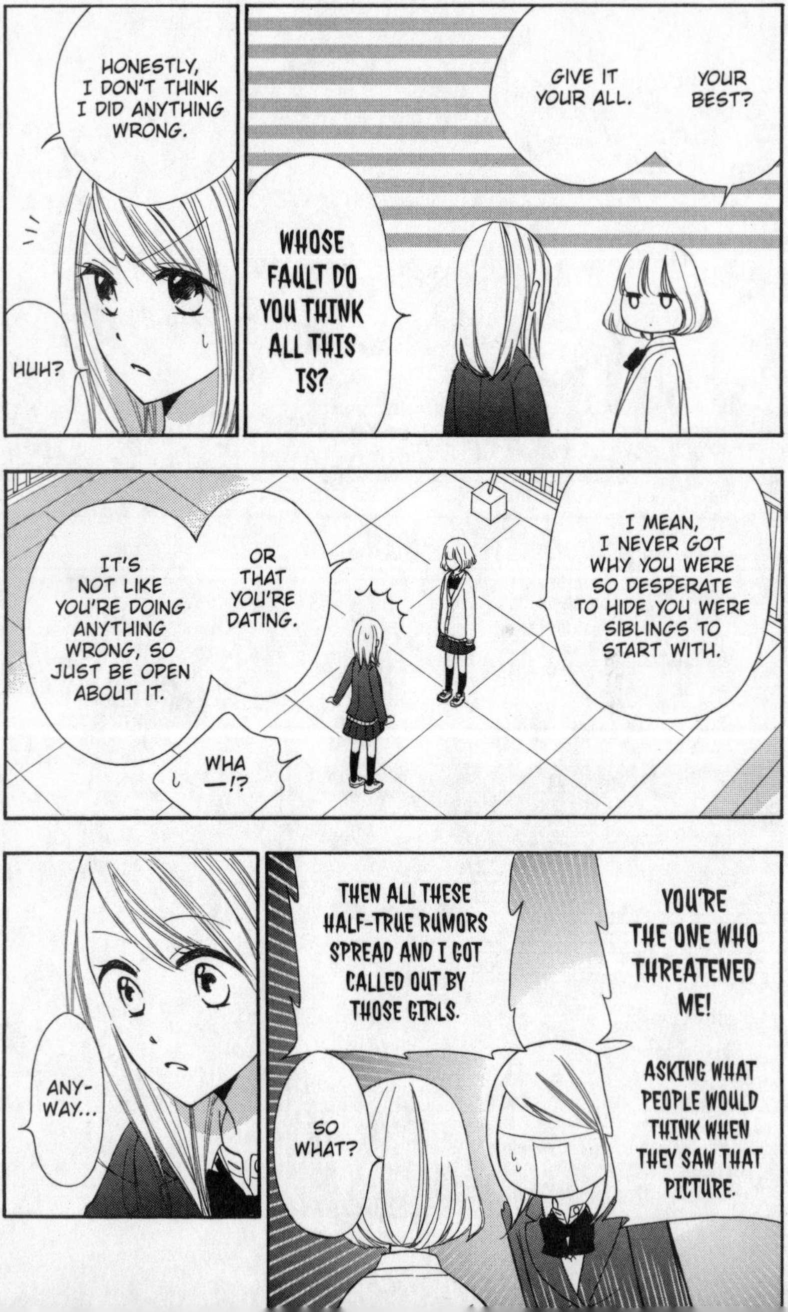
YOUR BEST?
GIVE IT YOUR ALL.
WHOSE FAULT DO YOU THINK ALL THIS IS?
HONESTLY, I DON'T THINK I DID ANYTHING WRONG.
HUH?
I MEAN, I NEVER GOT WHY YOU WERE SO DESPERATE TO HIDE YOU WERE SIBLINGS TO START WITH.
OR THAT YOU'RE DATING.
IT'S NOT LIKE YOU'RE DOING ANYTHING WRONG, SO JUST BE OPEN ABOUT IT.
WHA—!?
YOU'RE THE ONE WHO THREATENED ME!
ASKING WHAT PEOPLE WOULD THINK WHEN THEY SAW THAT PICTURE.
THEN ALL THESE HALF-TRUE RUMORS SPREAD AND I GOT CALLED OUT BY THOSE GIRLS.
SO WHAT?
ANY-WAY...

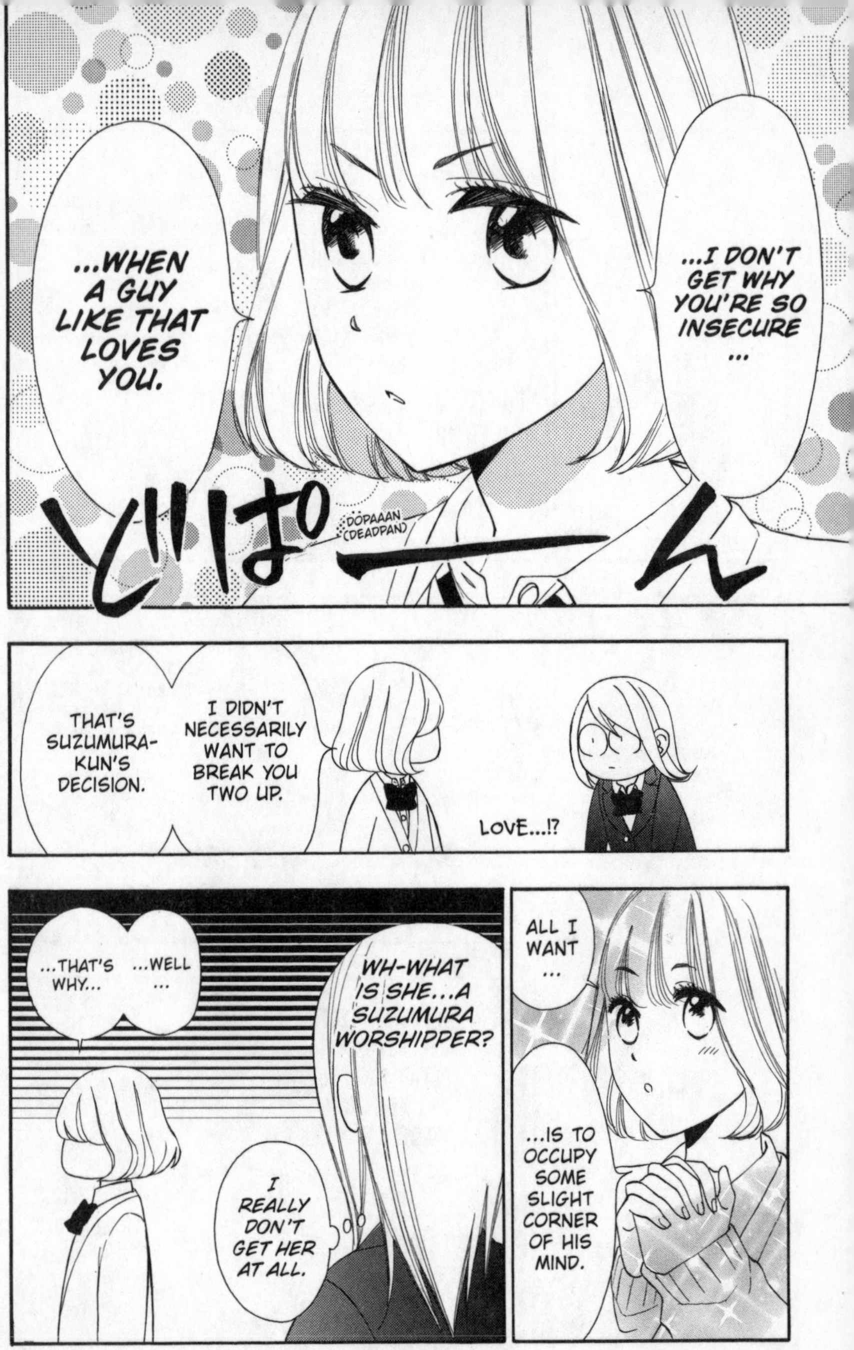
...I DON'T GET WHY YOU'RE SO INSECURE ...
...WHEN A GUY LIKE THAT LOVES YOU.
どぱーん
DOPAAAN (DEADPAN)
LOVE...!?
I DIDN'T NECESSARILY WANT TO BREAK YOU TWO UP.
THAT'S SUZUMURA-KUN'S DECISION.
ALL I WANT ...
...IS TO OCCUPY SOME SLIGHT CORNER OF HIS MIND.
WH-WHAT IS SHE...A SUZUMURA WORSHIPPER?
...WELL ...
...THAT'S WHY...
I REALLY DON'T GET HER AT ALL.

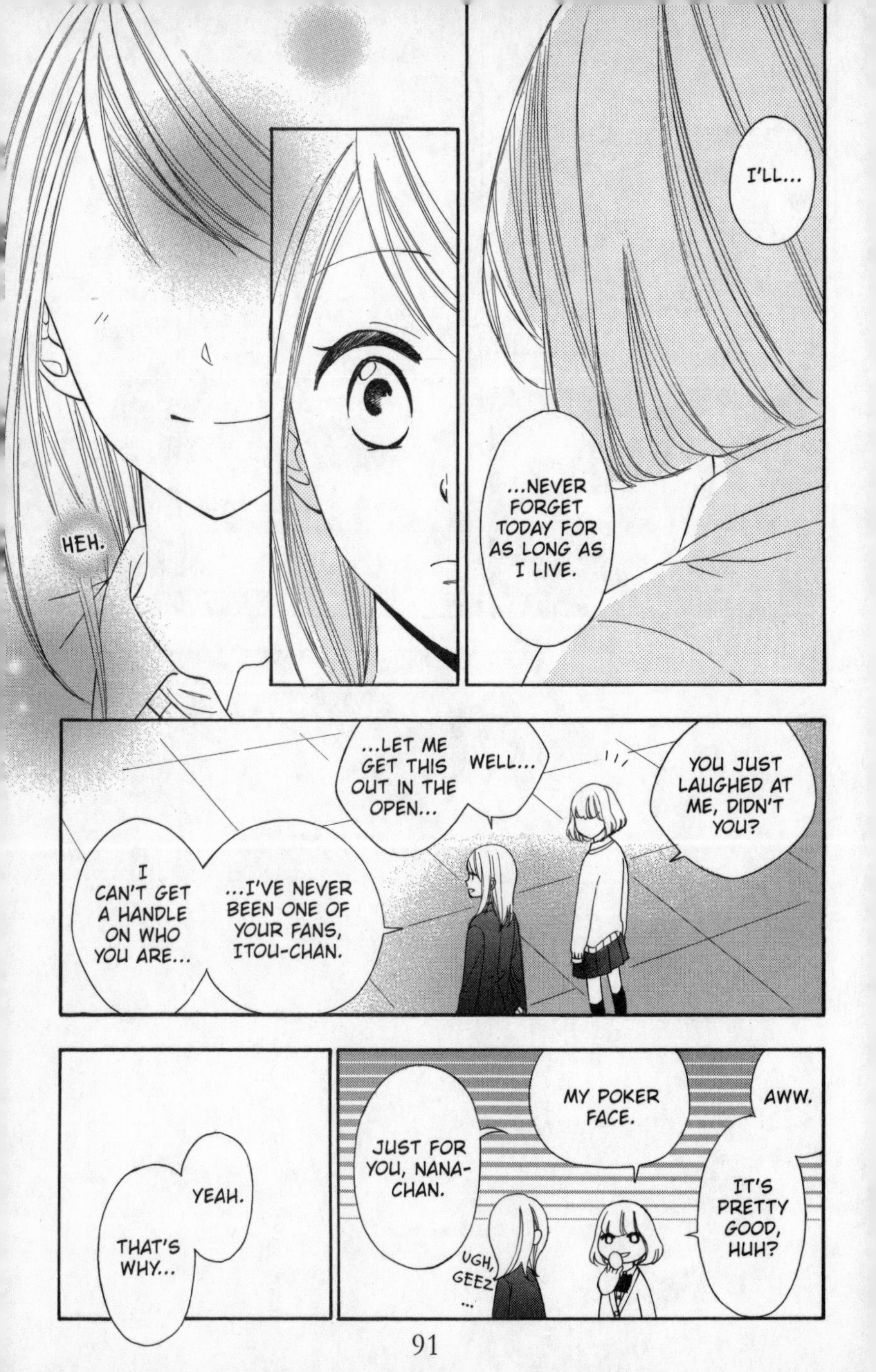
I'LL...
...NEVER FORGET TODAY FOR AS LONG AS I LIVE.
HEH.
YOU JUST LAUGHED AT ME, DIDN'T YOU?
WELL...
...LET ME GET THIS OUT IN THE OPEN...
...I'VE NEVER BEEN ONE OF YOUR FANS, ITOU-CHAN.
I CAN'T GET A HANDLE ON WHO YOU ARE...
AWW.
IT'S PRETTY GOOD, HUH?
MY POKER FACE.
JUST FOR YOU, NANA-CHAN.
UGH, GEEZ...
YEAH.
THAT'S WHY...

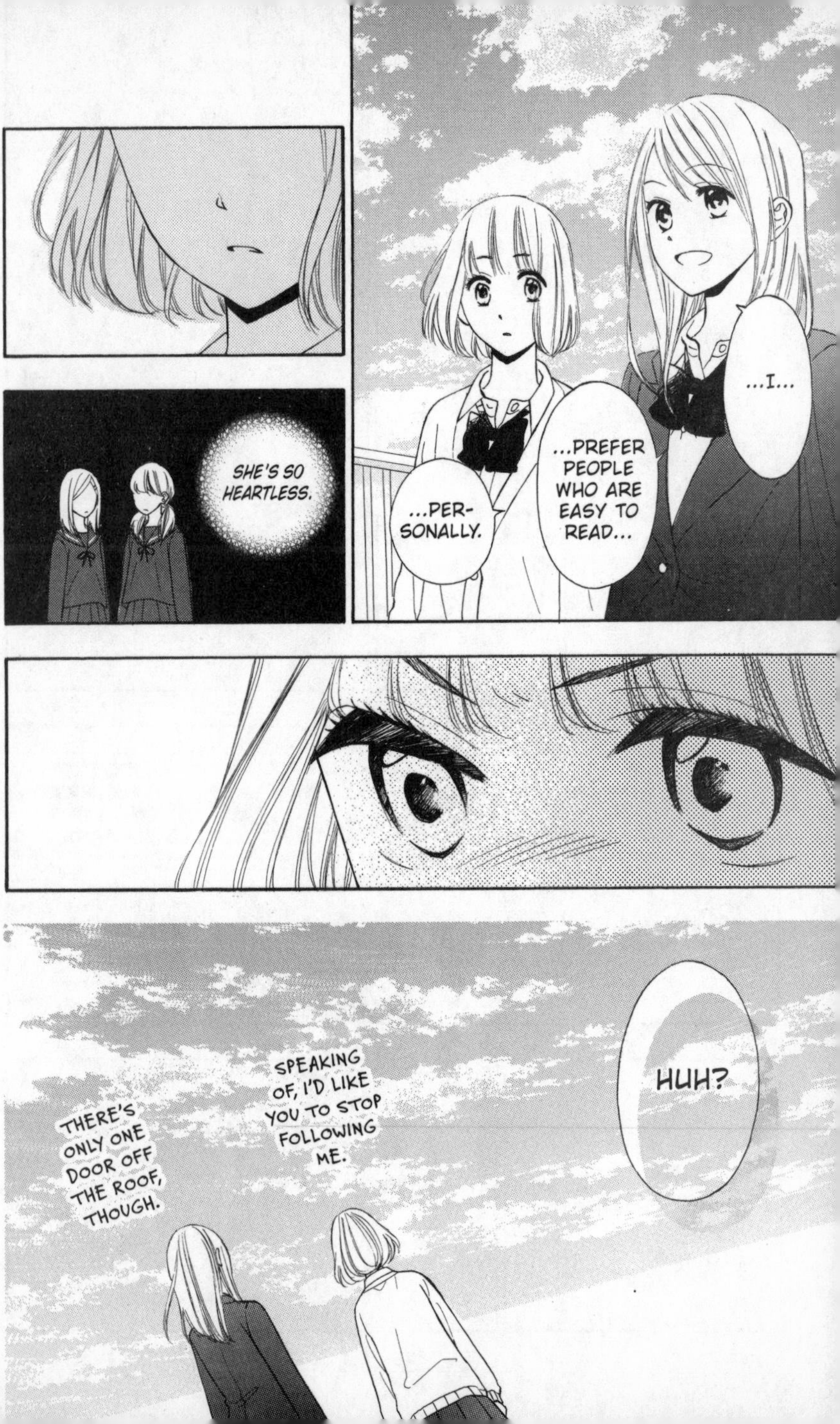
...I...
...PREFER PEOPLE WHO ARE EASY TO READ...
...PER-SONALLY.
SHE'S SO HEARTLESS.
HUH?
SPEAKING OF, I'D LIKE YOU TO STOP FOLLOWING ME.
THERE'S ONLY ONE DOOR OFF THE ROOF, THOUGH.

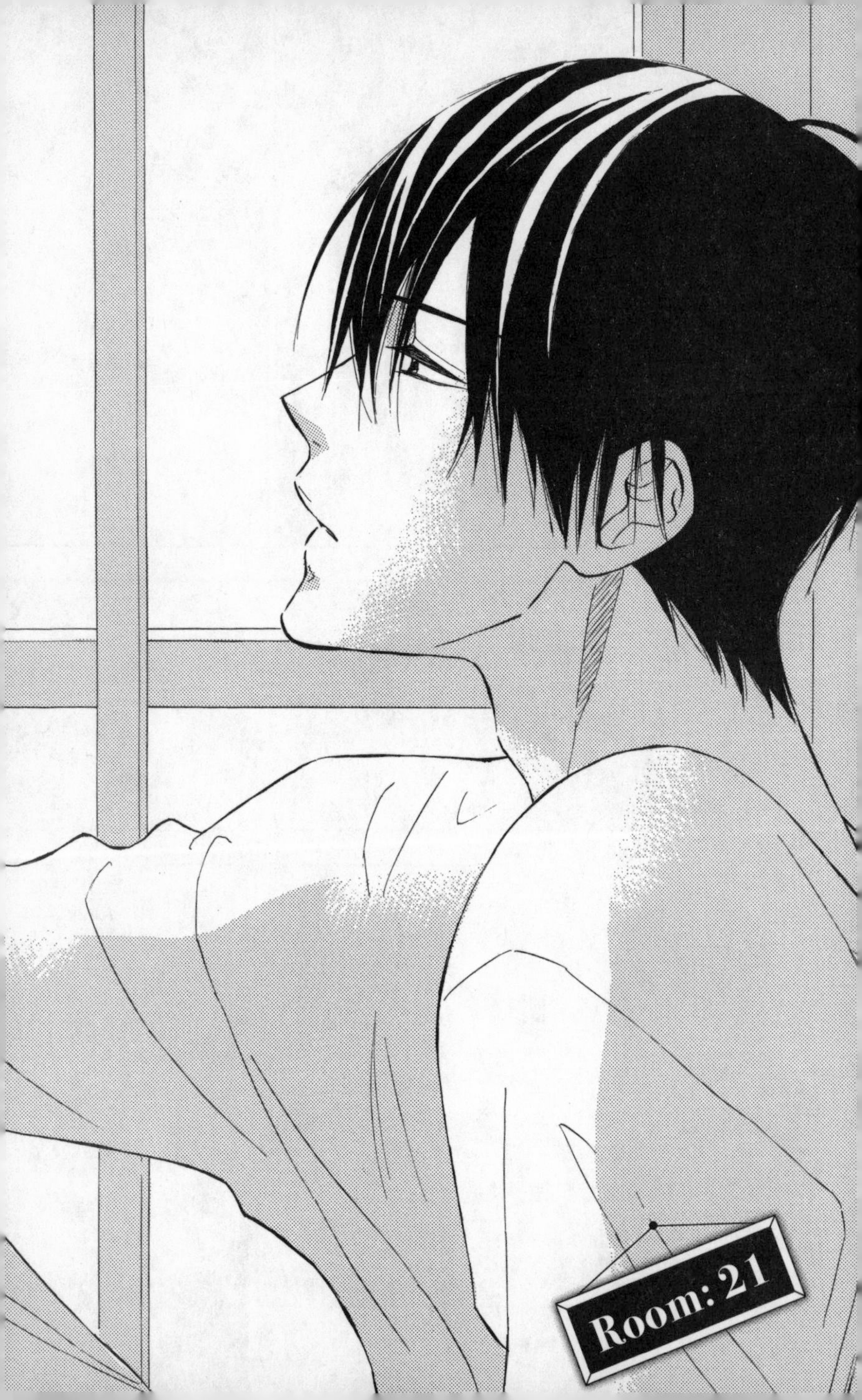
Room: 21

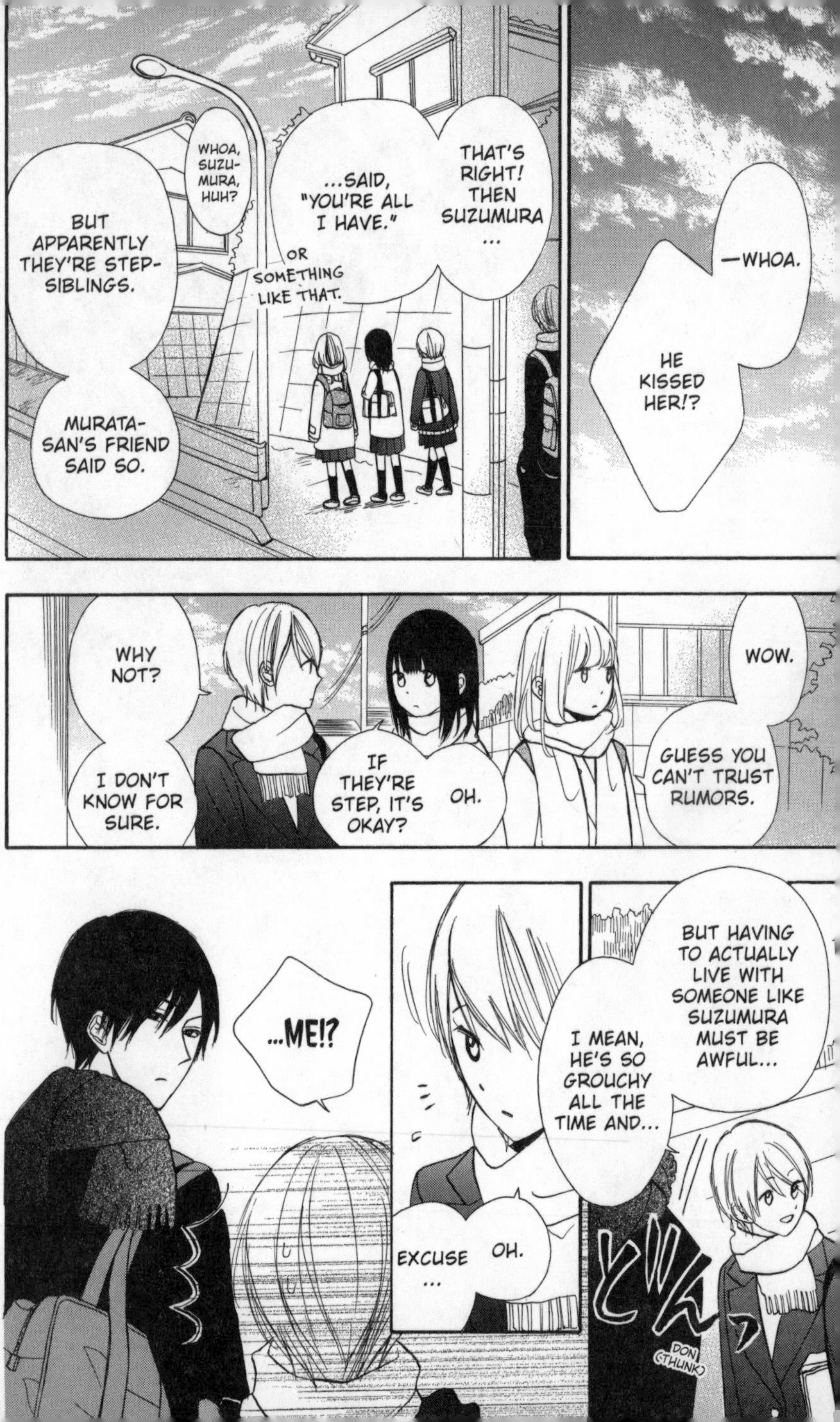
—WHOA.
HE KISSED HER!?
THAT'S RIGHT! THEN SUZUMURA ...
...SAID, "YOU'RE ALL I HAVE."
OR SOMETHING LIKE THAT.
WHOA, SUZUMURA, HUH?
BUT APPARENTLY THEY'RE STEP-SIBLINGS.
MURATA-SAN'S FRIEND SAID SO.
WOW.
GUESS YOU CAN'T TRUST RUMORS.
OH.
IF THEY'RE STEP, IT'S OKAY?
WHY NOT?
I DON'T KNOW FOR SURE.
BUT HAVING TO ACTUALLY LIVE WITH SOMEONE LIKE SUZUMURA MUST BE AWFUL...
I MEAN, HE'S SO GROUCHY ALL THE TIME AND...
DON (THUNK)
OH.
EXCUSE ...
...ME!?

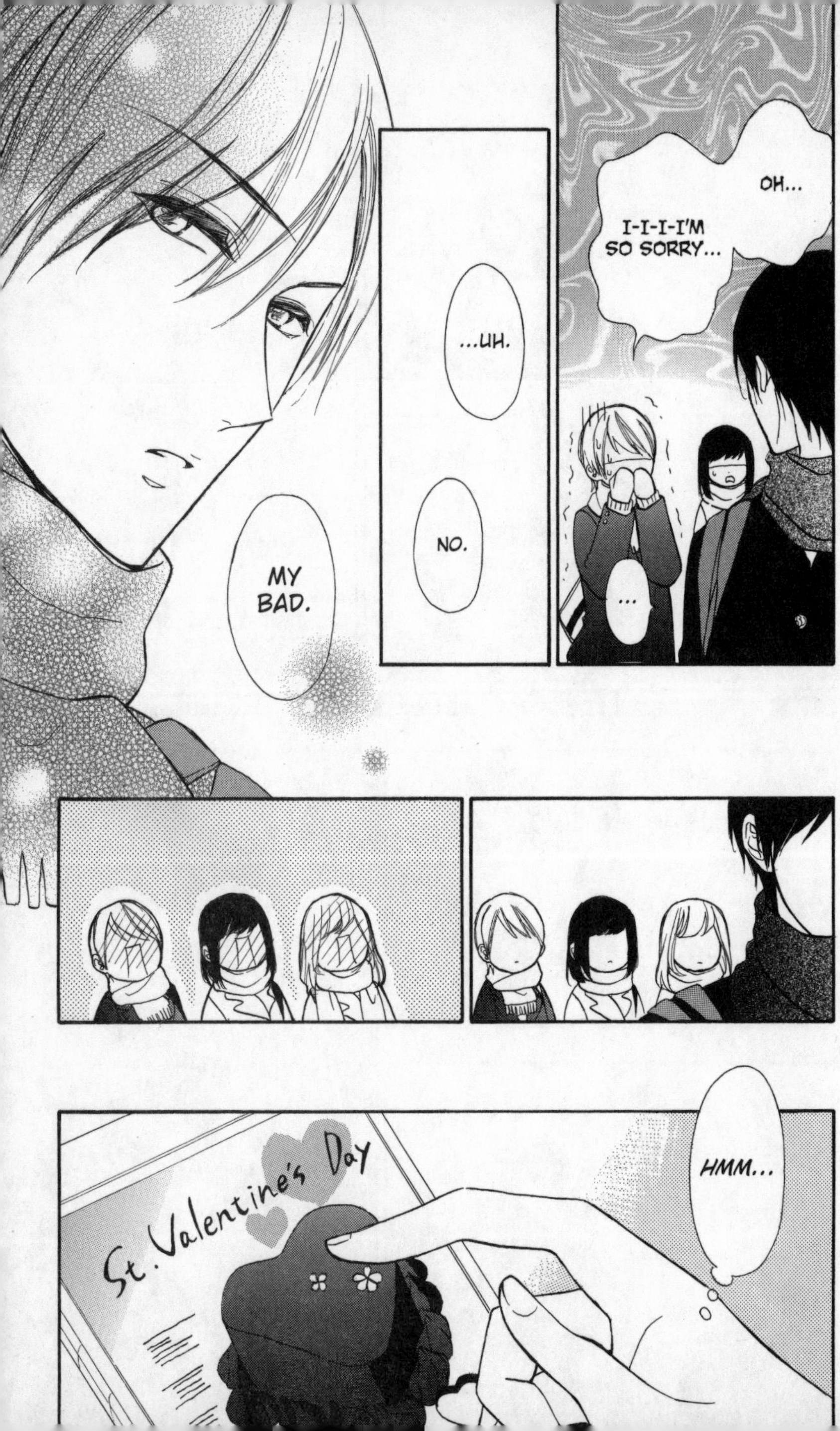
OH...
I-I-I-I'M SO SORRY...
...
...UH.
NO.
MY BAD.
HMM...
St. Valentine's Day

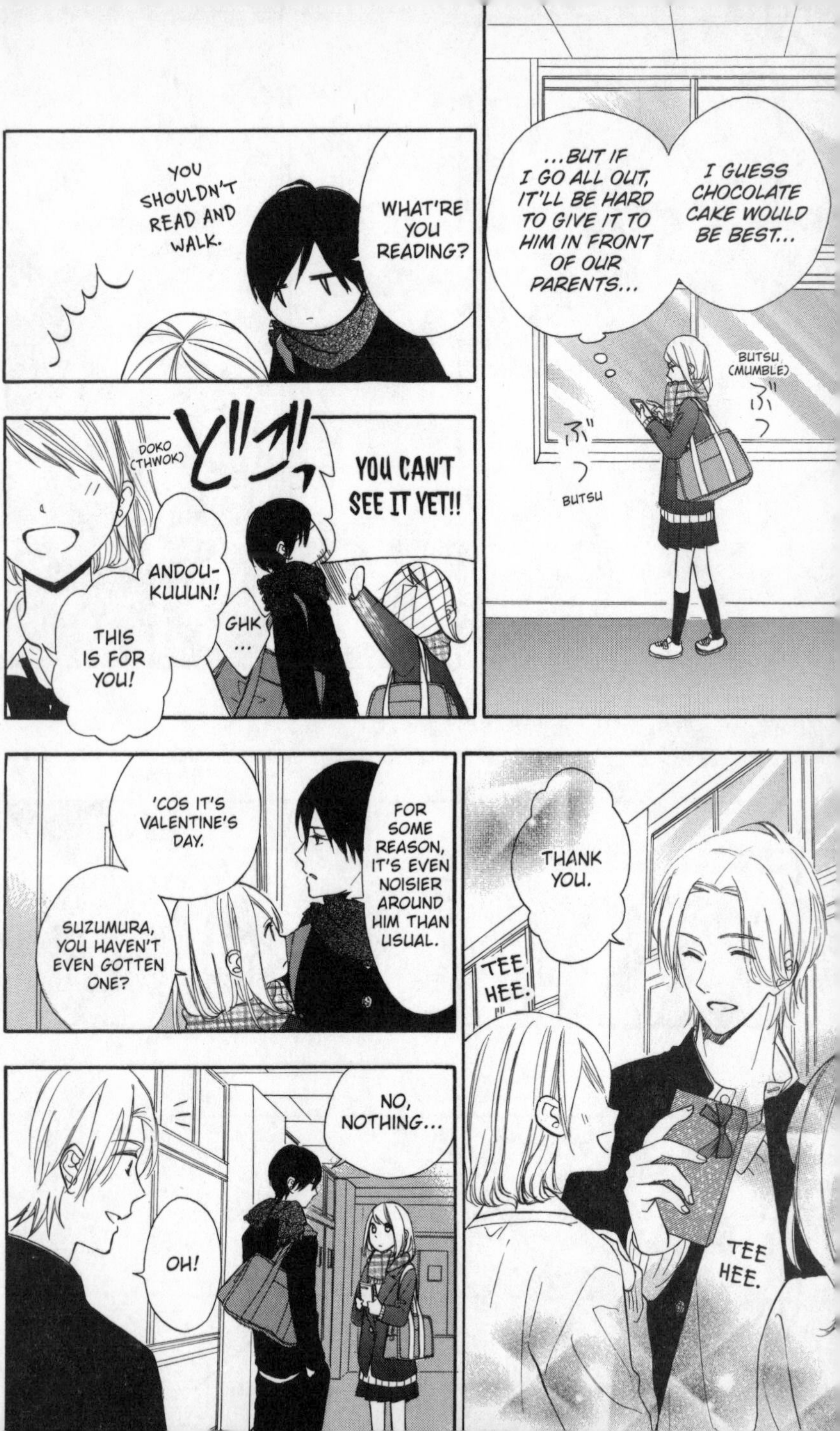
I GUESS CHOCOLATE CAKE WOULD BE BEST...
...BUT IF I GO ALL OUT, IT'LL BE HARD TO GIVE IT TO HIM IN FRONT OF OUR PARENTS...
BUTSU (MUMBLE)
BUTSU
WHAT'RE YOU READING?
YOU SHOULDN'T READ AND WALK.
YOU CAN'T SEE IT YET!!
DOKO (THWOK)
GHK...
ANDOU-KUUUN!
THIS IS FOR YOU!
THANK YOU.
TEE HEE.
TEE HEE.
FOR SOME REASON, IT'S EVEN NOISIER AROUND HIM THAN USUAL.
'COS IT'S VALENTINE'S DAY.
SUZUMURA, YOU HAVEN'T EVEN GOTTEN ONE?
NO, NOTHING...
OH!

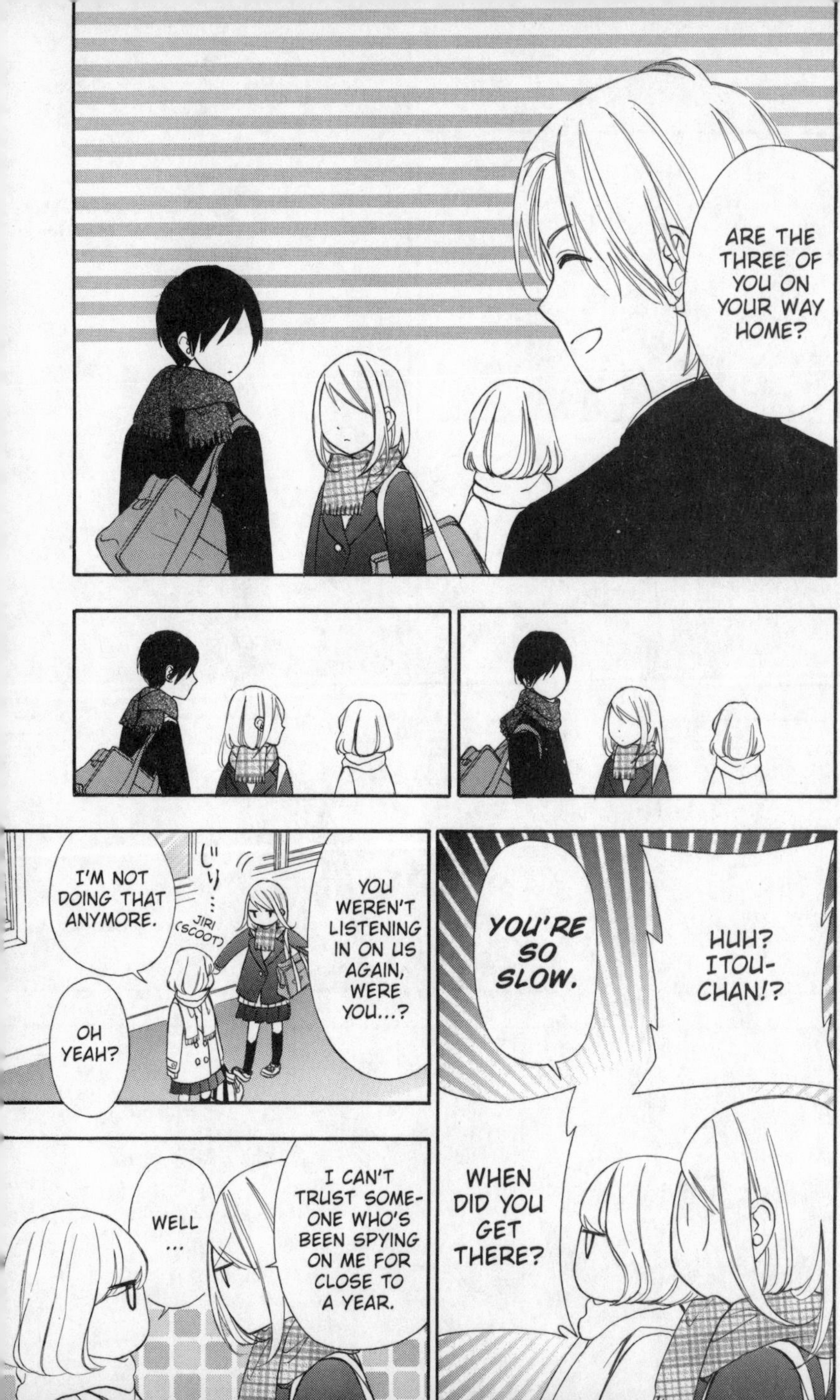
ARE THE THREE OF YOU ON YOUR WAY HOME?
HUH? ITOU-CHAN!?
YOU'RE SO SLOW.
WHEN DID YOU GET THERE?
YOU WEREN'T LISTENING IN ON US AGAIN, WERE YOU...?
JIRI (SCOOT)
I'M NOT DOING THAT ANYMORE.
OH YEAH?
I CAN'T TRUST SOMEONE WHO'S BEEN SPYING ON ME FOR CLOSE TO A YEAR.
WELL ...

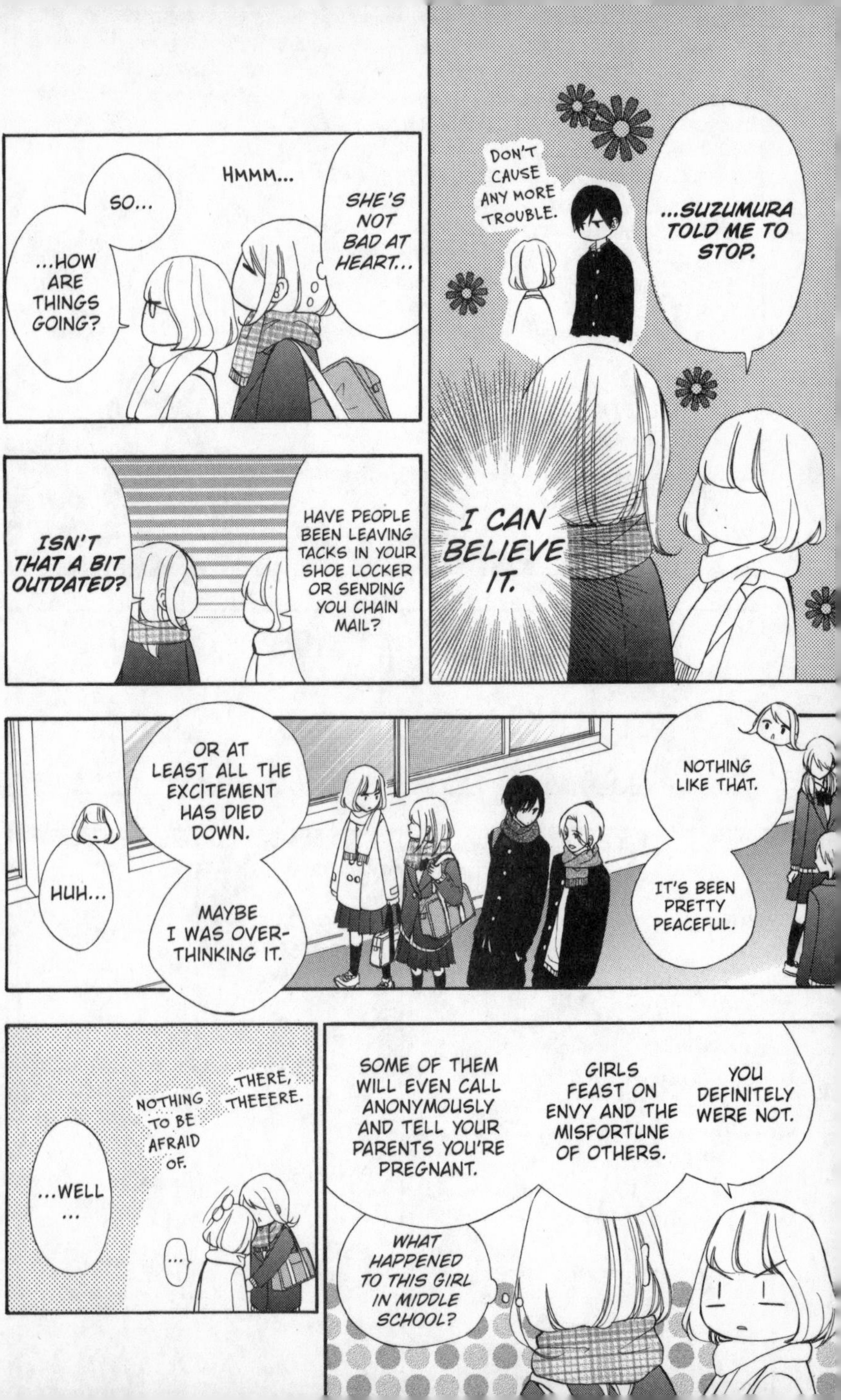
...SUZUMURA TOLD ME TO STOP.
DON'T CAUSE ANY MORE TROUBLE.
I CAN BELIEVE IT.
SHE'S NOT BAD AT HEART...
HMMM...
SO...
...HOW ARE THINGS GOING?
HAVE PEOPLE BEEN LEAVING TACKS IN YOUR SHOE LOCKER OR SENDING YOU CHAIN MAIL?
ISN'T THAT A BIT OUTDATED?
NOTHING LIKE THAT.
IT'S BEEN PRETTY PEACEFUL.
OR AT LEAST ALL THE EXCITEMENT HAS DIED DOWN.
MAYBE I WAS OVER-THINKING IT.
HUH...
YOU DEFINITELY WERE NOT.
GIRLS FEAST ON ENVY AND THE MISFORTUNE OF OTHERS.
SOME OF THEM WILL EVEN CALL ANONYMOUSLY AND TELL YOUR PARENTS YOU'RE PREGNANT.
WHAT HAPPENED TO THIS GIRL IN MIDDLE SCHOOL?
THERE, THEEERE.
NOTHING TO BE AFRAID OF.
...WELL ...
...

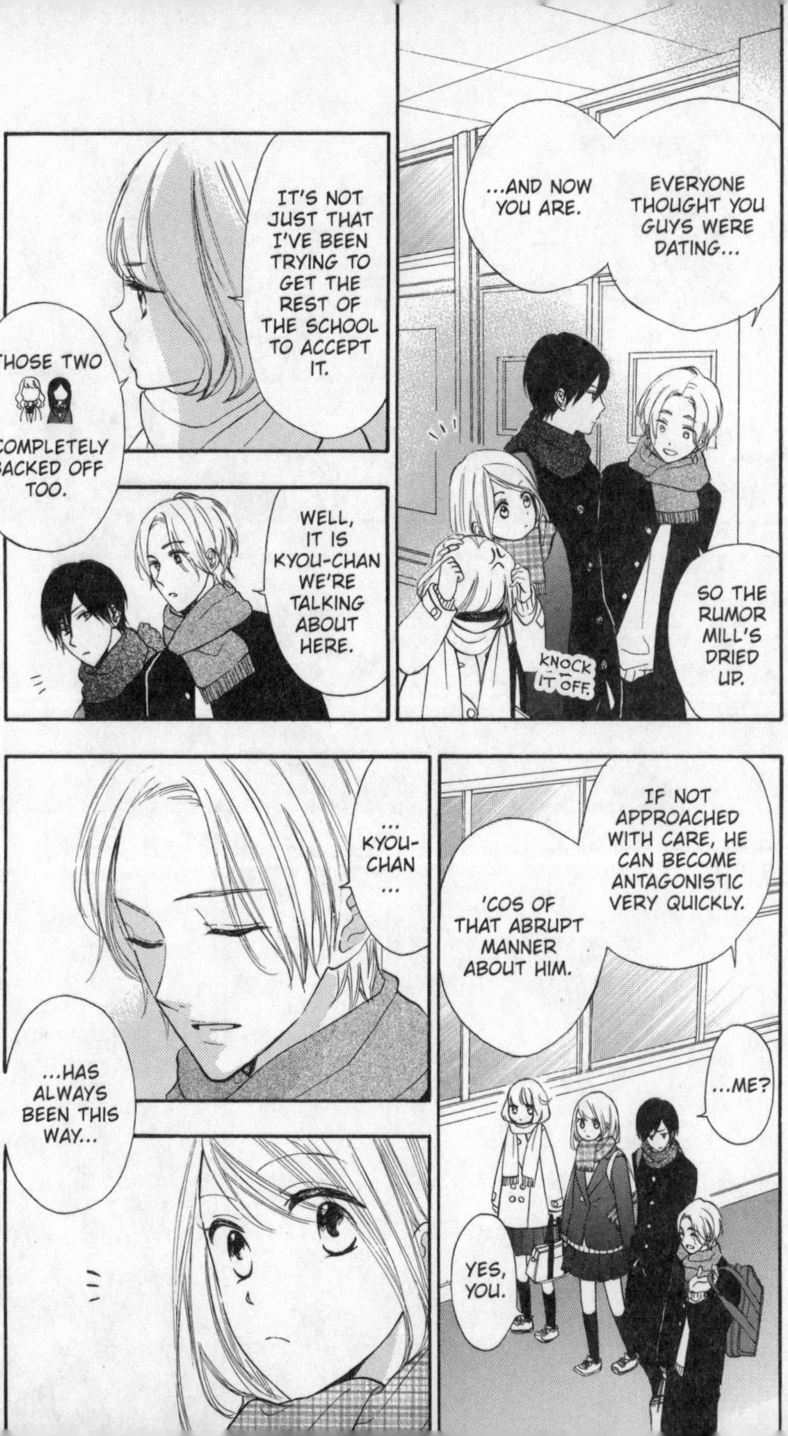
EVERYONE THOUGHT YOU GUYS WERE DATING...
...AND NOW YOU ARE.
SO THE RUMOR MILL'S DRIED UP.
KNOCK IT OFF.
IT'S NOT JUST THAT I'VE BEEN TRYING TO GET THE REST OF THE SCHOOL TO ACCEPT IT.
THOSE TWO COMPLETELY BACKED OFF TOO.
WELL, IT IS KYOU-CHAN WE'RE TALKING ABOUT HERE.
IF NOT APPROACHED WITH CARE, HE CAN BECOME ANTAGONISTIC VERY QUICKLY.
'COS OF THAT ABRUPT MANNER ABOUT HIM.
...ME?
YES, YOU.
...KYOU-CHAN...
...HAS ALWAYS BEEN THIS WAY...

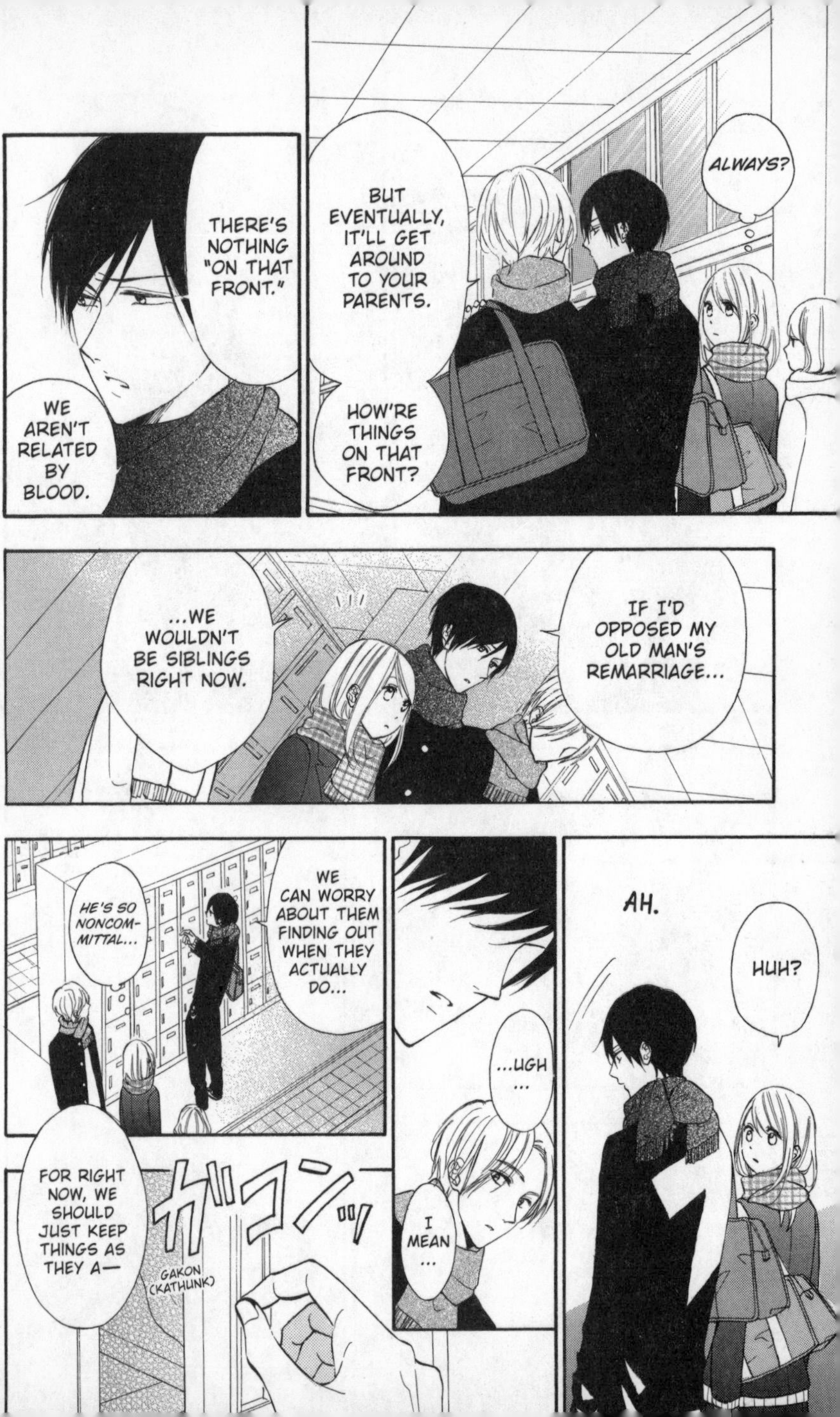
ALWAYS?
BUT EVENTUALLY, IT'LL GET AROUND TO YOUR PARENTS.
HOW'RE THINGS ON THAT FRONT?
THERE'S NOTHING "ON THAT FRONT."
WE AREN'T RELATED BY BLOOD.
IF I'D OPPOSED MY OLD MAN'S REMARRIAGE...
...WE WOULDN'T BE SIBLINGS RIGHT NOW.
AH.
HUH?
...UGH ...
I MEAN ...
WE CAN WORRY ABOUT THEM FINDING OUT WHEN THEY ACTUALLY DO...
HE'S SO NONCOMMITTAL...
FOR RIGHT NOW, WE SHOULD JUST KEEP THINGS AS THEY A—
GAKON (KATHUNK)

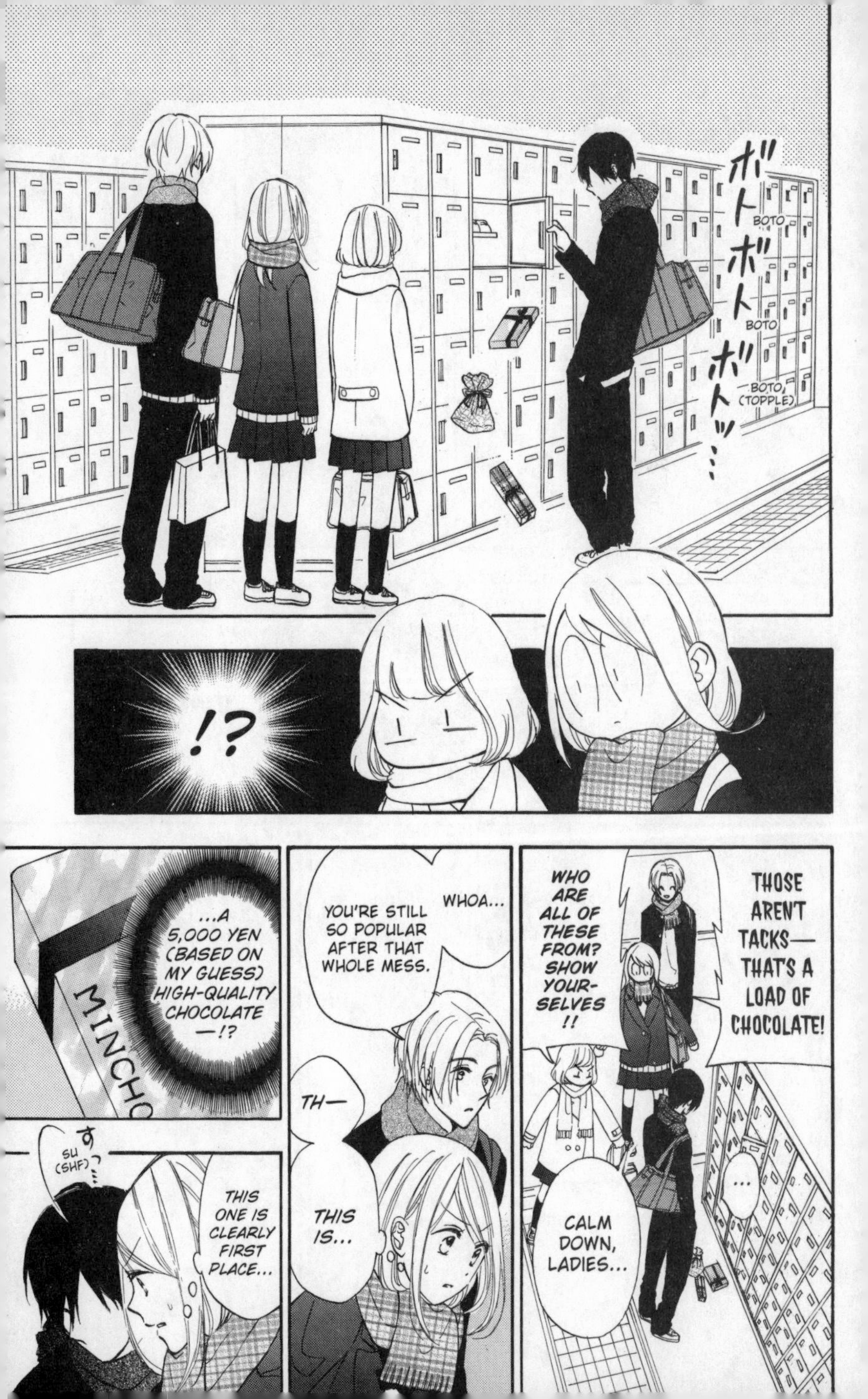
ボト
BOTO
ボト
BOTO
ボトッ…
BOTO (TOPPLE)
!?
THOSE AREN'T TACKS—THAT'S A LOAD OF CHOCOLATE!
WHO ARE ALL OF THESE FROM? SHOW YOURSELVES!!
CALM DOWN, LADIES...
...
WHOA...
YOU'RE STILL SO POPULAR AFTER THAT WHOLE MESS.
TH—
THIS IS...
...A 5,000 YEN (BASED ON MY GUESS) HIGH-QUALITY CHOCOLATE—!?
MINCHO
す
SU (SHF)
THIS ONE IS CLEARLY FIRST PLACE...

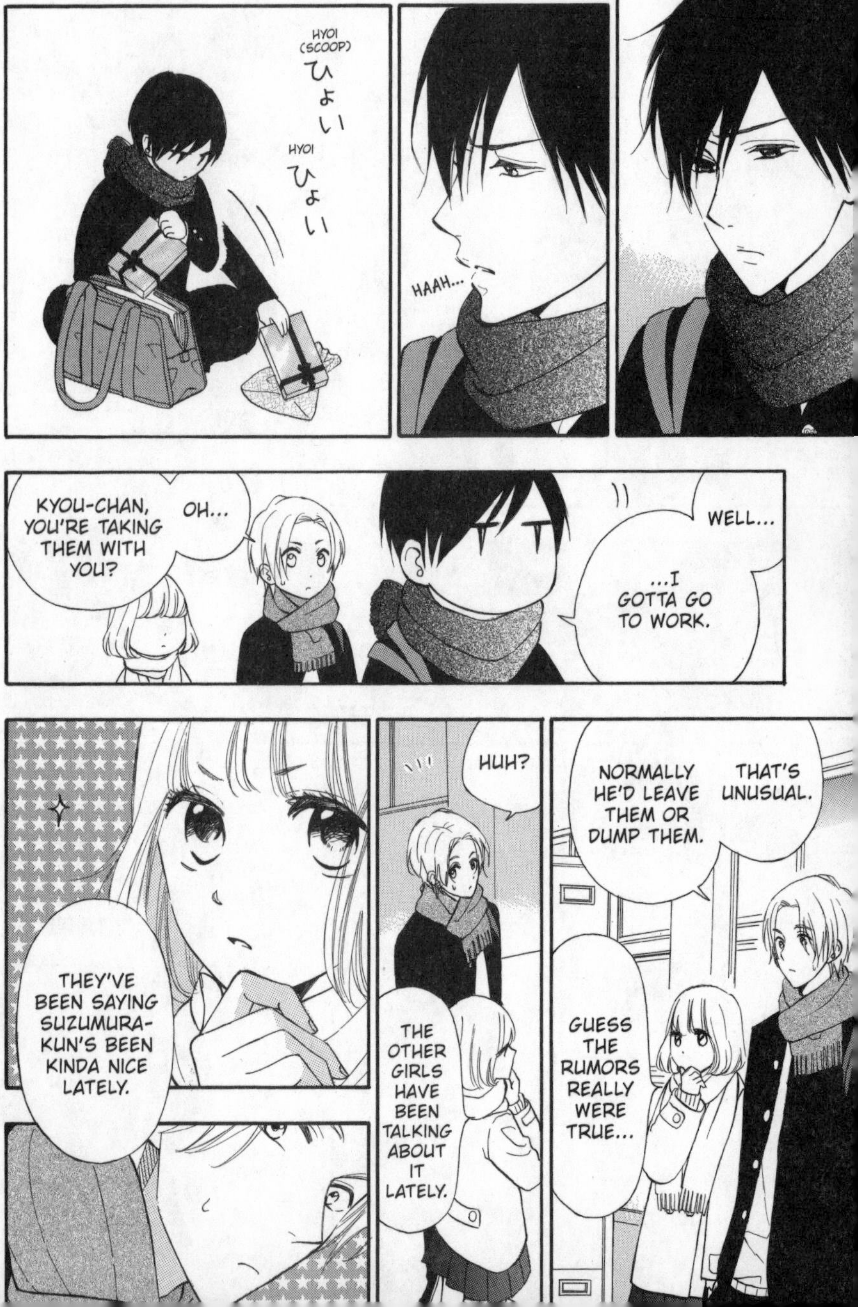
HAAH...
HYOI (SCOOP)
ひょい
HYOI
ひょい
WELL...
...I GOTTA GO TO WORK.
OH...
KYOU-CHAN, YOU'RE TAKING THEM WITH YOU?
THAT'S UNUSUAL.
NORMALLY HE'D LEAVE THEM OR DUMP THEM.
GUESS THE RUMORS REALLY WERE TRUE...
HUH?
THE OTHER GIRLS HAVE BEEN TALKING ABOUT IT LATELY.
THEY'VE BEEN SAYING SUZUMURA-KUN'S BEEN KINDA NICE LATELY.

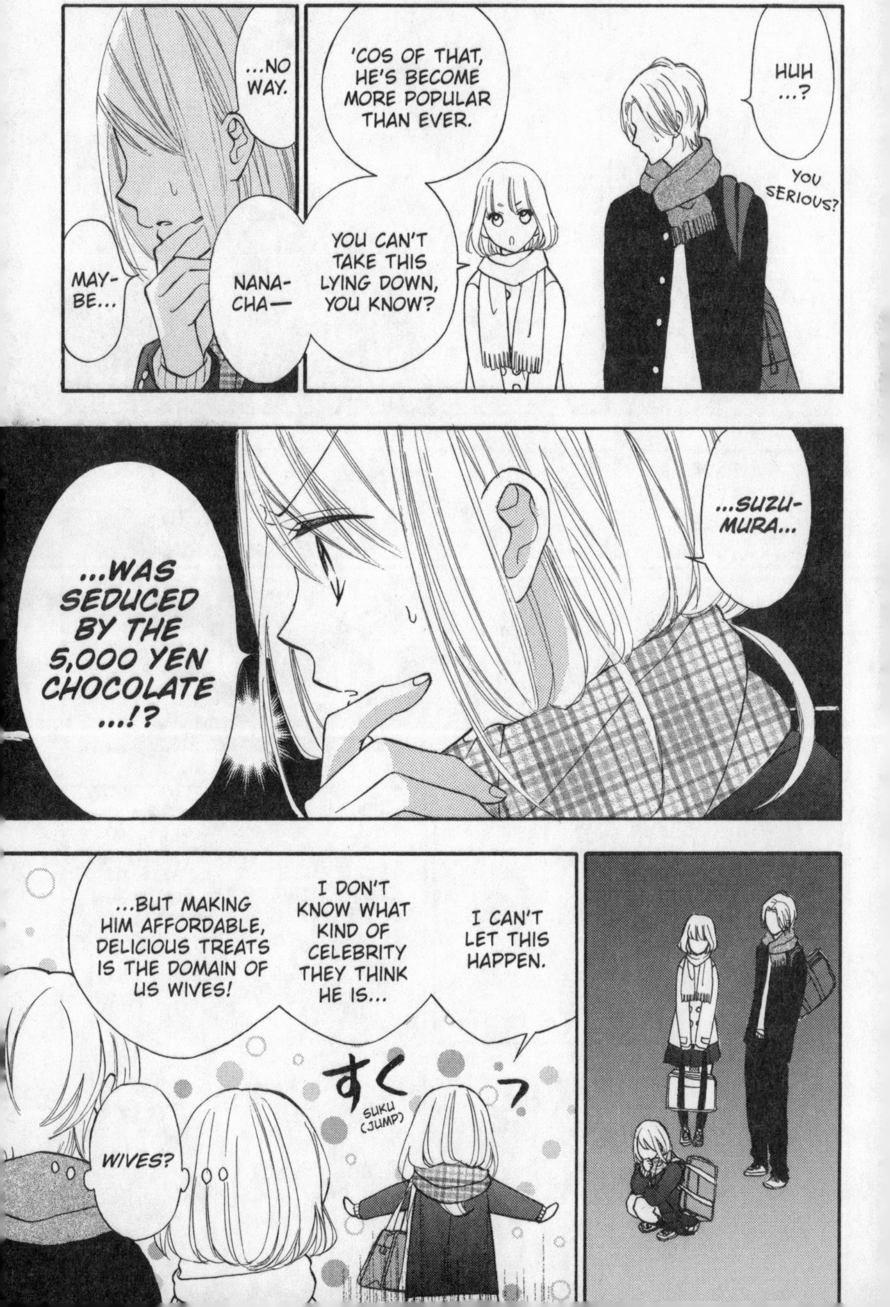
HUH ...?
YOU SERIOUS?
'COS OF THAT, HE'S BECOME MORE POPULAR THAN EVER.
YOU CAN'T TAKE THIS LYING DOWN, YOU KNOW?
NANA-CHA—
...NO WAY.
MAY-BE...
...SUZU-MURA...
...WAS SEDUCED BY THE 5,000 YEN CHOCOLATE ...!?
I CAN'T LET THIS HAPPEN.
I DON'T KNOW WHAT KIND OF CELEBRITY THEY THINK HE IS...
...BUT MAKING HIM AFFORDABLE, DELICIOUS TREATS IS THE DOMAIN OF US WIVES!
すく
SUKU (JUMP)
WIVES?

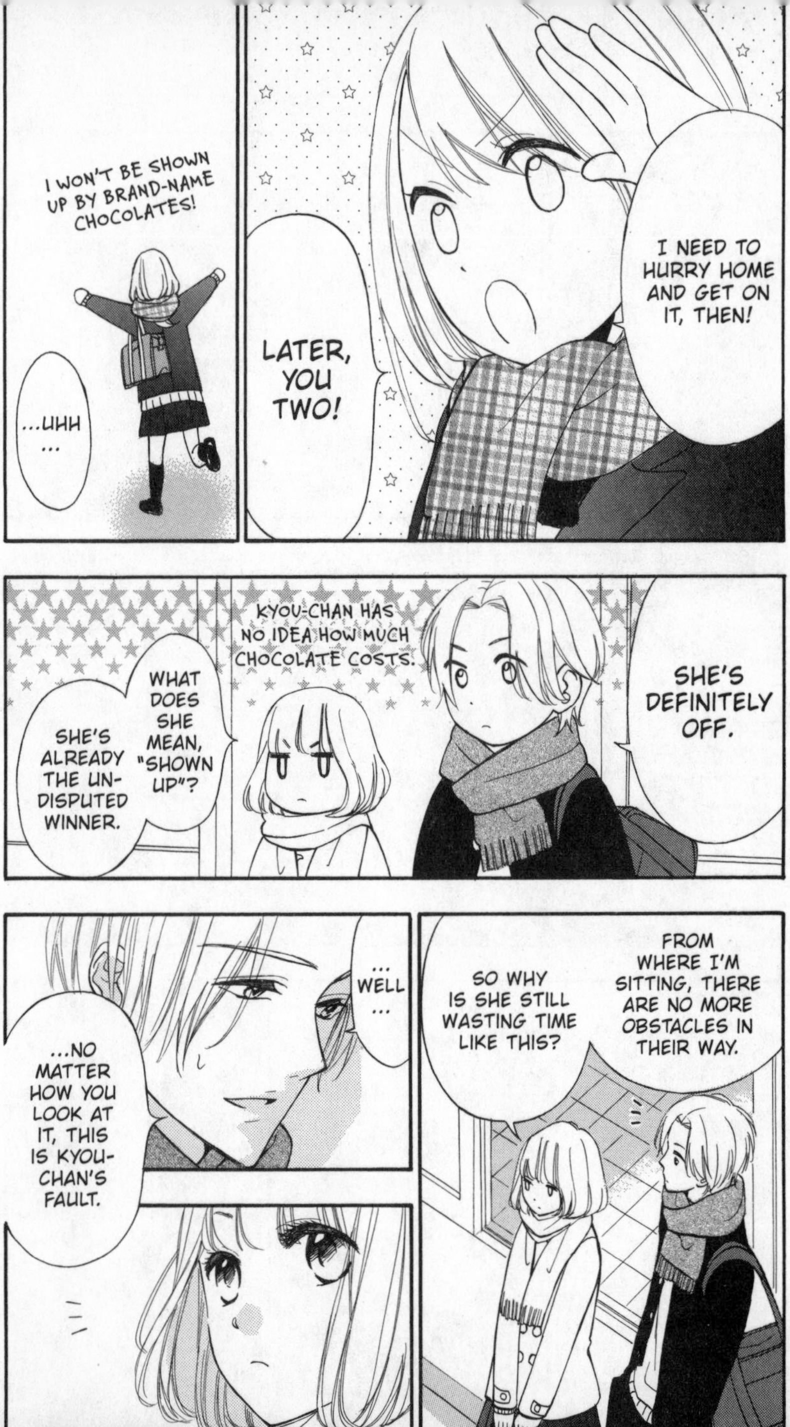
I NEED TO HURRY HOME AND GET ON IT, THEN!
LATER, YOU TWO!
I WON'T BE SHOWN UP BY BRAND-NAME CHOCOLATES!
...UHH ...
SHE'S DEFINITELY OFF.
KYOU-CHAN HAS NO IDEA HOW MUCH CHOCOLATE COSTS.
WHAT DOES SHE MEAN, "SHOWN UP"?
SHE'S ALREADY THE UN-DISPUTED WINNER.
FROM WHERE I'M SITTING, THERE ARE NO MORE OBSTACLES IN THEIR WAY.
SO WHY IS SHE STILL WASTING TIME LIKE THIS?
... WELL ...
...NO MATTER HOW YOU LOOK AT IT, THIS IS KYOU-CHAN'S FAULT.

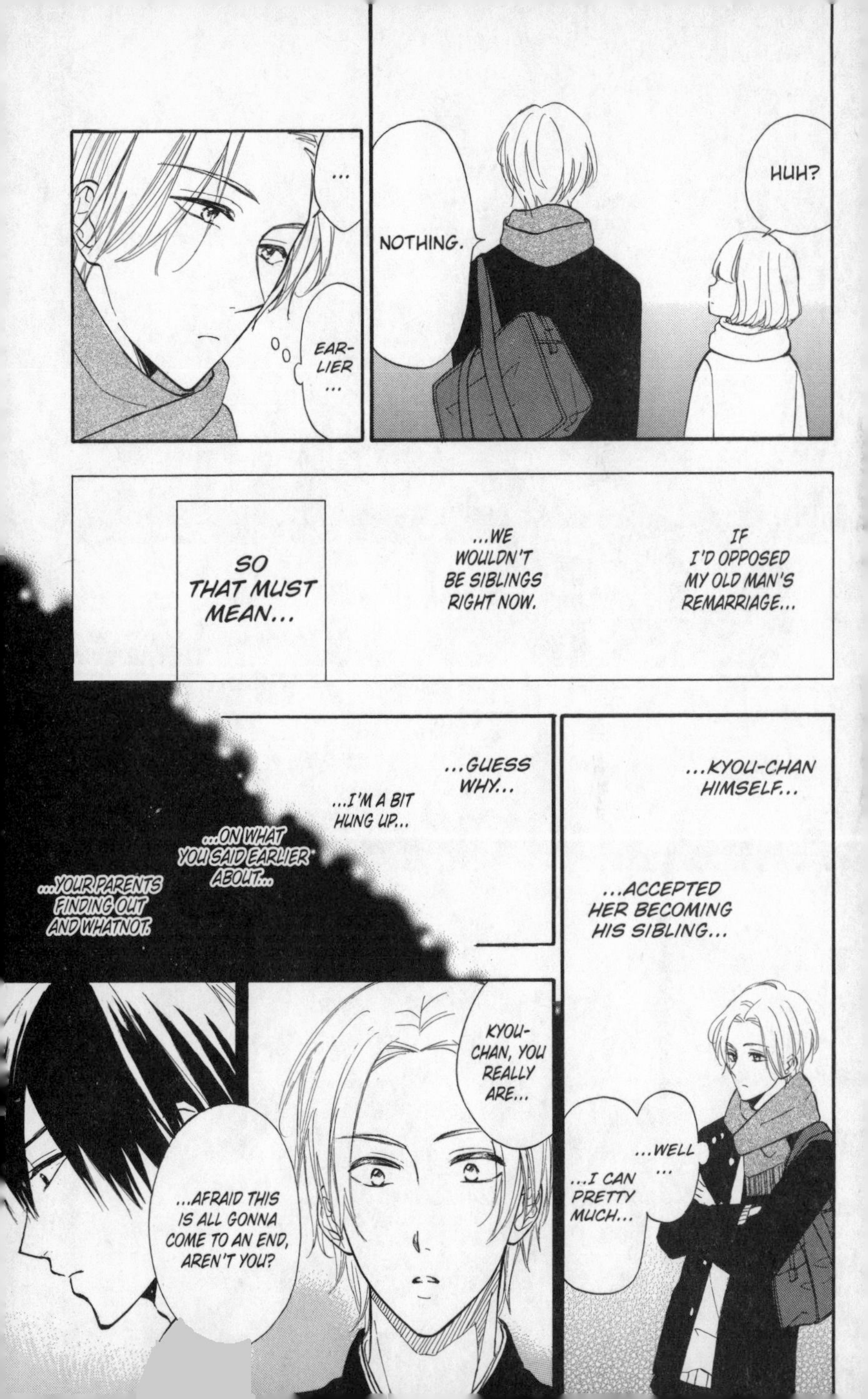
HUH?
NOTHING.
...
EARLIER...
IF I'D OPPOSED MY OLD MAN'S REMARRIAGE...
...WE WOULDN'T BE SIBLINGS RIGHT NOW.
SO THAT MUST MEAN...
...KYOU-CHAN HIMSELF...
...ACCEPTED HER BECOMING HIS SIBLING...
...WELL...
...I CAN PRETTY MUCH...
...GUESS WHY...
...I'M A BIT HUNG UP...
...ON WHAT YOU SAID EARLIER ABOUT...
...YOUR PARENTS FINDING OUT AND WHATNOT.
KYOU-CHAN, YOU REALLY ARE...
...AFRAID THIS IS ALL GONNA COME TO AN END, AREN'T YOU?

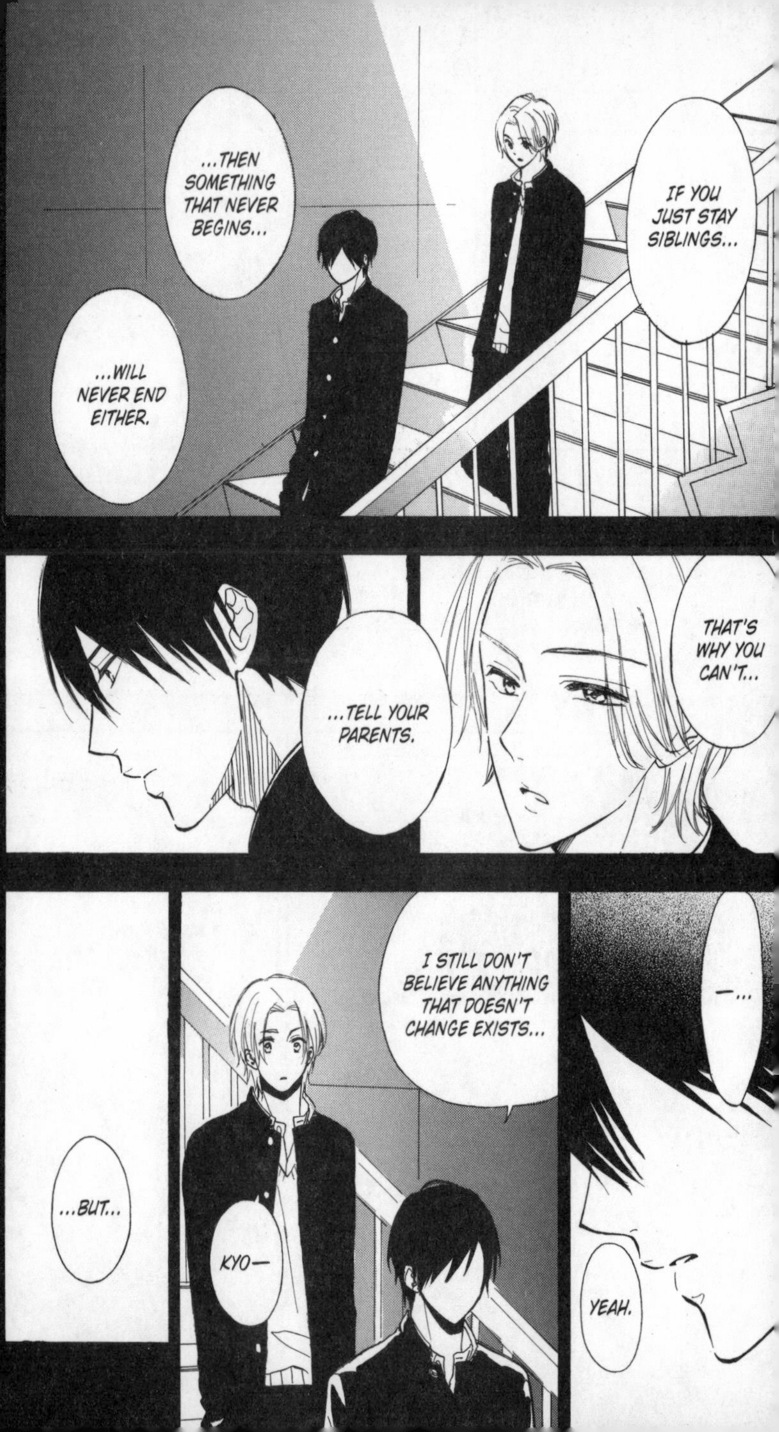
IF YOU JUST STAY SIBLINGS...
...THEN SOMETHING THAT NEVER BEGINS...
...WILL NEVER END EITHER.
THAT'S WHY YOU CAN'T...
...TELL YOUR PARENTS.
—...
YEAH.
I STILL DON'T BELIEVE ANYTHING THAT DOESN'T CHANGE EXISTS...
KYO—
...BUT...

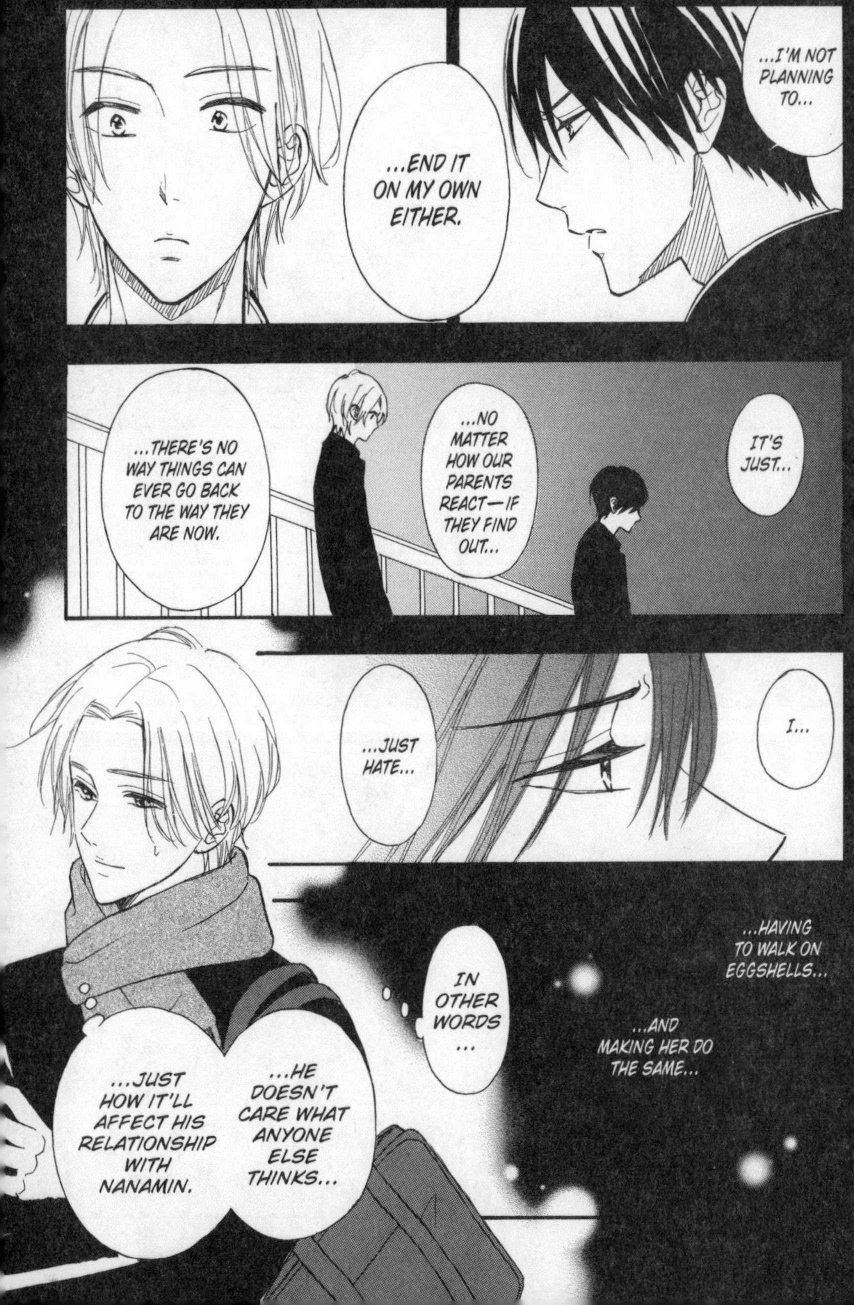
...I'M NOT PLANNING TO...
...END IT ON MY OWN EITHER.
IT'S JUST...
...NO MATTER HOW OUR PARENTS REACT—IF THEY FIND OUT...
...THERE'S NO WAY THINGS CAN EVER GO BACK TO THE WAY THEY ARE NOW.
I...
...JUST HATE...
...HAVING TO WALK ON EGGSHELLS...
...AND MAKING HER DO THE SAME...
IN OTHER WORDS...
...HE DOESN'T CARE WHAT ANYONE ELSE THINKS...
...JUST HOW IT'LL AFFECT HIS RELATIONSHIP WITH NANAMIN.

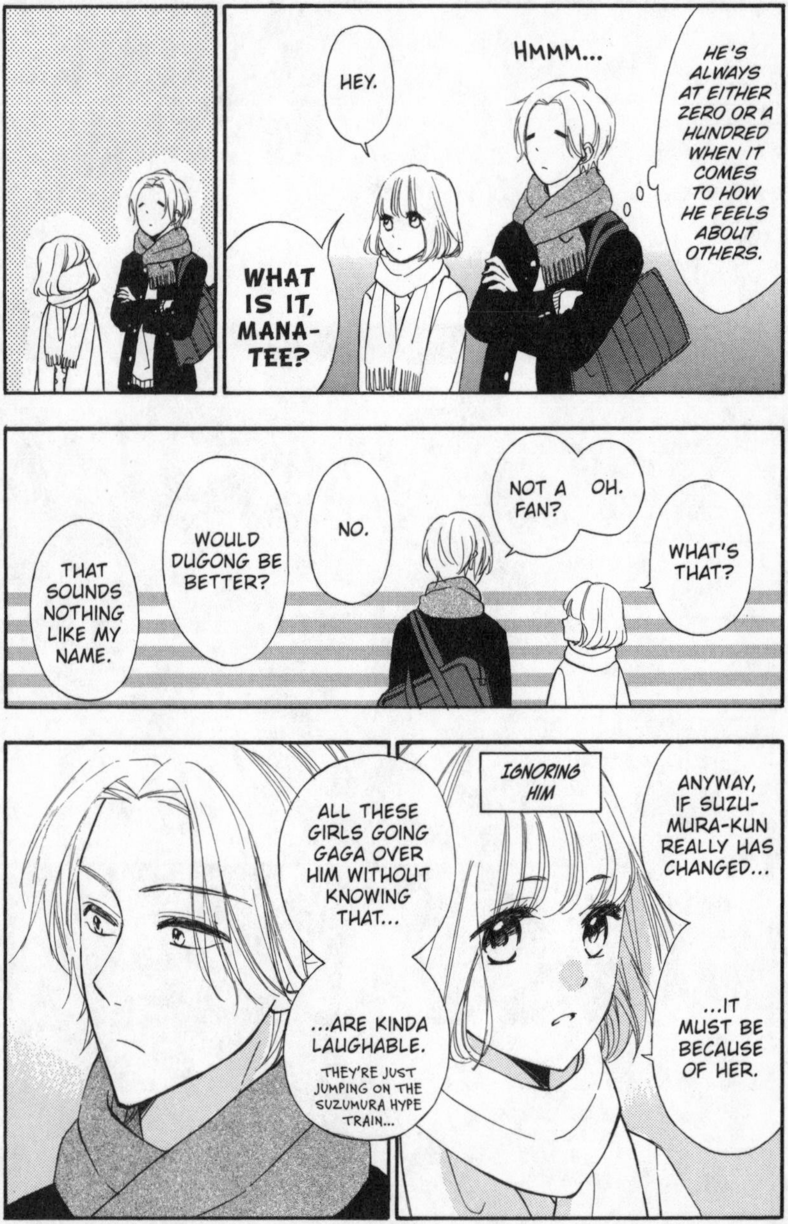
HE'S ALWAYS AT EITHER ZERO OR A HUNDRED WHEN IT COMES TO HOW HE FEELS ABOUT OTHERS.
HMMM...
HEY.
WHAT IS IT, MANA-TEE?
WHAT'S THAT?
OH.
NOT A FAN?
NO.
WOULD DUGONG BE BETTER?
THAT SOUNDS NOTHING LIKE MY NAME.
ANYWAY, IF SUZU-MURA-KUN REALLY HAS CHANGED...
IGNORING HIM
...IT MUST BE BECAUSE OF HER.
ALL THESE GIRLS GOING GAGA OVER HIM WITHOUT KNOWING THAT...
...ARE KINDA LAUGHABLE.
THEY'RE JUST JUMPING ON THE SUZUMURA HYPE TRAIN...

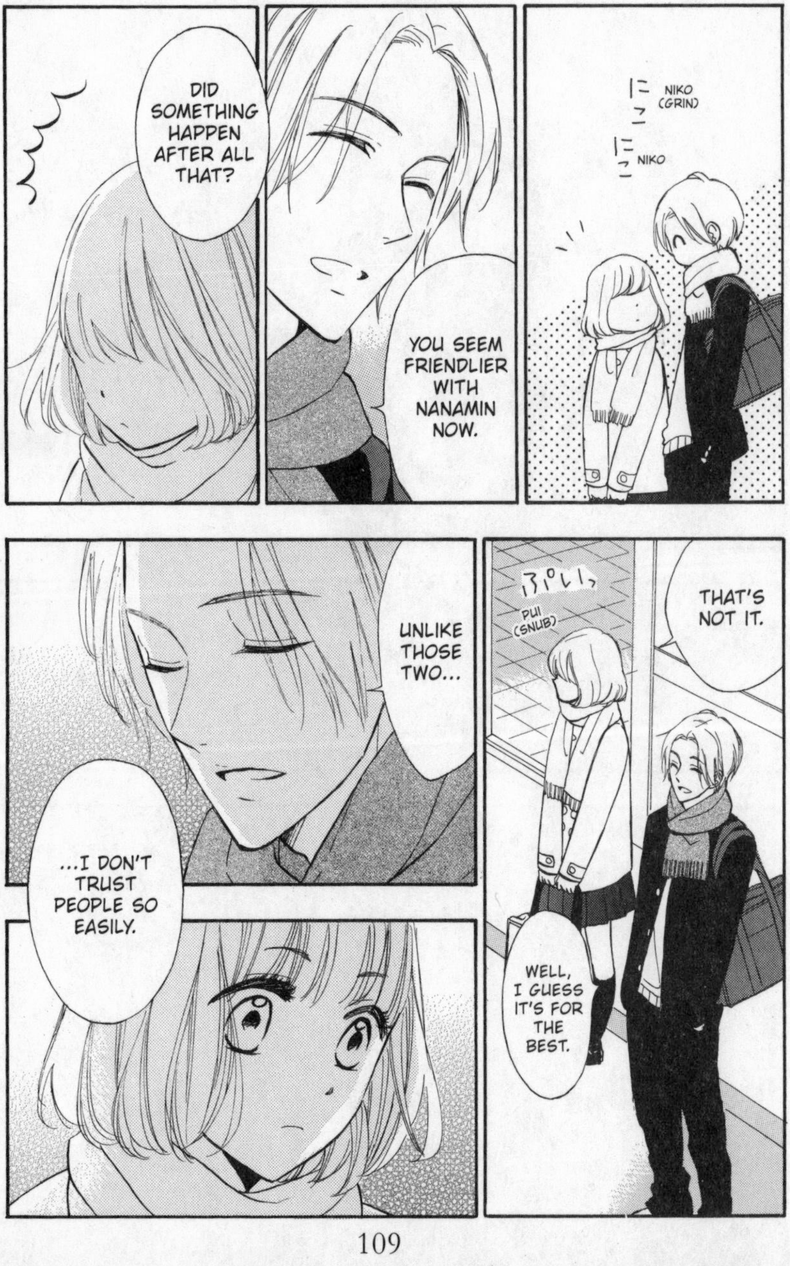
にこ
NIKO (GRIN)
にこ
NIKO
YOU SEEM FRIENDLIER WITH NANAMIN NOW.
DID SOMETHING HAPPEN AFTER ALL THAT?
THAT'S NOT IT.
ぷいっ
PUI (SNUB)
WELL, I GUESS IT'S FOR THE BEST.
UNLIKE THOSE TWO...
...I DON'T TRUST PEOPLE SO EASILY.

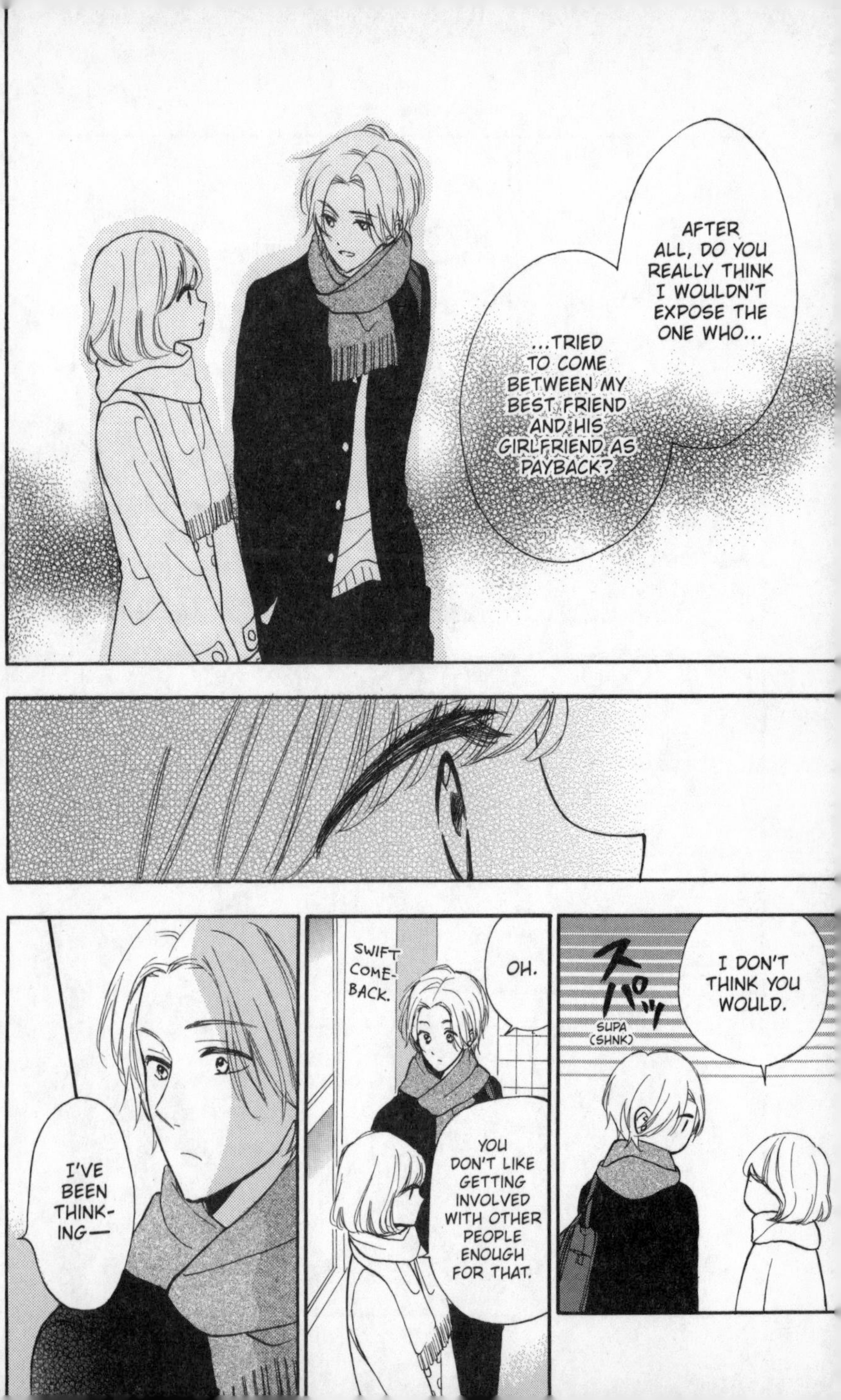
AFTER ALL, DO YOU REALLY THINK I WOULDN'T EXPOSE THE ONE WHO...
...TRIED TO COME BETWEEN MY BEST FRIEND AND HIS GIRLFRIEND AS PAYBACK?
I DON'T THINK YOU WOULD.
スパッ
SUPA (SHNK)
OH.
YOU DON'T LIKE GETTING INVOLVED WITH OTHER PEOPLE ENOUGH FOR THAT.
SWIFT COME-BACK.
I'VE BEEN THINK-ING—

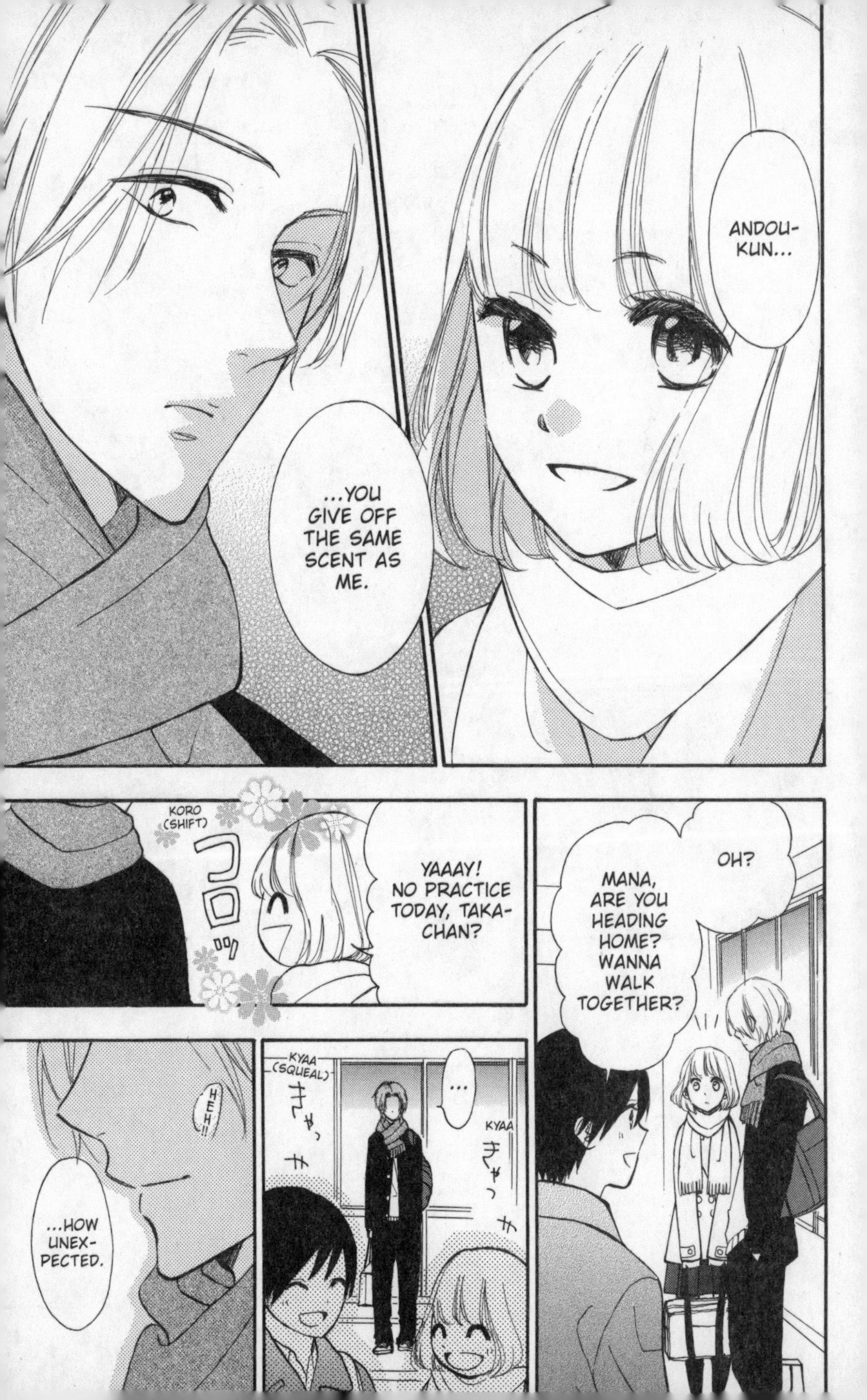
ANDOU-KUN...
...YOU GIVE OFF THE SAME SCENT AS ME.
OH?
MANA, ARE YOU HEADING HOME? WANNA WALK TOGETHER?
YAAAY! NO PRACTICE TODAY, TAKA-CHAN?
KORO (SHIFT)
KYAA
...
KYAA (SQUEAL)
HEH!!
...HOW UNEXPECTED.

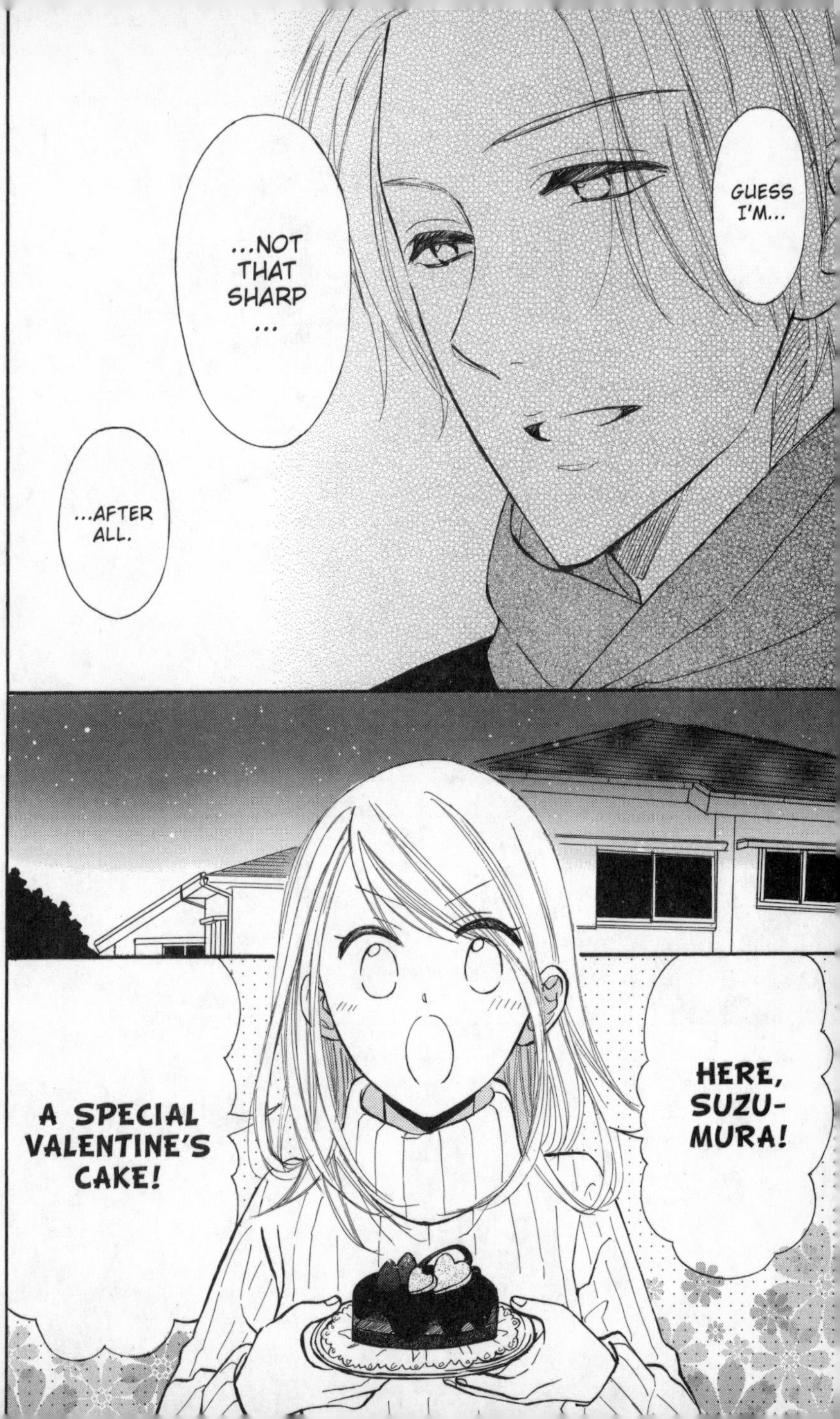
GUESS I'M...
...NOT THAT SHARP...
...AFTER ALL.
HERE, SUZU-MURA!
A SPECIAL VALENTINE'S CAKE!

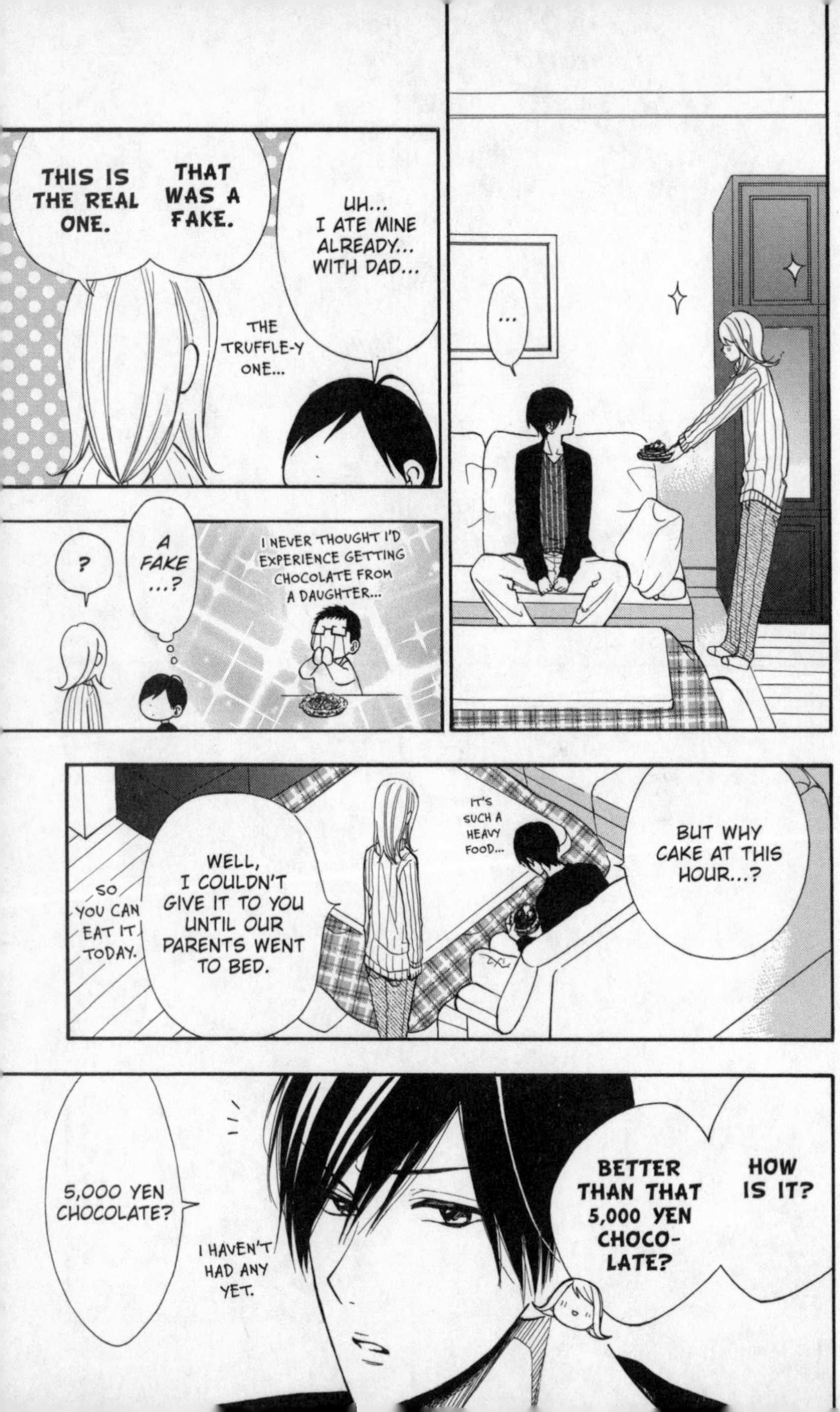
...
UH... I ATE MINE ALREADY... WITH DAD...
THAT WAS A FAKE.
THIS IS THE REAL ONE.
THE TRUFFLE-Y ONE...
I NEVER THOUGHT I'D EXPERIENCE GETTING CHOCOLATE FROM A DAUGHTER...
A FAKE ...?
?
BUT WHY CAKE AT THIS HOUR...?
IT'S SUCH A HEAVY FOOD...
WELL, I COULDN'T GIVE IT TO YOU UNTIL OUR PARENTS WENT TO BED.
SO YOU CAN EAT IT TODAY.
HOW IS IT?
BETTER THAN THAT 5,000 YEN CHOCO-LATE?
5,000 YEN CHOCOLATE?
I HAVEN'T HAD ANY YET.

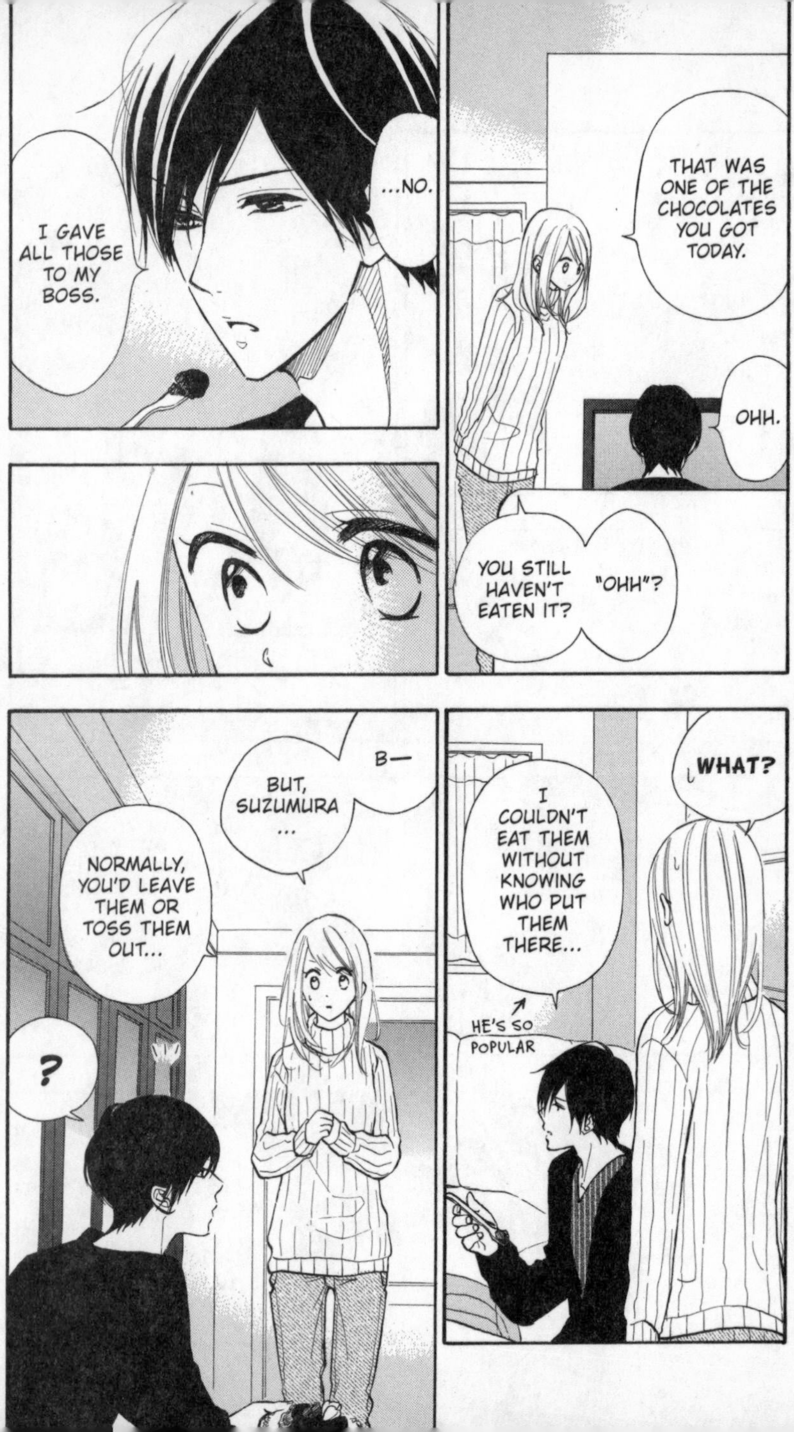
THAT WAS ONE OF THE CHOCOLATES YOU GOT TODAY.
OHH.
"OHH"?
YOU STILL HAVEN'T EATEN IT?
...NO.
I GAVE ALL THOSE TO MY BOSS.
WHAT?
I COULDN'T EAT THEM WITHOUT KNOWING WHO PUT THEM THERE...
HE'S SO POPULAR
B—
BUT, SUZUMURA ...
NORMALLY, YOU'D LEAVE THEM OR TOSS THEM OUT...
?

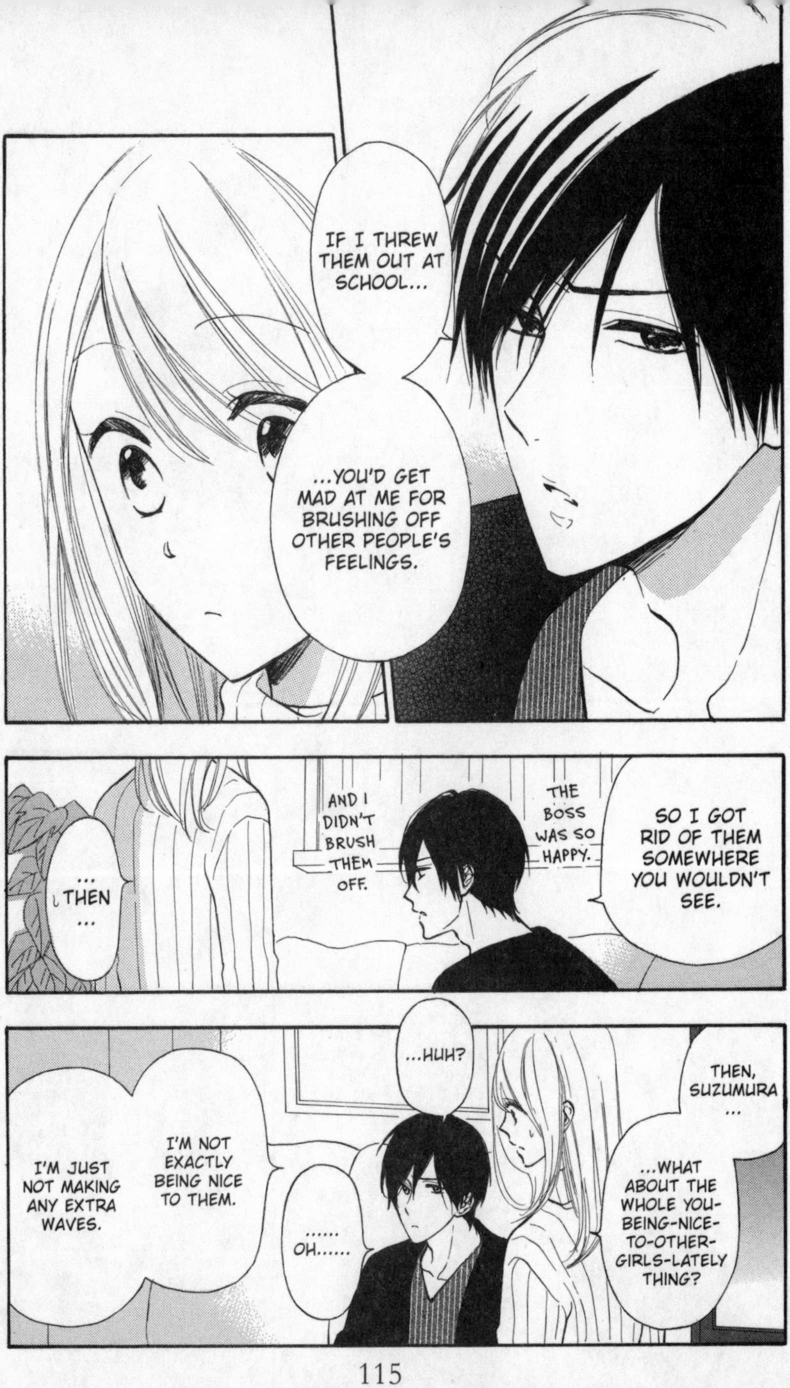
IF I THREW THEM OUT AT SCHOOL...
...YOU'D GET MAD AT ME FOR BRUSHING OFF OTHER PEOPLE'S FEELINGS.
SO I GOT RID OF THEM SOMEWHERE YOU WOULDN'T SEE.
THE BOSS WAS SO HAPPY.
AND I DIDN'T BRUSH THEM OFF.
...THEN...
THEN, SUZUMURA...
...WHAT ABOUT THE WHOLE YOU-BEING-NICE-TO-OTHER-GIRLS-LATELY THING?
...HUH?
......OH......
I'M NOT EXACTLY BEING NICE TO THEM.
I'M JUST NOT MAKING ANY EXTRA WAVES.

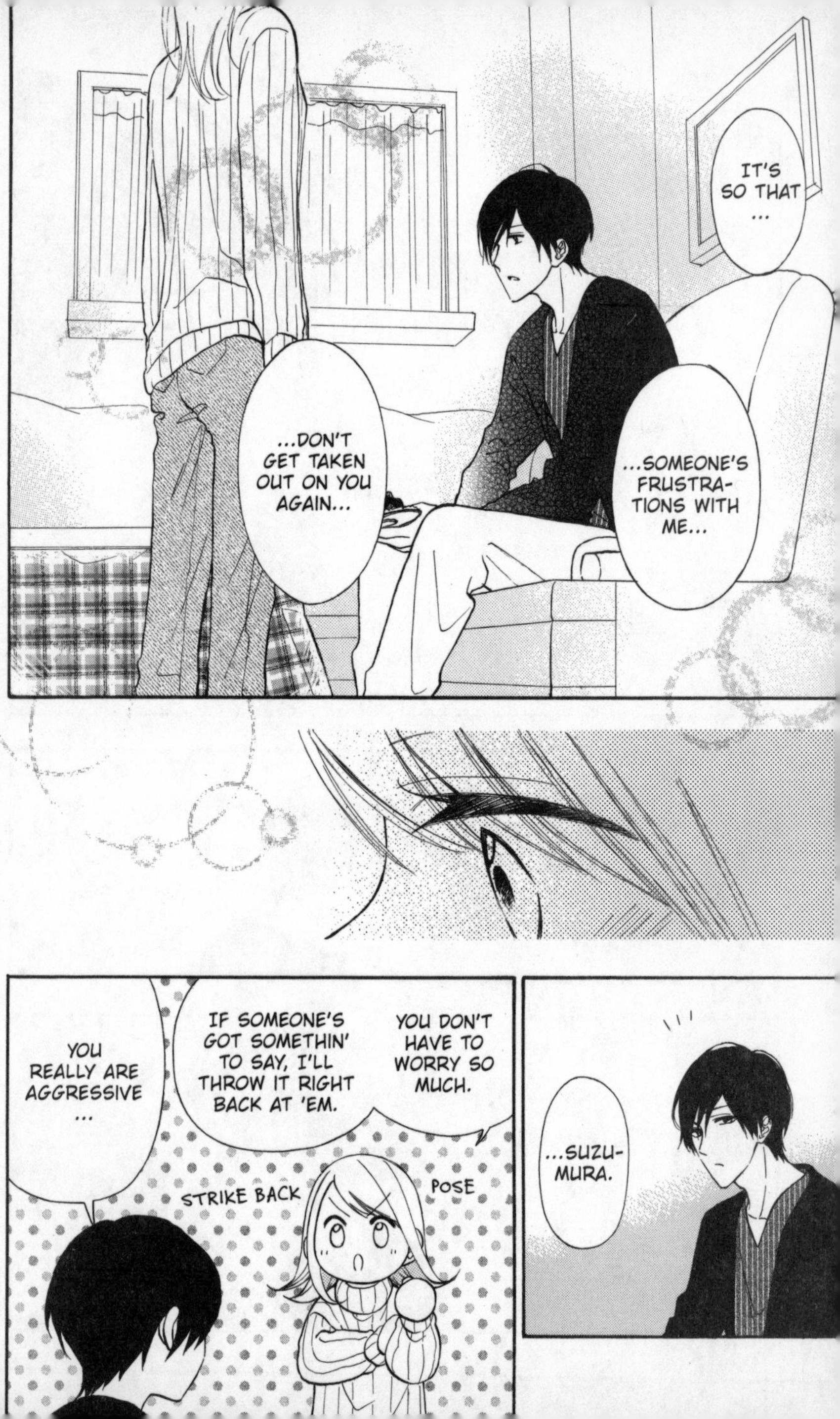
IT'S SO THAT ...
...SOMEONE'S FRUSTRA-TIONS WITH ME...
...DON'T GET TAKEN OUT ON YOU AGAIN...
...SUZU-MURA.
YOU DON'T HAVE TO WORRY SO MUCH.
IF SOMEONE'S GOT SOMETHIN' TO SAY, I'LL THROW IT RIGHT BACK AT 'EM.
POSE
STRIKE BACK
YOU REALLY ARE AGGRESSIVE ...

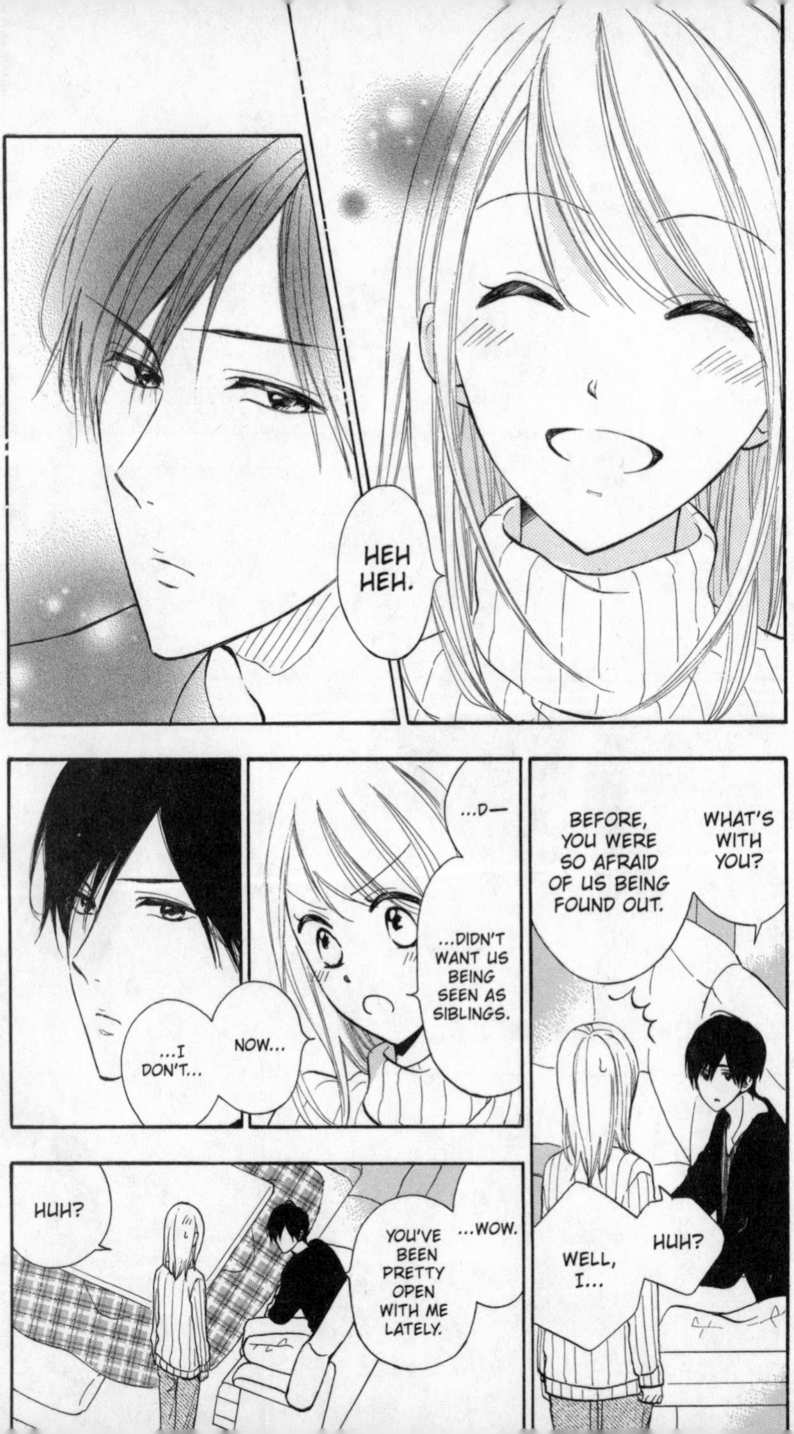
HEH HEH.
WHAT'S WITH YOU?
BEFORE, YOU WERE SO AFRAID OF US BEING FOUND OUT.
HUH?
WELL, I...
...D—
...DIDN'T WANT US BEING SEEN AS SIBLINGS.
NOW...
...I DON'T...
...WOW.
YOU'VE BEEN PRETTY OPEN WITH ME LATELY.
HUH?

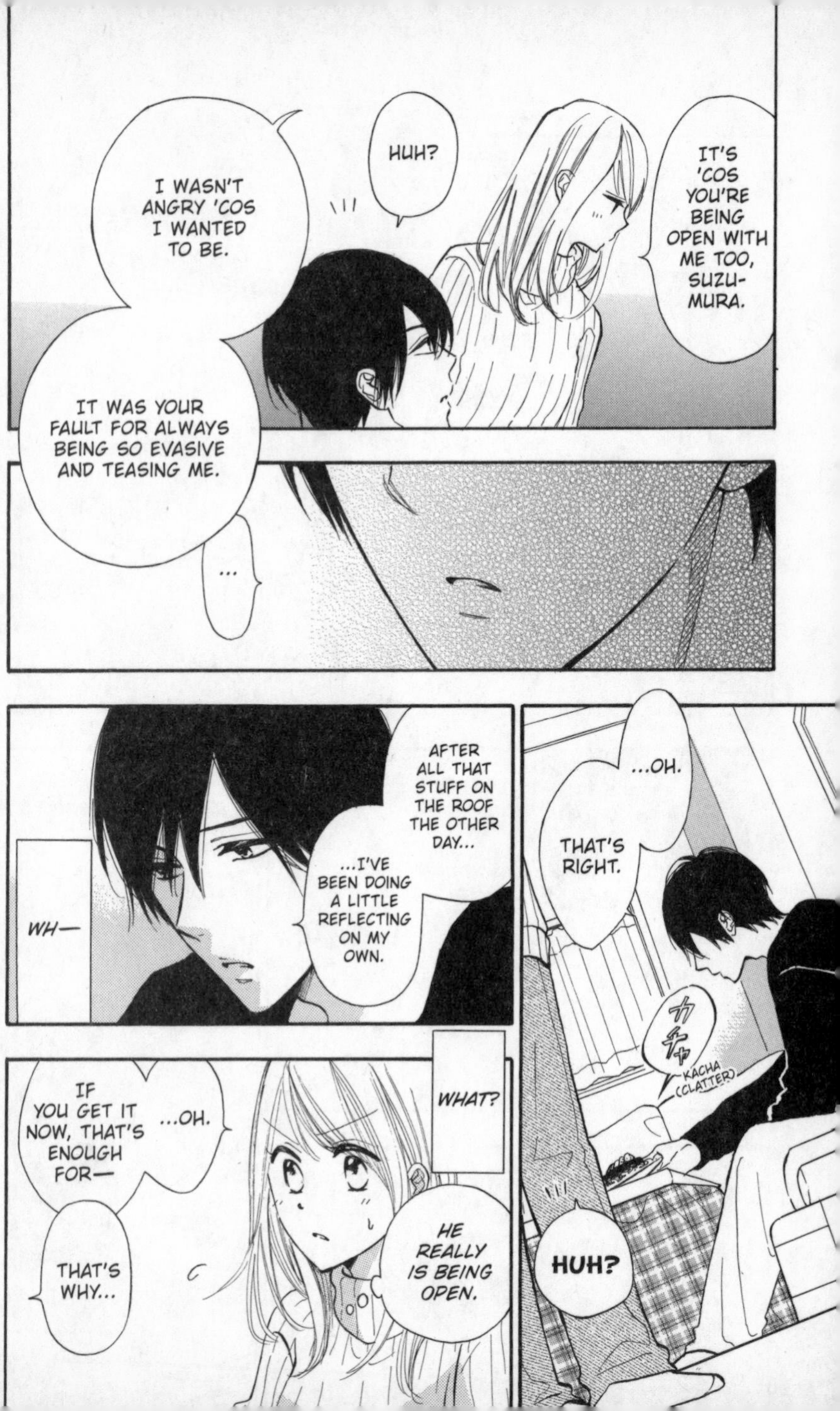
IT'S 'COS YOU'RE BEING OPEN WITH ME TOO, SUZUMURA.
HUH?
I WASN'T ANGRY 'COS I WANTED TO BE.
IT WAS YOUR FAULT FOR ALWAYS BEING SO EVASIVE AND TEASING ME.
...
...OH.
THAT'S RIGHT.
カチャ
KACHA (CLATTER)
HUH?
AFTER ALL THAT STUFF ON THE ROOF THE OTHER DAY...
...I'VE BEEN DOING A LITTLE REFLECTING ON MY OWN.
WH—
WHAT?
HE REALLY IS BEING OPEN.
...OH.
IF YOU GET IT NOW, THAT'S ENOUGH FOR—
THAT'S WHY...

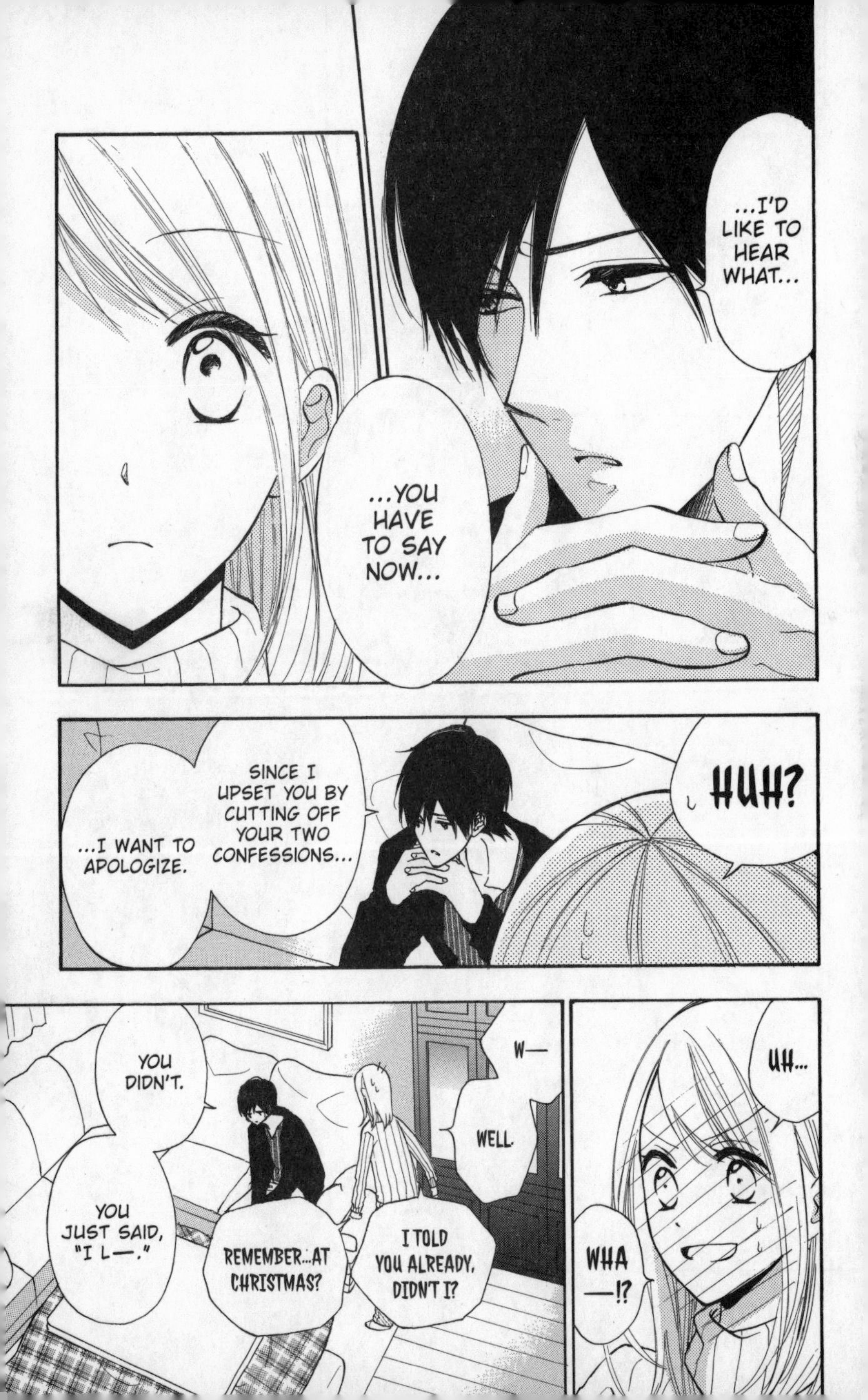
...I'D LIKE TO HEAR WHAT...
...YOU HAVE TO SAY NOW...
HUH?
SINCE I UPSET YOU BY CUTTING OFF YOUR TWO CONFESSIONS...
...I WANT TO APOLOGIZE.
UH...
WHA—!?
W—
WELL.
I TOLD YOU ALREADY, DIDN'T I?
REMEMBER...AT CHRISTMAS?
YOU DIDN'T.
YOU JUST SAID, "I L—."

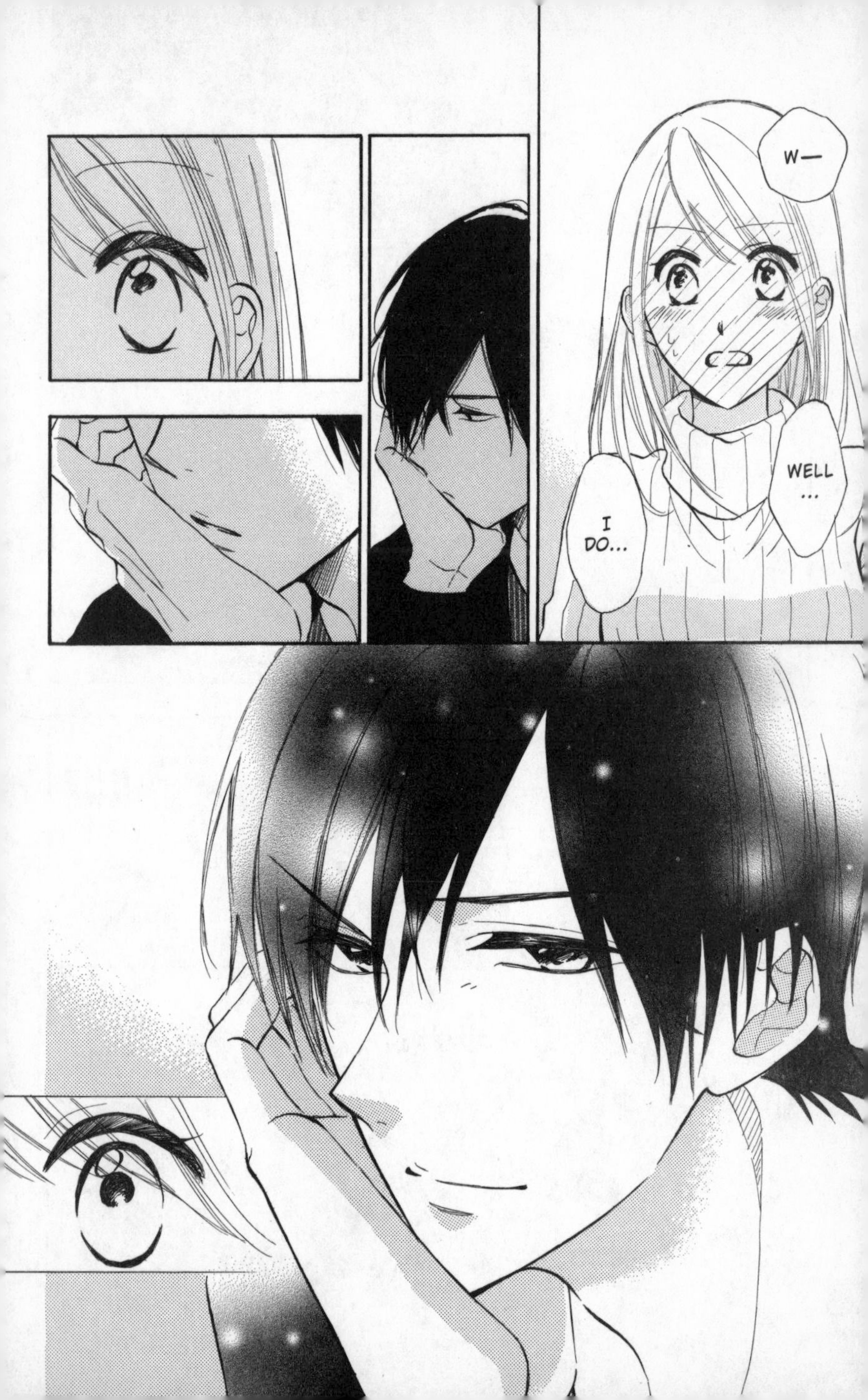
W—
WELL ...
I DO...

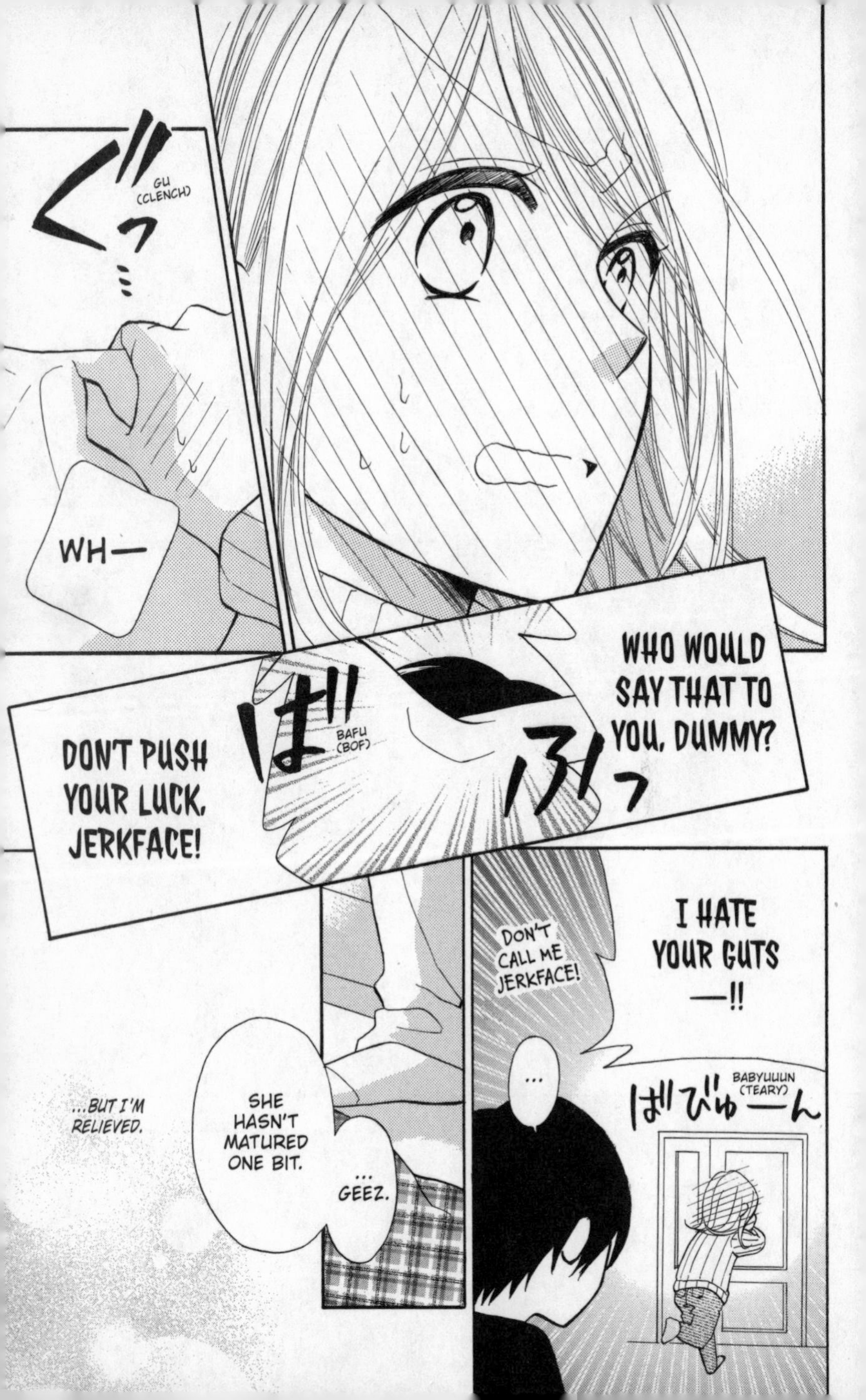
ぐっ
GU (CLENCH)
WH—
WHO WOULD SAY THAT TO YOU, DUMMY?
ばふっ
BAFU (BOF)
DON'T PUSH YOUR LUCK, JERKFACE!
I HATE YOUR GUTS —!!
DON'T CALL ME JERKFACE!
ばびゅーん
BABYUUUN (TEARY)
...
SHE HASN'T MATURED ONE BIT.
...GEEZ.
...BUT I'M RELIEVED.

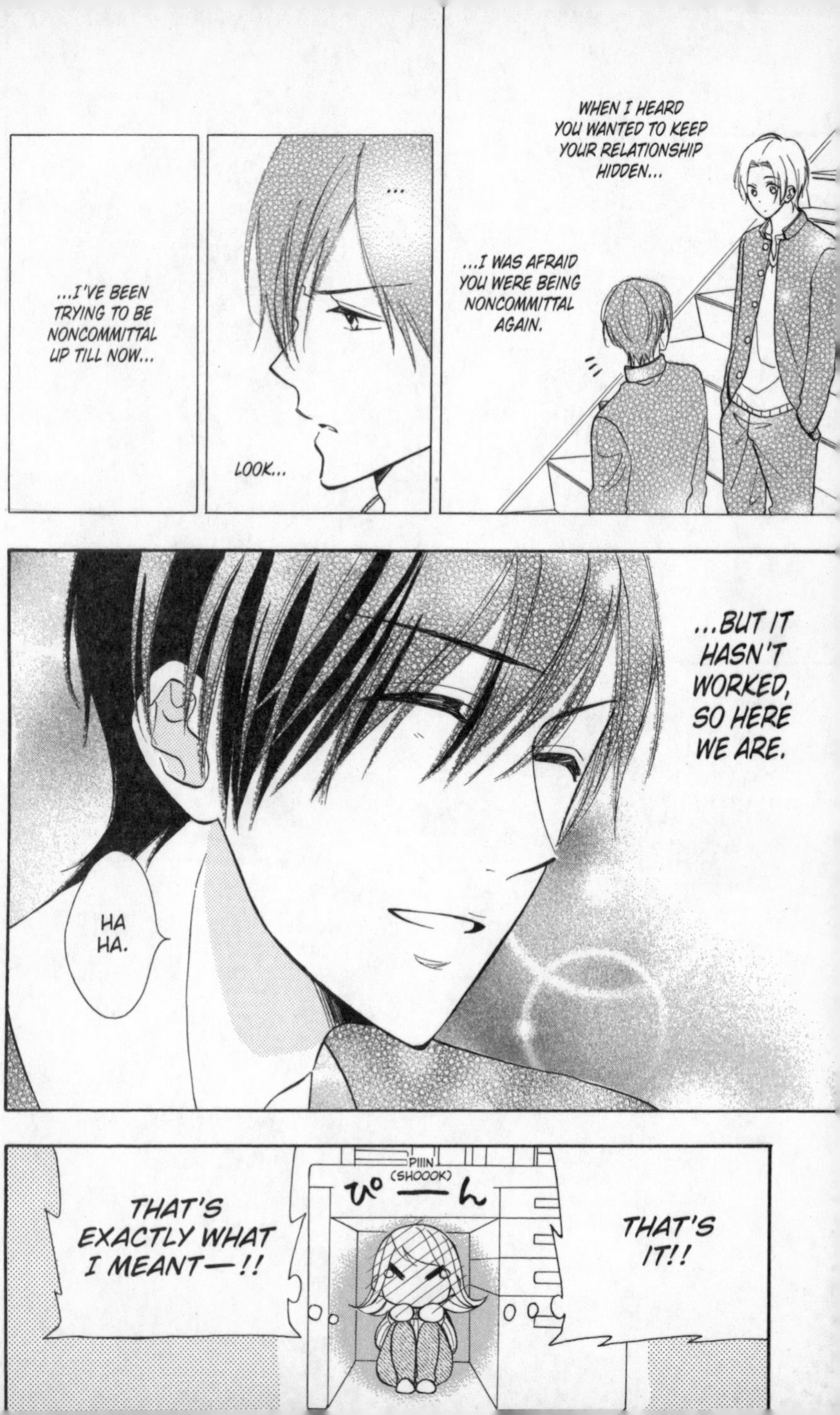
WHEN I HEARD YOU WANTED TO KEEP YOUR RELATIONSHIP HIDDEN...
...I WAS AFRAID YOU WERE BEING NONCOMMITTAL AGAIN.
...
LOOK...
...I'VE BEEN TRYING TO BE NONCOMMITTAL UP TILL NOW...
...BUT IT HASN'T WORKED, SO HERE WE ARE.
HA HA.
THAT'S IT!!
ぴーん
PIIIN (SHOOOK)
THAT'S EXACTLY WHAT I MEANT—!!

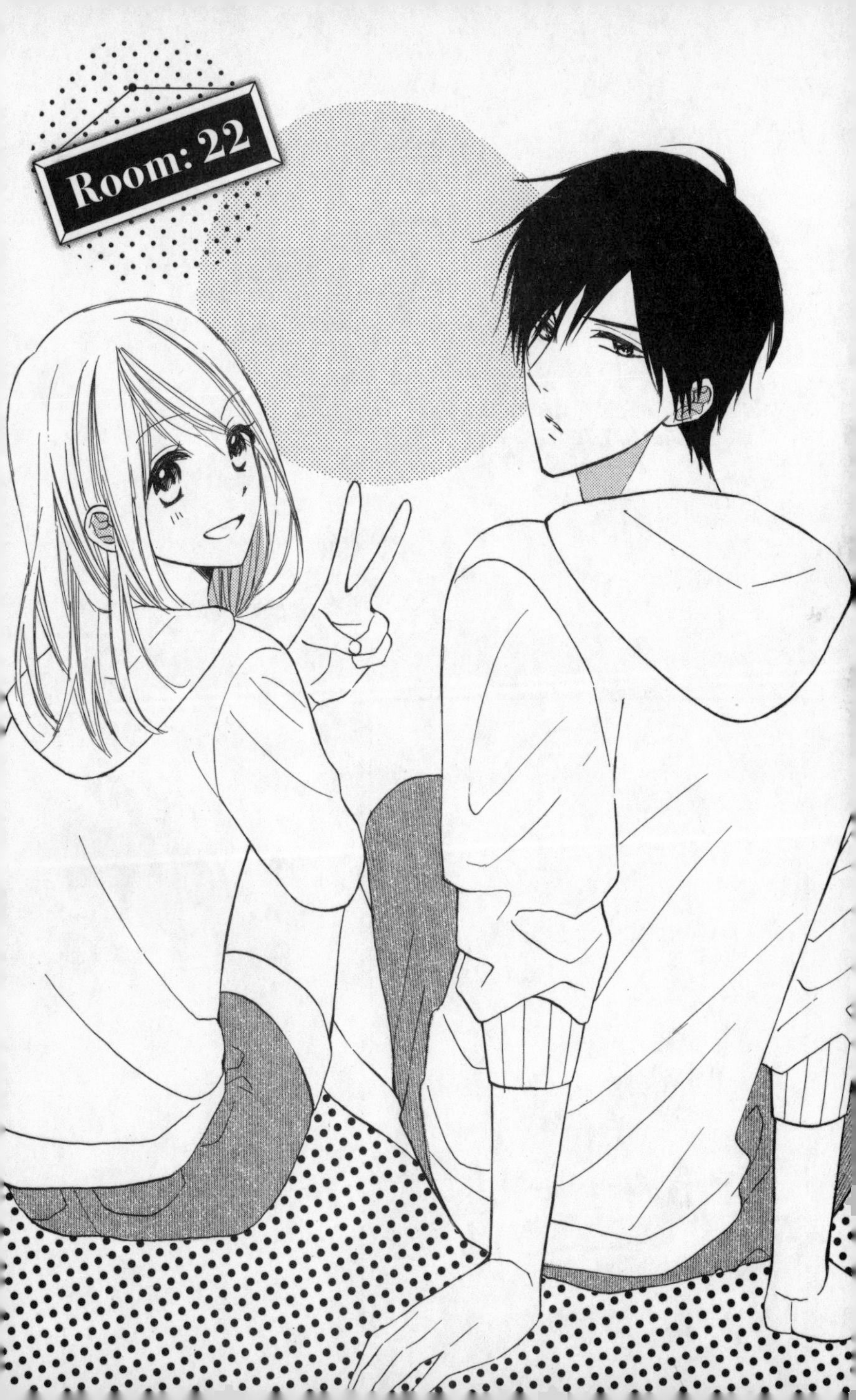
Room: 22

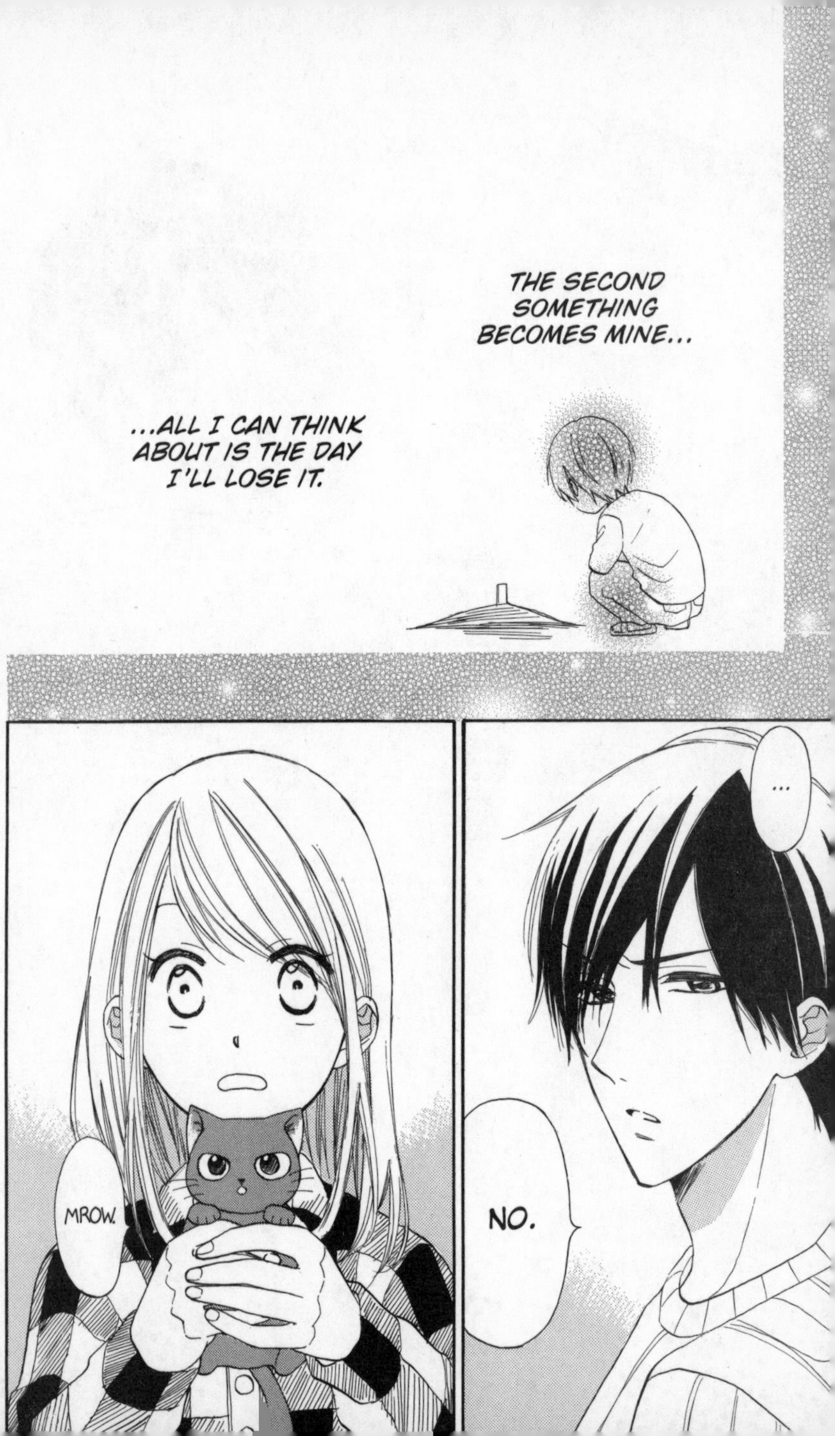
THE SECOND SOMETHING BECOMES MINE...
...ALL I CAN THINK ABOUT IS THE DAY I'LL LOSE IT.
...
NO.
MROW.

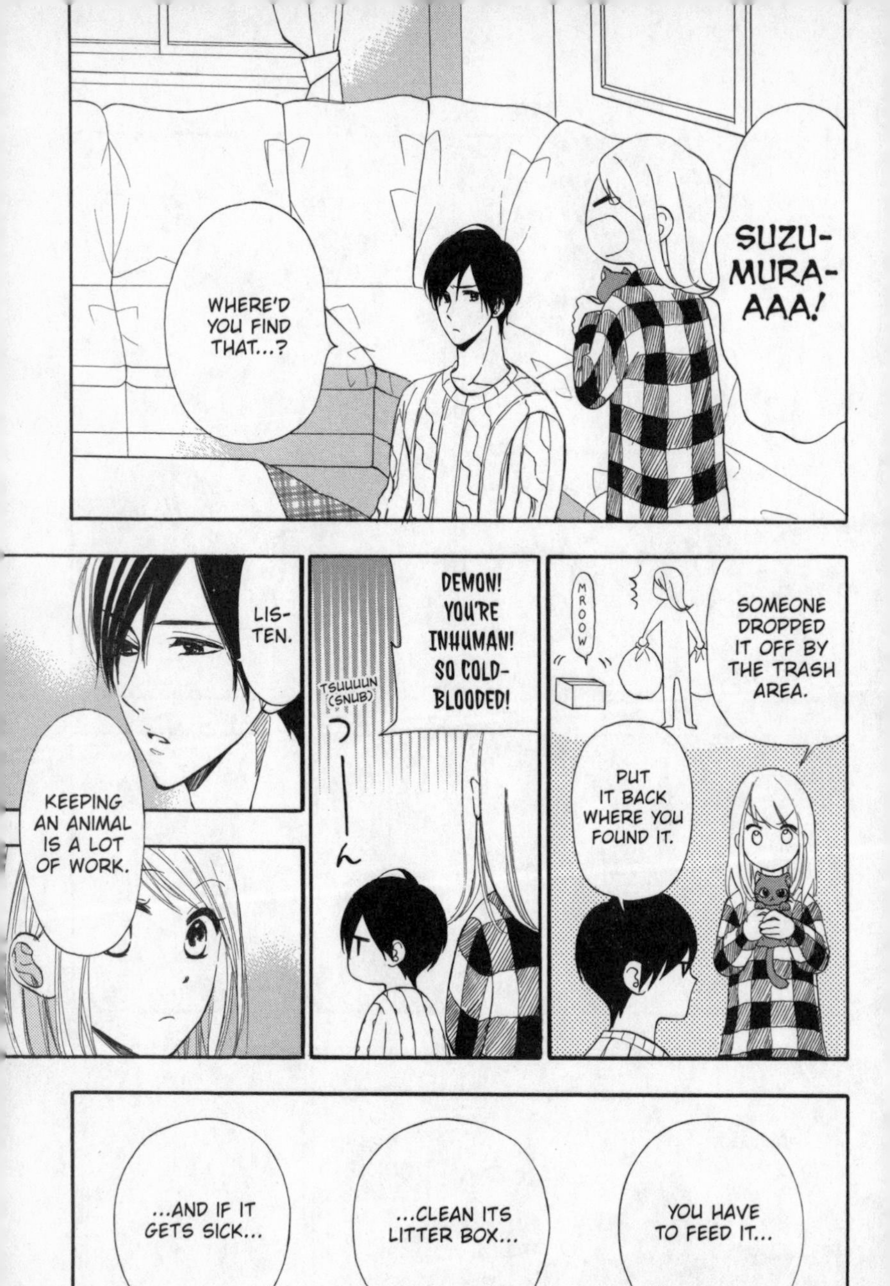
SUZU-MURA-AAA!
WHERE'D YOU FIND THAT...?
SOMEONE DROPPED IT OFF BY THE TRASH AREA.
MROOW
PUT IT BACK WHERE YOU FOUND IT.
DEMON! YOU'RE INHUMAN! SO COLD-BLOODED!
TSUUUUN (SNUB)
LIS-TEN.
KEEPING AN ANIMAL IS A LOT OF WORK.
YOU HAVE TO FEED IT...
...CLEAN ITS LITTER BOX...
...AND IF IT GETS SICK...

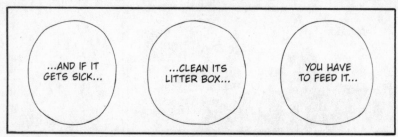

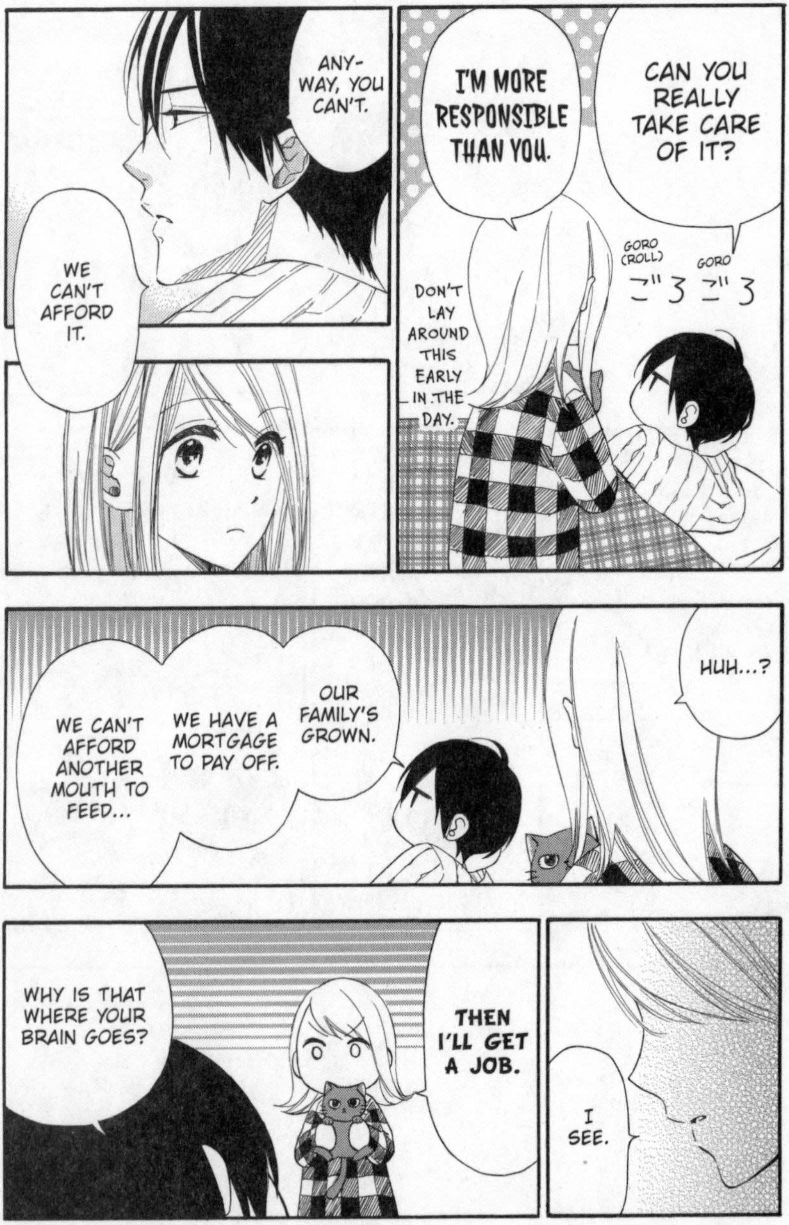
CAN YOU REALLY TAKE CARE OF IT?
I'M MORE RESPONSIBLE THAN YOU.
GORO (ROLL) GORO
ごろごろ
DON'T LAY AROUND THIS EARLY IN THE DAY.
ANY-WAY, YOU CAN'T.
WE CAN'T AFFORD IT.
HUH...?
OUR FAMILY'S GROWN.
WE HAVE A MORTGAGE TO PAY OFF.
WE CAN'T AFFORD ANOTHER MOUTH TO FEED...
I SEE.
THEN I'LL GET A JOB.
WHY IS THAT WHERE YOUR BRAIN GOES?

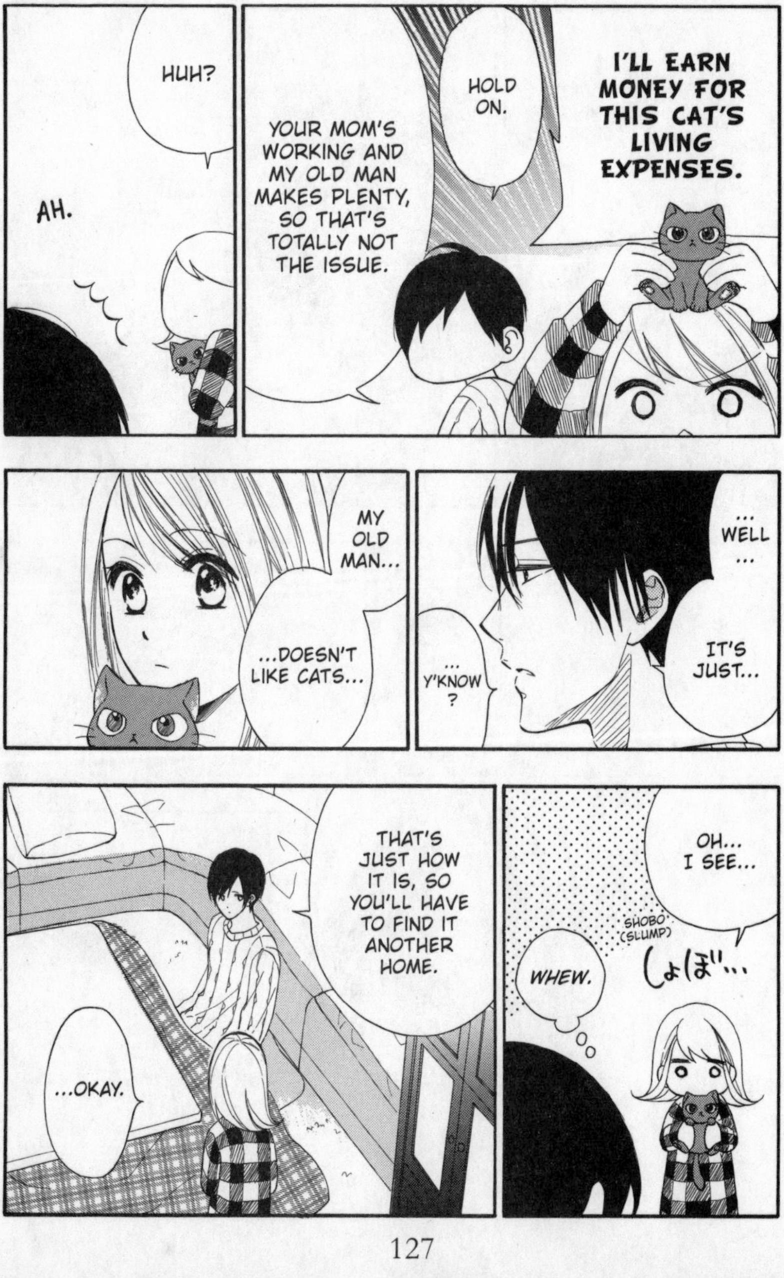
I'LL EARN MONEY FOR THIS CAT'S LIVING EXPENSES.
HOLD ON.
YOUR MOM'S WORKING AND MY OLD MAN MAKES PLENTY, SO THAT'S TOTALLY NOT THE ISSUE.
HUH?
AH.
...WELL...
IT'S JUST...
...Y'KNOW?
MY OLD MAN...
...DOESN'T LIKE CATS...
OH... I SEE...
SHOBO (SLUMP)
しょぼ…
WHEW.
THAT'S JUST HOW IT IS, SO YOU'LL HAVE TO FIND IT ANOTHER HOME.
...OKAY.

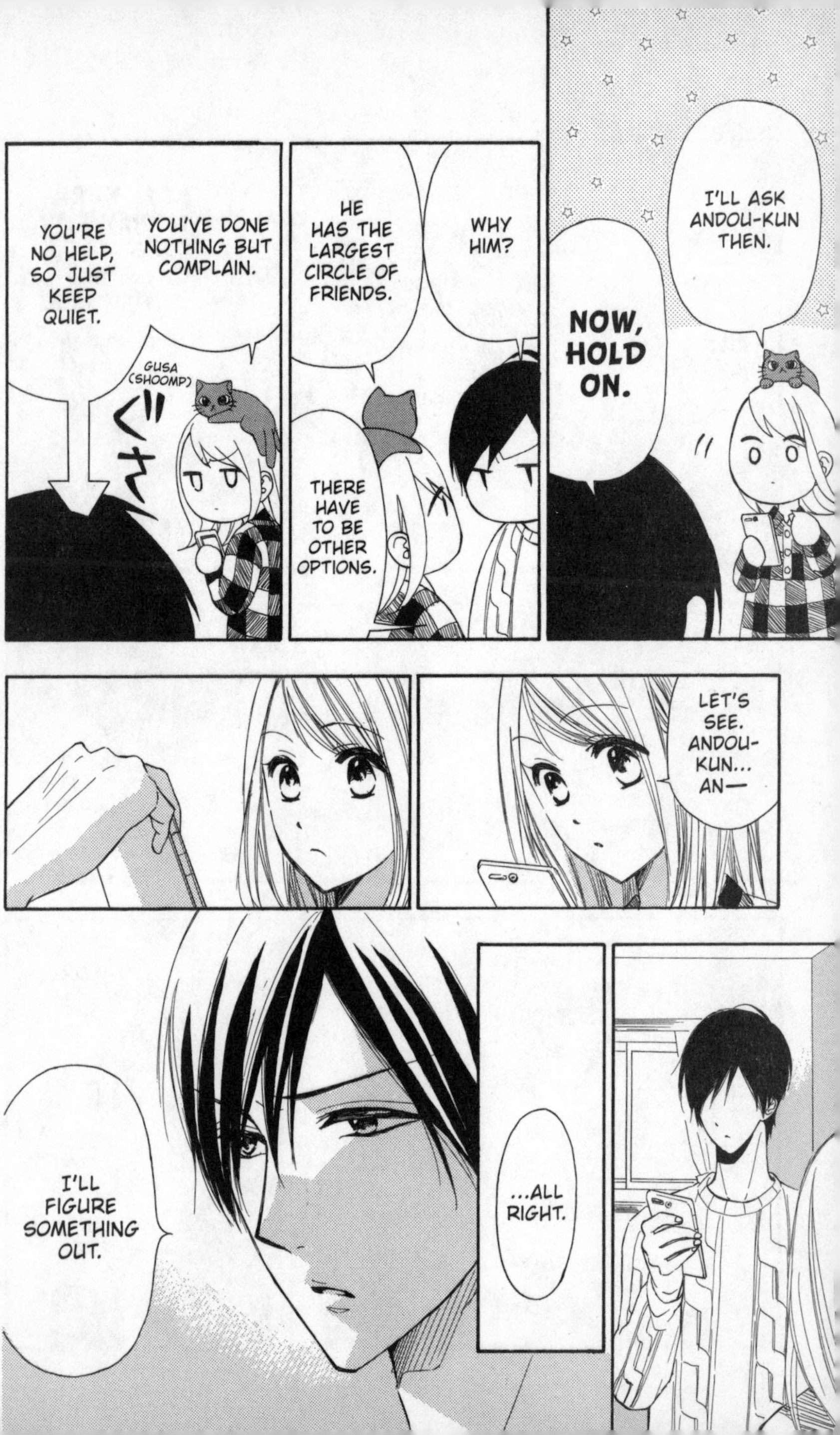
I'LL ASK ANDOU-KUN THEN.
NOW, HOLD ON.
WHY HIM?
HE HAS THE LARGEST CIRCLE OF FRIENDS.
THERE HAVE TO BE OTHER OPTIONS.
YOU'VE DONE NOTHING BUT COMPLAIN.
YOU'RE NO HELP, SO JUST KEEP QUIET.
GUSA (SHOOMP)
LET'S SEE. ANDOU-KUN... AN—
...ALL RIGHT.
I'LL FIGURE SOMETHING OUT.

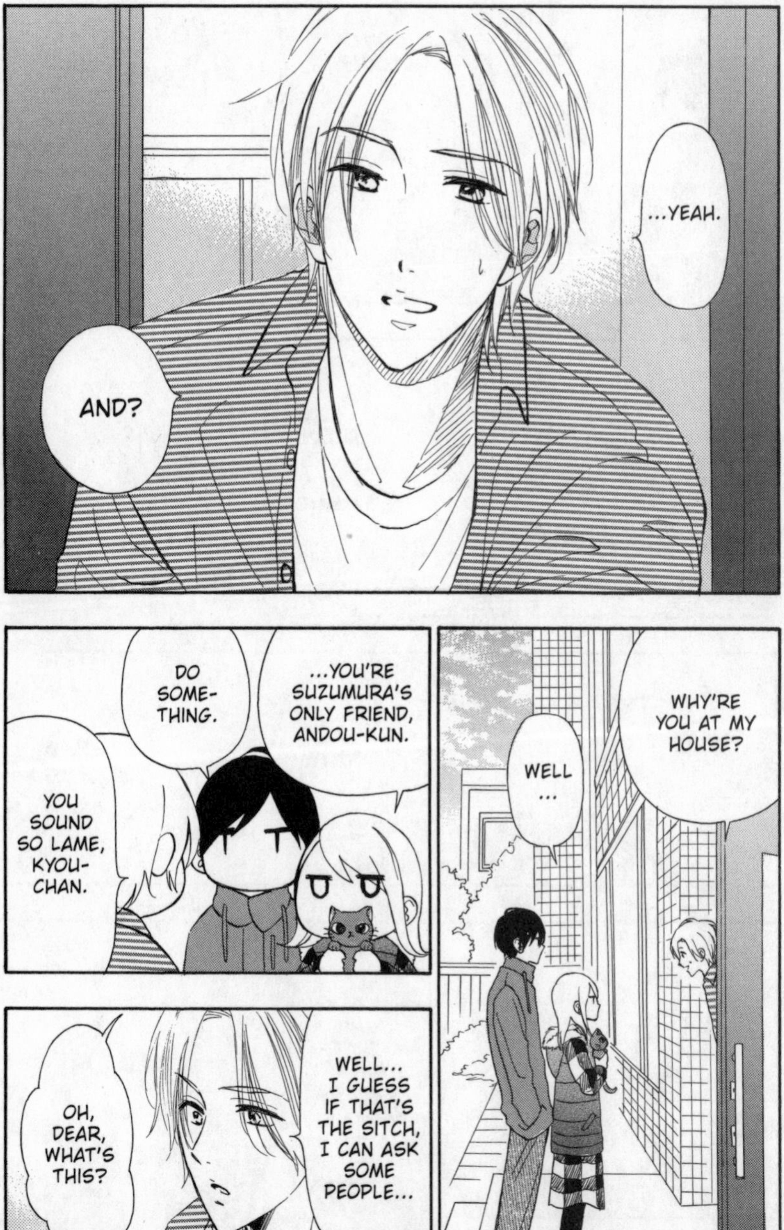
...YEAH.
AND?
WHY'RE YOU AT MY HOUSE?
WELL ...
...YOU'RE SUZUMURA'S ONLY FRIEND, ANDOU-KUN.
DO SOME-THING.
YOU SOUND SO LAME, KYOU-CHAN.
WELL... I GUESS IF THAT'S THE SITCH, I CAN ASK SOME PEOPLE...
OH, DEAR, WHAT'S THIS?

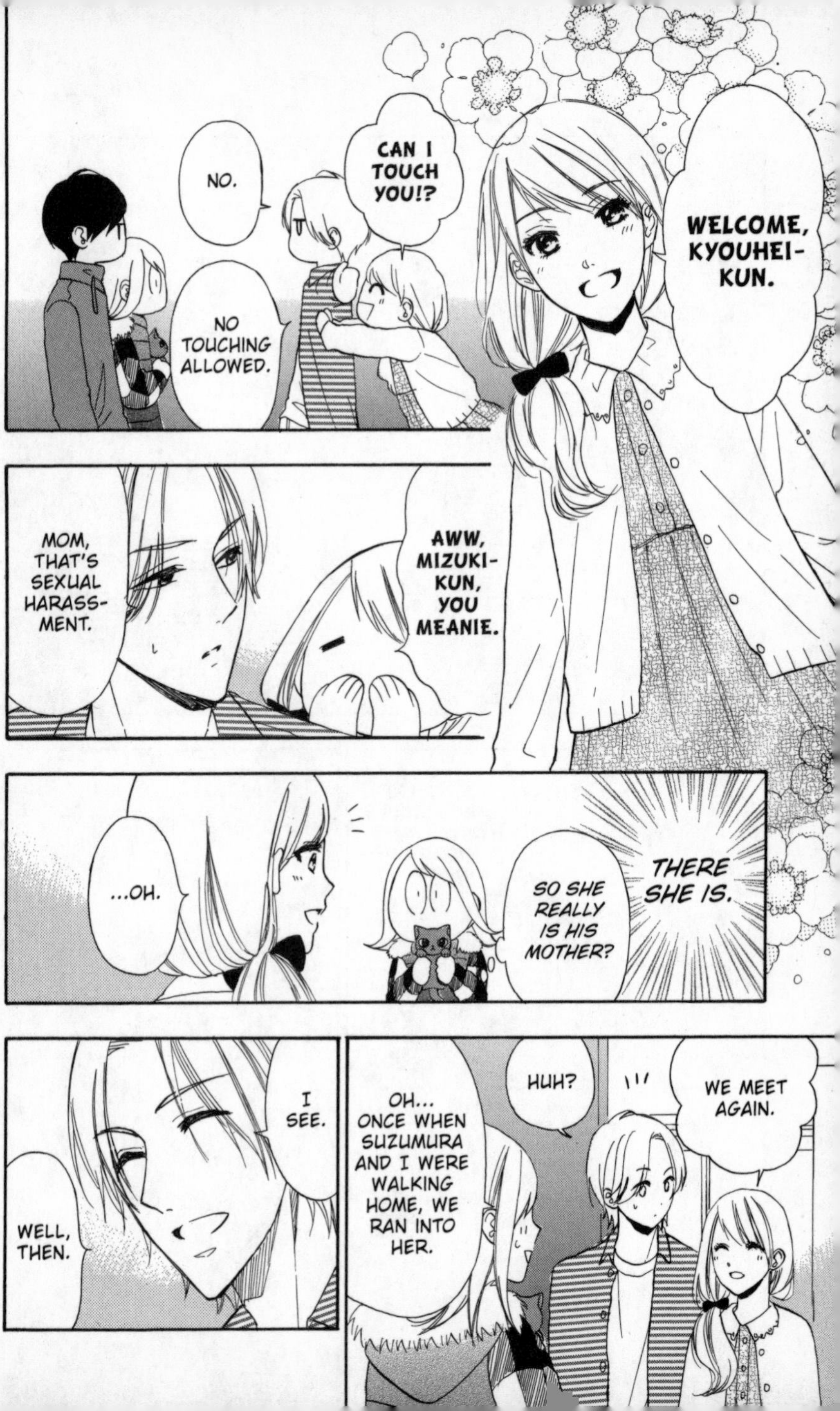

WELCOME, KYOUHEI-KUN.
CAN I TOUCH YOU!?
NO.
NO TOUCHING ALLOWED.
AWW, MIZUKI-KUN, YOU MEANIE.
MOM, THAT'S SEXUAL HARASS-MENT.
THERE SHE IS.
SO SHE REALLY IS HIS MOTHER?
...OH.
WE MEET AGAIN.
HUH?
OH... ONCE WHEN SUZUMURA AND I WERE WALKING HOME, WE RAN INTO HER.
I SEE.
WELL, THEN.

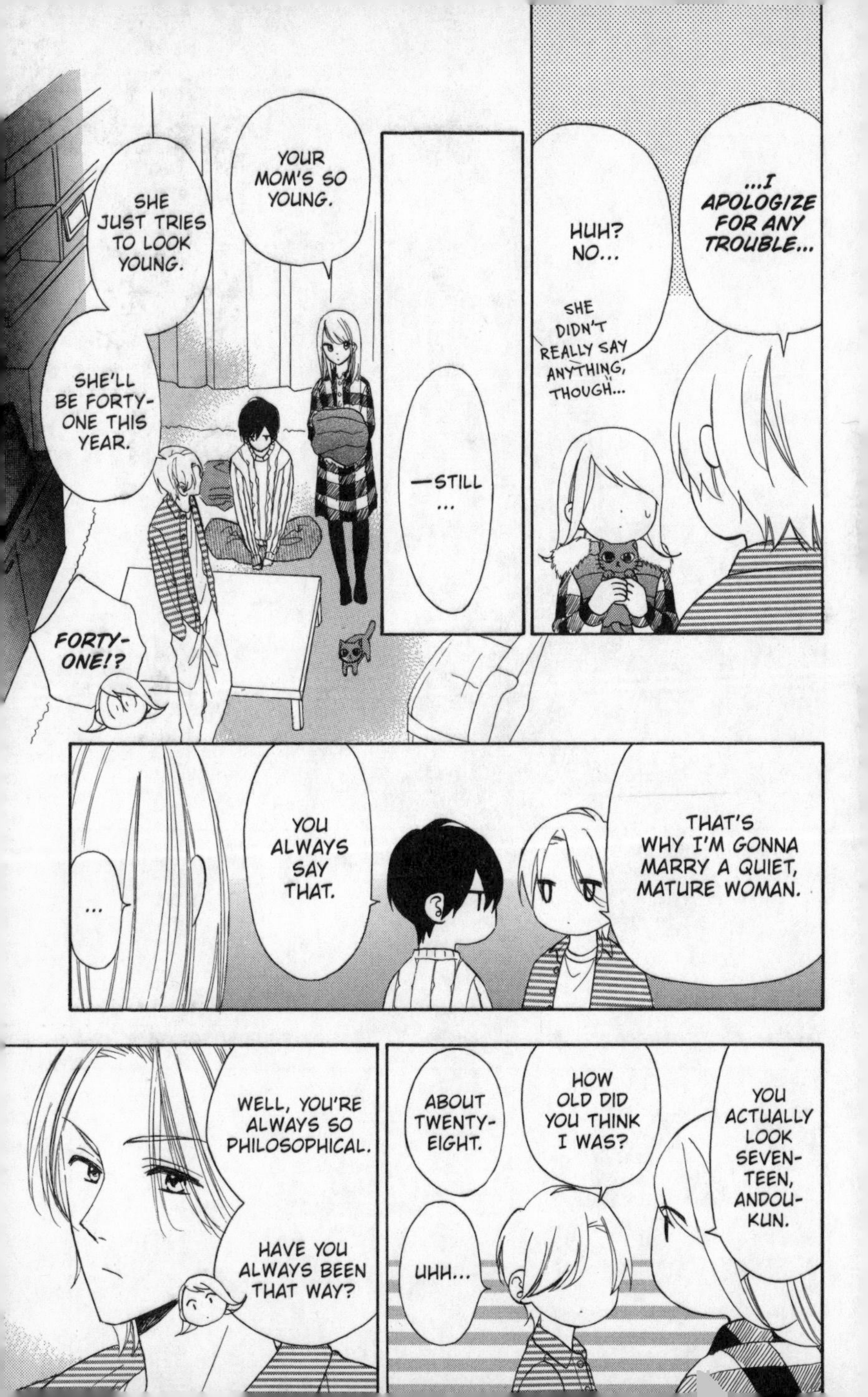
...I APOLOGIZE FOR ANY TROUBLE...
HUH? NO...
SHE DIDN'T REALLY SAY ANYTHING, THOUGH...
—STILL ...
YOUR MOM'S SO YOUNG.
SHE JUST TRIES TO LOOK YOUNG.
SHE'LL BE FORTY-ONE THIS YEAR.
FORTY-ONE!?
THAT'S WHY I'M GONNA MARRY A QUIET, MATURE WOMAN.
YOU ALWAYS SAY THAT.
...
YOU ACTUALLY LOOK SEVENTEEN, ANDOU-KUN.
HOW OLD DID YOU THINK I WAS?
ABOUT TWENTY-EIGHT.
UHH...
WELL, YOU'RE ALWAYS SO PHILOSOPHICAL.
HAVE YOU ALWAYS BEEN THAT WAY?

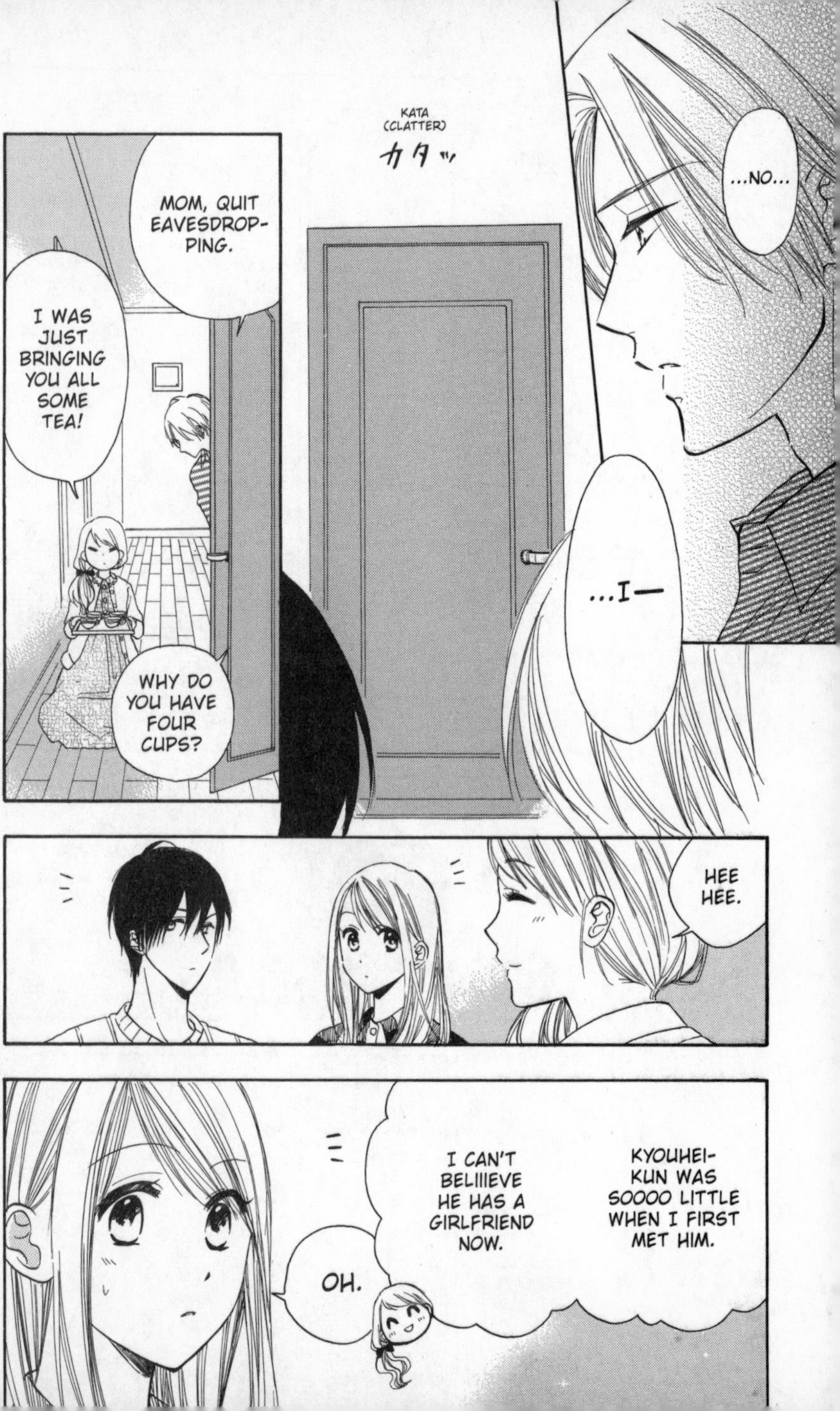
...NO...
...I—
KATA (CLATTER)
カタッ
MOM, QUIT EAVESDROPPING.
I WAS JUST BRINGING YOU ALL SOME TEA!
WHY DO YOU HAVE FOUR CUPS?
HEE HEE.
KYOUHEI-KUN WAS SOOOO LITTLE WHEN I FIRST MET HIM.
I CAN'T BELIIIEVE HE HAS A GIRLFRIEND NOW.
OH.

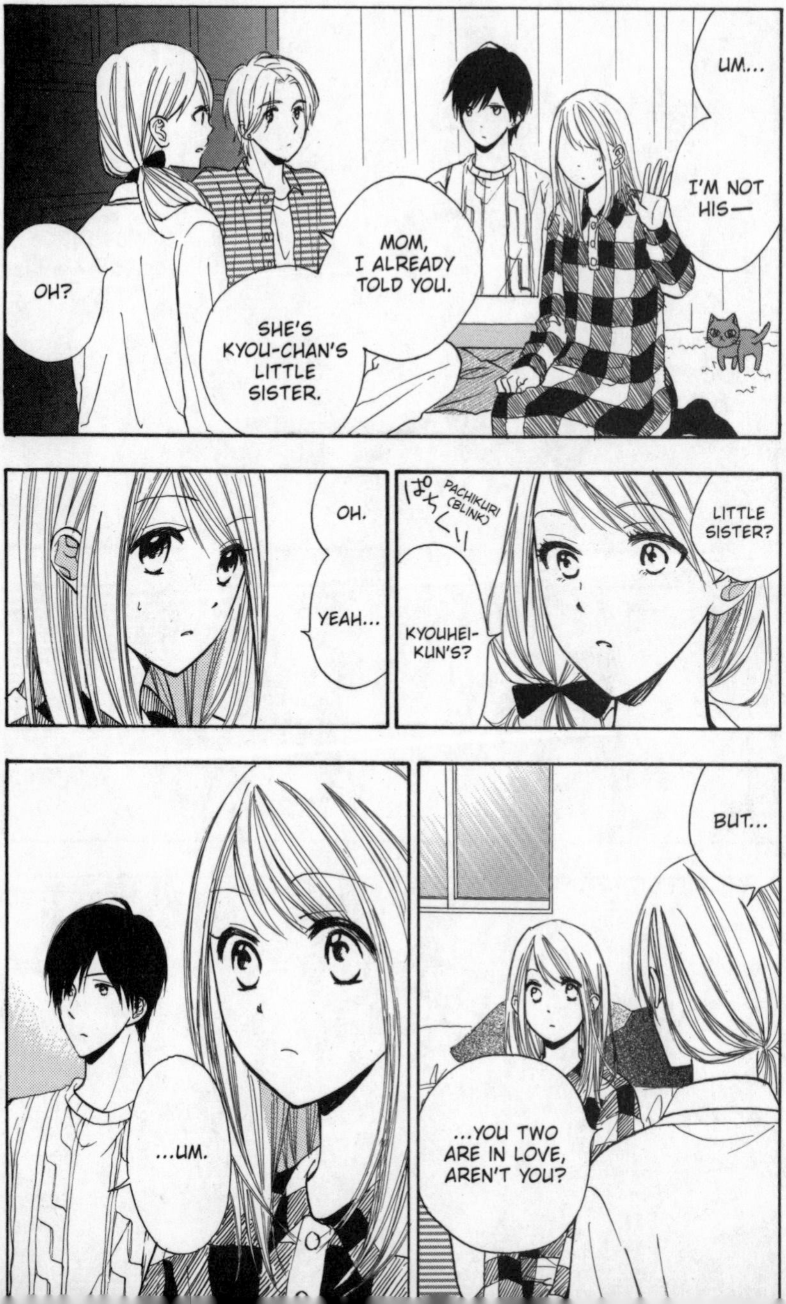
UM...
I'M NOT HIS—
MOM, I ALREADY TOLD YOU.
SHE'S KYOU-CHAN'S LITTLE SISTER.
OH?
LITTLE SISTER?
ぱちくり
PACHIKURI (BLINK)
KYOUHEI-KUN'S?
OH.
YEAH...
BUT...
...YOU TWO ARE IN LOVE, AREN'T YOU?
...UM.

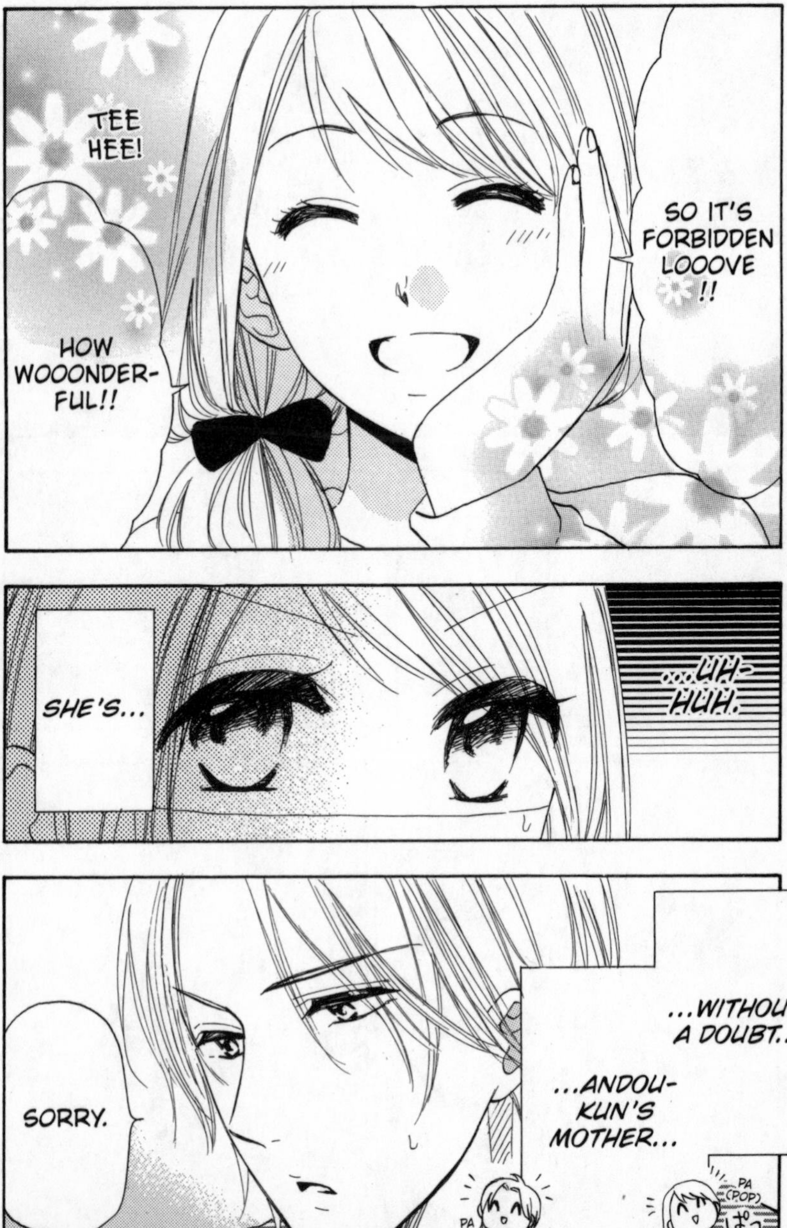
SO IT'S FORBIDDEN LOOOVE!!
TEE HEE!
HOW WOOONDER-FUL!!
...UH-HUH.
SHE'S...
...WITHOUT A DOUBT...
...ANDOU-KUN'S MOTHER...
PA (POP)
ぱっ
SORRY.
PA
ぱっ

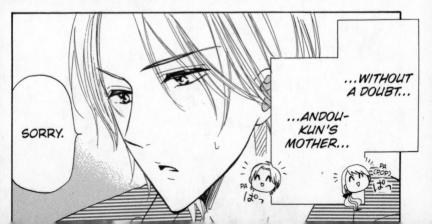

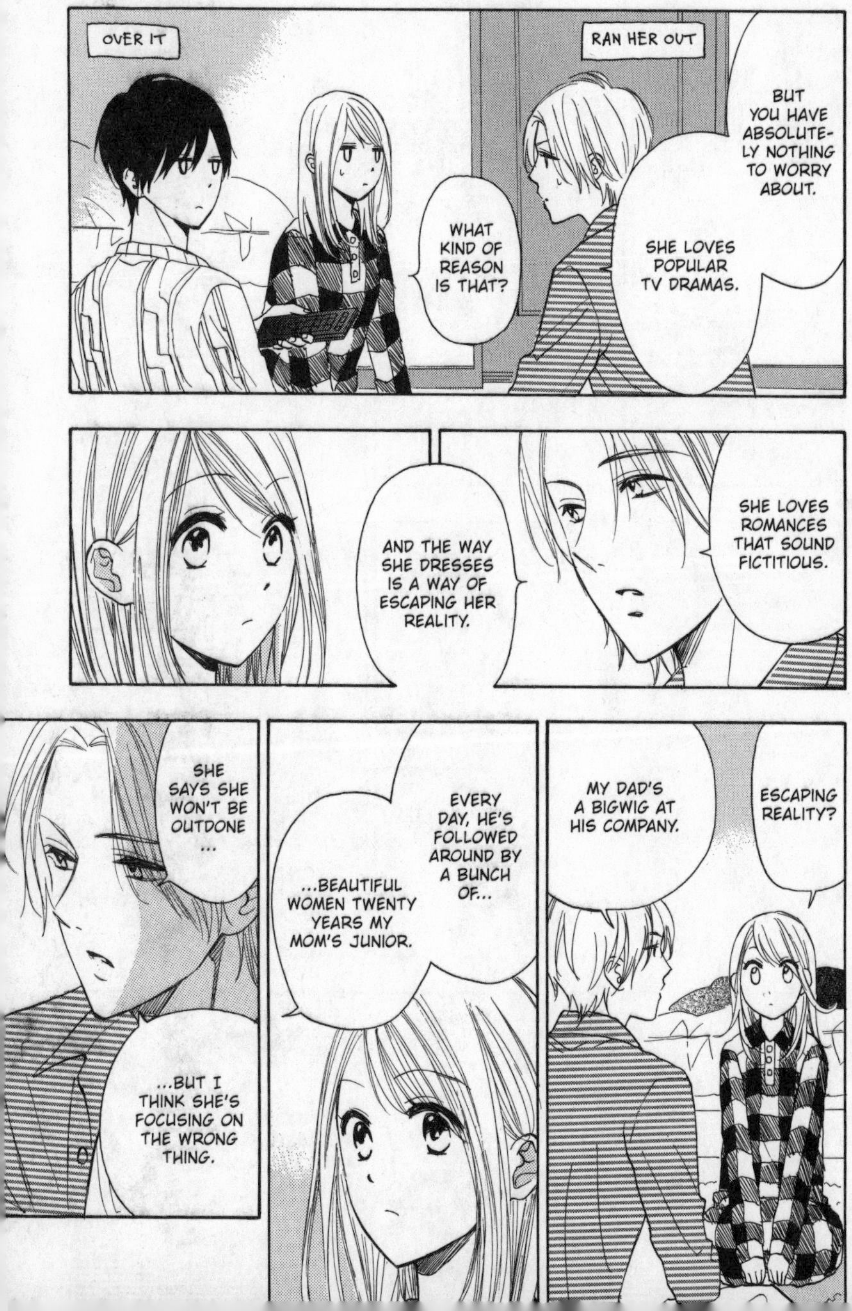
RAN HER OUT
BUT YOU HAVE ABSOLUTELY NOTHING TO WORRY ABOUT.
SHE LOVES POPULAR TV DRAMAS.
WHAT KIND OF REASON IS THAT?
OVER IT
SHE LOVES ROMANCES THAT SOUND FICTITIOUS.
AND THE WAY SHE DRESSES IS A WAY OF ESCAPING HER REALITY.
ESCAPING REALITY?
MY DAD'S A BIGWIG AT HIS COMPANY.
EVERY DAY, HE'S FOLLOWED AROUND BY A BUNCH OF...
...BEAUTIFUL WOMEN TWENTY YEARS MY MOM'S JUNIOR.
SHE SAYS SHE WON'T BE OUTDONE...
...BUT I THINK SHE'S FOCUSING ON THE WRONG THING.

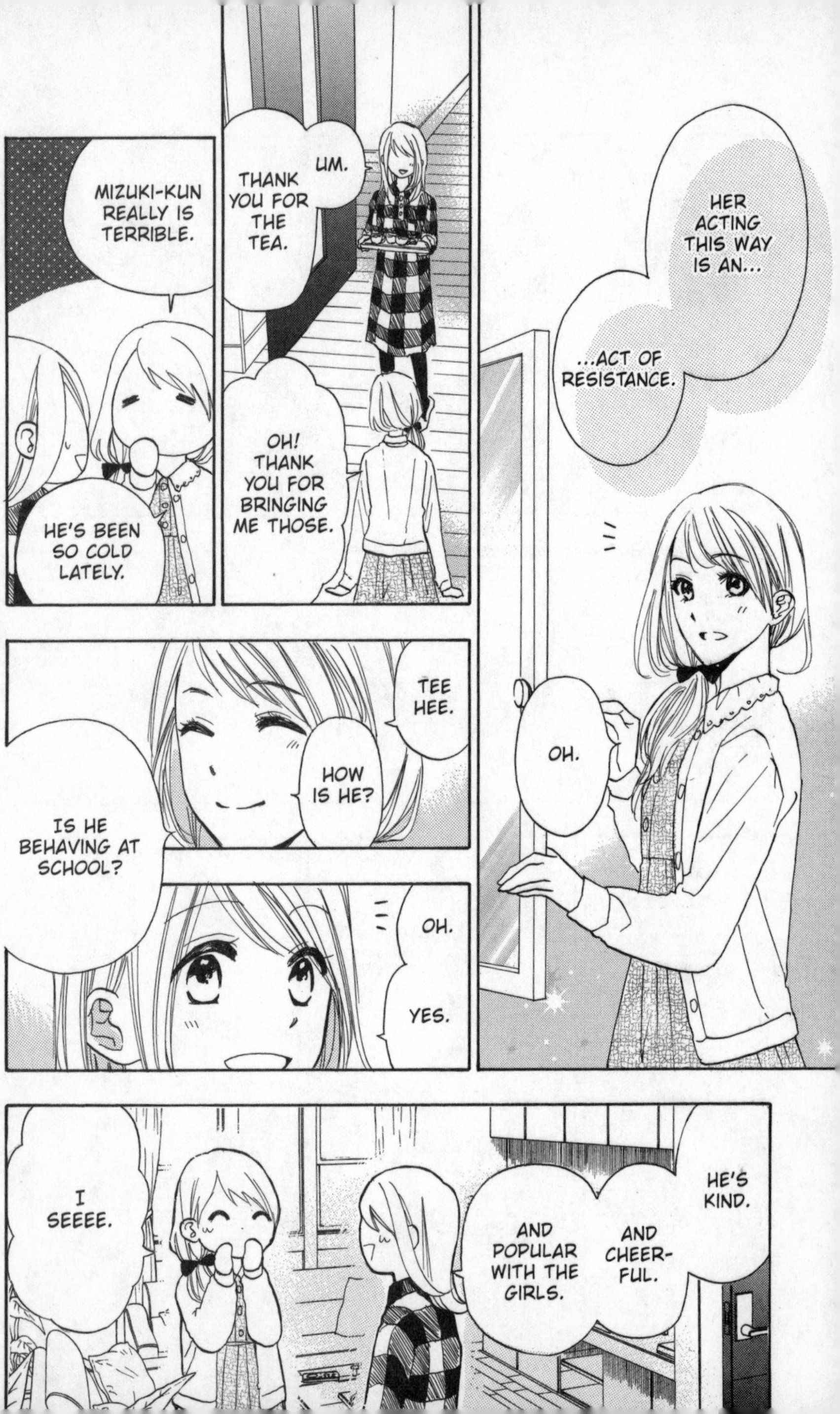
HER ACTING THIS WAY IS AN...
...ACT OF RESISTANCE.
OH.
UM.
THANK YOU FOR THE TEA.
OH! THANK YOU FOR BRINGING ME THOSE.
MIZUKI-KUN REALLY IS TERRIBLE.
HE'S BEEN SO COLD LATELY.
TEE HEE.
HOW IS HE?
IS HE BEHAVING AT SCHOOL?
OH.
YES.
HE'S KIND.
AND CHEERFUL.
AND POPULAR WITH THE GIRLS.
I SEEEE.

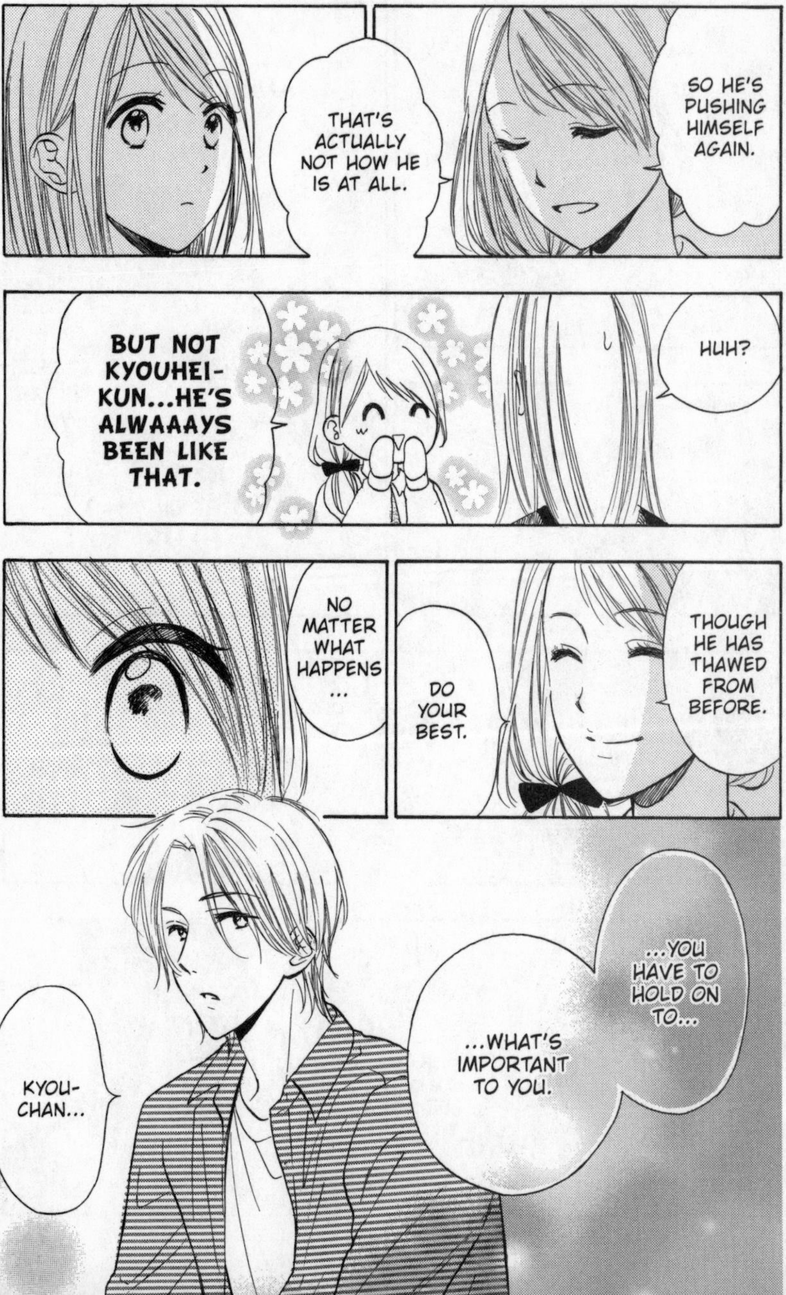
SO HE'S PUSHING HIMSELF AGAIN.
THAT'S ACTUALLY NOT HOW HE IS AT ALL.
HUH?
BUT NOT KYOUHEI-KUN...HE'S ALWAAAYS BEEN LIKE THAT.
THOUGH HE HAS THAWED FROM BEFORE.
DO YOUR BEST.
NO MATTER WHAT HAPPENS...
...YOU HAVE TO HOLD ON TO...
...WHAT'S IMPORTANT TO YOU.
KYOU-CHAN...

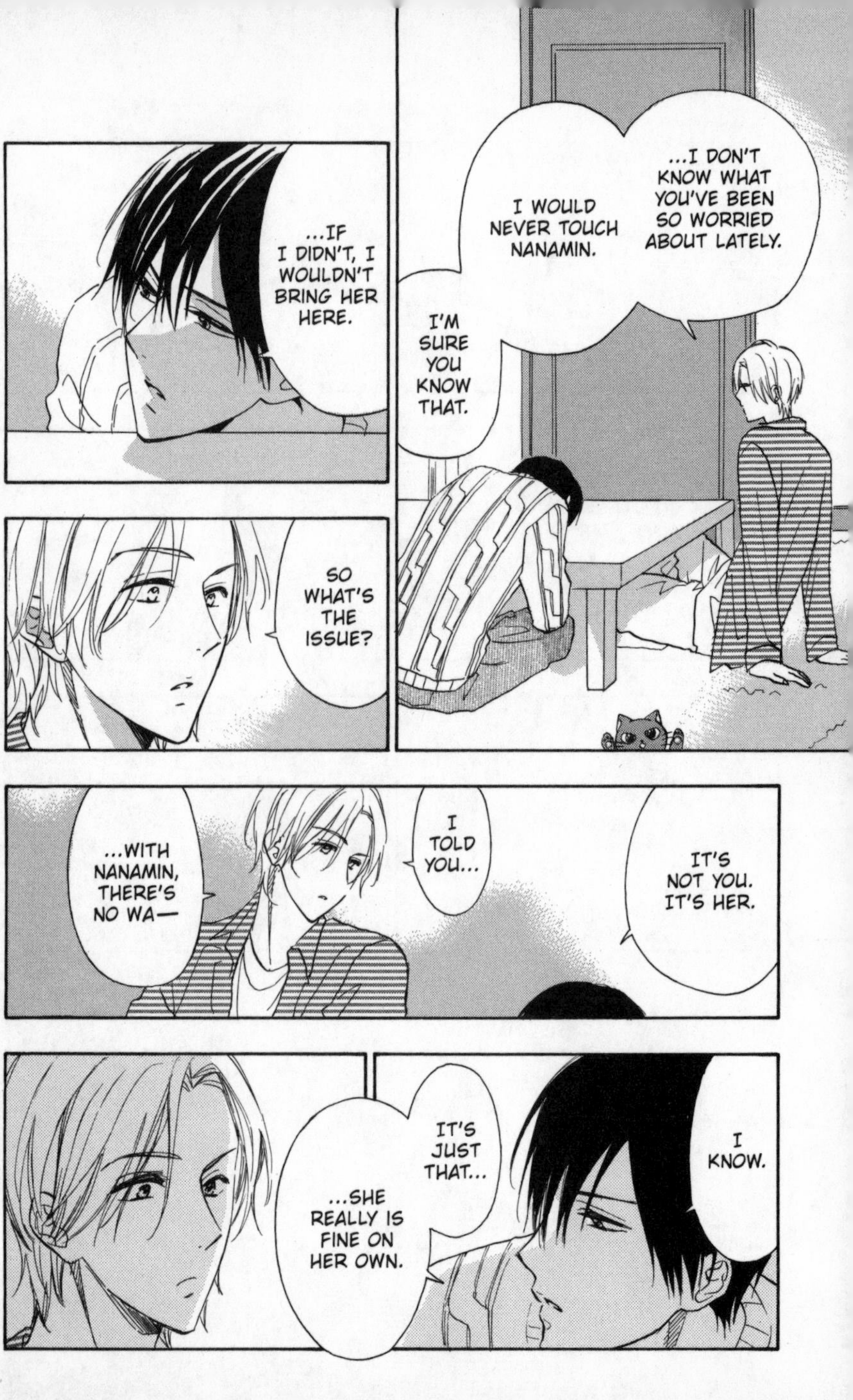
...I DON'T KNOW WHAT YOU'VE BEEN SO WORRIED ABOUT LATELY.
I WOULD NEVER TOUCH NANAMIN.
I'M SURE YOU KNOW THAT.
...IF I DIDN'T, I WOULDN'T BRING HER HERE.
SO WHAT'S THE ISSUE?
IT'S NOT YOU. IT'S HER.
I TOLD YOU...
...WITH NANAMIN, THERE'S NO WA—
I KNOW.
IT'S JUST THAT...
...SHE REALLY IS FINE ON HER OWN.

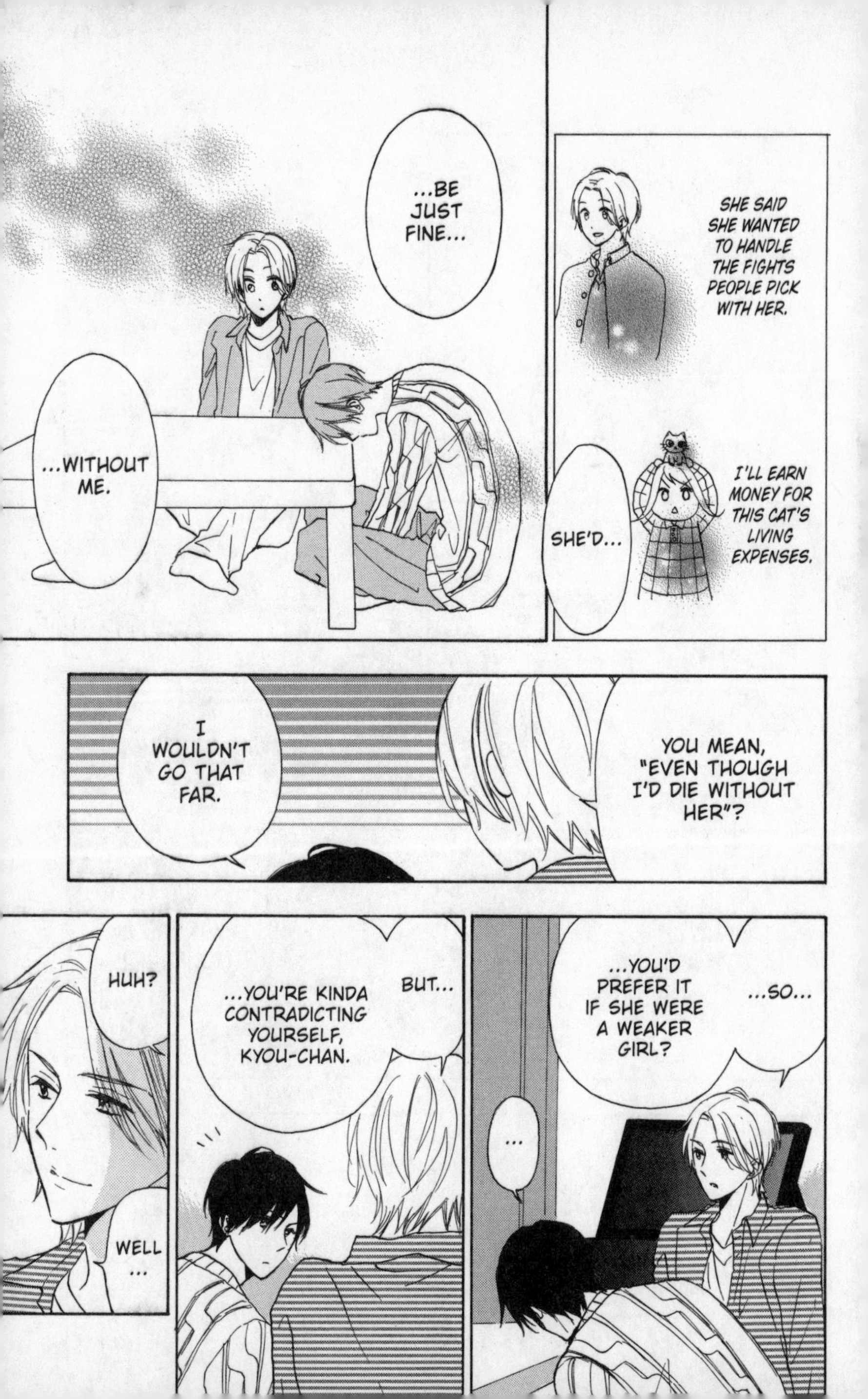
SHE SAID SHE WANTED TO HANDLE THE FIGHTS PEOPLE PICK WITH HER.
I'LL EARN MONEY FOR THIS CAT'S LIVING EXPENSES.
SHE'D...
...BE JUST FINE...
...WITHOUT ME.
YOU MEAN, "EVEN THOUGH I'D DIE WITHOUT HER"?
I WOULDN'T GO THAT FAR.
...SO...
...YOU'D PREFER IT IF SHE WERE A WEAKER GIRL?
...
BUT...
...YOU'RE KINDA CONTRADICTING YOURSELF, KYOU-CHAN.
HUH?
WELL ...

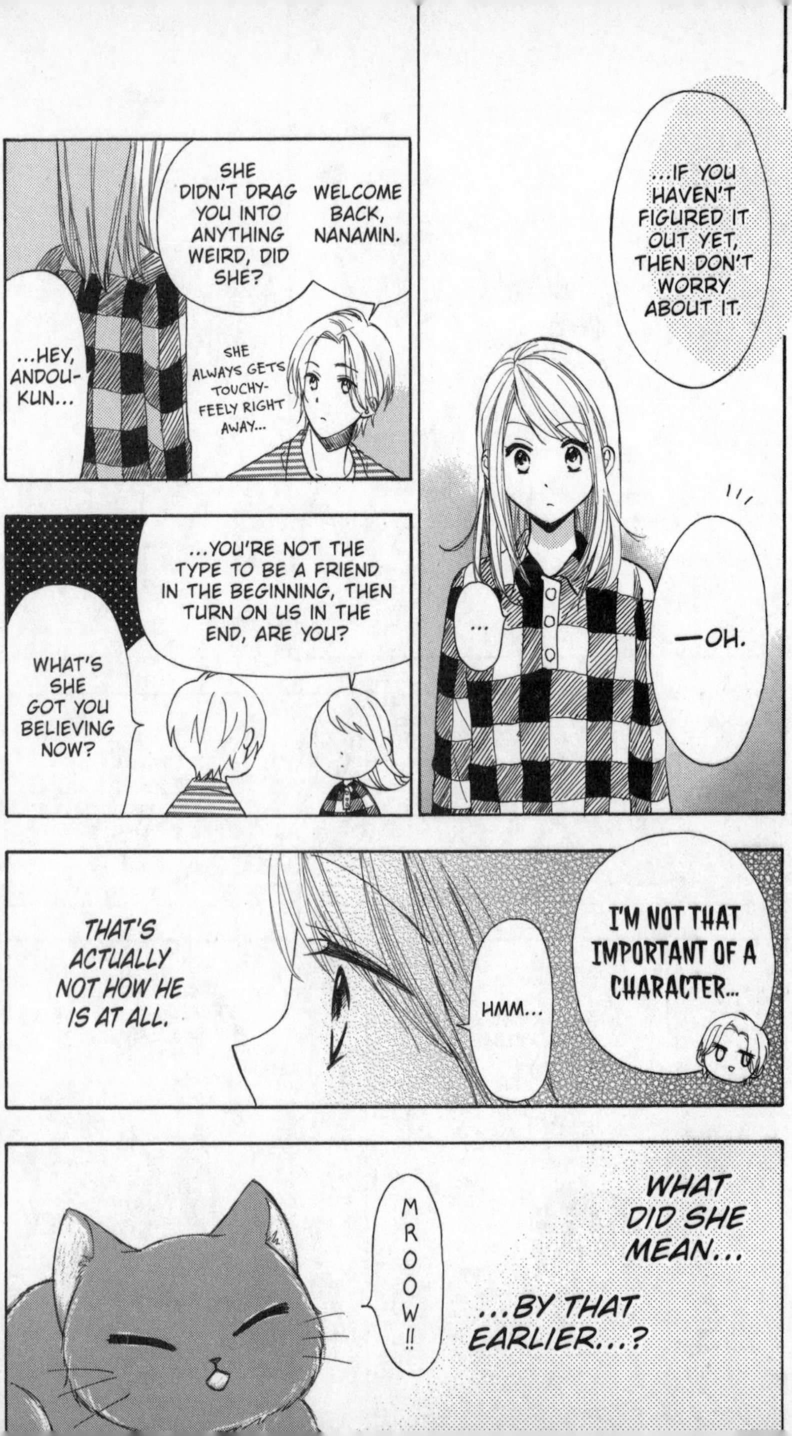
...IF YOU HAVEN'T FIGURED IT OUT YET, THEN DON'T WORRY ABOUT IT.
—OH.
...
WELCOME BACK, NANAMIN.
SHE DIDN'T DRAG YOU INTO ANYTHING WEIRD, DID SHE?
SHE ALWAYS GETS TOUCHY-FEELY RIGHT AWAY...
...HEY, ANDOU-KUN...
...YOU'RE NOT THE TYPE TO BE A FRIEND IN THE BEGINNING, THEN TURN ON US IN THE END, ARE YOU?
WHAT'S SHE GOT YOU BELIEVING NOW?
I'M NOT THAT IMPORTANT OF A CHARACTER...
HMM...
THAT'S ACTUALLY NOT HOW HE IS AT ALL.
WHAT DID SHE MEAN...
...BY THAT EARLIER...?
MROOOW!!

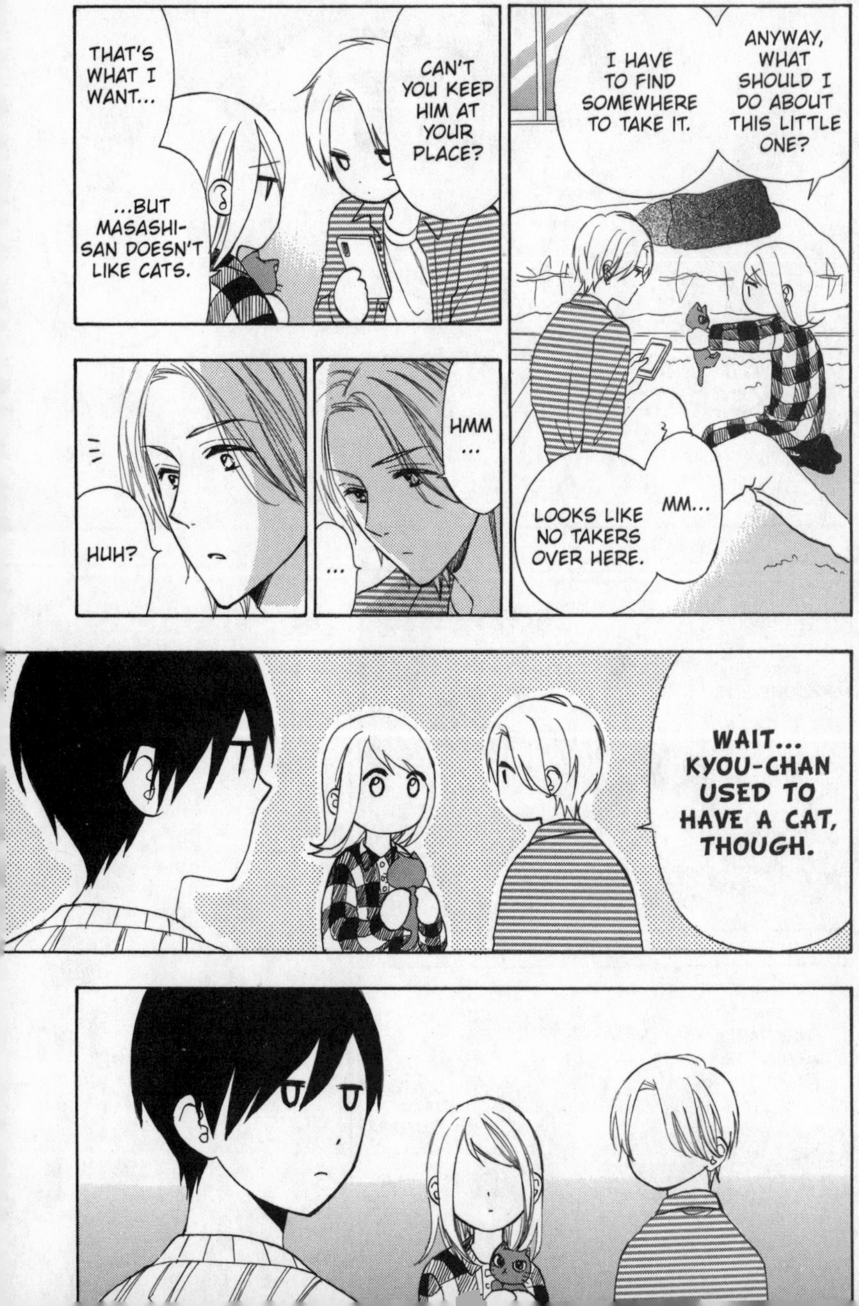
ANYWAY, WHAT SHOULD I DO ABOUT THIS LITTLE ONE?
I HAVE TO FIND SOMEWHERE TO TAKE IT.
MM...
LOOKS LIKE NO TAKERS OVER HERE.
CAN'T YOU KEEP HIM AT YOUR PLACE?
THAT'S WHAT I WANT...
...BUT MASASHI-SAN DOESN'T LIKE CATS.
HMM ...
...
HUH?
WAIT... KYOU-CHAN USED TO HAVE A CAT, THOUGH.

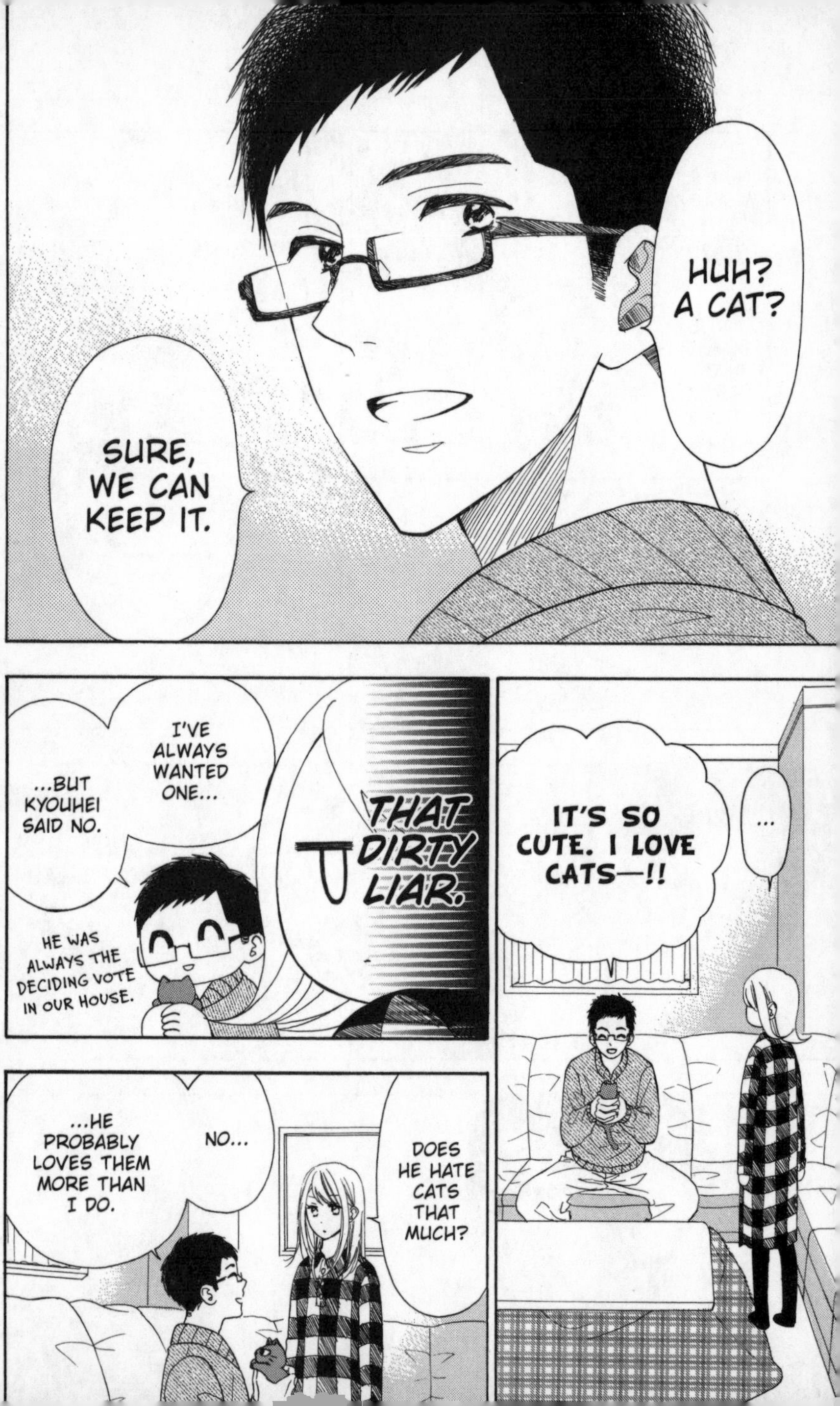
HUH? A CAT?
SURE, WE CAN KEEP IT.
IT'S SO CUTE. I LOVE CATS—!!
...
THAT DIRTY LIAR.
I'VE ALWAYS WANTED ONE...
...BUT KYOUHEI SAID NO.
HE WAS ALWAYS THE DECIDING VOTE IN OUR HOUSE.
DOES HE HATE CATS THAT MUCH?
NO...
...HE PROBABLY LOVES THEM MORE THAN I DO.

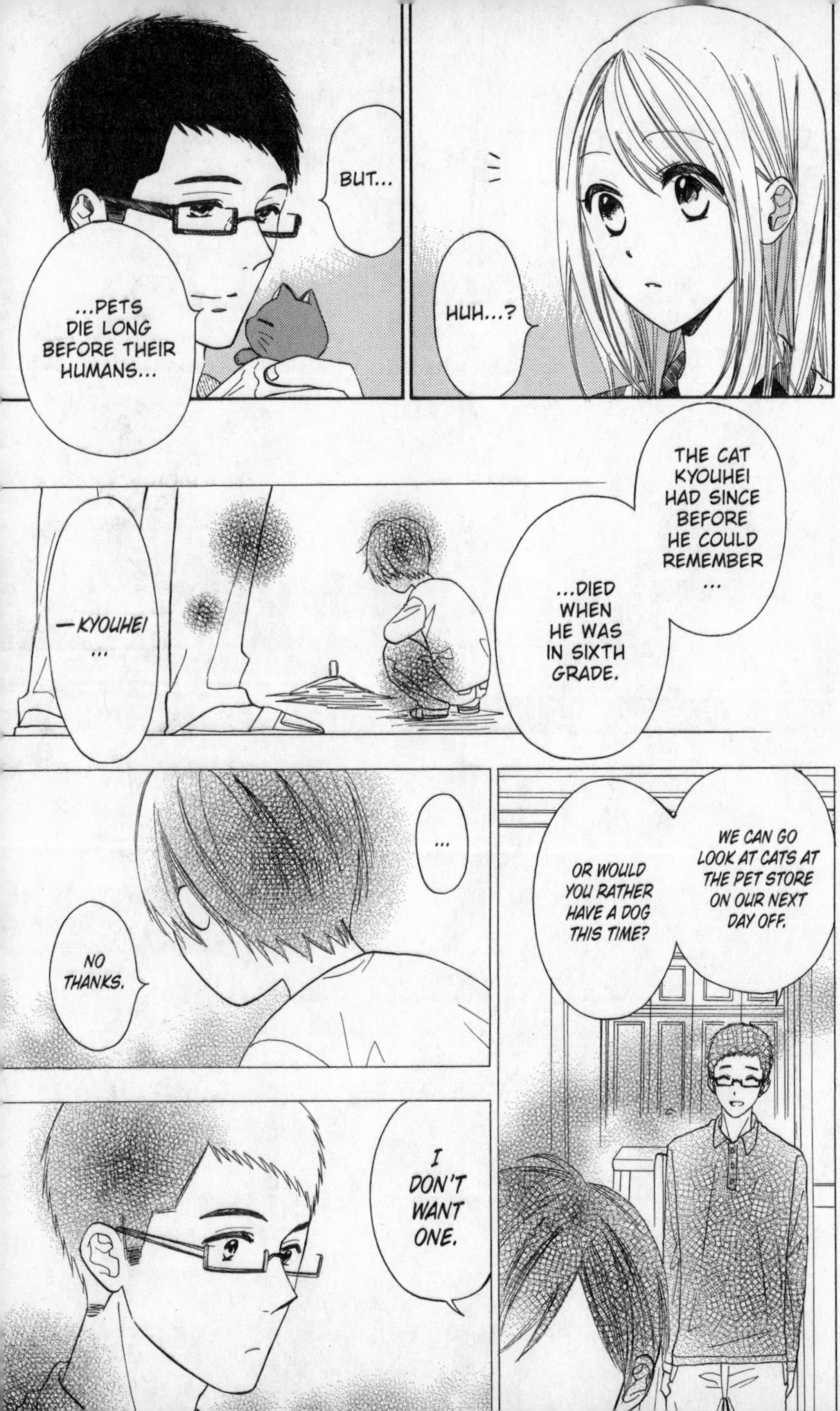
HUH...?
BUT...
...PETS DIE LONG BEFORE THEIR HUMANS...
THE CAT KYOUHEI HAD SINCE BEFORE HE COULD REMEMBER ...
...DIED WHEN HE WAS IN SIXTH GRADE.
—KYOUHEI ...
WE CAN GO LOOK AT CATS AT THE PET STORE ON OUR NEXT DAY OFF.
OR WOULD YOU RATHER HAVE A DOG THIS TIME?
...
NO THANKS.
I DON'T WANT ONE.

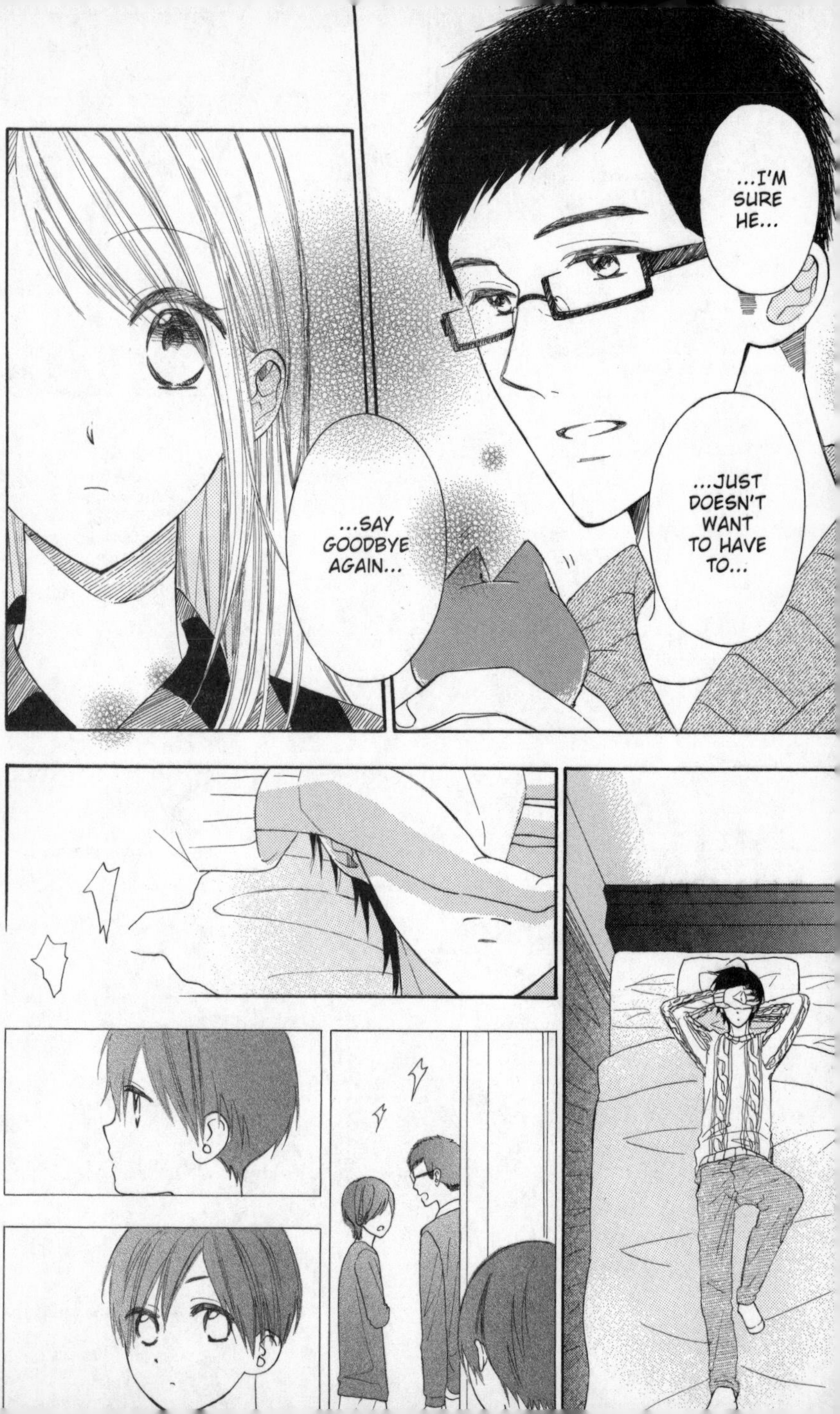
...I'M SURE HE...
...JUST DOESN'T WANT TO HAVE TO...
...SAY GOODBYE AGAIN...

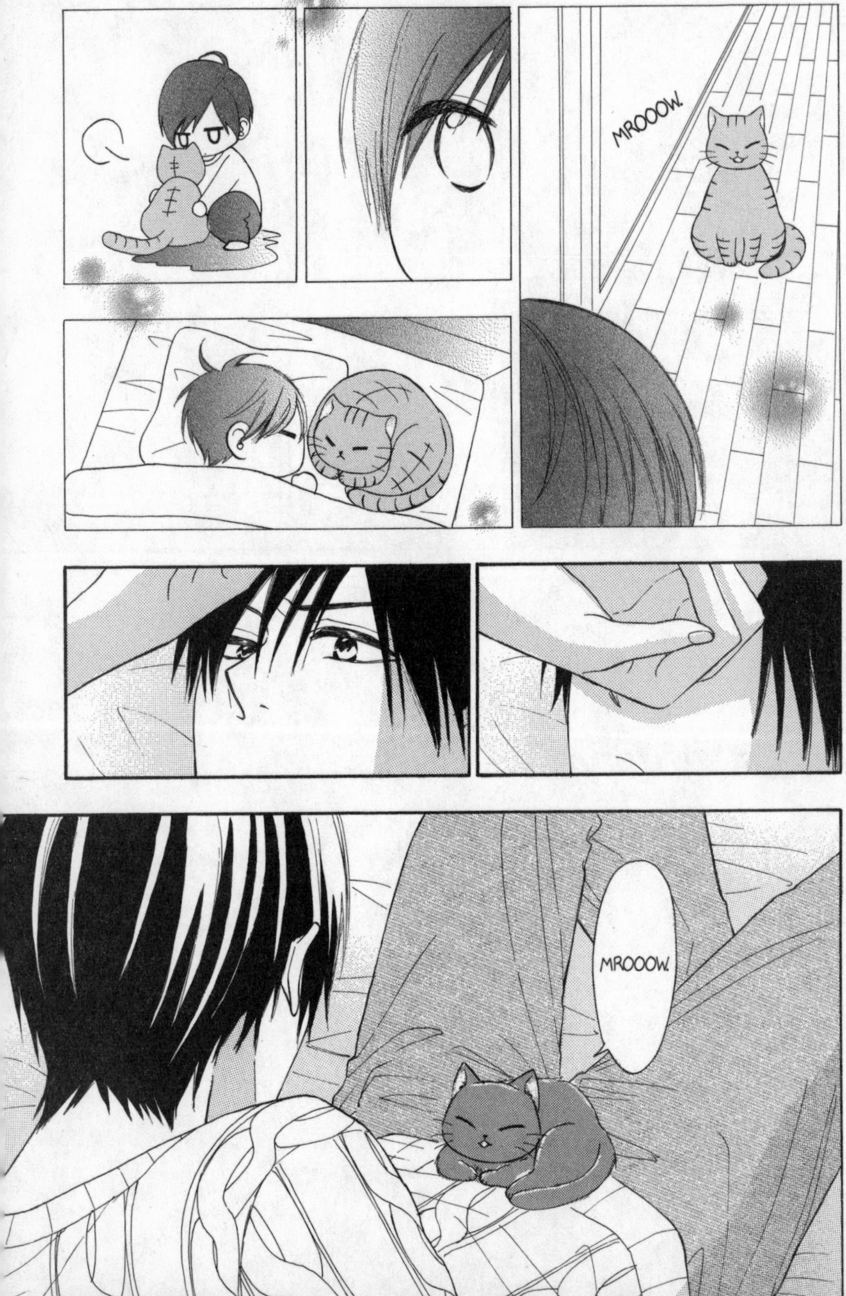
MROOOW.
MROOOW.

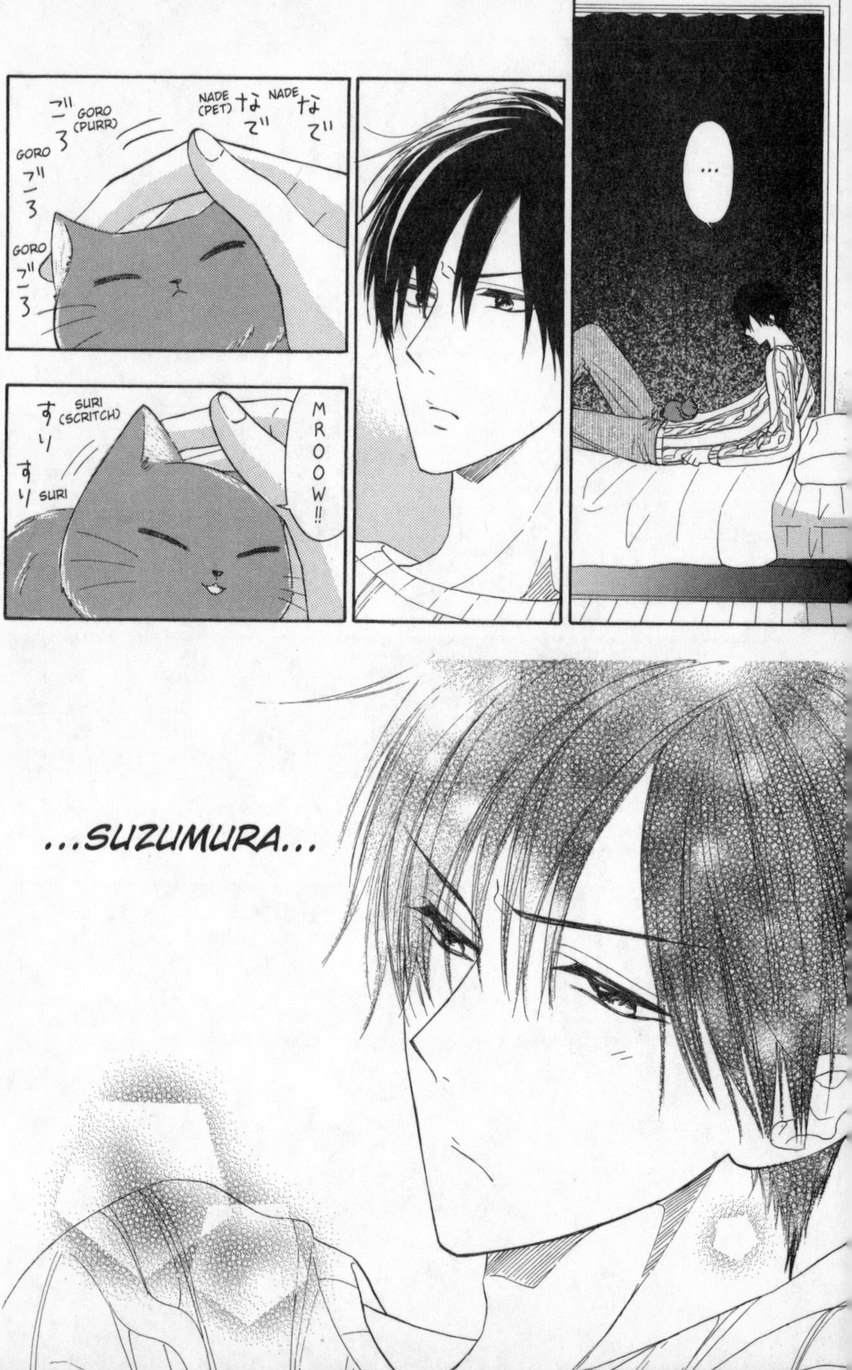
...
NADE なで
NADE (PET) なで
ごろ GORO (PURR)
GORO ごろ
GORO ごろ
MROOOW!!
SURI (SCRITCH) すり
すり SURI
...SUZUMURA...

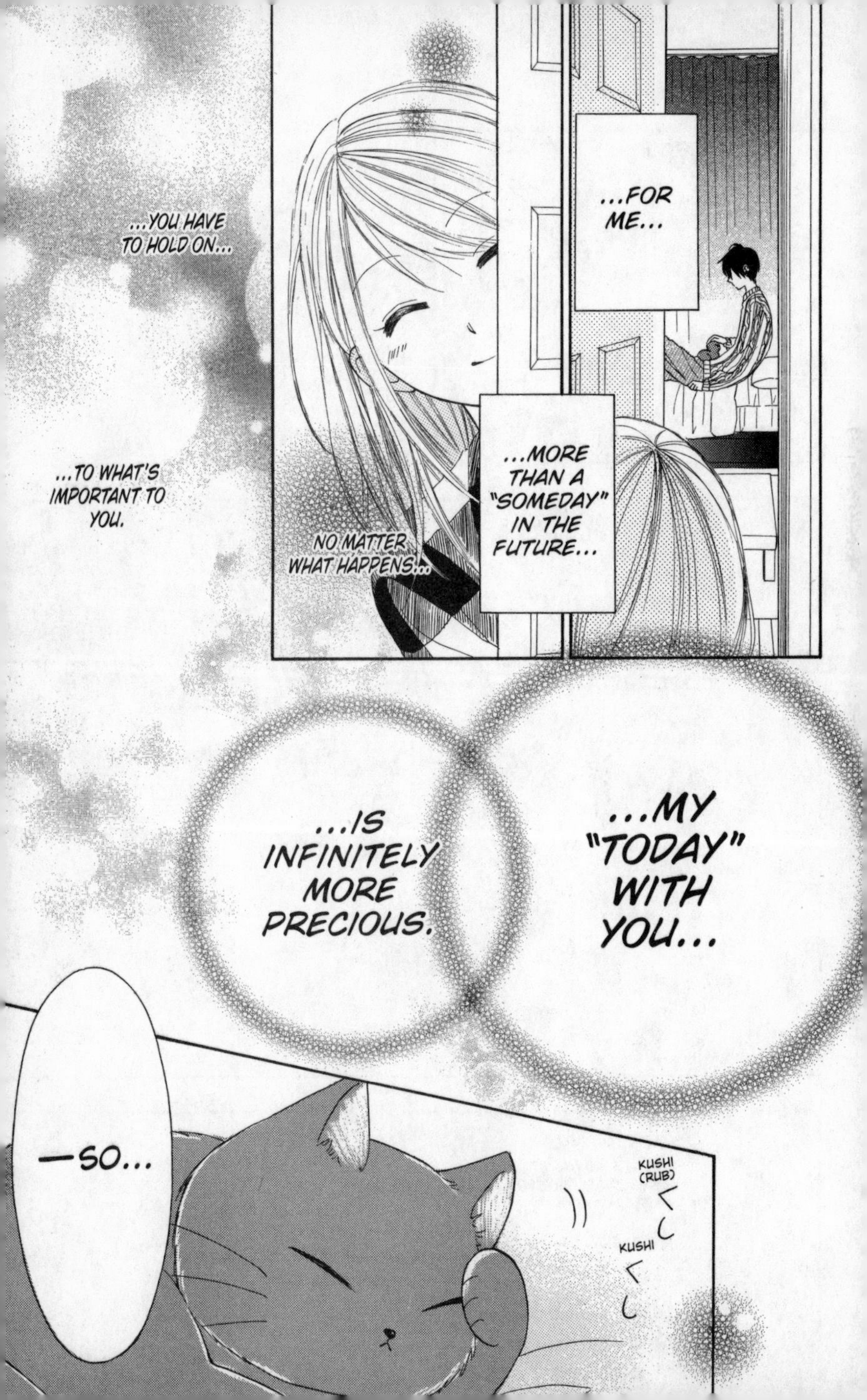
...FOR ME...
...MORE THAN A "SOMEDAY" IN THE FUTURE...
...MY "TODAY" WITH YOU...
...IS INFINITELY MORE PRECIOUS.
NO MATTER WHAT HAPPENS...
...YOU HAVE TO HOLD ON...
...TO WHAT'S IMPORTANT TO YOU.
KUSHI (RUB)
KUSHI
—SO...

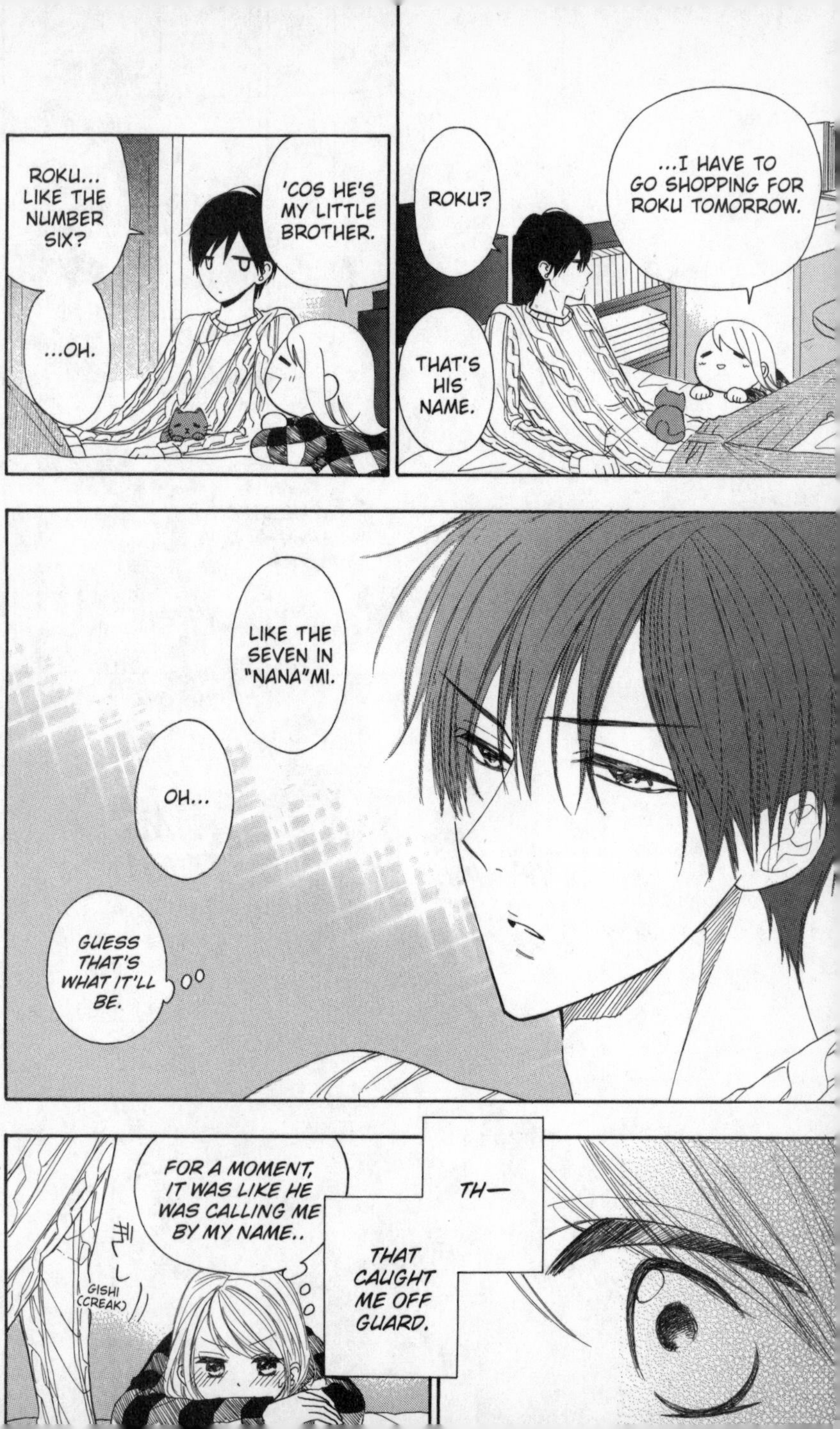
...I HAVE TO GO SHOPPING FOR ROKU TOMORROW.
ROKU?
THAT'S HIS NAME.
'COS HE'S MY LITTLE BROTHER.
ROKU... LIKE THE NUMBER SIX?
...OH.
LIKE THE SEVEN IN "NANA"MI.
OH...
GUESS THAT'S WHAT IT'LL BE.
TH—
THAT CAUGHT ME OFF GUARD.
FOR A MOMENT, IT WAS LIKE HE WAS CALLING ME BY MY NAME..
ぎし
GISHI (CREAK)

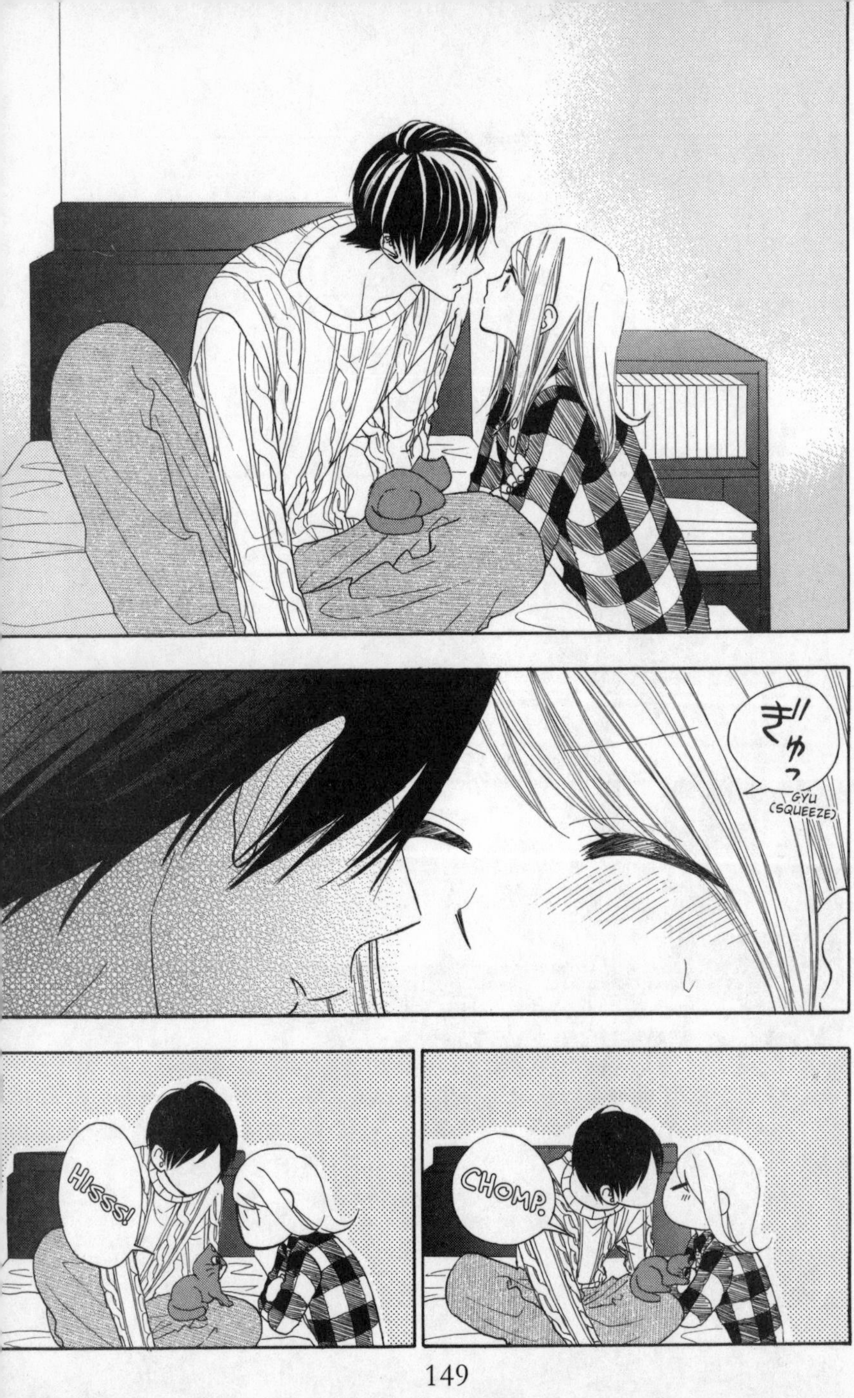
ぎゅっ
GYU (SQUEEZE)
CHOMP.
HISSS!

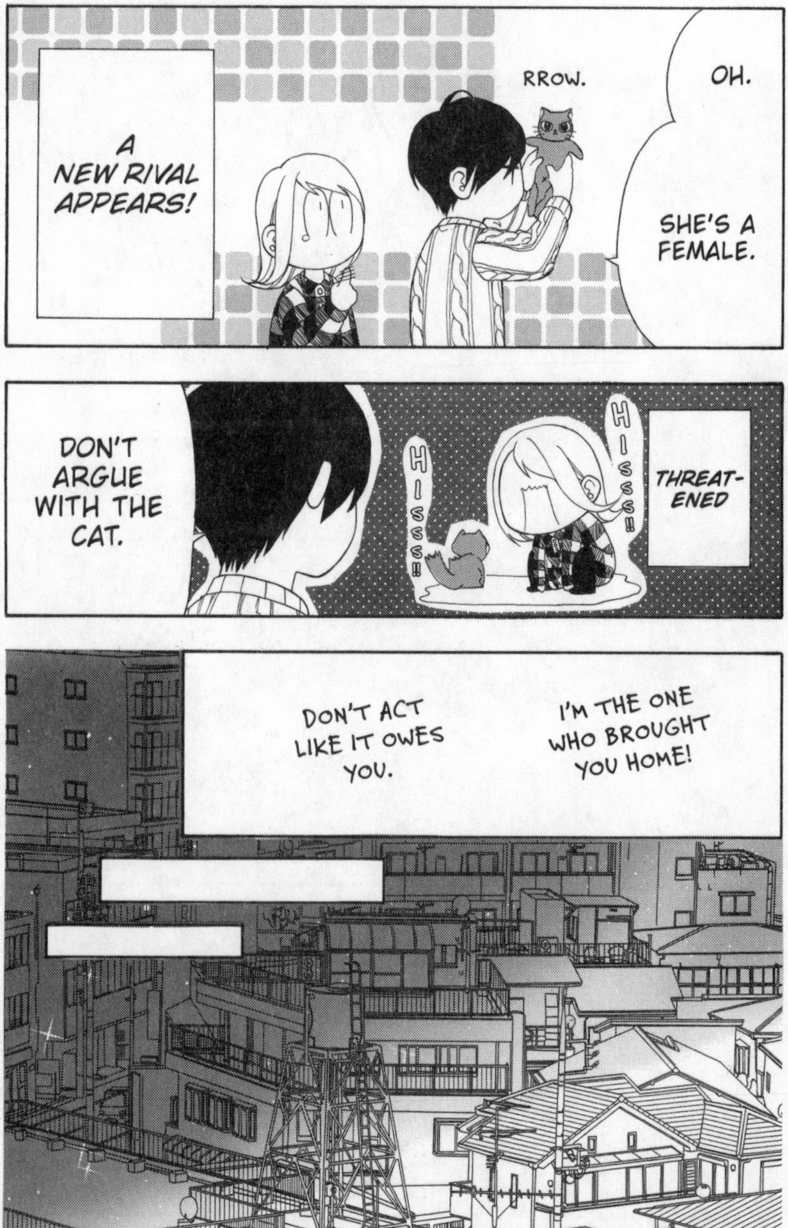
OH.
SHE'S A FEMALE.
RROW.
A NEW RIVAL APPEARS!
THREAT-ENED
HISS!!
HISS!!
DON'T ARGUE WITH THE CAT.
I'M THE ONE WHO BROUGHT YOU HOME!
DON'T ACT LIKE IT OWES YOU.

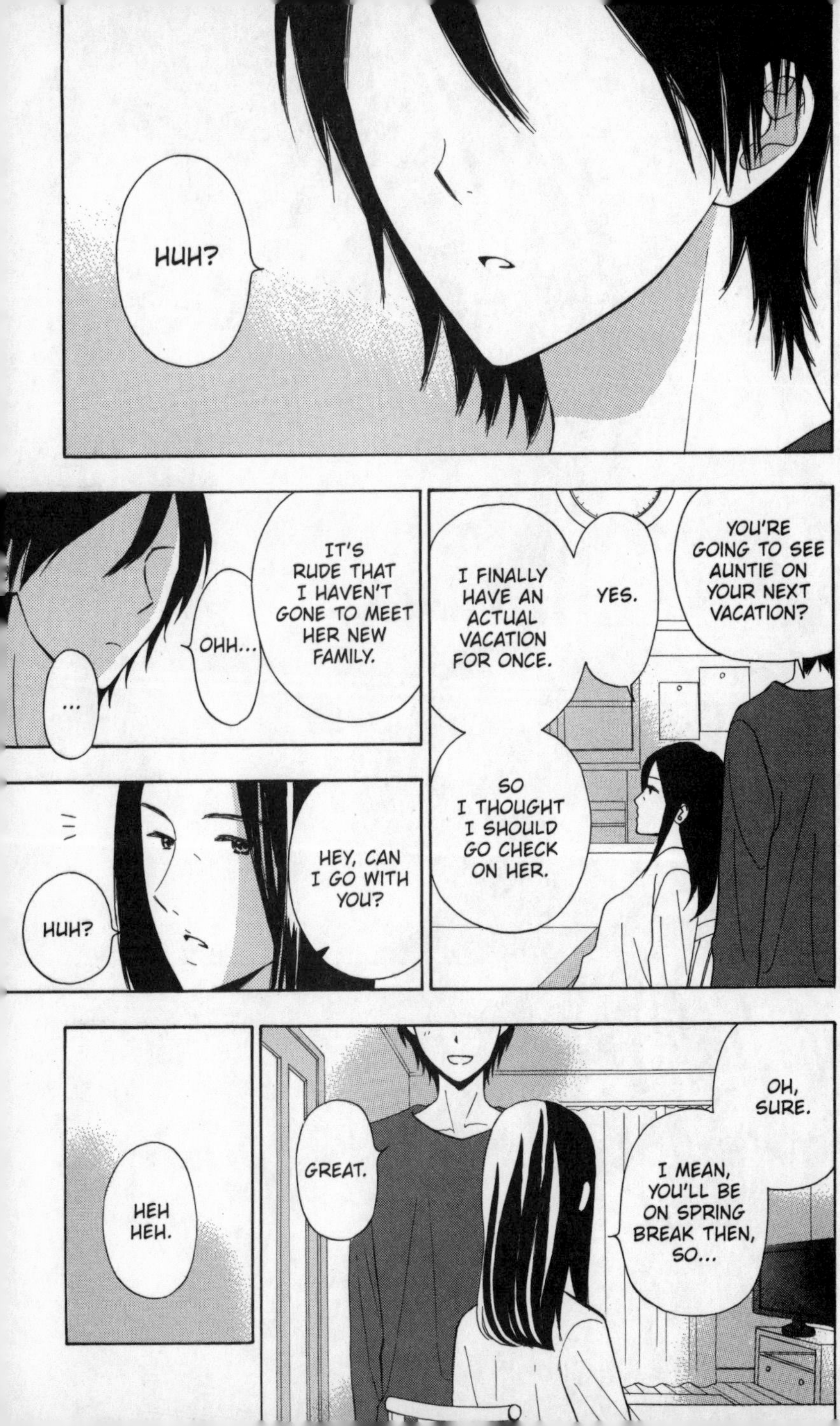
HUH?
YOU'RE GOING TO SEE AUNTIE ON YOUR NEXT VACATION?
YES.
I FINALLY HAVE AN ACTUAL VACATION FOR ONCE.
SO I THOUGHT I SHOULD GO CHECK ON HER.
IT'S RUDE THAT I HAVEN'T GONE TO MEET HER NEW FAMILY.
OHH...
...
HEY, CAN I GO WITH YOU?
HUH?
OH, SURE.
I MEAN, YOU'LL BE ON SPRING BREAK THEN, SO...
GREAT.
HEH HEH.

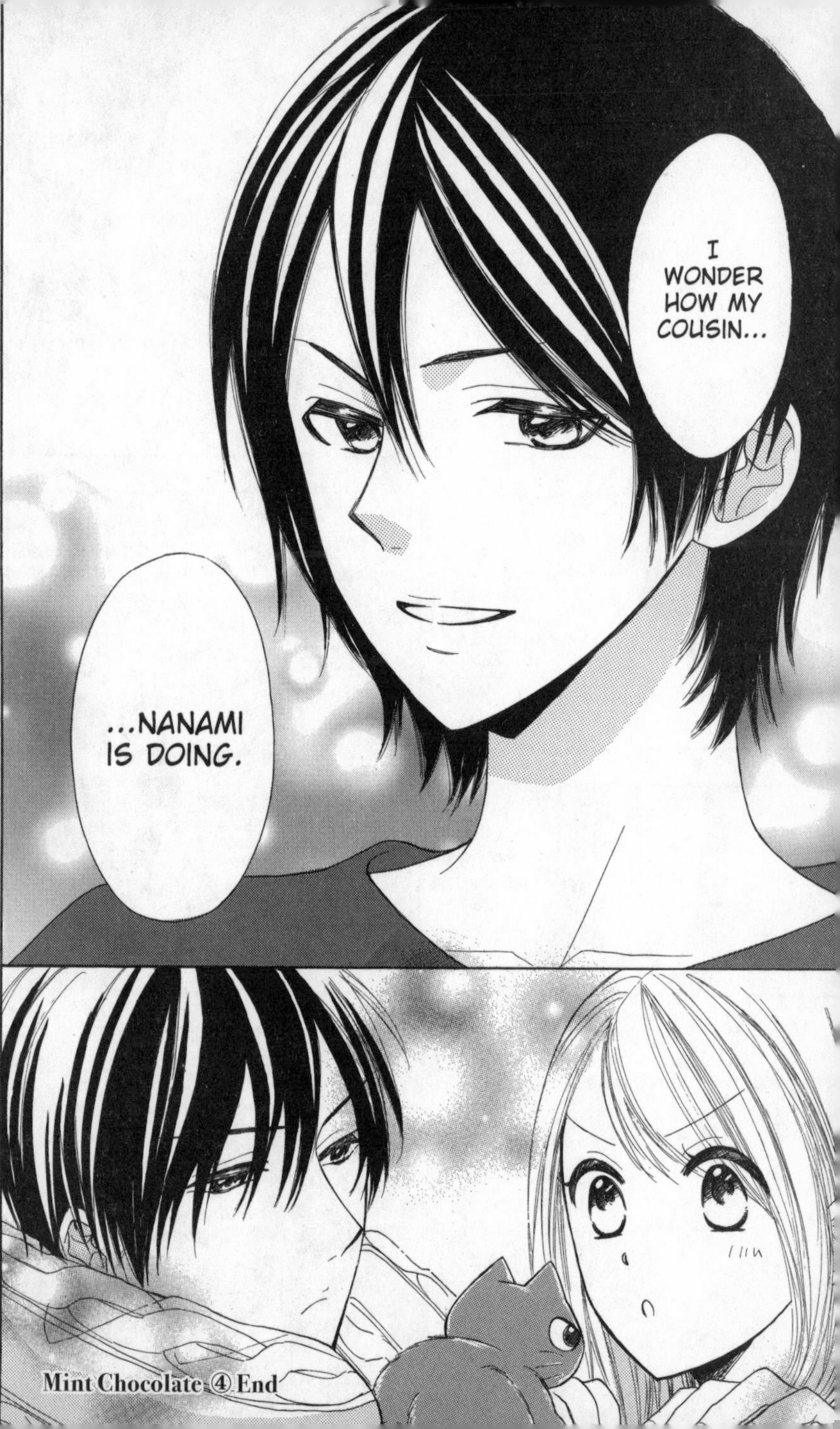
I WONDER HOW MY COUSIN...
...NANAMI IS DOING.

Mint Chocolate ④ End

White Day Special

March 14th

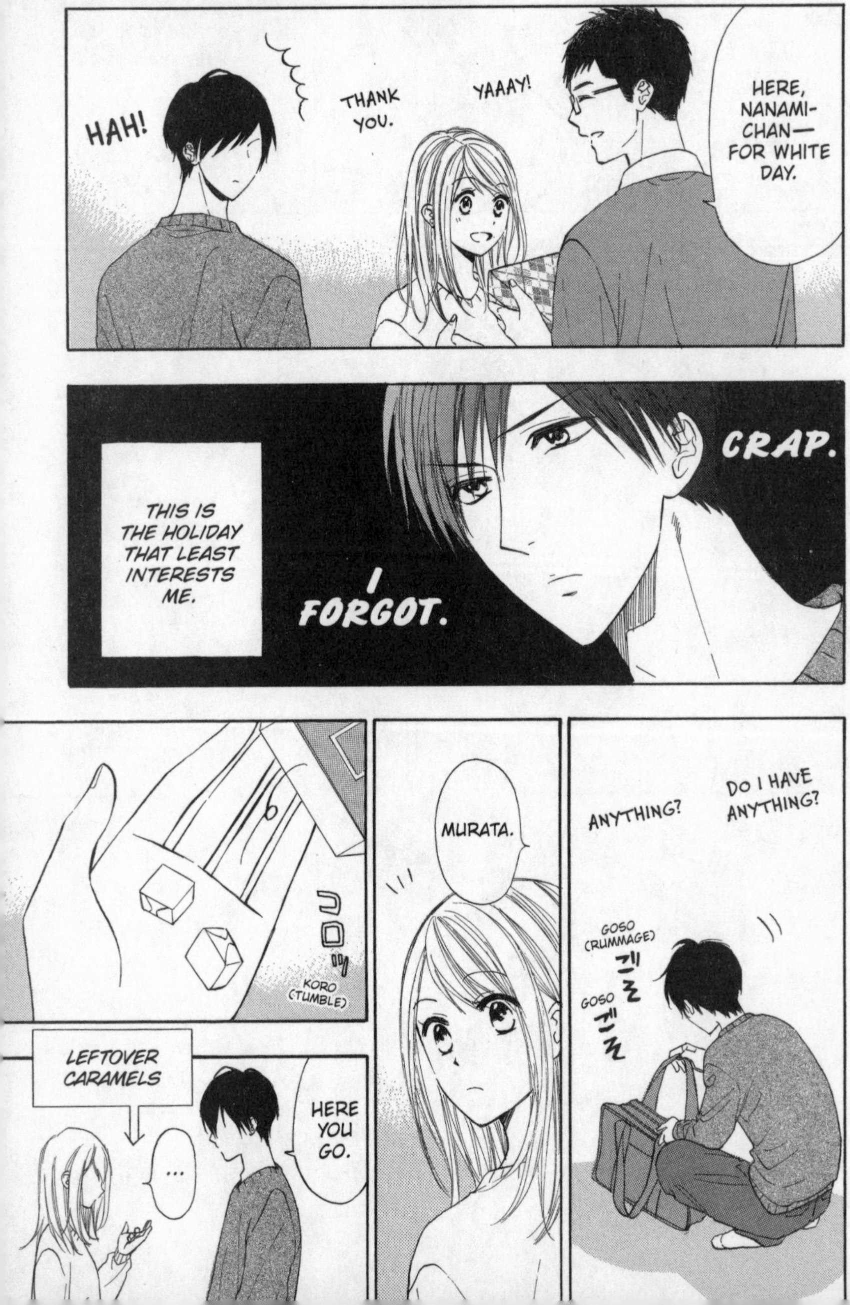

HERE, NANAMI-CHAN— FOR WHITE DAY.
YAAAY!
THANK YOU.
HAH!
CRAP.
I FORGOT.
THIS IS THE HOLIDAY THAT LEAST INTERESTS ME.
DO I HAVE ANYTHING?
ANYTHING?
GOSO (RUMMAGE)
GOSO
MURATA.
KORO (TUMBLE)
HERE YOU GO.
...
LEFTOVER CARAMELS

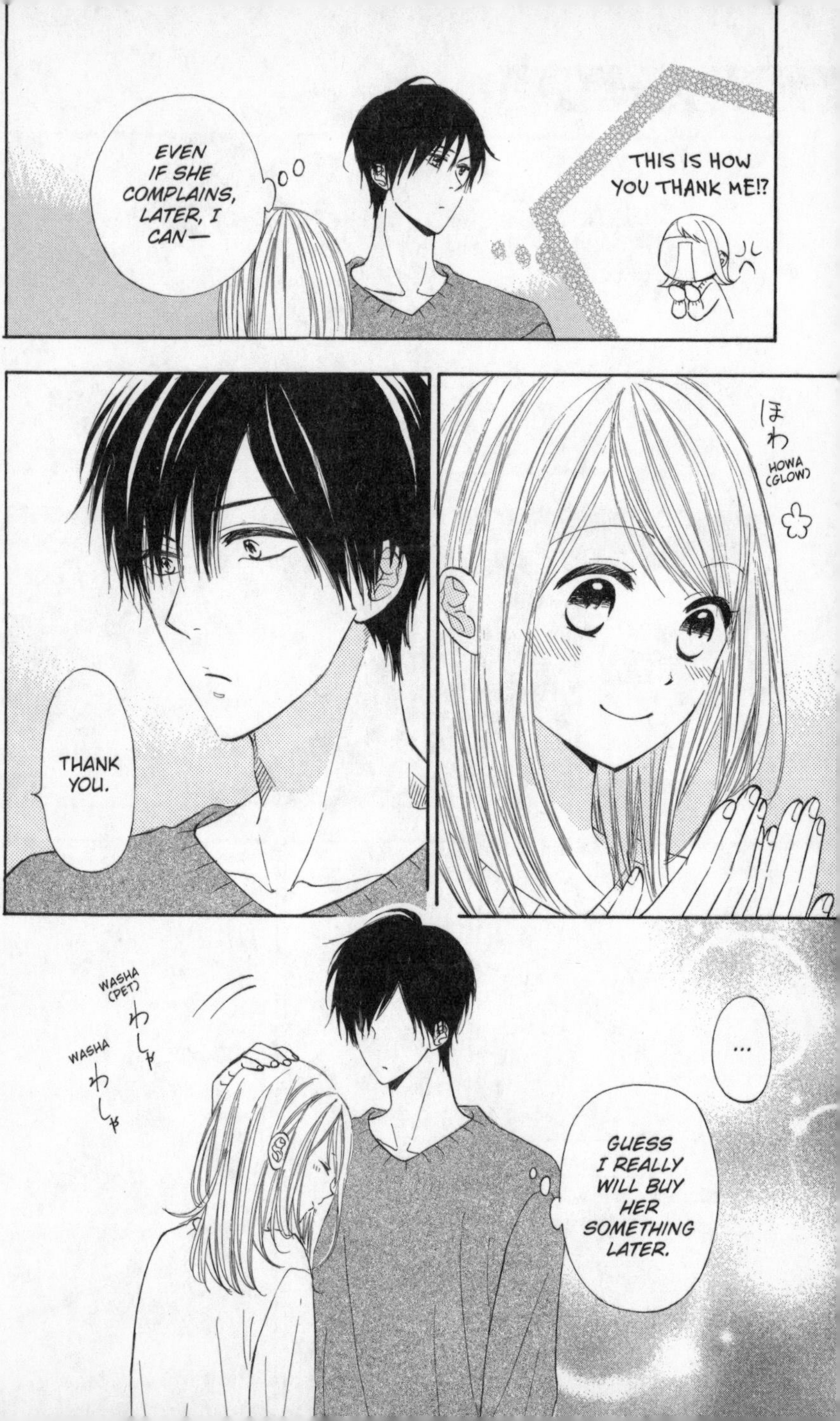
THIS IS HOW YOU THANK ME!?
EVEN IF SHE COMPLAINS, LATER, I CAN—
ほわ
HOWA (GLOW)
THANK YOU.
...
GUESS I REALLY WILL BUY HER SOMETHING LATER.
わしゃ
WASHA (PET)
わしゃ
WASHA

The Next Day

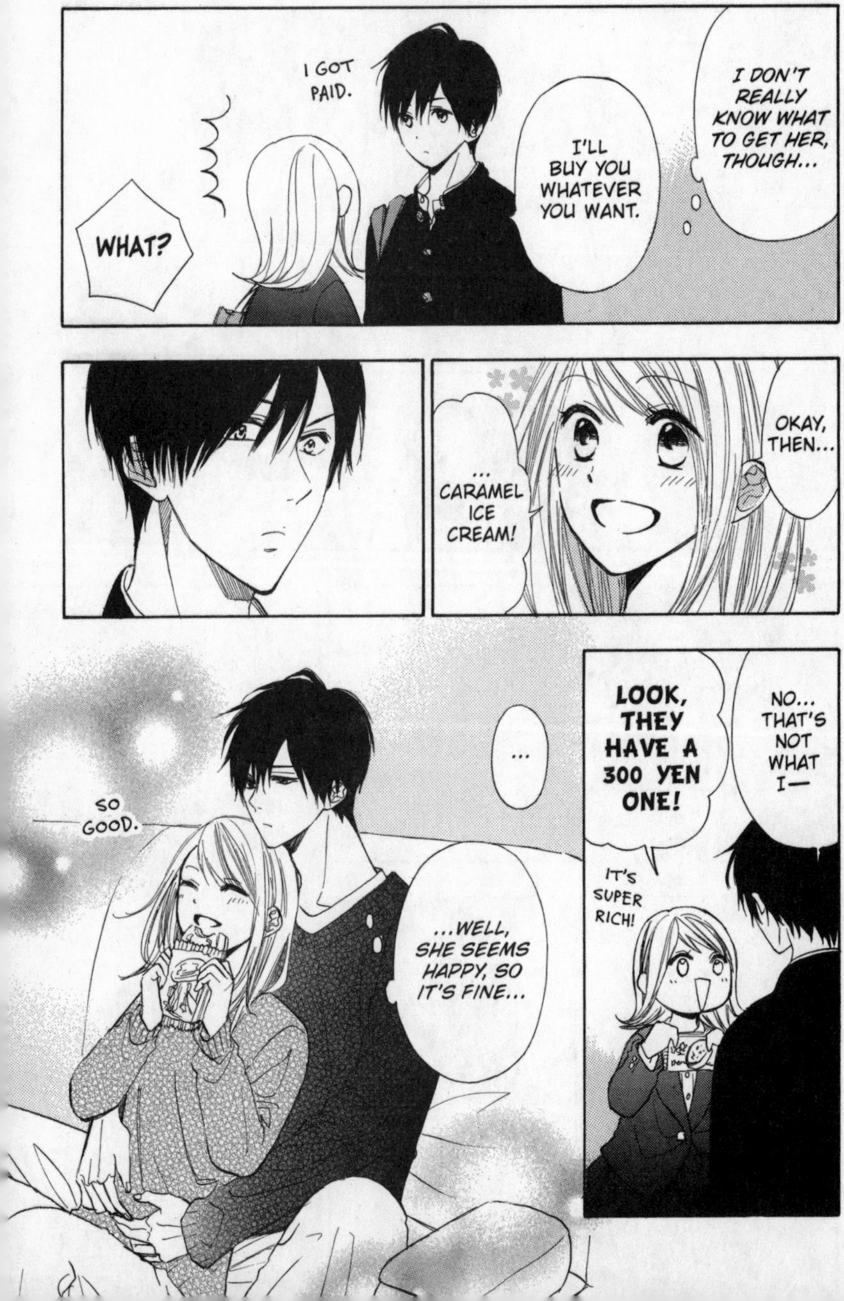
I DON'T REALLY KNOW WHAT TO GET HER, THOUGH...
I'LL BUY YOU WHATEVER YOU WANT.
I GOT PAID.
WHAT?
OKAY, THEN...
...CARAMEL ICE CREAM!
NO... THAT'S NOT WHAT I—
LOOK, THEY HAVE A 300 YEN ONE!
IT'S SUPER RICH!
...
...WELL, SHE SEEMS HAPPY, SO IT'S FINE...
SO GOOD.

Bonus Chapter

After Kyouhei Bought Her Ice Cream

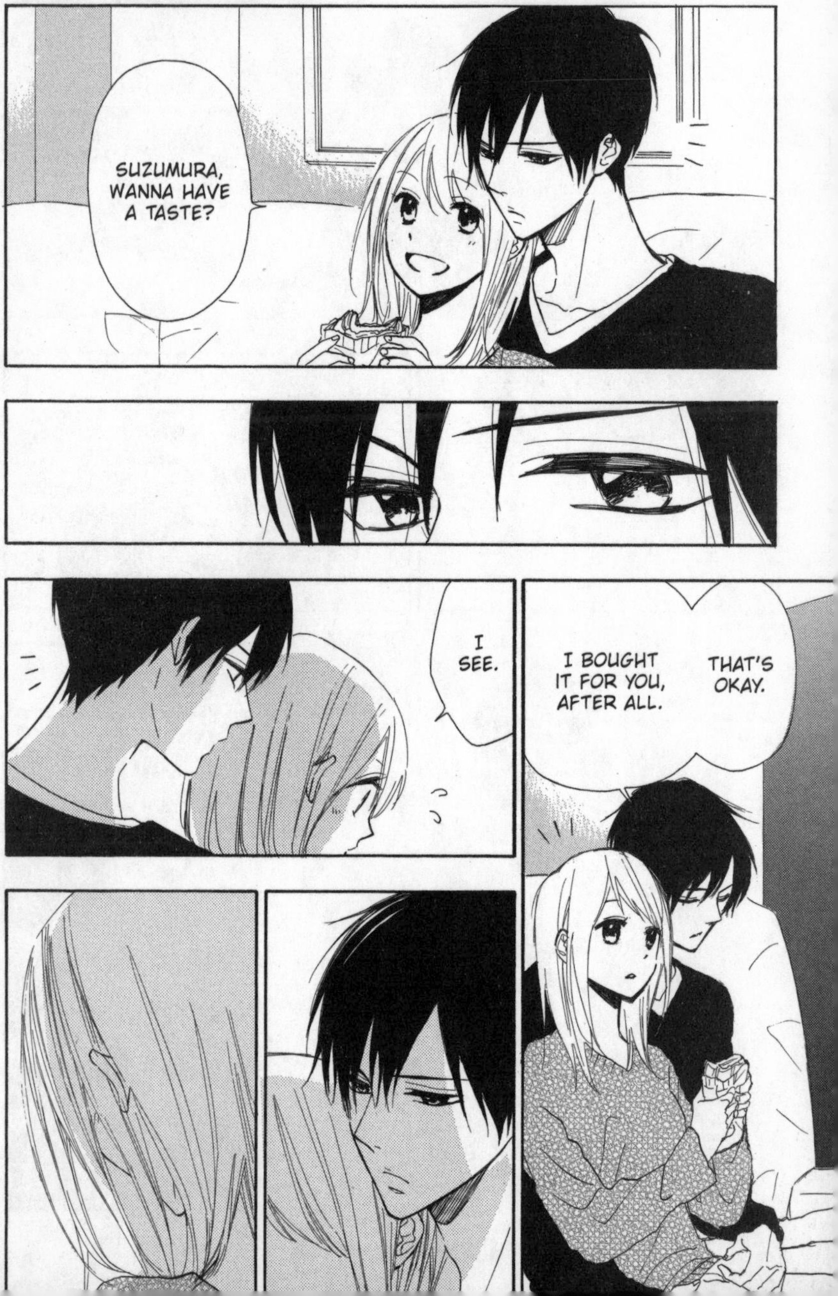
SUZUMURA, WANNA HAVE A TASTE?
THAT'S OKAY.
I BOUGHT IT FOR YOU, AFTER ALL.
I SEE.

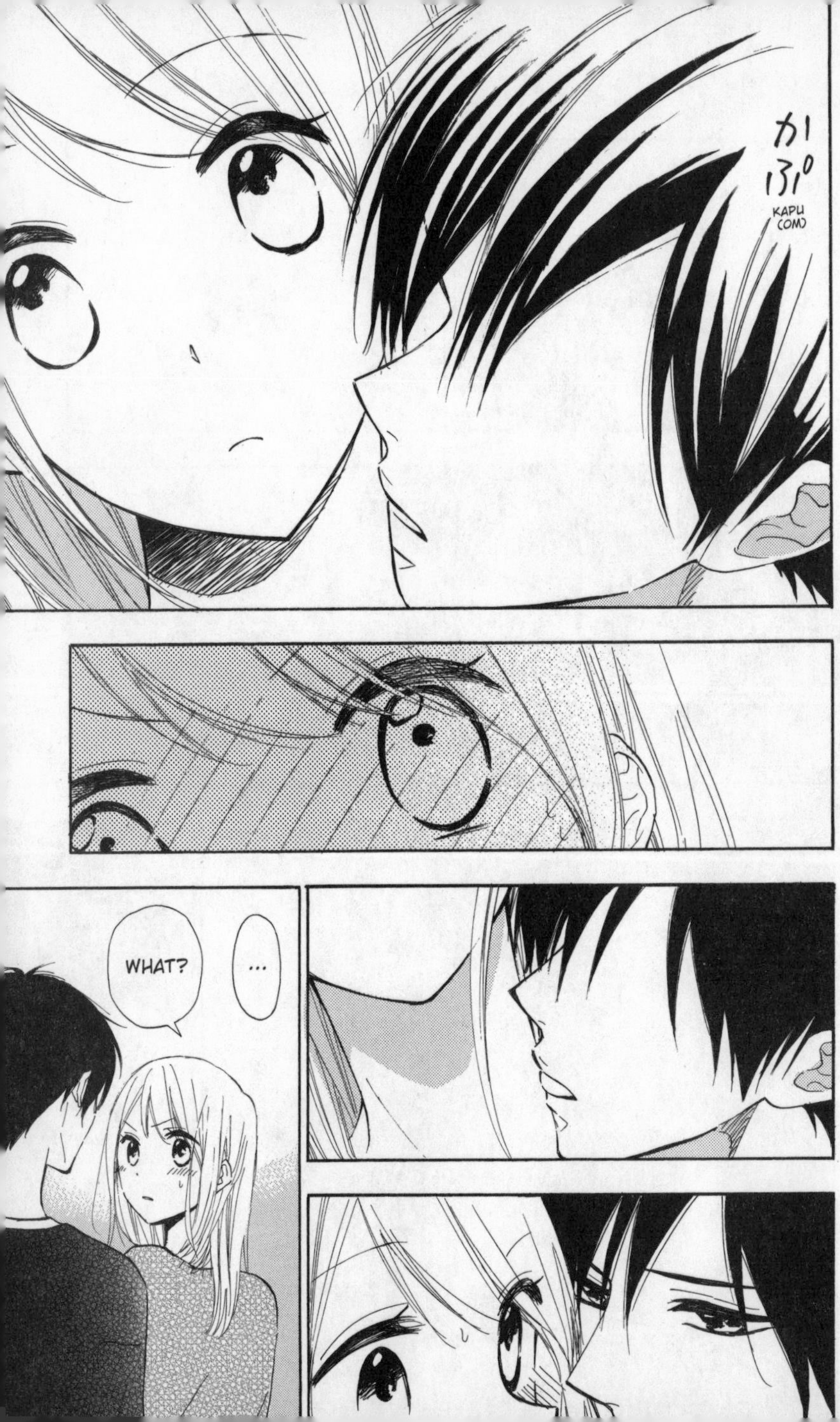
かぷ
KAPU
(OM)
...
WHAT?

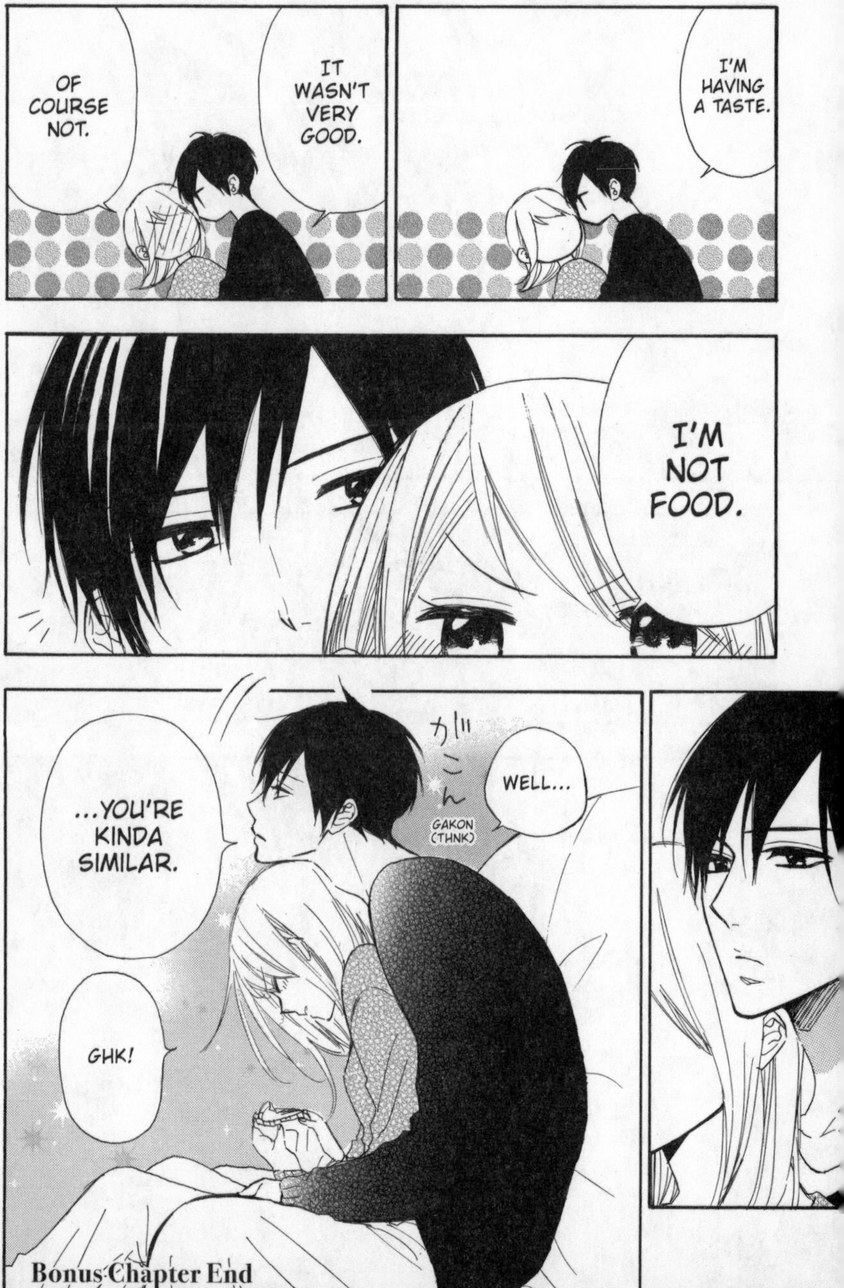
I'M HAVING A TASTE.
IT WASN'T VERY GOOD.
OF COURSE NOT.
I'M NOT FOOD.
WELL...
ガこん
GAKON (THNK)
...YOU'RE KINDA SIMILAR.
GHK!

Bonus Chapter End